WINNING WAYS

Dermot Reeve

with

Patrick Murphy

B🌿XTREE

To my Mum with thanks

This paperback edition first published in 1997 by Boxtree

First published in the UK in 1996 by Boxtree
an imprint of Macmillan Publishers Ltd
25 Eccleston Place, London SW1W 9NF and Basingstoke
Associated companies throughout the world

Copyright © Boxtree Ltd.

ISBN: 0 7522 2400 X

10 9 8 7 6 5 4 3 2 1

Typeset by SX Composing DTP, Rayleigh, Essex.
Printed and bound in Great Britain by Mackays of Chatham plc, Chatham, Kent

A CIP catalogue entry for this book is available
from the British Library

Contents

1

The Lara Factor

'Brian, don't!'
    'F*** off! Go on f*** off!'
    'Brian, don't tell me to f*** off.'
    'I'm telling you to f*** off – now f*** off!'
    And with that, the world's greatest batsman turned away from his captain, and in front of his team-mates, repeated his terse message twice more. The rest of the side melted away in embarrassment, leaving the captain to deal with a superstar out of control. I was that captain, the incident was at Northampton in late June 1994, the year of Brian Lara's supreme batting for the West Indies and my county, Warwickshire. It was also a summer when Lara's cavalier attitude to playing county cricket put me under severe pressure and made me think seriously about giving up the captaincy at a time when we were in the process of making championship history, with the prospect of a clean sweep of four domestic trophies.
    That flashpoint out in the middle at Northampton was the worst example of player indiscipline I have experienced in my career. I had never heard a team-mate speak like that to another, never mind a captain being on the receiving end. It led to the worst week of my cricketing life, as Warwickshire handled Brian Lara with kid gloves and made me realise I lacked support at the club. In the end, I had to swallow my pride, think about my own future and bite the bullet while the club kept a superstar happy. It cast a shadow over the rest of that historic season for me, and I was close to drifting out of the game because of Lara.

Brian's antics in midsummer were a far cry from the atmosphere of sweetness and light in April 1994, when he arrived at Edgbaston, off the back of his 375 against England in the Antigua Test a couple of weeks earlier. Even though he was now the world's highest scorer in Test history, he said all the right, modest things and seemed to have an ideal temperament for the inevitable trappings of mega-stardom that were bound to come his way. Brian had acquired an agent – Jonathan Barnett, who handled the business affairs of Waqar Younis and Wasim Akram – and there seemed no reason why the association with Warwickshire shouldn't be of huge mutual benefit. At the club, we were clapping our hands with glee, having signed Brian just before he scored that amazing 375. The phones jangled off the hook at Edgbaston after that, membership went through the roof, the sponsors loved all the exposure and the players and myself were thrilled to have such a player in our dressing-room. We were sorry to have lost our old mate, Allan Donald, to the South African side that was touring England, and I was intrigued to see how the side would fare with a world-class batsman replacing a top bowler.

I didn't realise what a phenomenal player Brian was until I saw him from the other end and, despite our serious differences, he remains the best batsman I have ever seen. The man is a genius, a truly great player. I have never seen someone able to find the gaps like Brian: he waits for the ball that little bit later than anyone, and just keeps piercing the field. Brian has so much control of the blade, despite the speed of his downswing from such a high backlift. It was a privilege to watch him bat and none of us in the Warwickshire dressing-room could believe his talent until we saw it in the flesh. Brian started off the season with a string of glorious hundreds, including the best innings I have ever seen in county cricket. In the second innings against Leicestershire at Edgbaston, we faced defeat on a fast wicket, with cracks developing all over the place. The odd ball was keeping low, others were taking off. Every other batsman was either getting rapped on the knuckles or jabbing down late on a shooter, but at the other end, Brian made it look a doddle. He adjusted so late that the shooters would be kept out easily and, if the ball took off, he'd either play it over the slips' heads or leave it alone. The bad delivery would just be dismissed to the boundary with no fuss. Brian farmed the bowling and got us what proved to be a valuable draw. At the end of that season, Leicestershire finished second to us in the championship and who knows how it all might have ended if they'd beaten us that day in May? We ended up 206/7, with Lara 120 not out, with the next top score just twenty. Brian just seemed from another planet as a batsman and we couldn't believe our good luck.

A few weeks later, he made history again, scoring 501 not out against Durham at Edgbaston. It was the highest first-class score in history, beating Hanif Mohammad's 499, and we just sat in awe. It was an amazing feat physically, because he had to concentrate for such a long time. At lunchtime on the final day, he was 285 not out, capitalising on a very flat pitch, a Durham side lacking David Graveney's spin bowling because of injury and the game going nowhere. I was disappointed that I hadn't been able to do a deal with Durham, so that they could set us a fourth innings target. We had lost the third day because of rain, and Durham decided just to play for bonus points. So when Lara said to me that lunchtime, 'You're not going to declare are you?' I was curious to know why. He told me about the record of 499, that he fancied it and I thought, 'This guy's a confident character – he's still got to get another 200-odd before the close.' Well he did, and despite so much being weighted in his favour, it was a phenomenal performance. We just watched open-mouthed as he kept hitting boundaries. I was even more impressed by his innings the next day in a Benson and Hedges Cup semi-final. I can only imagine the sense of anti-climax and release of adrenalin Brian felt as he came off the field that evening at Edgbaston with the world record in his pocket – and then he had to go through all the media razzamatazz for an hour.

After all that, he had to drive down to London to check into a hotel for the big game next day against Surrey at the Oval. The way he raised his game to score seventy in a tight finish was remarkable. Brian had to come in at number six, down the order, because he had felt dizzy in the field after his exploits, and had to go off and lie down. That was understandable, but by the time he came in, the match was in the balance. Somehow he found the reserves of energy and concentration and brought us to victory. It was his best one-day innings that season for us and I was hugely impressed.

So, after six weeks of the '94 season, everything seemed perfect for Warwickshire. We were into a Lord's final, we had the world record holder at Test and first-class level batting like a dream for us, and the crowds were flocking in. Our profile with the media was getting higher and higher and Brian was impressing outsiders as a mature, level-headed guy who had settled very quickly into our dressing-room and was proving a supportive team-mate to players who rightly revered him. The reality is that, even then, I was looking for the Elastoplast to hold things together. It was all too easy for Brian, and early on I realised that he didn't have a great deal of respect for county cricket. He started to look for ways to get out of fielding and made it clear he really only wanted to bat. That 501 not out seemed to convince him that the standard of county bowling was far inferior to that in the Caribbean, and soon he was in need of motivation when he turned up at the ground to play. With the inevitable commercial deals raining down on him, he soon lost his edge.

Brian might have kept up his commitment longer if he'd been captained by someone other than me. Right from the start, the chemistry wasn't right between us. From day one, we never had a beer together and he went out of his way to avoid me socially. Early on, I invited him round to my flat to share a bottle of champagne, to get to know each other, but he declined. I could live with that – a captain doesn't need to be liked, just respected – but it soon got back to me that he was making sniping comments about me on the field. Because of this daft rule about bowling a minimum of 18½ overs an hour in county cricket, the over rate is always a worry to captains, and the rest of the side would understand when I chivvied them along to move around quickly in the field. But Brian would saunter from slip to square leg when I moved him and I'd clap my hands and shout, 'Come on Brian – over rate!' He didn't like that, confiding to some of the lads that not even the West Indies captain, Richie Richardson, talked to him like that. He also questioned my tactics on the field to some of the other guys and inevitably it got back to me. So I thought I'd have a quiet word early on with our new chief executive, Dennis Amiss. His response was disappointing: 'Keep him sweet, Dermot, he's special, he's the best player in the world.' Fateful words that would eventually ruin my relationship with Lara and affect my captaincy and standing in the club. I turned to our coach, Bob Woolmer, a supportive friend. Yet Bob was in awe of Brian's remarkable talent, and his advice was equally disturbing: 'Handle him with kid gloves. It's only for this season. He's different.' To me that was just storing up trouble after just a few weeks of a season that was scheduled to run for four and a half months. I was proved right in the long run, and at a cost to my self-esteem.

We had our first spat in the third championship match down at Taunton and it stemmed from a harmless bit of fun that you experience in every county dressing-room. I'd been in the England squad for a one-day international so I turned up to watch the closing stages of our match against Somerset. It had been agreed that Warwickshire would feed some runs to Somerset for a few overs, then we'd embark on a run chase. That morning, Brian had just received a new mobile phone – appropriately the number was 375375 – and he took it onto the field with him to see if it would work. Now that's not exactly the done thing in English first-class cricket, but the atmosphere was going to be light-hearted for the first few overs as we gave them cheap runs. Just for a laugh I agreed with some of the other lads that I'd phone Brian as he went to his place at slip. Before a ball was bowled, as the batsmen were sorting themselves out, Brian answered his phone and heard me say, 'Brian, I think you're standing a bit close to Keith.' He looked up at the balcony, saw me and some of the other lads waving and promptly put the phone away. We had a chuckle and thought no more about it. A year later, I read in Brian's autobiography that I'd got him in trouble with the umpires for calling him on the mobile phone in the day's *second* over. That was nonsense: if he'd had a call then, it wasn't from me, I only called him before a ball was delivered. After the game (incidentally won by us with yet another wonderful hundred from Brian), the umpires told me to have a word with him, that you can't take calls during a first-class match. Brian was very sniffy with me about it and in his book he said I was having a joke at his expense. He didn't seem to realise that it was just a gentle bit of leg-pulling. After all, he kept saying that he was loving the dressing-room atmosphere, that he was just one of the boys – and a sense of humour has always been part of the Edgbaston atmosphere in my experience. I realised though that Brian would laugh at himself if the joke or quip was from others in the team, rather than me.

So, after a few weeks, there were various sub-plots swirling around Brian and me, with wounds already festering. Another one opened in the next championship match at Lord's against Middlesex. At one stage, on the final day, Keith Brown and Paul Weekes were blocking out for a draw and I decided to dangle the carrot, get Middlesex interested again in a run chase as I felt this would bring us a greater chance of victory. So I brought on Brian to bowl his leg-breaks. Now he's not the worst bowler and I thought he would either get a wicket or help boost the Middlesex run rate; either way, I wanted an attacking field and I had to put my foot down and insist. He was a little unlucky with a couple of deliveries, but he went for 31 in his two overs. I didn't mind that, because it perked up Middlesex and they went for the runs again. They finished 24 short with the last man, Angus Fraser, blocking the last three balls to deny us the match. Fair enough, a good effort from both sides and I would've been delighted if we had pulled it off. But Brian wasn't happy. As soon as he had finished his second over, he pointed to his knee, signalled to the umpire and walked off the field. In the dressing-room afterwards he had a go at me, saying he couldn't understand what I was playing at, putting him on without a run-saving field. I tried to explain to him that with 20 overs left I felt we needed to keep Middlesex interested in the target by feeding them some runs, but he wouldn't see it initially. After Brian left the dressing-room, Bob Woolmer told me that he also had tried to explain the tactics to him during those closing overs. Bob confided in me that Brian was unimpressed by my tactics but felt by the end of the game he could see what I was getting at. Bob said I wouldn't have been all that enamoured by Brian's remarks on entering the dressing-room, so it was clear to me then that he didn't value my captaincy all that highly.

By now, I was having to work at getting Brian on to the field on Sundays. He clearly didn't fancy the helter-skelter style of the Sunday League, he wasn't making runs in these games and he was trying hard to get a day off. 'I don't like Sunday cricket,' he would tell me, complaining about his sore knee. I would compromise by saying that I'd put him in certain positions that wouldn't tax his knee – yet when he really had to, Brian fielded like a gazelle and he still put in some tremendous sprints between the wickets when he was pushed. So I was taking all his protestations with a pinch of salt, trying to keep the lid on the whole situation for the good of the team, trying to ignore the fact that the star player didn't like or rate his captain. I called a meeting of our senior players to ask their advice. I was worried that team spirit might get eroded when they saw the amount of leeway Brian was getting, arriving late almost every morning when everyone else knew the time to be on parade. I told the players about Dennis Amiss' preference for the softly-softly approach and Gladstone Small said he'd have a word with Brian. We agreed the important thing was to get him on the field, and to make sure our own personal standards didn't drop. Obviously the cricket management couldn't come down on another player if he was late or unshaven – one of Amiss' new rules on becoming the boss. So when Paul Smith turned up half an hour late one morning and Bob Woolmer wanted to tackle him, I had to say, 'Let it go, Bob, you can't be hard on the others because Brian gets away with it. Let it go just for this year.'

But I was worried about this preferential treatment. The goal-posts had moved from the previous season, and I wondered how much indiscipline might creep in as the club tried to accommodate Brian. When Brian asked to miss a Nat West Cup game, I was really put on the spot. We were at home to Bedfordshire, a minor county, as we defended our trophy – on paper a doddle but I hate games like these, where the county side is on a hiding to nothing. Brian informed me he didn't want to play because his girlfriend was arriving that day from Trinidad. 'Listen, it's only a minor county, you'll beat them,' he said. I wasn't happy at all about the situation, but tried to find a compromise – after all it was what Dennis Amiss would have expected me to do. Brian said he was picking her up at Heathrow at 9 in the morning, and that he'd be back at the ground by the start at 10.30. I didn't believe that would happen for a minute, especially as there was a train strike on at the time and more traffic on the roads as a result. I told him to get back as soon as possible. He arrived 90 minutes late. Luckily Roger Twose and Dominic Ostler put on a big stand for the first wicket and Brian could bat in his usual number three position, but it was a totally embarrassing situation for the team. By now, the press boys were beginning to ask questions about why Brian was spending so much time off the field and I was having to bend the truth, to keep the peace. Brian was beginning to chance his arm with me and once he said, 'I've got to go and make a phone call to Trinidad', and raced off the field. I couldn't believe it. No one else would've thought about making such a request. Brian was being paid handsomely to play county cricket, yet he clearly didn't have a great deal of respect for it. I just bit my tongue, and let him get away with it. The sponsors and members were happy, we were bang in the public eye and I felt my hands were tied. I was honestly confused.

And so to Northampton, and that astonishing outburst from Brian at me on the second day. The events are absolutely crystal clear in my mind; it was a nightmare caused by allowing a great player to have his own way, with his captain being undermined. Now I've never been a shrinking violet on the field. I give out as much as I get and, in fact, the more the adrenalin flows, the more I like it and the better I seem to play. But Brian's behaviour over a three-day period still leaves me bewildered. He had started off the match with a brilliant 197 and his duel with Curtley Ambrose was fascinating. Ambrose had never got him out in first-class cricket and it was fantastic to watch these two proud West Indians squaring up to each other. Brian seemed fully motivated and, despite a blow on the helmet from Ambrose, batted as only he can. So much for the first day.

When Warwickshire came out to field on the second day, Brian had already been complaining about a headache and he was clearly in a grumpy mood as we set out to make Northants follow on in baking heat and on a flat wicket. We got two early wickets from Tim Munton but after that we were having to work hard for more success. During Tim's second spell, I was standing beside Brian in the slips, and we had the following exchange:

LARA: 'Take Tim off, you bowl him too much.'

REEVE: 'He's only bowled three overs, and if Tim doesn't get to bowl at least eight overs in this spell, he'll be disappointed.'

LARA: 'Why?'

REEVE: 'He needs rhythm – the more he bowls the better he gets. He always wants to bowl, he's a captain's dream.'

LARA: 'He's a bad captain's dream.'

I spotted the warning signals from that conversation and I realised I had to get out of the slips to concentrate on the game. It wasn't the time to unload a few home truths in Brian's direction, much as I wanted to. Rob Bailey started to bat well for Northants as I fielded at mid-off, hoping Tim Munton would get us another valuable breakthrough. Bailey edged one off Munton and it was taken low down by our wicket-keeper, Keith Piper. From mid-off, it didn't look right to me, but the slips all appealed and Keith claimed the catch. Then the square leg umpire Allan Jones intervened and said firmly, 'I saw the ball bounce – not out.' That should have been the end of it and it was for the rest of us. Except Brian. 'You must have f***ing good eyesight, then,' he shouted at Jones from slip. The umpire's reply was instant: 'There was nothing wrong with my eyesight when I gave you not out first ball yesterday – you concentrate on your batting and I'll do the umpiring.' That didn't please Brian at all and he carried on chuntering at slip, regularly looking over at Allan Jones in a hostile manner. His whole body language was disrespectful and dismissive of Allan Jones and I thought I'd better try to calm him down. So I went into the slips again and we had another frank exchange of views.

REEVE: 'Brian, you've got to be careful about umpires in this country.'

LARA: 'Why? What can he do? All he can do is give me out. So what?'

A few overs later, Bailey edged Graeme Welch to Keith Piper

and he was clearly out. As Bailey walked away and we ran to our bowler, Lara shouted over to Allan Jones, 'Well that one carried by three feet.' Luckily Jonah didn't hear that, otherwise Brian would really have been for the high jump, but he was still bristling with anger as we gathered around celebrating Bailey's dismissal. I simply said, 'Brian – don't', and that led to the torrent of abuse and four-letter words at me, in front of the whole team. I was determined not to swear back at him – something I was very tempted to do – but I instantly realised what an important moment this was. I knew all the boys were listening, as they slowly parted, and that my leadership was on the line, and my credibility in their eyes. After Brian had told me to 'f*** off' seven times, I said firmly, 'Brian, you're turning into a prima donna.' Those were my exact words and said in a clear voice, but not loudly. Some of the guys would have heard it, and certainly Brian, but I knew that I just had to try to douse the situation, appear non-confrontational and hope the club's administrators would back me up when we had the inevitable inquiry.

That incident remains precisely fixed in my memory, despite attempts from other quarters to put a gloss on it. The *Independent* newspaper carried a damaging piece shortly afterwards from its cricket correspondent, Martin Johnson, in which he stated that I had loudly informed Lara that he was 'a f***ing prima donna'. I took great exception to this, because I had deliberately tried to defuse the situation. I met up with Martin Johnson a few months later in Australia, and asked him who his sources were for that false information. He waffled on, saying he couldn't remember if it was a freelance journalist or one of my players. It was a false allegation from a serious newspaper's cricket writer who seemed to spend more time churning out funny asides than writing a match report, but Johnson didn't seem interested in setting the record straight.

But Brian Lara's interpretation of the incident was of more concern to me. At the end of the over, in which he had abused me and the umpire, he pointed to his knee and shouted to Allan Jones, 'Sore knee', and walked off the field. Yet in his book, Brian says he went off because he was feeling dizzy, that the spat was just a minor incident. He said there was no intention to abuse the umpire or dispute the decision to his face, that it was the kind of incident which happens occasionally in cricket, and is forgotten by the time the next interval comes around. That was nonsense.

That night, I tried to keep calm about that flashpoint, telling myself that some good might come of it, that the club's executives would at last realise that the captain had to be supported against the player. I knew the other players were concerned and they were watching me for a lead. I made it quite clear that I wanted serious discussions on the matter, that I expected some form of disciplinary procedure. I was also well aware that the press were sniffing around – can't say I blamed them! I would've loved to mark their cards but I thought it better to keep quiet for a time. In any case, we had an important weekend ahead of us. We'd bowled out Northants cheaply and made them follow on, and there was also a Sunday League game ahead, as we tried to make it six wins out of six.

On the third day of the championship game, it took a monumental effort by our bowlers to take seven Northants wickets after making them follow on. It was a great team effort, one that really pleased me as captain. Brian Lara spent the whole of that day under the dressing-room table resting. At lunch and tea, he roused himself sufficiently to ask the score, only to be told by Roger Twose, 'Why don't you get up and have a look at the scoreboard?' We just had to shut it out of our minds and concentrate on winning the game, which we did on the fourth evening, with a great run chase, with three balls to spare.

Before that, I had another traumatic experience with Brian on the Sunday, one that really disillusioned me. He was late arriving at the ground, after driving down from Birmingham. Brian then announced he wasn't fit to play, that his knee was sore, and that he was still complaining of headaches. Our physiotherapist, Stuart Nottingham, told me there was not much wrong with his knee in his opinion, but Brian insisted he wasn't fit to play, and I didn't see the necessity to coax him after his performance over the last two days. So I went off and told the team that Brian wasn't playing, and then tried to get on with my own preparations for the match. But Bob Woolmer came up to me and said,

'Have another word with Brian about playing.' I replied, 'Bob, he's said he's not fit. Come with me and hear it from him.' We went into the dining area and heard Dennis Amiss saying, 'Do it for me, Brian – please play.' Dennis had said to me earlier, 'Brian's got to play, the TV cameras are here', as if that should make a difference. Clearly Dennis didn't want the press to be alerted to further problems with Brian, and finally he persuaded him to turn out. I was astonished. I had told the eleven the batting order – without Brian – but Dennis was insistent that we must accommodate Brian at the last moment. That left me with the problem of telling Trevor Penney he wasn't playing – 20 minutes before the start, when everyone was waiting for me to go out and toss the coin. I felt desperately sorry for Trevor Penney and furious at the way Brian had been pampered into playing. I then watched him field brilliantly despite his earlier protestations about his sore knee. For once, I was speechless.

That evening, we had a showdown meeting in the physio's room, attended by Dennis Amiss, Bob Woolmer, Tim Munton, Brian and myself. Dennis said, 'We have to keep all this quiet, don't let anyone talk to the press. The official line is that Brian's suffering from the after-effects of a blow to the head. We have to sweep this under the carpet.' There were no apologies and the meeting was over in five minutes.

A day or two later, I had another meeting with the senior players about Brian. The general feeling was that we had to grin and bear it, otherwise he might just disappear on a plane to Trinidad and not come back. One of the guys said he'd happily string him up on a hook in the dressing-room if there was any more nonsense from him, but we all hoped it wouldn't come to that. The senior players agreed that they would handle it if Brian stepped out of line again, but I wasn't optimistic that it would work. On the moral aspect, they were all on my side – you just can't do what Brian did at Northampton and expect to get away with it – but in practical terms, I knew there were one or two players who wouldn't have been too perturbed that I lacked official backing. I wasn't having a great season in the championship with either bat or ball, and if I faded out of the picture it would open up a spot for someone. So I still felt a little isolated, and even more so when Dennis Amiss told me that Brian was demanding an apology from me. I was told that I had called him 'a prima donna' and that he was upset at that, and I should phone him. I was dismayed. Even though Lara's recent behaviour had fully justified the accusation of prima donna behaviour, I had been careful to tell him that he was '*turning into* a prima donna', which is not quite the same thing.

I pointed out to Dennis that Brian had told me to 'f*** off' seven times before I mentioned the word 'prima donna.' He replied, 'Yes we realise that and Brian is sorry for what he said. I've spoken with Brian and if you phone him and apologize, I'm sure he'll do the same.'

'Apologise for what?' I said. 'What are the club going to do about Brian's behaviour?' I was insistent about this, I couldn't believe my ears.

Dennis answered, 'He's having such a good season, we mustn't upset him. He's a great player, Dermot – let him have his way this season.'

At this point I felt so angry that I wanted to deliver this ultimatum: 'Brian apologises or you find a new captain.'

It was an effort to stay composed. My mind was racing with the repercussions of such a statement. I came to the conclusion that I didn't trust the club to stand by what was right or wrong, and support me.

At that point, Brian Lara was bigger than Warwickshire County Cricket Club. I felt that if I refused, I might not be backed up by the cricket committee. With my form below par, Brian was undeniably more productive than me, and they could allow me to fade away, with Tim Munton taking over the captaincy. My place in the side wasn't my concern but hanging over my head was a major consideration in keeping my mouth shut – the benefit system. That's always been one of the ways in which a county keeps a player sweet, as you wait to be granted one, keeping your nose clean. I was due a benefit and I knew that if I refused to play ball over the Lara situation, I might miss out.

I hated doing it, but my pride had to take a back seat, so I picked up the phone and dialled Brian. He was very quiet and non-committal at the start, until I said, 'Brian, I don't like to insinuate that anyone's behaving like a prima donna or turning into one. I'm sorry the incident happened, we have to get a working relationship going for the sake of the team. It doesn't matter if we're not mates.' I had phrased those words deliberately after chewing it over: I was determined not to give him a total apology. He thought it over for a few seconds and said, 'You're right, I'm sorry the incident happened.' That seemed to be a truce, but then he suddenly added, 'But you never wanted me here in the first place.'

I was stunned. It dawned on me that Brian had heard about all the discussions about an overseas player to replace Allan Donald and that he had thought I'd stuck out against signing him. This gave me some insight into why he had no time for me. I tried to explain that the previous August it had been unanimously decided to go for an all-rounder because we were worried about our bowling strength. I told him that top of the list was Phil Simmons, a West Indian opener who could bowl lively medium pace, but he wanted a two-year contract. Our next choice was Manoj Prabhakar, who was an excellent one-day cricketer who could swing the ball. The unanimous decision of the cricket committee was to go for Prabhakar but when he damaged his ankle in the spring of '94, we had to look elsewhere.

I told Brian that I would have preferred an all-rounder because of the balance of the Warwickshire staff and a year ago I didn't realise what a great player he was. I told him enthusiastically and honestly that he was the best batsman that I had ever seen and how lucky we were to have ended up with him. I stated that we must endeavour to make a satisfactory working relationship for the sake of the other players and Brian agreed. End of phone call.

According to Lara's book, this was the worst fortnight of his life. I wonder how he would have felt in my position. I was isolated, out of form as a player, getting no support on a serious disciplinary matter, and having to swallow my pride because I needed a benefit. My daughter Emily was very much in my mind at the time. After my marriage broke up, Emily went back to

Western Australia with her mother, and if I was lucky, I'd get out there to see her for a couple of months a year. If I had a successful benefit, I might be able to fly her over, or just hop on a flight to Perth on a whim. In the end, my love for my daughter helped me overcome the lowering of my self-esteem.

Yet Brian could still surprise me. On the morning of the Benson and Hedges Final, ten days after our phone conversation, he asked for permission to talk to the boys before the start of play. The Lord's dressing-room was hushed as Brian apologised to the team and to the captain for his recent behaviour, that it hadn't been fair on them. He shook hands with everyone and as I stuck out my hand, he embraced me. I was very surprised and moved by that gesture and by what he had said. I looked up and saw Roger Twose wiping away a tear and it was certainly a great way to get the boys together as a unit before going out to beat Worcestershire. What a pity Brian chose to re-write history in his book, preferring to say that newspaper articles had a lot to do with all the rumours that he had apologised, rather than hard fact. I quote from his book: 'I told the players that I considered myself part of the team, no different from anyone else, and assured them that I was still fully committed to playing with them.' That is pretty close but I'm afraid nowhere in that section does he mention that he in fact apologised to us for his behaviour. Well he did. Perhaps my vocabulary is more limited than Brian's, but I'm under the impression that the word 'sorry' means an apology.

Even after that Benson and Hedges Final, and his apology, Lara still didn't really seem motivated for us during the rest of that season. I felt county cricket was now too easy for him, and that he couldn't get inspired unless it was against a challenge such as Curtley Ambrose at Northampton and Devon Malcolm at Chesterfield, when he made two wonderful hundreds. The one-day game held little appeal for him, especially the Sunday League. A lot of my pre-match preparations on Sundays were spent trying to get him to play, even though we were going for the title and possibly the Grand Slam of all four trophies. I thought he was bluffing me about his sore knee and his fatigue, an impression confirmed when I saw him really motor in the field and whenever he'd disappear to play golf. Brian was bitten straight away by the golf bug when he joined us. After moaning during the day about his sore knee, and feeling tired, Brian would regularly be off out the dressing-room door like a shot to play golf. Towards the end of the season, I was openly asking our physio, 'Is golf good for his knee?' to be told, 'No – that's if the knee is a problem to him.' Try as he could, Stuart Nottingham couldn't find any serious damage to Lara's knee.

For the rest of that season, Brian and I kept a wary distance from each other. We had another flare-up early in August when we lost a Sunday League match in ridiculous fashion to Worcestershire. We only needed 183 in 38 overs and after Dominic Ostler and Neil Smith had put on 105 in just 14 overs for the first wicket, it ought to have been a stroll. But Brian got bogged down, struggling badly with his timing, for once. For some reason, he allowed Richard Illingworth to bowl maiden overs, not using his feet, nor milking him away for singles. In the space of five overs, Illingworth only conceded two runs. It was mystifying cricket from Lara, he just played straight and hit the field. It looked to me that he was having a net for the following Tuesday's Nat West semi-final against Kent at home, on the same wicket. The pressure built up, and I batted poorly when I came in at number seven. Both Brian and I got caught at mid-on and we lost by three runs.

It was a dreadful batting effort and in the dressing-room afterwards I had my first-ever general go at the side, saying we were too complacent after such a great start. I said, 'On that wicket, there's no way a spinner can bowl five overs and just go for two runs.' Lara obviously took that personally, snapping back at me, 'You cost us the game. I was playing well, you scored too slowly and you didn't get me on the strike enough. Can't a guy bowl maidens?' I said, 'No, not on that wicket'. Bob Woolmer asked for calm, telling Brian I wasn't having a go at him personally, but I was close to it. Perhaps I should have handled it differently, saying right away that I'd batted badly, but I was sick at the manner of the defeat and just wanted to talk it out. But Brian didn't appreciate such honest, open discussion, a feature of the Warwickshire dressing-room in recent years.

Even when we created history in September, winning the Sunday League down at Bristol, I got the impression that Brian didn't rate the achievement all that much. As we chased the treble, having won the championship and the Benson and Hedges Cup, Brian had been allowed to skip the championship match at Bristol and was given permission to drive down for the Sunday game. He arrived late and didn't take part in our pre-match practice. Afterwards, in the pumped-up atmosphere in our dressing-room, I looked over at Brian and thought, 'This doesn't mean much to you, mate. We've won three trophies in one season, but it doesn't look like it's been a great day for you, like it is for us.'

I breathed a sigh of relief when the season ended and it dawned on me that I might not have to captain Brian Lara again. With Allan Donald returning for the '95 season, it would be a pleasure to captain a model overseas player, a supreme profes-sional, who takes great delight in Warwickshire victories and in the success of his team-mates.

Within six months of celebrating our triple trophy success, I was dismayed to discover that Brian Lara was due back at Edgbaston for the '96 season, in preference to Allan Donald. I didn't think a decision was needed for at least a year on who would be our overseas player for the '96 season, and Donald would certainly get my vote, despite South Africa's hectic inter-national schedule. But in February '95 I had a phone call in Australia from Dennis Amiss, telling me that Lara was to return, ahead of Donald. I was shattered, especially when I heard that Brian had secured a three-year contract. I was very hurt that the club had not thought to tell me that discussions were imminent, or even ask my opinion. I asked Amiss if Allan Donald had been informed. 'Yes, he's in New Zealand with South Africa,' I was told. 'It's up to you and Bob Woolmer to motivate him now for this season.' So the captain does the motivation, but doesn't get consulted on such a serious cricketing matter. I was worried that Allan Donald might think I had something to do with all this, that I might now have a disillusioned overseas fast bowler on my hands, but I needn't have worried. When I saw Allan in South Africa on our pre-season tour, I told him I hadn't been consulted. He said, 'Skip, you don't have to worry – I'm going to get a hundred wickets and show them.' He was as good as his word and no one gave more to the cause of Warwickshire than Allan Donald, as we won two more trophies in 1995.

Throughout the summer of 1995, there were rumours that Brian Lara wouldn't be coming back the following year as our overseas player. As early as June, several umpires had told me he wasn't coming back, according to their particular grapevine – and that was the word from some West Indies players, as they toured England with Brian. He came to Edgbaston for a chat with club officials and for a private word with Allan Donald, and news seeped through that the club was thinking of alternating with Lara one year and Donald the next. I thought that was grossly unfair to Allan Donald, after all he had done for Warwickshire. He was a casualty of Brian's shilly-shallying as his agent pressed him to commit himself to Warwickshire while the player wanted prolonged rest from the self-induced treadmill of commercialism. In the end, Allan Donald took a lucrative package for '96 that involved league cricket in Lancashire and the post of fitness coach/bowling guru at Edgbaston, but I wish we could have acted more promptly to secure him as a player. He wanted it, the rest of the players wanted it and the South African Cricket Board would just have to realise that Allan preferred to play county cricket, instead of kicking his heels to avoid injuries and fatigue.

So Warwickshire fell between two stools for '96 and we lost both Donald and Lara. I was relieved when I heard that Brian was not returning because I would have resigned as captain. I never wanted to captain him again after the events of '94, even though he sent word back via the club's officials that he would have been perfectly happy to play under me. But what about my desire to captain him? I would still have been worried about his love for the game and passion for Warwickshire cricket, something that would never occur to me when considering Allan Donald. Brian Lara was very hard work for me as club captain and I didn't like the way it seemed as if he wasn't enjoying county cricket after his early dazzling performances. He'd sit in the dressing-room, moaning about fatigue, the demands on his time, the many autographs he had to sign – then if Dennis Amiss asked him to pop next door to do a press conference, he'd put on that angelic smile and tell the media how important it was for him to see his team do well. A genius isn't necessarily a great team man.

Life with Lara complicated my cricketing career at a time when I should have been enjoying the experience of holding up all those trophies to our supporters. It wasn't a scenario I'd envisaged 15 years earlier when I worked the scoreboard at Lord's on the MCC ground staff, just happy to get a game of cricket anywhere.

2

A Restless Lad

If I seem hyperactive now, you should have seen me as a kid. There never seemed enough hours in the day when I grew up in Hong Kong and used to spend all my time zipping around playing football or cricket in between classes, or after school, cramming in my homework whenever I could. One of the early attractions about cricket for me was that it lasted so long – football seemed to be over in a flash and I still had so much energy left. I was the youngest of four boys and one of my earliest memories is running around in the garden, shouting, 'Give it to me!' as my brothers played football, ignoring their little runt of a brother! Since then, I've always wanted to be in the game; it's much more fun being an all-rounder.

My parents were both teachers in Hong Kong, although born in England. Dad was headmaster of King George the Fifth School in Kowloon and Mum taught maths and physical education. We were a sports-mad family, with Mum the most competitive of the lot. She had trialled at netball for Lancashire and was an excellent all-round games player, and her attitude was that you played the game to win, within the rules. My father took the attitude that you played sport for fun – a surprising view from someone born in Yorkshire and an ex-Wimbledon footballer, but he was sincere about it. His favourite saying to me if I'd had a bad day on the sports field was 'Don't worry, it's good for the soul.' Mum would have none of that. She was furious at him one day when he gave me out lbw in a schools game. I blurted out to him that it was a pathetic decision and he agreed:

'I know you weren't out, but it would have looked bad if I'd let you off, because I'm your father.' Mum thought that was non-sense. Whenever we lost, you could see her struggling to cover up her disappointment.

Although my parents separated after 37 years of marriage, they remain totally supportive of all their four sons and my memories of our family life together in Hong Kong are very warm. Mum and Dad were always there for us, driving us around all over the island to play sport, always happy to go into the gar-den and play with a ball. Mum in particular has been amazingly supportive of my cricket career. Since I made my debut in first-class cricket for Sussex in 1983, she has missed barely ten days of my career in England – and then only because she had gone to see my eldest brother, Mark play cricket. When I made my England debut in New Zealand in 1992, she somehow managed to get out there at short notice. I knew where she was sitting in the stand when I went out to bat for England for the first time, and when I managed to get 50 in my first innings, I remember waving the bat in her direction, feeling very happy for her as well as myself. She even ended up as England's official scorer on the tour to India and Sri Lanka in 1993 when Clem Driver fell ill. I was delighted that she could then join us in the England team hotel, because I'd been a little worried that she'd been staying in a few dodgy places, keeping within her budget. Mum was in her element then, assisting players she had come to see as legends – excluding me of course!

No children could have asked for more from their parents than the Reeve boys, but the family atmosphere was a competi-tive one. We didn't have a television until I was 13, so we had to make our own entertainment and it was a struggle to get a word in edgeways around the table at night. Perhaps that's why I still talk so quickly, I'm expecting to be interrupted any second. As the youngest, I had to fight to get noticed by the others. Early on, I learned to play board games and cards and tried extra hard to beat my brothers. Mum tells me I could play chess at the age of three, and never gave anyone a moment's peace, always after a game. Because my brothers were that much older than me, I had to fight to get their attention when we played sport in the back garden, but by the time I was six Dad was whacking a ball at me, testing my reflexes and my catching ability.

All four brothers were sports-mad, but we've used that competitive streak to do pretty well in our chosen professions. Mark, the eldest, was a very good hockey player. He did officer training at Sandhurst and now he works in television advertising. Paul was deputy head boy at our school and just passed exams for fun – straight 'A's all the way. An excellent swimmer and rugby player, he became a doctor and practises in New Zealand. Phil, a good sprinter and footballer, studied at the London School of Economics, and works as a freelance photo-journalist for travel magazines when he's not playing in a rock band. We are still a very close family, there for each other at any time. I still see my father whenever I'm in Hong Kong, and we have a round of golf together. It's strange, though – he doesn't mind that much if I beat him. Not like the others in my family!

In Hong Kong, you get roped into all sports if you're co-ordinated and because space on the territory is very tight, you'd play wherever you could. Our cricket pitch was a mat laid down in the middle of a football field/athletics track, with holes in the outfield where the shot putt had landed. The boundaries either side were very short – about 40 yards – and that's where I learned to knock the ball square, one of the most productive areas of my batting when I became a professional in England. I was always hoicking it over square leg as a boy, style meant nothing to me – then and now! I made a point of watching how the best batsmen played and in Hong Kong they all seemed to have good eyes, with no desire to look all that elegant. So I'd also look to smash a ball on the off-stump over mid-wicket, a shot I continued to play, against the better judgment of some coaches when I came to England. At school in Hong Kong, we relied on the teacher's love of the game to find the time to coach us and I was very lucky with our master, David Clinton. David didn't bother too much with technique, but he was very encouraging, helping us to respect the game. He gave up a lot of his free time to help us, and I'll always be grateful to him for making me even more enthusiastic about cricket. The facilities were very rudimentary, so there was no detailed coaching. I found the need to watch and copy older and more successful batsmen. When bowling, I used to run up and try to bowl fast off-cutters, because that was the only way the ball would deviate off the matting. But no one showed me to hold the ball, or the technique needed to make it swing. It was a case of going out there to enjoy it.

At the age of 12, I made my debut in adult cricket for my school. We played Saturday and Sunday for seven months a year and that must have made me even more competitive, playing against men every game. My Mum would drive me all over the island, talking to me about how I should be playing, have a post-mortem on the way back if we'd lost or I'd failed – and I loved it. In club cricket over there, the convention was that you didn't bat and bowl, so I used to miss out on batting, which didn't please me. David Clinton batted me at number nine for a whole season, which didn't appeal to me too much, but after I'd nagged away at him, he put me in as opener the following year and I made some runs. I knew I wasn't a classical player but that didn't bother me – I just looked in the scorebook! I never looked at myself on a cricket video until I'd been at Sussex for a few years – which is just as well because it was then too late to change!

Apart from the support of my parents, the most significant part of my cricket development in Hong Kong came when a certain Geoffrey Boycott came to the territory. He visited our school to do some coaching as part of a deal with Cathay Pacific Airlines and we were in awe of the man. Hardly surprising when you consider his stature in world cricket at the time – and Geoffrey for one wouldn't disagree! At that time, I was only aware of Boycott the great batsman, rather than the quirky Yorkshireman with a fantastic knowledge of the game, who I've come to respect so much. It was an eye-opener when he first came to the school nets at Kowloon. For a start, he batted first – and stayed in the nets for an hour. His justification was typical Boycott: 'You can learn a lot from watching me.' He was right. We saw how high his left elbow was, how side-on he played, the way he respected every ball that was sent down to him. He hardly lofted a shot, he'd defend a straight ball that was doing nothing at all if it was on a good length, and if it was slightly over-pitched, he'd lean into a classical drive. He was so disciplined: if the ball was short, he'd lean back and crack it, but everything else would be played with a straight bat unless it was wide. He was just working on his technique, getting into a groove, and it was unbelievable for schoolboys to watch him at close quarters. I realised then just what a great player looks like. It was the first time I'd been anywhere near a serious, disciplined cricketer and I was dumbstruck with admiration.

After his prolonged masterclass in the nets, he gave us a few minutes of catching practice before making it clear he was done with us. As he was collecting his gear, he said, 'Right, who wants a pair of batting gloves then?' Quick as a flash, I shot up my hand and he said, 'Right, that'll be 90 dollars.' Now that was a lot of money, but I didn't care, nor did I know about Boycott's reputation as a Yorkshireman who was careful with his money. When Mum came to pick me up, I bubbled on about the nets and that Geoffrey Boycott of all people had offered to sell me his batting gloves: how could she refuse? I saw her misgivings, but she handed over a 100 dollar note to Boycott, who said, 'You won't want change, then?' Mum shot back: 'Yes, I do, thanks very much – I'm married to a Yorkshireman.' Geoffrey obviously realised he'd met his match, handed her the change and they got on well after that.

Years later, I had the great thrill of bowling at him in my first season in county cricket. It was at Headingley, and as we walked off the field at lunchtime, I saw him eyeing me. He eventually said, 'Where have I seen you before?' and I answered, 'You coached me in Hong Kong.' It quickly dawned on him and he said, 'Oh aye, the one with the moother. Well done, lad.' He wasn't so pleased later that day, though, when I got him lbw. He was convinced he wasn't out (he has been known to offer that view, hasn't he?) and he didn't speak to me for the rest of the match! I was on cloud nine, though, and Mum was chuffed when I told her the story.

Geoffrey Boycott paid another visit to our school in Hong Kong when I was about 16. He must have had a great deal with Cathay Pacific! This time, he made an even bigger impression on me. By now, I was really getting into cricket, loving its challenges, wondering how I could improve. Boycott showed me his way to improve in no uncertain terms. He took us for a coaching session and started by telling us to play the backward defensive shot. One boy was doing it with his arms and hands away from his body and Boycott walked up to him, jabbed him on the chest and shouted, 'The ball can hit you here – and it hurts.' The boy's eyes were watering from the painful jab, and so we were even more keen on having no gap between body and bat as he walked down the line. Later, one of my pals bowled me a bouncer and I ducked out of the way of it. I smiled, picked up the ball and threw it back. Boycott spotted me grinning as I said, 'You missed' to the bowler. He stopped the net and shouted, 'What are you doing?' My answer ('Batting, Mr Boycott') didn't amuse him and he said in front of everyone, 'You don't coom to my nets to smile and enjoy yourself, you coom here to work. You enjoy it afterwards if you win. You're here now to learn.' That wiped the smile off my face, and although Mum, who was watching, told me to take no notice of him – she is Lancastrian, after all – I could see what he meant. I could see his focus even then, when I knew nothing at all about what was needed to make the grade. He respected the game so much, he knew how technical it was, how difficult it could be. He told us, 'The most important stroke is the forward defensive. Learn to play it, otherwise you'll get out and it's not as enjoyable a game watching others bat. If you can play the forward defensive, you can survive in club cricket.' That advice has stayed with me and I still use it when I coach. It's vital to be able to play it in county cricket if you're trying to save the game and when you first come in to bat. When I first go in, I block it, to get myself attuned to the pace of the pitch. That applies even when we're in a run chase, because I need to get into rhythm and a groove before I can try to play shots. The forward defensive is the key to that for me.

I know Geoffrey Boycott gets up some people's noses in the game, but for me he has been very influential, from my schooldays and when I played for England. He was on television duty when we toured India in 1993 and I was very impressed by the analytical, precise way he talked about batting. He was very quick to praise, as well as point out defects, which will surprise those who think he is too negative and knocking. Boycott is brilliant at getting you in the right focus, at channelling your mind while at the same time getting you relaxed in your body, so that you play the shot properly. All those years previously, he had made me realise what was needed by a cricket-mad kid if he even aspired to play professional cricket. Boycott was determined to have a great net against a bunch of schoolkids, even though he was a world-class player. It was an amazing insight into the mental hardness and self-discipline top sportsmen have to acquire.

I didn't even think about such self-sacrifice for myself at that stage, all I wanted to do was play cricket every day. When I first went to England at the age of 14, I was thrilled to be able to spend a summer playing cricket. One of the many advantages of having parents who are teachers is that they get long holidays, so we would spend long periods of the English summer in the London area, where there was so much cricket available. I joined Mike Gatting's old club, Brondesbury in North London, so I was in my element -cricket all the year round. Up to five games a week, plus evening social games, and I was doing OK. The lads at the club called me 'Yank', because I didn't have an English accent. Must have been all that American stuff on Hong Kong television I'd been watching!

So the pattern was set for me over the next couple of years. I got to play so much cricket in Hong Kong and London that I couldn't help but improve, yet I was still raw, lacking in technical skill, relying on a good eye for batting and aggression when bowling. My parents knew this and when I came back to London at the age of 16, Mum arranged a couple of nets for me at Lord's. I was totally over-awed at the facilities and, after the poor surfaces back home. I couldn't believe the quality of outdoor and indoor nets at Lord's and I wanted to bat and bowl all day, every day. When I had my first indoor net – paid for by my parents – the coach kept telling me to play straight. But it was a perfect surface; the bounce was even and I kept clubbing the slow bowlers and the medium pacers over mid-wicket, like I did in Hong Kong. Eventually the coach, an Australian, came up to me and said, 'You've got the best eye of any young player I've seen.' He said I would have to tighten up my game when I got outside, on wickets that would see the ball jag around, but he encouraged me. That's what young players need above all; he realised you must play to your strengths, instead of applauding politely if you blocked a straight ball that should have disappeared.

Mum could see how much I looked forward to my sessions at Lord's and eventually she wangled regular nets for me, alongside the MCC Young Cricketers. They are deemed to be the elite of the young players in the country, spotted at an early age, earmarked by the various county clubs, some of them destined for international honours, most of them with a very good chance of at least playing first-class cricket. For a raw teenager from Hong Kong with no obvious technical ability, it was a thrill just to be in the same net as them, drinking in the wisdom of the head coach, Don Wilson, a great character who had played for Yorkshire and England. I arrived three months later than the others, but I got on very well with them. They called me 'Hong Kong Phooee', and we had a lot of fun. That year's intake included Norman Cowans, Mark Feltham, Asif Din, Paul Smith and Neil Williams. I knew I wasn't in their class, but I made up for that with enthusiasm. Mum would drive me as far as Kent for the games and, whenever there was nothing on at Lord's, she'd somehow organise a net or a match for me somewhere. She was fantastically supportive, she knew how happy I was playing cricket all the time. What I didn't know at the time was that she was trying to get me taken on as an MCC Young Cricketer for the following year. I didn't think I was any good as a player, especially when I watched the other lads at close quarters, but I was delighted to stay on in September 1980 for an extra month, playing for the Cross Arrows at Lord's. I'd made my way up from the fourth team to the firsts at Brondesbury and that helped my confidence. I'd also won the fielding prize for the club that year, probably because of my enthusiasm but also because I had a strong throwing arm in those days. Times have certainly changed . . .

I went back to Hong Kong with a faint hope that I might be taken on at Lord's next year, but well aware that a lad from Hong Kong with little technical ability couldn't really compare himself with guys of his own age who had looked so impressive in the same side and in the nets. I wasn't surprised when Don Wilson rang to say that I hadn't made the final selection, but I was next in line. Don told my parents that my enthusiasm and spirit were the reasons why I had got so close and that he was impressed by my keen attitude, so I suppose that was some consolation as I settled down to my 'A' Levels and club cricket in Hong Kong. Then, out of the blue, he rang the following March. Chris Lethbridge had been taken on by Warwickshire and there was a vacancy. My parents, even though they were teachers, didn't advise me about getting my 'A' Levels, because they knew that such an opportunity for a boy living in Hong Kong wouldn't come around again. After a frenzy of packing and last-minute organising, I arrived at Lord's at the start of a momentous season for English cricket – 1981, the year of Botham's Ashes. Ian Botham had been a member of the ground staff just eight years earlier and his achievements were a godsend to head coach Don Wilson as he tried various ways to inspire us. 'Just look at what Botham's done,' he'd tell us. 'That could be you.' That was stretching it a little, but typical of Don's positive thinking. Ian Botham was already a hero to me because of the way he approached the game. I'd only read one cricket book – 'by Tony Greig' – but I knew how I wanted to play the game, despite my respect for Geoffrey Boycott's disciplined professionalism.

Don Wilson was absolutely brilliant with us at Lord's. He was so enthusiastic, so knowledgeable and very funny. Every Friday night, after getting paid (£32 a week), we'd all go to the bar in the Indoor School and Don would hold court after buying us all a drink. One lad made the mistake of ordering a soft drink, which led Don to question his sexual orientation. 'Eee lad, there's a couple of other things that are as important as cricket – and one of them's having a drink! You'll have a pint!' Don liked us all to muck around together off the field as well, and he was brilliant at fostering team spirit, an aspect of the game that to me is very important and is one of the reasons for Warwickshire's success.

The MCC Young Cricketers had a huge fixture list, which was ideal for us – so much better than working the scoreboard or selling programmes during the big matches at Lord's. Although I was pleased to be selling scorecards one day at Lord's during a Test Match, because I got to speak to Mick Jagger. That's putting it a little strongly, I suppose. He said, 'Thanks' when I handed him the scorecard and grinned when I said, 'See ya, Mick!' as he walked away. I pushed my luck and asked him to sign a scorecard, and he happily obliged. What a life! Playing cricket every day, getting paid for it – and meeting Mick Jagger . . .

I struggled to make an impression in my first year. I found the bowlers far faster than anything I'd been used to – I soon bought a helmet! At last someone told me about where to place the wrist when you bowl, how to impart swing, when to bowl the bouncer; for someone from the cricketing backwoods of Hong Kong, it was a very, very steep learning curve when you consider the quality of the other young players on the staff. There were the Australians Tim Zoehrer, Wayne Phillips and Mark O'Neill, the great New Zealand batsman Martin Crowe and home-grown players like Phillip DeFreitas. Every day I'd be first in the nets to choose a good ball from the box, so that it would swing. I'd rub away at it to get a good shine, make sure I held up the seam properly, and keep trying to master the outswinger. None of that seemed to matter though when Martin Crowe batted against me; he was just on a different level, with awesome ability. I'd look at the gulf between those guys and me and never dream about playing county cricket, unlike all the rest of the ground staff. I'd look out over the hallowed turf at Lord's and daydream about playing just once on that immaculately kept surface. Just once – I didn't believe I could justify anything more than that. A first-class career was out of the question, but perhaps I could nip in for a friendly game in late September?

The height of my ambition in that summer of 1981 was just to be retained for another year. I savoured every moment of it,

I didn't find the atmosphere at all stuffy, not even when we had to bowl at the members. Don Wilson used to say, 'Right lads, you're finished for the day, but does anyone want to stay on to bowl at the members?' I was there like a shot, because I loved it all so much and it was bound to help my bowling. I even got tipped a quid now and then . . .

While I struggled to master the intricacies of swing bowling, I learned an awful lot about the mechanics of batting by watching players like Martin Crowe. I noticed how low he stayed while playing the cover drive, how he would bat for rhythm, getting accustomed to the pitch and the bowling before opening out. Even though I batted very low in the order that first year, I was taking it all in, telling myself that I'd put everything into practice if I ever got the chance for a long innings.

When I went back to Hong Kong after that first summer at Lord's, I broke some domestic records and a lot started falling into place for me. So much that I had picked up in England seemed to have been absorbed subconsciously and for the first time I felt I wasn't a bad player. I was then picked to play for Hong Kong against Singapore, one of the rare matches to be played on a grass wicket. I managed to take six wickets with the new ball, mainly due to my newly-discovered outswinger. I was then selected for Hong Kong in the ICC Trophy competition that saw us playing for a few weeks in the Midlands in 1982, and I loved that. For me, it was just a case of doing my best for whatever team I was in, enjoying the day and getting ready for the next match, wherever it was.

Not for the first time, my Mum had greater ambitions for me. She had watched me closely and decided that cricket in Hong Kong was no longer stretching me enough. Mum was very determined and she phoned her sister in Perth, Western Australia, to say that I wanted to play club cricket out there. I'd already met a guy from Perth called Tony Taylor in London who had told me his club, Claremont Cottesloe, had four sides: that was good enough for Mum. Off I went to Western Australia to find out just how good I was at cricket in a very tough environment. I was 19. Three times a week, my uncle Walter would drop me off at the nets and I'd cadge a lift back. Eventually, I

moved into a flat with Tony Taylor and started to enjoy the
Australian way of life. I started off in the second team at
Claremont Cottesloe, following in the footsteps of David
Gower, Norman Cowans and Nick Cook. Mind you, they'd
played in the first team. They were England players, after all –
what could I expect?

I quickly had to learn to play off the back foot on those fast
wickets and my bowling needed more variety because the new
ball soon lost its shine and hardness on the dry surfaces. I spent
nine seasons playing grade cricket in Western Australia, and
there's no doubt it was a vital stage in my development, not just
as a cricketer pure and simple, but in mental terms. I really had
to toughen up straight away. Before I went to Australia, the
game of cricket was such a joy to me that I'd have a permanent
smile on my face out in the middle, loving the privilege of playing a great game. In Australia, there isn't any room for such sentiments. It's hard, unrelenting and losing is not an option.
Cricket out there was so much more vocal than anywhere else I
had played. I was teased about being a Pom, first because I was
based at Lord's (their attempts at a posh English accent were
very amusing), then because they thought I was no good.

The sledging on the field never stopped, and I admit that I
brought those experiences with me to county cricket as I became
more self-confident. It was so intense. The midweek practice sessions were very organised and intensive, with everything geared
up to 90 overs that coming Saturday, with the return innings of
90 overs the following Saturday. It took a while to get used to
being out in the field for 90 overs in the heat of Perth, but it was
all part of the toughening-up process for me. The sides would
enjoy victory afterwards among themselves, but there was rarely
a sense of enjoyment or pleasure on the pitch during the game.
And the post-mortems could be very serious and bitter. One
day, Robin Smith turned a game against us, winning it with a
brilliant innings. In the dressing-room afterwards, the inquest
went along predictable lines: 'We're just not good enough,
we've got to work harder.' Yet we hadn't played badly, we just
lost to a great knock, in my eyes, but they didn't see it that way.
If you lose, there must be reasons for it. They also didn't believe

in mixing with the opposition, whatever the result. They'd sing in the shower if they'd won, take it badly in defeat – and always go back to their own clubhouse and mix with all the teams from their own club. The Australian concept of 'mateship' is very strong and perhaps that's why they gel as a team more than in other countries. For me, it was just a case of getting used to a different cricketing philosophy. I didn't think one view was preferable to the other, just different.

There's no doubt that playing out there made me a better cricketer and, as I moved to a higher standard of cricket in Perth, I was pleased that my own game improved in the nine years I spent there. I was named Western Australia's Grade Cricketer of the Year for two seasons, and that meant a great deal to me. It's an award on the recommendation of the umpires for consistency throughout the season, so for them to give it to a Pom must count for something. Also, the State players like Mike Veletta, Bruce Reid and Graeme Wood (all Test cricketers) were regulars in the competition, so doing well against that lot was great for me. The same goes for Alec Stewart, who also won the award in Western Australia. Interesting that some English experts have sometimes accused Alec and me of going over the top on the field at times. Australians would just say we were fair dinkum cricketers!

My second summer with MCC Young Cricketers showed a distinct upturn and I put that down to my experiences in Australia. I was even more battle-hardened when I came back in 1983 after a season in Perth that saw me make a double hundred in grade cricket. I was beginning to think I wasn't such a bad cricketer after all, and I was chuffed when picked at short notice to go on an MCC tour of Holland and Denmark. Vanburn Holder had dropped out and I think they only chose me because it was convenient, but I wasn't complaining. It was a terrific trip. The cricket talk from the old pros was an eye-opener for me, and I took all the leg-pulling in good part. They called me 'Boy' as I fetched and carried their bags for them, but it was all in good fun.

Unknown to me, Sussex had made an approach to the MCC on my behalf when I was on that tour. It all came about in a way that's convinced me that luck is vital to any cricketer. At the end of April, MCC played the champion county, Middlesex, at Lord's in the traditional curtain-raiser to the English season. It rained all three days and not a ball was bowled. So the players needed some practice, and they went to the Indoor School at various stages for a net. Ian Gould was there when I was bowling and I offered to send a few down at him. Gould had been on the England tour to Australia a few months earlier, and as wicket-keeper/batsman with Sussex, he was highly regarded. So I tried my very best to impress and with a successful season in Perth behind me, I was full of confidence. I was mentally harder, physically stronger and I was doing more with the ball. My bouncer worked well against Gould, I rapped him on the pads several times with late swing, and made the odd one go across him. I bowled really well at Gould that afternoon, but thought no more about it after he'd gone. After the game was washed out on the third day, I happened to be walking past the pavilion door as the players were leaving. Gould, on his way to a county match, bumped into me, and when I said 'Cheerio', he stopped, recognised me and asked my name. He said he'd recommend me to his county, Sussex. I thanked him, but thought there must be far better young cricketers than me around to interest a county. Little did I know that Sussex were about to suffer a series of injuries to their seam bowlers and that a vacancy would soon arise.

After Gould's recommendation, I played a couple of second team games for Sussex. Then I went on the MCC tour to Holland and Denmark.

When I got back from that tour, I was summoned to the office of Donald Carr, the Test and County Cricket Board secretary. Sussex had offered me a contract but the question of my appearance the previous year for Hong Kong in the ICC Trophy was a worry. Mr Carr wanted to know how English I was. Would my Hong Kong birthplace count against me in registration terms? Well, I put on my most pukka English accent for Mr Carr, but it was more relevant that both my parents had been born in England. I was in the clear and allowed to sign for Sussex. Within a few weeks, I made my county debut – at Hove against Somerset.

Looking back, it was an unbelievable sequence of events that got me into professional cricket. Strokes of luck everywhere. Chris Lethbridge being signed by Warwickshire, allowing me a place on the ground staff. Don Wilson having faith in me because of my enthusiasm, nothing else. That MCC game against Middlesex being washed out. The fact that I was bowling when Ian Gould came into my net at Lord's. Bumping into him as he was leaving the ground on that last day. Would he have done anything about me if I hadn't said 'Cheerio'? The fact that his county suddenly became short of seam bowlers, so short that they had to turn to a 20-year-old who was just coming to terms with the basics of seam and swing bowling. They could have snapped up many more cricketers of the same age, with greater maturity and ability. I just happened to be in the right place at the right time. People say that you make your own luck in life, but that wasn't so for me in the summer of 1983. I should have done the pools every week!

3

The County Novice

If I was lucky to get on to a county staff, I was even luckier to slip into the Sussex first team within a week or so of arriving at Hove. They signed me as cover for some of their seamers, especially Imran Khan – not much of a challenge that! The great man had a stress fracture of the shin and was playing as a batsman. Adrian Jones, who ought to have been next in line from the second team, was also injured and then, after I had played just two games for the seconds, Ian Greig's freak injury gave me my first-team chance. Greig had played for England the previous year and was obviously a key all-rounder for Sussex. At the start of June, during the home county game with Kent, he had broken his leg, trying to get into his flat. The front door key had snapped off in the lock, and as he tried to climb in through the first-floor window, the ledge gave in and he fell. Greig only played eight championship matches that season, so within a couple of days of that accident, I was making my county debut, at Hove against Somerset.

I hadn't even met my county captain, John Barclay, until the morning of my debut. He couldn't have been nicer. He asked what I bowled and said, 'Don't worry, we'll work it out, just enjoy it – and good luck.' Johnny was like that all through my Sussex career, a marvellous enthusiast who made you want to do well for him as well as yourself.

We fielded first, I came on first change and bowled every ball as fast as I could. I wasn't confident enough to hold the seam up the right way, trying to swing it: all the Lord's Indoor School stuff went out the window, I just wanted to get it down the other end as quick as possible. I took five wickets in the game, which we won, and I was chuffed to bits. The wicket was superb, by the standards I had been used to, and I was pleased to have battled my way to 16 at number nine, after I had come in on a hat-trick. Those five wickets were a huge thrill though, even if Somerset were without Viv Richards and Ian Botham, who were playing in the World Cup at the time. I did my sums quickly and thought, 'If I carry on like this, I'll get over seventy wickets this season!' Then it dawned on me that it might rain, and I might get carted around, or get injured, or dropped. I was so naive – but thrilled to be playing county cricket, and not being humiliated.

The Sunday League game was terrific that weekend. There was such a buzz at the ground, and I remembered the advice of the coach, Stewart Storey – 'You've got to attack the ball in the field.' I was running around at full tilt, hurling the ball in, and the crowd applauded me: the adrenalin flowed and I was really pumped up. It was great fun and was the first time I'd played in front of a large, vocal crowd. I loved that atmosphere. That Sussex team had some excellent fielders – Alan Wells, Gehan Mendis, Paul Phillipson and, above all, Paul Parker. Only Trevor Penney comes near to Paul Parker as a fielder in my experience. He worked so hard at his fielding that he became, in effect, an all-rounder – someone who bats and fields, saving runs and taking wickets. You would put Paul where you knew it would be busy and just rely on him to intimidate the batsman. He'd worked out a new method of fielding, the slide/pick-up that was faster than picking up the ball, then throwing on the turn. I saw him outwit Richard Hadlee with that new method, tempting him for the second run and when Hadlee was coasting, Paul threw the stumps down on one knee. It was a brilliant piece of work and typical of Paul's professional approach to fielding. He never saw it as a chore and his displays would lift the whole side.

I stayed in the first team after my debut, playing 17 championship games that season. John Barclay said he couldn't drop me, because I had done so well, which was very good of him. I'm not sure how popular it made me with some of the second team, though. There was this feeling that you had to serve your time in the seconds before getting a chance in the first team, but here was I – a young sprog from Lord's – walking straight in, and staying in the side. I was also disappointed early on with the attitude of several of the senior players. There was a surprising amount of back-stabbing, an attitude that astonished me, because I thought it was just a privilege to be playing county cricket, and that everyone must feel the same. I realise now that my boyish enthusiasm must have annoyed some of the older guys. Whenever it rained, I was so disappointed, whereas most of the others were pleased. Sussex weren't going to win the championship and they saw little motivation in playing after the halfway mark in the season. Whenever I looked out of the dressing-room window and said, 'Great lads – it's stopped raining!' the only ones to share my enthusiasm were Paul Parker and the captain, John Barclay. Paul clearly bothered some of the senior players with his professional approach to cricket and his overall integrity. One night, early in that first season, I went out for a few drinks with Colin and Alan Wells and Chris Waller, and they spent some time putting the boot into Paul Parker, saying he was probably tucked up in bed early, reading a book. I said nothing, sipped my beer and within a week I was having dinner with Paul, asking his advice, respecting his approach to his profession. Clearly Paul's dedication disconcerted some of the senior Sussex players; they felt shown up by him. Paul wanted to be the best fielder and batsman, and so he worked harder than anybody, to graft consistency onto his natural talent. I soon realised that you have to be yourself, even in a team game. Do what suits you best in terms of preparation and don't knock those who have a different perspective.

I tried too hard to please in that first season with Sussex. I was so keen, so naive – I'd say the first thing that came into my head, and the senior guys would tease me. Soon I became the butt of their humour as my mouth tended to run away, with my brain ten minutes behind (a fault I still have, I'm afraid!). County cricket was a far harder school mentally than I realised. In my first season, I was bowling against Middlesex and, I thought, doing okay. Mike Gatting was at the non-striker's end, watching with exasperation as I kept Wilf Slack quiet. Gatt couldn't take much more of this and shouted out, 'Come on Slacky – this bloke can't bowl!' Some of my team-mates enjoyed that, but it was one of many harsh introductions for me to the county grind. I didn't forget that moment. Gatt has become a friend over the years, and we enjoy the jousts on the field, but whenever I get him out I shout, 'Huh! Can't bowl, eh? Take a shower!' It was sink or swim and I was going to toughen up, because I loved playing county cricket so much.

I was soon physically shattered in that first season. Garth le Roux couldn't bowl after August because of a groin problem, and soon the guys nicknamed me 'Jesus' (as in 'the Saviour'), because I was always so keen to bowl. From my debut in late June, I sent down 470-odd overs in the championship alone, stayed in the side for the Sunday League, and my body was very stretched. I was wiry, but not physically strong enough for all that bowling; and I relied on adrenalin to get me through, because I still couldn't believe my luck that I was playing for a county side so soon. John Barclay was a fantastically supportive captain. I felt he was a man who was genuinely interested in my career. He had a lovely way of dealing with his players. He'd sidle up and confide in me in that classy Old Etonian accent: 'I'd simply love it if you could possibly give me another over. Can you?' and you'd run through the proverbial brick wall for him. I lost respect early on for some of the senior players, realising that you do it for yourself, the captain and the club, not for the knockers in the side – but for John Barclay I had total respect. I'm not at all surprised he has done well in the England set-up on tours. He was so encouraging, he'd always pick up on something positive. If you'd had a bad day in the field, you'd apologise to him – he deserved that at least – and Johnny would say, 'Not at all, you did your best. What about that late outswinger in your fourth over – beautiful ball that one. If you'd got a wicket then it would've all been different. Keep going.' He'd leave you on a high, feeling better. Johnny had a marvellous cricket brain, a deep knowledge of where opposition batsmen liked to play the ball, and he was bloody-minded enough to follow the ball, by altering his field if he felt a batsman was going to keep playing the ball into certain areas. He was worth his place in the side as a gutsy batsman, who could bowl useful off-spin. Sadly his gutsiness with the bat reduced his ability to spin his off-breaks, as he kept getting hit on the fingers because of the way he batted. He would take a huge stride on the front foot, and the blows kept coming to the hand, but Johnny never flinched. I remember a 60-odd he made against Malcolm Marshall at his best, which was so impressive. Johnny's commitment and positive attitude never wavered and when I eventually became a county captain, I tried to instil his supportive, positive methods of man-management into the Warwickshire set-up.

Johnny's relationship with Imran Khan in the Sussex side was at times amusing, sometimes frustrating and always fascinating. When I joined Sussex, Imran was the most charismatic cricketer in the world. Imran wasn't just a top all-rounder, a successful captain with Pakistan, a player who would improve any side in the world, he was a classy guy – and I'm sure he wouldn't disagree with that assessment. We lesser mortals in the Sussex dressing-room would read about his playboy activities with a mixture of envy and admiration, but there were no doubts about his success with women, his prominence in London social circles that we could only read about, or that county cricket appeared fairly low on his list of priorities. Imran would decide when he was coming on to bowl, not John Barclay. There were times when I had just got a wicket and I'd be bustling in, full of my usual optimism and then I'd hear that familiar drawl, 'Johnny – bring me on now.' The captain would come up to me and say, 'You've done really awfully well to get us our breakthrough, but Imran's our strike bowler. Hope you understand.' I did, but I'd be pissed off – especially when Imran would then decide he'd had enough after four overs and I'd be brought back on to bowl at a guy who had been in for half an hour.

In my first season, I saw Imran's pride and his insensitivity at close quarters in one county game, at Edgbaston. We were playing Warwickshire and Alvin Kallicharran was batting like a millionaire. I came on to bowl and immediately had him dropped by Imran at slip. He didn't say a word to me by way of apology. Then I had two big shouts for lbw against Kalli, only for the umpire, Bill Alley, to say, 'I can't give him out – I've never seen him bat so well, I'm enjoying this.' Thanks very much, umpire – what ever happened to the laws of cricket? When it came to our turn to bat, Imran copped a stack of bouncers from Paul Smith. It was clearly 'payback time' for previous encounters, with Paul realising this time that Imran wouldn't be able to retaliate, because of his shin problem. He was in the side purely as a batsman, so Imran got bouncers and verbals aplenty. He was furious. When we fielded again, he was still fired up and called for his bowling boots. 'I want to bowl, Johnny, I'm going to have Smith.' Barclay said, 'Are you sure?' but that was just an irrelevance. Imran had decreed he would bowl.

He came off his short run, but still fired them down at the speed of light. Every time a new batsman came in, we'd say, 'This is him – here's Smith!' and he'd snort and bowl bouncers at everyone, as he suffered from mistaken identity. Winding him up worked a treat, because he ended up with 6/6, including a hat-trick, and the wicket of Paul Smith. Honour was satisfied as far as Imran was concerned, and he looked forward to a comfortable victory, as we chased just over two hundred. Unfortunately, our batsmen failed Imran, despite his stylish 64. Soon we were in danger of defeat, which did nothing for Imran's mood. He was even less impressed when he walked out of our dressing-room to find D.A. Reeve padded up. He stopped, stared at me, took a look at the scoreboard and said, 'Oh shit.' He called for our captain and, in front of the other guys, said, 'Johnny, Dermot can't bat, put him in at number eleven and put Wally ahead of him at ten.' With that he went back into the dressing-room. Barclay said, 'Good idea, Imran', and as I fought back the urge to say something derogatory to Imran, I was demoted to last man and 'Wally' – Chris Waller – who boasted a career average of eight and an aversion to fast bowling, went in ahead of me. Sadly for me, there is no happy ending to this story. I was given out lbw for nought – by Bill Alley, the umpire with a selective attitude to lbw appeals – and we lost by 21 runs. Afterwards, Imran really made my day when he said, 'Johnny, I told you so – Dermot can't bat.' I was almost in tears and I only wish I had stood up to him. Imran's behaviour was something I would never do to a team-mate and another lesson I took with me when I became Warwickshire's captain – never belittle a colleague over his cricketing ability, or lack of it.

That incident might have destroyed me. Yet I realised that it was just Imran's way of speaking, reflecting his inbuilt confidence. He didn't mean to denigrate me, although it was hard to believe that at the time, especially as I knew I wasn't a huge favourite in the Sussex dressing-room because of my sudden arrival in the first team, with a few of their pals left behind in the second team. In fact, Imran went out of his way to help me after that Edgbaston game. He was very thoughtful about how to cope with the lifestyle of being a county cricketer, about the right type of food to eat and the need to avoid too much alcohol. Imran would call Ian Gould 'Lagerboots – you can hear Gouldy sloshing around behind the stumps', and Gouldy would have to take that from him. Imran told me that too many players succumb to the social pressure of drinking pints of lager because the others are at it and if you don't join in, they'll tease you. His advice was to drink mineral water if that's what you prefer and don't give in to mild bullying. He set a great example in that regard, looking after his physique. He would do weight exercises on his arms, because he felt that he needed strength for his heavy bat. That is one of the reasons why Imran could hit the spinners out of sight, because he was so strong. He also gave me some good advice about injecting extra pace into my bowling: jump higher. That was how he was transformed into a quick bowler. Mind you, Imran was always pretty keen on a jump, wasn't he?!

Imran had this massive self-belief. One day, he hit Jack Simmons for a huge six over long-off and his batting partner, Alan Wells, came down to congratulate him. Imran simply said, 'That's an easy shot for me', and he meant it. In a Sunday League game against Derbyshire, he came unstuck against Geoff Miller's off-spin and scored slowly. We only managed about 140 in our 40 overs and Imran just couldn't get Miller away. In the bath afterwards, Imran was, for a second or two, apologetic. He said, 'I had a nightmare. They're going to call for a stewards' and they're going to blame me.' He then walked into the dressing-room and called for attention. 'Guys, it's all my fault, I stuffed up. But Miller was bowling so well that I thought I'd see him off. If I couldn't get after him, surely no one else in the side could. My plan was to hit Michael Holding when he came on. I'm sorry, guys, but don't forget all the other games I've won for you.' That was typical Imran – a sincere apology by his standards, a kick in the teeth to the rest of us about our batting inadequacies and the conviction that he'd be able to smash Michael Holding around. And he believed it all!

He did it again at Ilford, when we were following on against Essex. I was nightwatchman, batting at number three, and the obvious danger man for us was their left-arm spinner, John Childs. Or, in the words of Imran, 'John Childseese'. The boys found it amusing to hear Imran mispronounce Childs' name. Half an hour before the start of play, Imran announced in his most imperious tone, 'Johnny, I must talk to the players – I have something really important to tell them.' Johnny Barclay, of course, agreed and we settled down at the feet of the great man. 'Listen to me, fellas, I grew up on these kind of pitches in Pakistan, so I know what I'm talking about. The danger bowler is this John Childseese, so don't leave your crease, otherwise you'll be stumped. The ball is turning too much, so just stay in your crease, wait for the short ball, and cut it for four. It's that simple – thank you, Johnny.' As Imran stood back, our captain replied, 'Well, Imran, thanks awfully for that – it was inspirational. Well, chaps, looks like we're batting all day, making around 400 and no one's getting out. Good luck then, do your best. On, on!'

I thought for a split second about the joys of running Imran out when we batted together but I decided against it for the good of the side. Anyway, it would be part of my cricket educa-tion to see the master at close quarters, dealing with a fine spin-ner. The Imran masterclass didn't last very long – he was stumped off John Childseese for just four. I was at the other end, as he skipped down the crease, missed the turning ball by a long way and was stumped by a yard. I thought back to his team talk and had to stop myself from laughing out loud. I was waiting for his explanation afterwards and wasn't disappointed. 'It was a half volley, I lifted my foot a little. That's all.' Not a word about trying to hit him over the top for six, something he had expressly forbidden in his inspirational team talk.

Imran did have a sense of humour, though. He was particularly taken with Cockney rhyming slang. When Ian Gould, a cheery southerner, used to say, 'Mornin' lads, I had a skinful last night. Sunk a few pints down the old Gregory', Imran would stare at him, trying to work it all out. Finally, he said, 'Gouldy, where is this pub, the Gregory – are there any nice chickies there?' Gouldy would sigh, 'I've told you before, it's slang – Gregory – Gregory Peck – neck. A few pints down the old Gregory! Geddit?' Imran slowly digested this and got the last laugh. 'Oh, thank you, Gouldy – my old china plate.' With that, we went out to field.

Imran went to fine leg and Garth le Roux started to bowl. As he was running up, Imran shouted, 'Stop, Garth! Stop!' He sounded so panicky that fielders, batsmen, umpires all stopped dead in their tracks and turned to Imran at fine leg. His advice to Garth was 'Bowl him a bouncer.' Someone shouted back, 'Why?' and Imran replied, 'To hit him in the Gregory!' We fell apart, Garth couldn't bowl for laughing and Imran was tickled pink for the rest of the day. For a time he really got into the Cockney slang. He'd stride into the dressing-room and inform us, 'Guys, I went to this fabulous Mori last night.' Someone would say, 'Mori, what's that?' and Imran would summon up his most arrogant stare and say, 'Mori – Moriarty – Party. God, you're so thick.' I found it hilarious to hear this proud Pakistani, born in Lahore, educated at Oxford University, speaking in Cockney rhyming slang.

Imran had a way of making you feel respected by him, then he'd bring you down without realising the impact of his words. I bumped into him one year in Australia, where I'd been playing grade cricket. He was with the Pakistan side, but he stopped to chat and asked how my cricket was going. I told him about the double hundred I'd just scored in grade cricket, an innings that really delighted me. He looked at me and said, 'You mean the whole team got two hundred?' I corrected him and he said, 'Dermot, why do you make these things up, to impress me?' A team-mate alongside me confirmed that I had actually scored a double hundred and Imran asked about the standard of the game, about the wicket. Finally he said, 'Dermot, you must be joking. I played grade cricket in Sydney and I never even got a hundred!' The following season in England, I got a fair number of runs in county cricket and for a time I played pretty well. Imran wasn't playing all that much for us – the society season was in full swing in London at the time and Ascot, then Wimbledon probably called – but he came back to play in one match, where I scored just 18. When I walked in after getting out, he said, 'Well played', and I answered, 'But I only got 18.' I told him to piss off, that I'd been playing well and scoring runs. Imran said, 'Have you really? I haven't seen the scores lately.' I resisted the temptation to point out that the county cricket scores aren't published in *Tatler*, but it was another example of Imran's thoughtlessness, that he was on a totally different plane to his Sussex team-mates.

To be fair to him, he often tried to make amends to me. I think he was genuinely interested in my cricket career. He knew it hadn't been easy for me when I first came into the Sussex side, and I knew he valued the fact that I was an individual and wouldn't go with the herd in social terms. I remember he was the first to try to teach me the intricacies of reverse swing, where the ball will go in the opposite direction to where it's expected. Imran knew all about this from playing in Pakistan, where the ball gets scuffed up early and is therefore difficult to swing traditionally. I just couldn't grasp what Imran was on about, even though I asked him several questions. In the end, he said, 'I give up – Johnny, he won't listen.' That day, Trevor Jesty hit me for 14 in an over and I wished Imran had got through to me about reverse swing. At least he had tried, though.

A few years after Imran and I both left Sussex, we played against each other on the biggest stage of all – the World Cup Final, at Melbourne, in 1992. On the eve of the game, I had first-hand experience of Imran's distinctive sense of humour. The England and Pakistani sides had been invited to a big bash, and the Australian hosts had put on a satirical show. Some Aussie came on, dressed as the Queen, and proceeded to satirise the Royal Family. That was too much for Ian Botham, who walked

out during the soup. Our captain, Graham Gooch, followed him
out, as did Alec Stewart, and soon it looked as if the whole
England team would walk out. I looked at Allan Lamb and he
joked: 'For goodness' sake, Dermot – we haven't drunk any of
this wine yet, and it's good stuff, man.' I stayed there, as the
Fergie and Diana jokes came out, and although it was close to
the bone, because we were representing our country the next
day, I thought the guy's comic technique was good. During the
show, I couldn't help noticing that on the nearby table, Imran
was in hysterics. I went over and sat down beside him, and the
tears were flowing down his cheeks. Finally, he managed to
speak and said, 'Dermot, it's so funny – only the real English
have walked out. The colonials don't know what to do!' With
that, he dissolved into more helpless laughter and I looked
around to see which English players were still there. Sure
enough – there was Graeme Hick, Robin Smith, Allan Lamb,
Derek Pringle, Chris Lewis, Phillip DeFreitas, Gladstone Small
and Dermot Reeve. All born abroad. Some from what might be
termed a 'colonial' background. Of the English-born, only Neil
Fairbrother and Richard Illingworth were still there. I thought
it was very smart of Imran to spot that.

Next day, we lost the Final and you could see Imran's pride at
the achievement as he stood on the podium, and his joy at the
realisation that now he could get the financial support for his
cancer hospital. Later I went into their dressing-room to congratulate the Pakistan team and Imran motioned to me to sit
down beside him: he does have this regal manner! He said,
'Dermot, I must tell you, I'm very happy for you, you've done
so well to get so far in the game.' Then a crucial pause and the
killer phrase – 'for someone of your limited ability.' There I was,
thinking for a fleeting second that he was being nice to me, then
he takes away the compliment. He really knows how to make a
guy feel special! The trouble is, he actually meant what he was
saying. He had never rated me on talent, but he liked the way I
had made a career for myself on application and character. I suppose I ought to have been flattered.

I shall always be grateful though to Imran Khan for one thing.
That distinctive, aristocratic voice of his has given me rich

pickings when I do after-dinner speeches. I'm lucky enough to have an ear for accents, and to be able to impersonate some. When I grew up in Hong Kong, there were 28 different nationalities at school and I could somehow manage a few of the accents. As a boy, I'd do impersonations in Chinese or Indian while reading poems out loud and they seemed to work. So when I heard a new accent, I'd try to do that one. When I joined Sussex, I'd walk around trying out new voices, and I was particularly taken by Imran's. So was everybody else in the dressing-room and Imran finally got very shirty about it. One day he shouted, 'Why do all of you guys think you sound like me? It's pathetic, just be yourselves. Dermot is the only one who remotely sounds like me.' I took that as a licence to impersonate him, but he still wasn't too happy about it. He finally cracked at Lord's, as I was going through my routine, trying to get his distinctive drawl just right. Imran said, 'Listen, you little shit, if you go on like that I'm going to punch you on the head!' John Barclay overheard him and said, 'Oh there's nothing like a great team spirit is there, chaps?' and disappeared to lunch! After that, I was wary about doing Imran in his presence, but I was extremely grateful to him in his absence one day in 1992. I was a guest at the dinner marking the Hong Kong Sixes event, and the master of ceremonies knew I was a bit of a closet mimic. Anyway, he sprung it on me, telling the audience I was going to do my impersonations. I was struck dumb with terror, because I had nothing prepared and genuinely thought I was there just for the fun. I managed to get through 20 minutes of Brian Johnston and Imran Khan impersonations, and although it was the longest twenty minutes of my life, it went fairly well. Since then, I have managed to organise some sort of party piece for my after-dinner work, and Imran features regularly. So thanks for everything, Imran – especially that voice.

Imran didn't play at all for Sussex in my second season, in 1984, but we soldiered on, rising several places up the championship table to sixth place. I was well aware that 'second seasonitis' might strike me, so there could be a reaction to my first, satisfactory season, but I did quite well. I averaged 27 with the bat and 25 with the ball in first-class cricket (compared to 12 and 28 the year before) and at one stage I managed to get as high as number seven in the batting order. A hundred against Surrey as nightwatchman helped, I suppose, but in the end, I had to be content with number eight or nine in a strong batting side. Looking back on those years now, I realise I tried too hard on the field. By that I mean I was too keyed up, too full of nervous tension, so that I didn't focus properly on the ball. With greater experience, I now understand that to do well as a batsman, you have to watch the ball as closely as possible, but you can't do that unless you're relaxed at the right moment. Your mind needs to be relaxed, yet focused when it really counts. You also need to be in an encouraging environment if you're a young player and that wasn't the case for me, with the exceptions of John Barclay, Paul Parker, Colin Wells and Gehan Mendis. There were too many petty jealousies, too much conformist thinking. If you expressed a contrary view, you were pigeon-holed as a cocky youngster who had only been in the game five minutes.

In my early years at Sussex, a local radio reporter interviewed me, and asked my ambitions. I said what any self-respecting young professional ought to say – that I would dearly love to play for England one day. I didn't at any stage suggest I was good enough, but some of my team-mates heard the interview and used it as ammunition. I particularly recall the words of Alan Wells: 'You ought to just concentrate on staying in the first team, getting your cap, hoping for a benefit at the end of it all. You'll never play for England.' I just gave him a look but inside I was angry. I believe his attitude was wrong, that you have to aspire to a goal, even if you might fall short for lack of talent. I knew I didn't look all that special on the cricket field, that I wasn't the finished, polished article. When I first saw myself on video as a Sussex player, I wasn't at all impressed – but it was the best I could manage and I was more concerned about effectiveness than style. Alan Wells was far more elegant than me as a batsman, but he was a long way from England selection when he tried to cuff me down.

Years later, when I first played for England – and scored 59 on my Test debut – I recalled that quote from Alan Wells and smiled to myself. When I eventually captained Warwickshire, I tried to use incidents like that one with Alan Wells to get the guys properly motivated. I'd tell them at no stage should they even think about coasting. If you're looking to score a certain number of runs in a month and you get there with a week to spare, you revise your target and keep pushing yourself. Simplify the game, take it one over at a time, never look ahead to the last day. Don't conform or settle for your county cap and possibly a benefit ten years later. Make it happen for you. If I'd taken Alan Wells' words to heart, I probably would have drifted out of county cricket soon afterwards.

I seriously thought about retiring after a couple of years with Sussex. I was still the butt of a few influential senior players, and although most of it could be construed as the usual dressing-room banter, I was sensitive and no one ever said, 'Don't worry, it's just a bit of fun.' Ian Greig once threw my kit out of the dressing-room, which I found childish from such a mature guy, but also significant: I was obviously a threat to him in his eyes as the side's all-rounder. I remember being bitterly disappointed when he was picked ahead of me against the Australians in 1985 and John Barclay's consoling words ('You'll get a chance to play against them in the future') didn't cut much ice. Any young player surrounded by such experience would be a little sensitive, but I felt there wasn't enough encouragement. In one game against Essex, I got myself out badly – a loose shot to cover off Derek Pringle after I had batted away against Neil Foster, picking up sore ribs, but I left Ian Gould high and dry at the other end. As soon as I walked in, our coach Stewart Storey tore a strip off me, telling me it was a bloody awful shot. It dawned on me then that there was a right way and a wrong way to get out. I remember being caught at short leg off an off-break from Mike Watkinson that turned, only to be told 'bad luck' by the coach. Yet when Colin Wells swept Watkinson straight to deep square leg, he was told it was a waste of a wicket and a bad shot. Now to my mind, I was more guilty than Colin, because at least he was trying an attacking shot, while I was just defending. Yet my dismissal looked better than Colin's and I didn't get the rollicking. When I came to Warwickshire I decided I would bat with more freedom, that if I got out, at least it would hopefully come from playing positively. My experiences of being bawled out in front of my team-mates at Sussex also influenced me in choosing the right way to talk to someone who has been brainless on the field – in private, face-to-face, long after the heat of the moment has passed. That player doesn't need to be told he has stuffed up as soon as he walks off the field.

Stewart Storey wasn't always hard, though. He was aware of Ian Greig's attitude to me and he sympathised. He told me about one young player from his days with Surrey, who was finally hounded out of the game by the older pros. They were insecure about their own futures, the prospect of a benefit, their declining prowess, and they made this lad a whipping boy. He stood it for a time and then gave it away. Stewart said he was worried I'd be going the same way, and I admitted I was thinking about it, because I just wanted to enjoy myself and keep improving. I didn't need the back-stabbing. He told me to stick at it, that it was a hard profession and to develop thick skin. Of course, he was right, but I do think I was in an insensitive environment and I started to wonder if I would enjoy my cricket somewhere else on the county circuit.

Ian Greig wasn't retained at the end of the 1985 season, but that didn't necessarily smooth the way for me in my ambition to move up the batting order. The wickets at Hove were now so good that I didn't expect to get many innings there in championship matches, unless we were in trouble. After my hundred as a nightwatchman against Surrey, I put together a few good scores and I suggested to Stewart Storey that perhaps I could open if we were involved in a run chase, so that the better players could come in later, with the pressure eased if I managed to pull off a few shots. He made it clear that I would never open the innings, which disappointed me. It seemed a depressingly conformist attitude: did that mean you never open the bowling with a spinner? Young David Wood was trying to make his way as an opener for Sussex in those days, but even if he was short of form and confidence, he would still be the opener even in a run chase – because he was categorised as an opener. So I was pigeon-holed as a lower order batsman, whose main task was to bowl. There seemed little awareness that circumstances change, that you have to be flexible: the sort of dynamic attitude that helped Sri Lanka win the World Cup.

I loved the occasion of the big match and when Sussex won the Nat West Final at Lord's in 1986, I was in my element. I won the Man of the Match Award because I was determined to enjoy the day and not freeze. I wanted the ball to come to me all the time in the field, and when I made a good stop in the second over, I just felt I was going to do well. I took 4/20 coming on third change, including my old Sussex team-mate Gehan Mendis out lbw, and then I ruined the day for the Lancashire fans and the neutrals by getting Clive Lloyd out lbw for nought. It was big Clive's farewell game, and many hoped he'd sign off with a major innings, but umpire Ken Palmer wasn't to be swayed and he supported my appeal. Lloyd out second ball; I've always rated Ken Palmer as an umpire! We cruised to a seven-wicket win and I was so pleased for my Dad, because I got the award from his special hero, Sir Leonard Hutton, who was the match adjudicator. Dad was there to see it, so that was a great day for both of us to savour. I can't explain why I managed to do so well on such a high-pressure day, other than being able to relax at the right time and not let the tension drain me. I just smiled my way through the entire day, and I felt fresh as a daisy. If you go with the flow, and manage to switch on the concentration when it's needed, you can do yourself justice on big occasions like a Lord's Final. I find that if you are too tense, nothing happens when you press the button.

A year after that Lord's Final, I had decided to leave Sussex. It was purely a case of ambition, certainly not money. I wasn't enjoying it at Sussex as much as I had hoped. It was more fun playing as an amateur, when I used to look forward to every game as if it was going to be my last. When you do it for a job, all that changes and it becomes hard work every day. I could understand how so many of the senior players at Sussex had become jaded by mid-season, and that only increased my admiration for John Barclay and Paul Parker, who were still so enthusiastic. They must have been superb actors, because I rarely saw them listless, apart from one day when Paul Parker got himself out. He was in a rich seam of form at the time, batting for hours, and playing really well until he had had enough. When he finally got out, he almost crawled back to the dressing-room and said, 'Dermot, for the very first time, I'm glad I'm out.' He was dead on his feet because of the daily workload, a rare admission from someone like Paul Parker. I could sympathise with that, but I wanted a fresh challenge if I was going to stay in the game and face days like that one which exhausted Paul so much.

Basically, I left Sussex because I wanted to improve as a cricketer and I wasn't getting very far. When I first went there, the wickets encouraged the faster bowlers and I did quite well behind the likes of Imran, Garth le Roux and Tony Pigott. I learned to swing the ball, because I swiftly realised I lacked the physique to be able to bowl flat out, over after over, day after day. Gradually the Hove wickets changed in texture; they became abrasive, and you couldn't keep the shine on the ball essential for the traditional swing bowler. This was my main reason for leaving Sussex. It was literally a case of the grass being greener elsewhere. In those days I was playing more as a bowler than an all-rounder, but I was struggling to get wickets in the home games. My 1987 bowling statistics make the point: my average at Hove was 46 which would have placed me 128th in the national averages, while for away games it was 21.07 which would have placed me 12th. My overall average was 29.52 placing me 65th. It wasn't just one freak season either, in 1986 the statistics were alarmingly similar.

I was also getting little chance of batting. In the Nat West Final of '86, I was down to bat at number nine. I honestly thought I was a better player than that, and that I could get a thousand runs a season if I went up the order. Yet, after five years in the first team, I was still going in at seven and lower. After five years of championship cricket, I was averaging 25 with the bat, but getting only one innings per match. I wanted to improve as a cricketer, to see how far I could push myself towards my dream of playing for England. When the news came out that I had asked to be released, there were some daft rumours flying around that I had fallen out with the captain, Paul Parker. That was nonsense, I had the greatest respect for Paul. In fact he rang me up asking me to stay, offering me the new ball for the following season. I had to point out to Paul that I wasn't an opening bowler any more, that I wanted to go to a home ground where the ball would still swing after a lot of overs and where I could bat in the middle order. We parted on the best of terms as far as I'm concerned, and I shall always be grateful to the example set by Paul Parker in my early years in county cricket. It was typical of Paul that he was still playing county cricket for Durham at the age of 38, still fielding brilliantly, batting stylishly and supporting his team-mates to the hilt.

Kent and Warwickshire were two counties who expressed keen interest in me and I plumped in the end for Warwickshire. I felt that Kent had enough seam and swing bowlers on their staff, which might have restricted my first-team chances, and I liked the potential at Edgbaston. I'd played a second team game there in my final season with Sussex, and I noticed that the ball was still swinging after 60 overs. The outfield was lush, helping to keep the shine on the ball and I felt that it would be a good place for a swing bowler. Andy Lloyd, the Warwickshire captain, seemed very keen to sign me and I liked that. It was time for a change of scenery. It proved a good decision.

4

A Change of Scenery

I came to Edgbaston at just the right time for my career. I was 25, ambitious, eager to learn more about the game, but I didn't want to be dragged down by the old-stagers in the dressing-room who had seen it all before and didn't take kindly to lippy lads with views of their own. There was a freshness about life at Edgbaston at the start of the 1988 season. Players like Norman Gifford, Alvin Kallicharran, Dennis Amiss and Geoff Humpage had given great service to the club, but they had either just retired, or were drifting out of the game. Warwickshire had fin-ished third bottom of the 1987 championship table and at the foot of the Sunday League, so the only way was up as far as I was concerned. The new brooms – the captain Andy Lloyd and the coach, Bob Cottam – felt the same way. They knew we weren't a great side, but they were determined to be more positive in their approach. It seemed that avoiding defeat had been the main priority in previous seasons, but Andy was having none of that. A keen gambler on all sports, particularly on the horses, he was the right guy to captain us. He knew that you could draw every game and finish bottom of the table. He was very keen on group discussions to analyse how we could win a match, how we could maximise our assets, rather than worry about the opposi-tion. At least we'd have a go.

Judging by the way Andy Lloyd negotiated with me to per-suade me to come to Edgbaston, I was his type of player and that meant a lot to me. I had been frustrated by the selfishness of some of my Sussex colleagues and I wanted greater input in team discussions. I felt there were a lot of cricketing conventions that should be challenged; too many senior players just conformed in the way they approached and played the game. The wickets and conditions at Edgbaston would also be beneficial to my bowling, compared to Hove. When you're a swing bowler and the ball comes back off the boundary boards without any alteration in shape or shine, you feel you've got a chance of swinging the ball consistently, especially with lush outfields like you get at Edgbaston. In my last year with Sussex, I had taken 7/37 against Lancashire in conditions that were ideal for my type of bowling: low cloud, moisture in the air, green outfield. That was at Lytham, though – not at Hove. I couldn't keep hoping that a few times a season I'd encounter conditions that suited me, I wanted to enjoy the prospect regularly on my home ground. Edgbaston seemed perfect for that, and I knew that the policy towards the pitches there was going to change under the new captain. They would help the faster bowlers more than the traditional Edgbaston featherbeds which favoured batsmen, yet gave little hope of positive results.

It was no coincidence that Warwickshire hadn't won a trophy since 1980, or the championship since 1972: their pitches just didn't lead to a positive, dynamic approach. Lloyd had experienced all that in his ten years at the club, and he was determined to see a fresher attitude, with the bowlers getting more encouragement from the home wickets. It was something that many other county sides had done for years, and become successful as a result, and I saw no reason why we shouldn't do the same. That's been the general policy at Edgbaston since I've been at the club and although traditionalists and other counties moan about our 'result' pitches, it's not as if we have been the first to prepare pitches that play to our strengths. We've also won a lot of matches away from home, in all sorts of conditions, but that is conveniently overlooked.

We finished sixth in the 1988 championship season and only the champions, Worcestershire, picked up more bowling bonus points. It was a great season for our fast bowlers – Allan Donald, Tony Merrick, Tim Munton and Gladstone Small – but, sadly, I played little part in our bowling revival. I could only bowl less than 300 overs in championship matches, because of a shoulder injury that has proved a worry over the years. In my last month with Sussex, I had a cortisone injection in my right shoulder, but within six weeks, I couldn't even brush my teeth or lift a tea cup. I had a scan in Australia, and that showed an abnormality of the joint and a tear to a tendon. By the time I reported to Edgbaston for the next season, it had healed, but I still needed an operation that August. It took a yard off my pace, and I bowled just under a hundred overs in the 1989 championship summer. It was very frustrating, at a time when I was looking to bowl a lot of overs, and it hampered my throwing in the field as well. After a season with Sussex, I realised that I'd never be a tearaway fast bowler, but I still had to bang the ball in to take advantage of the indifferent bounce that Edgbaston offered. Losing that yard of pace was a blow, but I still worked at my swing bowling. I used to watch and admire the techniques of Ian Botham, Kevin Cooper, Terry Alderman and Richard Ellison, as they timed the release of the ball, using their wrist and fingers to control the late swing, experimenting at either end of the crease. But that shoulder injury delayed my progress as an all-rounder at Edgbaston, at a time when I should have been developing.

I was lucky, though, that Bob Cottam was an exceptional bowling coach. He did a great deal for the likes of Tim Munton, helping him to learn how to swing the ball. Munton became an absolute rock to Warwickshire after that, a reliable, hard-working bowler who could get the best players out because he could now swing the ball late. Cottam was the ideal coach at the time for Warwickshire. He liked guys who would get stuck in at the crease, who didn't flinch at the short stuff, and played the hook shot whenever it was on. He thought it was fine to show disappointment when you were out, because that meant you cared. Diving around in the field was also a must for Cottam; as a former England bowler himself, he knew the need to encourage the bowlers with a high degree of commitment in the field. I knew I was Bob's type of cricketer, visual and hyperactive. Bob warmed to vocal, aggressive cricketers and didn't have much time for anyone moping around, feeling sorry for themselves.

Within two years of coming to Edgbaston, Bob had made me

the vice-captain, but not before we had a few disagreements. Bob's a very hot-blooded guy, who wears his heart on his sleeve. As a coach, he was bursting with knowledge and opinions, many of them stimulating and imaginative, but he wasn't a calm watcher. At times he would get too emotional when viewing a game and that didn't help the players relax. His successors, Bob Woolmer and Phil Neale, have been able to cope with that in different ways – Wooley would take himself off to the gym and eff and blind at us out on the field, while Phil is a very relaxed guy in those situations, rightly pointing out that it's now the captain's responsibility.

Bob Cottam was more vocal, he judged players very quickly, in black and white terms: he would always be a Gooch man rather than a Gower man, for example. One day I was very upset at Bob's emotions running away from him. It was a Sunday League game against Northants and I was bowling at David Ripley. I had bowled five 'dot' balls in a row at David Ripley and as I walked back I thought, 'The last thing he'll expect now is the slower ball.' It had been working well for me that summer, so I tried it – out of the back of my hand. Ripley smashed it for six. Well played to him, I thought – he'd spotted it. In the dressing-room immediately after the end of the Northants innings, Bob tore a strip off me in front of the others, demanding what the hell I thought I was doing against Ripley. It was all done in front of the team and I asked to see him in his office. He was still red in the cheeks as I explained quietly yet assertively that I'd done my best and there was no need for such confrontational action, especially with my team-mates sat beside me. He calmed down and we got on fine after that, but it was another lesson I took with me when I became captain. Rollickings should be handed out calmly, in private, without the player being denigrated publicly.

As well as Bob Cottam's expertise as a bowling coach, he was excellent at spotting young talent. As long as they played with guts and energy, Cott would push them forward. He spotted and developed many of the players who came through the ranks to become regulars in our successful sides, when we picked up six trophies in three seasons. The likes of Keith Piper, Roger

Twose and Trevor Penney were all spotted and signed by Bob Cottam. I was particularly impressed with Bob's coaching of the bowlers, including Allan Donald, who was fast but erratic in his early days at Edgbaston. Cott put him on the road to streamlining his action and adding control to that natural talent to bowl fast. He topped the national bowling averages in 1989, and it was a major plus to have him firing away on pitches that helped him.

Slowly things were starting to gel at Edgbaston and it was a huge boost to our confidence to win the Nat West Trophy in 1989. It took the pressure off Andy Lloyd, who had been coming under fire for our erratic performances earlier in the season, and it brought a thawing in the relationship between captain and coach. They were both strong-minded characters, not afraid to voice their opinions, and there were times when we weren't totally focused in the same direction. The batting let us down consistently, but it all came good on a dark evening at Lord's in September, when Warwickshire won a Final for the first time in 21 years. I got the Man of the Match Award for a tight spell of bowling and 40-odd in a low-scoring match, and that pleased many of cricket's statisticians. It meant I had become the first player to pick up the award for two different counties. I didn't set much store by that, because it was only because I had moved to another county, but I was happy with two finals, two victories and two "Man of the Match" awards.

It was much more vital to win, especially as we were up against Middlesex, one of the best one-day sides in the game, on their home ground. On a slow pitch, we only needed 211 in our 60 overs, but against the likes of Norman Cowans, Angus Fraser and John Emburey, that was never going to be easy. I was run out by an inch at the bowler's end, and although *Wisden* and the TV commentator said I was backing up too far, that was because my partner, Asif Din, said, 'Yes', then 'No', and therefore I didn't have time to beat the throw from mid wicket. Never mind, it's one of those things that regularly happen in one-day cricket and, due to the cool head of Neil Smith, we got home.

Smith was a great selection by Cottam and Lloyd. Roger Twose, a left-handed batsman, had pushed hard for selection but Neil had made 161 the day before against Yorkshire, batting as a nightwatchman, so he was in confident form with the bat. Although only 22, he was a very mature cricketer. His father, Mike (better known as M.J.K.), was chairman of our cricket committee, but as you'd expect from a former captain of England and Warwickshire, was only interested in what Neil could do on the field, rather than adding to the Smith family name. Neil had bowled his off-spin very well in their innings, bowling the dangerous Desmond Haynes, but when he came in to bat, it was a situation that would have tested the most experienced player. I had been run out, with 20 needed off 18 balls, and after Neil Smith, we were down to the bowlers. He and Asif Din had to do it – and it was so dark now! The last over was to be bowled by Simon Hughes, a good choice at the death, because he bowled a full length, and for variation possessed an excellent slower ball. With ten needed in that last over, you would have backed Middlesex. Neil got the strike for the second ball and he made contact with Hughes' slower one. Bob Cottam was sat alongside me on the dressing-room balcony and shouted, 'Where's it gone?' For some reason, I saw it clearly: 'It's six, it's six!' Neil had hit it superbly and the ball soared back over the bowler's head, to hit the covers, a good 20 yards over the long off boundary. What a shot, at the perfect time! Then Hughes bowled a legside wide, and fumbled a straight drive from Neil, and we were home with two balls to spare. It was a great party that night!

The heart we had shown to win that Final must have made a lot of people in the game sit up and take notice. On paper, Middlesex were clear favourites, with the experience and the quality in their side. We were in transition, but we fielded well and supported each other all the way through. It was particularly gratifying to see a young player come in at the death and play with such calmness. The environment at Edgbaston was beginning to suit those with a bolder approach, and that great win was an important staging post for the club and those players who went on to share so many trophies a few years later.

We didn't build on that famous victory straight away, though. The following season was a good one for me personally, as I at last made a decent contribution as an all-rounder, with wickets, slip catches and a batting average of over 50. Batting as high as number 5 gave me more opportunity and I made almost 1,500 first-class runs, but the side still wasn't clicking, even though we finished fifth in the championship. Our record in the one-day games was dreadful, and that ought to have been the area where we did well, considering the ability the players had but our fielding was letting us down and we played spin poorly. The cricket committee boxed itself into a corner about our two overseas players, Tom Moody and Allan Donald. Only one could play at a time, and for the following season, only one could be registered – so which one would it be? There was a lot of shilly-shallying around, complicated by Tom Moody's awesome batting form, but in the end the cricket committee made the right decision to keep faith with Donald. That had to be right. Tom proved a top player for us, a great guy in the dressing-room, but it's well-known that a class fast bowler wins you more matches, especially on pitches like Edgbaston where speed through the air and off the pitch can be deadly with uncertain bounce. Looking back now on Warwickshire's record under my captaincy, I can only thank those on the cricket committee who saw the sense of keeping Allan Donald. He has been a model professional for us, an inspiration to the rest of the staff – and a matchwinner consistently.

Soon after the 1990 season, Bob Cottam left. He had several run-ins with the cricket committee over policy matters, and he didn't want to stay. It was no secret that his relationship with the captain, Andy Lloyd, wasn't all that harmonious, but I was sad to see Cott leave. His part in Warwickshire's resurgence shouldn't be forgotten as he breathed new life into the playing staff in his three years at Edgbaston and his successor, Bob Woolmer, was grateful for his legacy.

Of all the coaches I have worked with, Bob Woolmer has been the best. He was also great fun to have around in his four years at Edgbaston. Bob had the knack of being apart from the players at the right times, giving them their space, but he was accessible and ready to laugh at himself. No one ever spent more time with the hairdryer in our dressing-room than Bob, and the amount of work he put in at the gym did nothing for his splendid paunch – all he managed was a very strong pair of legs! Bob took all the ribbing in good part and he helped foster a great team spirit, where young players were encouraged to debate the pros and cons openly, without being talked down by the elders.

Bob's passion for cricket was only surpassed by his love of food, and we spent many evenings down at T.G.I. Fridays restaurant in Birmingham, talking about the game, hatching plans, and bouncing ideas off each other. I was a single guy at the time and Bob's family were usually at home in South Africa, so we had time to spend with each other to shoot the breeze. I loved his bright, open thinking, his readiness to take on new ideas, to take a more scientific approach to professional cricket. Andy Lloyd deserves a lot of credit for recommending Bob Woolmer. Obviously Andy had played against Bob, who was a fine batsman for Kent and England, but he got to know him particularly well out in South Africa. He recognised a coach with imagination, hunger to succeed and the ability to put over his ideas. His greatest asset is that he has a very young nature – he'd say, 'Come on, I'm learning as I go along as well, you guys can come with me.' That was appreciated by the Warwickshire boys. His relaxed way concealed a formidable cricket brain, a terrific memory and a passion to improve. Bob Woolmer's part in our success at Edgbaston cannot be over-estimated. England lost a great coach when they overlooked him, allowing him to go to South Africa as the national coach. I find it amazing that Bob was never even offered an 'A' tour, despite his excellent record at Edgbaston in such a short space of time.

As soon as he arrived, Bob made an immediate impression on me for his innovative attitude. At Trinidad, of all places, we had a team meeting that was to have significant repercussions over the next few years. I had studied our statistics, talked to Bob and we came to the conclusion that the side had to change the way we batted against spinners. Bob said we all should learn how to play the sweep shot, and also the reverse sweep. We pointed out that players such as Mike Gatting, Graham Gooch and Chris Cowdrey were superb players of the sweep, bringing them thousands of runs in their careers. It was all very well thinking about

playing defensively with a straight bat against the sharply turning ball, but that kind of delivery may still get you out and if
you're playing defensively you've got little chance of scoring
runs. By sweeping, you can actually take the ball on the full or
smother the spin and still be in your crease, avoiding the chance
of being stumped. We also talked about playing the reverse
sweep if there was a gap behind square on the offside.

The first time I saw that stroke played was in 1984 by, of all
people, Malcolm Marshall. John Barclay was the bowler and
Marshall's two strokes turned the game. Barclay wasn't
impressed, saying the stroke should be banned, but I remember
thinking, 'There's an off-spinner who doesn't like that shot, so
that must be a good option.' It made sense to combat an off-
spinner who's bowling to a right-hander with six men on the
legside and three on the off. If you play it well, a man has to be
brought over from the legside to plug the gap on the offside –
and then you can pick up runs in the orthodox manner, playing
with the off-break on to the legside, finding the gap. For years,
off-spinners like Nigel Cowley, Jack Simmons, Geoff Miller,
Eddie Hemmings and John Emburey had been some of the
most economical bowlers in one-day cricket because they had
been played mostly in orthodox fashion. The ball would be fired
in around middle and leg, and the batsman would only get a
single if he managed to pierce the legside field of six. The bowler
would make sure he didn't bowl with a short legside boundary,
so was rarely hit for six. It was about time the off-spinner was
played in a different manner.

Of course, there were many diehards who were totally against
the reverse sweep. Peter May, the chairman of selectors, was very
unimpressed when Ian Botham played it against Greg Matthews
in 1985 and got himself out against Australia in a one-day international. The chairman said sniffily that it wasn't a shot in the
MCC Coaching Book, the implication being that it therefore
shouldn't be played. That ignored the fact that Peter May would
have needed to find different ways of scoring quickly against
tight spin bowling if he had been playing in 1985, more than 20
years after his retirement. It also insulted Ian Botham's daring,
positive qualities that made him such a great player. Take away

Botham's bravado and you dilute his effectiveness.

Mike Gatting also got a lot of stick for playing the reverse sweep in the 1987 World Cup Final, getting out to Allan Border as soon as he came on. It was suggested by many that Gatting lost us the World Cup with that single stroke. There was nothing wrong with the principle of the shot, just the execution. You can look a prat when the reverse sweep gets you out, but what about the countless times you see batsmen bowled by an offspinner giving themselves room for the cut shot? I reckon I've got out three times in my career to the reverse sweep, two of them on successive Sundays in 1993, but that didn't stop me playing it if the circumstances demanded it. Too many people are worried about getting out the wrong way. It's acceptable to be caught at short leg from an off-break but dismissal from the reverse sweep has the journalists rushing to their laptops and the committee members shaking their heads. Effectiveness ought to be the crucial factor, not style.

Bob Woolmer struck a chord with me as we debated the issue in that first meeting in Trinidad. A few of the lads were against changing the way we batted against spin, but I had felt that since I came to Edgbaston we had been missing out. Our top batters played the quicks very well, but we were too passive against the spinners. We didn't work the ball around, we were content just to wait for the loose ball, but against a good spinner it seldom comes. A good finger-spinner would just toy with us as we played him from the crease. Woolmer said we had to look to dominate the spinners from the first ball, that no longer do we look to play out maidens, even in championship cricket we should be more assertive. Andy Lloyd was equally concerned about that, and from then on he played very positively, with the side's best interests paramount. At a late stage in his career, he started to sweep the spinners quite well, and that was important; the younger players could see a senior batsman having success with a new approach, and that would help persuade them it was the right way to play the spinners.

After that Trinidad meeting, we tried a bolder approach in our next match on that tour – and we lost! They had two spinners and we struggled against them on the matting surface, especially as their wicket-keeper kept loosening the mat when the spinners were on. I was out lbw playing the sweep, and in our next team meeting we had an interesting difference of views. Gladstone Small, who had been sceptical about the new approach, pointed out that I'd got out to the sweep, only to be told by Andy Lloyd that I was also the top scorer, having got a few runs with the sweep shot. It was all a matter of degree, of stroke selection, of intensive practice. The cricket management were adamant that this was the way forward but it was obviously going to take time to implement. I'd seen the likes of Gatting and Gooch destroy spinners over the years, and Bob Woolmer felt the same way. He had seen Alan Knott, Chris and Colin Cowdrey sweep and paddle the slow bowlers to distraction and he was convinced it was a vital tool in combating tight bowling and the increasingly athletic fielding in the county game. The players needed to be educated, and it took some time to win over the likes of Gladstone, and Neil and Paul Smith – but over the years they came to admire the way the boys played the sweep and the reverse. When Tim Munton played it during the game against Hampshire when we won the 1994 championship, I was very chuffed. It was great to see such a positive, flexible approach from our number eleven batsman. As long as you practise it before using it in a match, I see it as a business stroke with little more risk attached than any other.

It became a personal crusade for me and Bob Woolmer over the next few years, and we knew that we had to win over influential people on the Warwickshire cricket committee, as well as some sceptical players. After Dominic Ostler had worked hard on the reverse sweep in winter practice, he played it at last out in the middle, and it got him runs. We were delighted with that, and so was Dominic, because the hard work had paid off for him. He could see the point of the shot, how it messed up the bowler's field and improved his run rate. As we talked about it in the dressing-room, Dennis Amiss walked in. He was chairman of the cricket committee at the time, having retired after a great career when batting had been more straightforward on flat Edgbaston wickets. He said, 'Dominic, I don't like you playing that shot. I used to try to come down the wicket and play the off-spinner over extra cover.' Bob Woolmer and I weren't impressed by what we saw as interference by Dennis, and we asked him not to raise it again with Dominic. We didn't want Dominic to face a dilemma – does he listen to his captain and coach or to the chairman of cricket, who had scored a hundred hundreds, and would have a big say in deciding whether he was going to get a new contract? Fortunately Dennis saw the point and I was impressed with Bob's assertiveness, as Dennis was a very good friend. I knew that guys play better when they're not getting too much strife. It was important for me to get this across to Bob, so that he could help create a relaxed ambience, where players aren't chastised strongly for making a mistake. Bob enjoyed a meeting of minds over cricket matters, and he would take enormous amounts of time to get his message across. The insistence on playing spinners differently was, in my opinion, the most vital element in Warwickshire's subsequent success. You can forget all that stuff about 'Larashire', and my captaincy, and Allan Donald's brilliant example: getting after the spinners set us apart from other sides, because we all did it, not just a few batsmen who were fine players of spin. There was a collective approach which stemmed from the cricket management encouraging everyone to play with spirit and freshness as long as the hard work had been done in the nets.

Bob was excellent on non-cricketing matters such as nutrition and a scientific approach to fitness. He brought with him not just a thorough knowledge of cricket and its techniques, but also the breadth of practical experience that would make us better cricketers. I had been concerned at the standard of fielding since I'd been at Edgbaston and Bob was onto that straight away. He knew that your skills suffer when you get tired, so he demanded greater levels of fitness, so that our fielding would stand up to a long day out in the middle under the sun. He brought in experts from Birmingham University to advise us on the proper diet, how to improve our flexibility, how to maintain stamina – all the things that other counties are embracing now, several years on. Bob was shrewd enough to realise that if he talked on and on about such matters, the lads would get bored, because they heard enough from him anyway, so an expert on such matters would automatically get their attention and the message would get home.

In cricketing terms, Bob would talk to every player on the staff at the end of the season, asking them what area constituted a weakness. He would identify it, then tell them to go away to work on it, and come back for next season, with that weakness turned into a strength. Roger Twose is just one example of the success of that approach. Bob felt he had a weakness against the short ball and told Roger to work on it in the winter. He came back with a revised technique and greater confidence against short-pitched bowling. By the time opposition bowlers had realised he was no longer vulnerable against that line of attack, Roger was scoring a lot of runs and enjoying a great season. A weakness had been turned into a strength by hard work and imaginative coaching.

When I first came to Warwickshire, Asif Din was our best fielder – yet in the modern game, Asif would only be classified as an average fielder, not an outstanding one. That was an indication of how far we needed to improve as a fielding side, even allowing for the inevitable weeding out of some senior players who weren't very good at that discipline. Bob Woolmer worked us hard in improving our catching and he did it in a typically imaginative way – with a tennis racket. He knew that a tennis ball is harder to catch than a cricket ball when you're working in close. A tennis ball can bounce out of your hands, and taking it cleanly really teaches you how to give with the ball at the moment of impact. Constant catching practice with a hard cricket ball can give you sore hands, so that when the chance comes out in the middle, you might subconsciously fail to go all the way for the snick. Bob would hit 50 catches a time to your left hand with a tennis ball, then another 50 to your other hand. He would advise you to go for a catch in the middle with both hands whenever possible, but his reasoning behind one-handed catching in practice was that it was harder: you would feel safer and more relaxed going for the chance with both hands in the field after gaining confidence with one-handed takes of a tennis ball. We knew that if the team's percentage of catching was high, it would be easier to win the championship. The high standard of our close catching in recent years has given us a head start over other counties and when I saw the Lancashire coach, David Lloyd, using the tennis racket in practice in the 1995 season, I felt proud that Warwickshire had been ahead of them by several years in that respect.

Our first season under Woolmer's coaching, in 1991, saw an immediate improvement. We batted much more positively, even if we didn't score massively. Our seam bowling attack of Allan Donald, Tim Munton, Gladstone Small and myself brought us 244 championship wickets between us, and I was pleased with my all-round efforts, averaging almost 49 with the bat and 21 with the ball. I relished batting as high as number five, and I was beginning to think my burning ambition to play for England wasn't as fanciful as I had thought, especially with Ian Botham in decline, as injuries piled up for him. It was more important, though, for the side to do well and we finished second in the championship, 13 points behind Essex, who were admittedly a stronger all-round unit with top quality spinners. The fact that we pressed them so hard, leading the table for three months, was a great consolation to us, justifying the positive way we played our cricket. We won as many games as Essex and our 11 victories would have brought us the title in five of the previous six years. Our tally of five away wins was the same as at Edgbaston (the other coming at Coventry), so we couldn't be accused of relying on favourable home conditions to get so close to the championship. At least, so we thought; we would have to get used to generalisations about the Edgbaston pitches and their effect on our continued success. That 1991 season was the first time we encountered the reluctance of so-called experts to give us credit for being a good side, rather than one which needed home advantage to win matches.

Andy Lloyd set the right example as captain in the field, always looking to force a win with positive field placings, keeping Allan Donald under wraps till he was needed, rather than over-bowling him. When he batted at number three, Andy played shots right from the start, making sure we had enough runs at speed to get among the opposition with our strong seam attack. Four-day cricket demands you get a fair quantity of runs at a good pace, otherwise you will struggle to get 20 wickets for victory especially if rain intervenes. I think Warwickshire realised that quicker than most counties, and Lloyd and Woolmer sorted out the correct strategy right from the off.

They also had no qualms about giving young players a chance. Jason Ratcliffe, at the age of 22, opened the innings most of the games in the championship, while 20-year-old Dominic Ostler was given the chance and the encouragement to bat at number four, and he responded magnificently. The fielding also improved greatly with so many young players coming through. That helped us in one-day competitions, with some success in all of them, even though we fell down at crucial times. Still, it was a very important season for this developing Warwickshire side. We responded eagerly to Woolmer's innovative ideas, to Lloyd's bold captaincy, and we were starting to gel as a unit. There was a lot of fun in the dressing-room as well, with the players enjoying the tension-free atmosphere – but we were also learning when to dig in and really concentrate at key moments in the match.

For me, it was a pleasure to be part of such a positive set-up, with plenty of give and take, easy banter, but a professional approach when needed. I hadn't regretted my move from Sussex at all, and I was sure Warwickshire were on the verge of great things. Success doesn't just happen overnight, and the contributions of Andy Lloyd, Bob Cottam and Bob Woolmer won't be forgotten by those of us who sprayed a lot of victory champagne around a few years later.

5

County Captain

At the end of the 1992 season, I succeeded Andy Lloyd as Warwickshire's captain. The news leaked out in a rather messy way, with two championship games left. Andy had been struggling with his form and fitness, and the club felt an announcement had to be made sooner rather than later, to avoid speculation. It didn't do much for morale in our dressing-room, though, and the way we subsided in our last match, against Kent, showed there was much to do. They got over 600 in their innings and bowled us out cheaply to win by an innings and plenty. We needed to show guts to hang in for a draw, but all we did was play shots and get out, as if we had given up. I felt our younger players needed to be harder mentally: Keith Piper seemed more pleased with the six he hit than anything; he seemed to ignore the fact that he had got out cheaply in the first innings and we had lost badly. It seemed as if we didn't care in that Kent game; that attitude would have to change.

I had been attracted to captaincy in my Sussex days and John Barclay had encouraged me, telling me to keep thinking and make contributions. I hadn't forgotten the stick I took for voicing my England ambitions, though, so I just kept making mental notes and trying to work out what my captains were thinking of when they made key decisions. I enjoyed the bluff and counter-bluff of captaincy, trying it on with the opposite number, feeling each other out in the negotiations you often had with three-day cricket. In the short game, you often had to rely on nods and winks, especially if rain had interrupted the game. You'd agree a target on the third and final morning, with the batting side scoring runs to set up a target for the fourth innings. One game at Edgbaston when I was playing for Sussex showed up the dilemma.

Asif Din and Alvin Kallicharran tossed up some stuff that was supposed to give us 150 more runs before the declaration. Unfortunately for us, we lost wickets and when Tony Pigott and I came together we were seven down and still 80 short of the target before declaring. Suddenly, Warwickshire's captain, Norman Gifford, realised he could bowl us out cheaply, leaving them to chase around 200, rather than the negotiated 250, and he started to play proper cricket. He took off the part-time spinners, dispensed with the attacking field, daring us to take risks. I blocked out two maiden overs from Gifford and he started to chunter. But I knew what he was trying to do. Tony Pigott continued to swing his bat, as Gifford said, 'You're doing the right thing, Tony – but what about the other bloke?' Pigott said, 'I agree with you, Giff' but I chipped in, 'I know what you're trying, Giff', and he eventually threw the ball back to Asif Din in disgust. Pigott was happy – he got his maiden hundred – and we ended up setting them exactly the amount agreed. My captain, Paul Parker, said I was absolutely right to play it the hard way, to have spotted that Gifford had changed his tactics.

I had definite aims when I took over the Warwickshire captaincy. The aggression that Andy Lloyd had instilled into the side, and his desire to go hard for the win, were qualities that I had valued. We needed to be fitter, though, and Bob Woolmer and I decided more attention to detail in that area was needed. Fielding had to improve, and that begins with increased fitness. I also wanted the players to be more respectful of each other in certain areas. Racist remarks have always annoyed me; I've never understood why people think racist jibes are funny, and sometimes in our dressing-room I had seen that one or two of our players had been upset at a few comments that were tactless and disrespectful. To me, that affected morale and it had to stop. I also wanted us to stop mickey-taking on cricketing matters. Now I'm all for leg-pulling and lively banter, but I don't think it's good for team morale if a player's defects as a cricketer get highlighted and he is denigrated in front of others. It's a fine line, I agree, but players are more sensitive about their game than they usually let on.

There'd been times when I had to keep the peace in the slips between Dominic Ostler and the wicket-keeper Keith Piper over the responsibility for a catch. I'd be at first slip, the edge would travel between myself and Keith and Dominic would say, 'Don't you want to catch them today then, Keith?' Now Keith has a quick temper and I worried that he wouldn't be focused on the next ball because of Dominic's remark. Incidentally, Dominic would only be retaliating to Keith calling him 'Costus', when he had dropped a catch earlier – 'Costus' as in 'That could cost us the match'. It all seems fairly trivial but I have seen many a young player's composure suffer because of mickey-taking. I also didn't like it when Jason Ratcliffe came up with a new nick-name for Roger Twose – 'Boards,' as in 'The ball keeps getting hit to the boards.' This came after Roger had been carted around during a bowling spell. That one soon spread to any suffering bowler. On the face of it, a guy might take it well and spit back with a cutting remark of his own, but what was it doing inside his head? Was it reducing his morale and effectiveness as a cricketer?

Early on, the new attitude to cricketing defects didn't work all that well. The brain often lags behind the quick mouth – it certainly does with me at times! – and I'd be pulling the guys up all the time. 'That's a cricketing issue,' I'd say, 'you can't take the piss on that.' I then went the other way, saying it was open season, and I'd go round the dressing-room sledging everyone for their cricketing frailties. The point of that was to underline that we all have cricketing defects and it was up to all of us to overcome them – together. It was all designed to protect a player's confidence: when that ball's in the air for a vital catch, I want that fielder to be shouting 'Mine, Mine!', wanting the ball to come to him, not pulling up the ladder to leave the responsibility to someone else.

At Sussex, I had seen how a negative atmosphere can affect a cricketer, so that he doesn't give of his best. Underneath that macho bravado, every professional cricketer is sensitive. We all question our ability. I certainly do it all the time. One day, when I was knocking up on the outfield, I was playing a few front foot drives, and Keith Piper came over to look, only to end up sniggering. Being laughed at while you're practising doesn't exactly help anyone's confidence and I told Keith so. I know I don't look pretty: I've gone into the indoor nets, armed with a video camera, and tried to bat like Mark Waugh, but it hasn't worked, it's not me. I used to suffer badly from fear of failure, even though my reputation is one of being supremely confident. I'm sure even the most confident and gifted players have flashes of self-doubt. For me, it was crucial that the Warwickshire players would be encouraged in those areas, in a supportive environment rather than one where everyone was on their guard, waiting for the next jibe.

The players needed to feel there was a genuine desire in the team for individuals to do well. It's hard for a senior player to change his attitude, as he becomes more introverted, worried about his form, whether he'll be kept on long enough to qualify for a benefit, with so many bright youngsters knocking on the door. We were lucky at Edgbaston with the senior players when I started as captain: they wanted success as much as I did, and we worked to create an atmosphere in which the younger players weren't intimidated, but made to feel equal and encouraged to speak their minds at team meetings. I wanted the younger guys to feel totally focused on winning the game for the team, rather than shining as individuals.

Early in his career, Keith Piper was too worried about what others were saying about him off the field. He'd want to impress the opposition with his batting, or the press when he kept wicket. We'd have to tell him just to forget what anyone else might be saying about him off the field. He's now a top wicket-keeper, not just because of his great natural talent, but because he's concentrating better.

In one of my early games at Edgbaston, Asif Din was at fault when running out Paul Smith in a tense one-day game. I was next man in and as I came to the wicket Asif said, 'What are they saying in the dressing-room about that run out?' I had to tell him to forget it, that was history, to focus on the rest of the game. Asif is a lovely, sensitive guy, but in those days he took too much notice of his cricketing environment, he was looking over his shoulder too much. Norman Gifford hauled him over the coals one day when he tried to hit the spinner over the top and holed out to mid-on, so he was afraid to try it again for a long time. He wasn't made to feel comfortable about his game, and above all he needed to be encouraged and backed by the management.

To me, it was a matter of self-esteem. I wanted my players to feel good about their efforts towards their game, and feel comfortable enough to speak up on cricketing issues in a team meeting. I didn't want anyone feeling they were too inexperienced to be entitled to make a contribution. I'd loved the way John Barclay had handled me at Sussex. He really wanted us to do well, he didn't have an ounce of professional jealousy in him. He'd create a framework whereby he'd encourage us as individuals in the desire that the team would gel as a unit. It wasn't Johnny's fault that some players were too selfish to go all the way with him. He'd talk so enthusiastically to me about my future: 'Yes, I really think you could play for England, and captain a county. Come up to me and talk any time, give me your views.' I couldn't believe that he was so interested in what I had to say when I wasn't exactly setting the county scene on fire, but he was so warm and supportive. At Edgbaston, I wanted to forge that kind of atmosphere, where the players were delighted for the individual who did well, where petty jealousies were absent, leading to an encouraging, successful environment.

I've been amazed at how slow some counties have been to cotton on to the necessity for a strong team spirit.

In 1995, I saw at first hand a terrible piece of man-management, and a young lad called Carl Crowe suffered. We were playing Leicestershire and young Crowe dropped a catch at cover off Gordon Parsons. The bowler shouted, 'Come on, what's going on!' and Alan Mullally said, 'How are we going to win games when you blokes can't catch?' Parsons eventually calmed down when Paul Nixon, their wicket-keeper, pointed out, 'Does he think we don't want to catch it?', but the damage was done for a lad making his first-class debut. He slunk around in the field, and you could tell he didn't want the ball to come near him.

That night, I went out for a drink and Mullally hinted that he'd like to come to Warwickshire. I said there was no way that I'd want him at Edgbaston with his attitude, because of the way he, a senior player, had treated a lad making his debut on the field. I told him, 'You made him feel inadequate and he's gone home, probably thinking you don't like him or rate him.' Mullally ended up apologising to me about the way he had treated his own team-mate! I told him not to apologise to me, because he had helped Warwickshire, but he ought to apologise to young Crowe next morning. I was also disappointed with Nigel Briers, the Leicestershire captain, over that incident. He clapped his hands and said, 'Come on boys, keep going', but he didn't seem to offer much consolation to Crowe. That wouldn't happen at Warwickshire. You must allow your players to relax, to feel you're all going in the same direction. No one drops a catch on purpose. County cricket can be very frustrating because of the bowlers' attitude to the batsmen and vice versa. That can develop camps and rifts in a team, as well as the destructive 'fear of failure' syndrome.

I was determined to eliminate tension as much as possible. So we brought in a 'smile break'. I'd read about laughter therapy classes, where psychologists have explained that laughing eases stress, relaxes the class, and leads to contagious laughter in the group. You feel good about yourself and upbeat about life if you laugh a lot. Presumably laughter releases a chemical in the body, it acts as a relaxing agent, and it helps you approach the job on an even keel. Instead of feeling tense about our lack of wickets when fielding, I'd say, 'Come on fellas, they've put on a hundred', and start laughing. We'd all join in, the opposition batsmen would look at us, puzzled, and it gave us a boost. Shouting didn't relieve the tension, but the team laugh certainly did, especially when we'd catch sight of Gladstone Small refusing to laugh out loud, but happy to compromise by smiling broadly.

Sometimes we'd play football with an imaginary ball, as the bowler walked back to the mark. Extra cover would chip the ball to mid-off, who would then control it on his chest and boot it over to mid-on, and so it would go on around the field, till the imaginary ball would come to Gladstone, who would kick it out of the ground – and that would start us all laughing. Sometimes it would be a basketball move, with the fielder spinning the imaginary ball on his finger. It may have looked daft at various times, but the trick is to laugh at yourself. On a hard day, when you're looking for some luck and a breakthrough, that feeling of togetherness, of fun, can lift the bowlers. You're sharing an experience, having a laugh – plus the opposition don't know what to make of it all.

I've always liked to win as a cricketer, because I also like to have a party, have a good time and relax with my team-mates. So when I became captain, I didn't have to alter my attitude to winning. But I had to become a better actor when we lost. It was important to avoid getting too morbid after a bad day, and here again I'd learned a lot from John Barclay's sunny attitude. The captain needs to act out the part, to say the correct upbeat things after a bad performance. So I'd say things like, 'Gee were we unlucky today! I can't believe it. Never mind, fellas, a better day tomorrow! Well tried! Have a good night out, and we'll be fresh for them tomorrow, a fresh start!' It sounds trite, but I felt the captain had to be up tempo, I didn't want the guys creeping around, feeling sorry for themselves.

I also wanted a lot of physical contact among the players out in the middle – lots of hugging and hand-slapping when we got a wicket. I know the old-stagers tut-tut and say, 'You're only doing your job, what's the big deal?' but I wanted to show that enjoying the game was important to us. It's great when the fielder at fine leg runs up to the bowler and says 'Well done', rather than sitting on the fence by the boundary, having a rest, looking around. I wanted us all to share in our successes, to be happy to be out there playing for Warwickshire, sharing the good moments.

To me, it was just a case of fine tuning when I took over as captain of Warwickshire. The raw materials were there. We had some fine young players coming through, and our fielding was getting better as a result, although it had to improve even more for my satisfaction. I was conscious that Allan Donald, our matchwinner, had to be handled as well by me as Andy Lloyd had done. When I first captained him, at Old Trafford, he really threw me. After two overs, Allan said he didn't want to bowl any more. I was astonished, because the hallmark of Allan Donald has always been a willingness to bowl. My strategy that day was to start with a good blast with the new ball by Allan and Gladstone Small, and I had to be firm with Allan. I was club vice captain at the time and it wasn't easy telling him he had to bowl. That was the only time I ever had a problem with him. Under the expert tutelage of Bob Woolmer, he grew in stature as a fast bowler and gave us a marvellous cutting edge.

I was disappointed in my first season as captain that we lost Allan's services for the last six weeks of the season. He had to go to Sri Lanka with South Africa, and with Tim Munton and Gladstone Small both suffering injuries, our seam attack was greatly reduced in effectiveness. Compare the statistics in 1991, when those three plus myself took 244 championship wickets. In 1993 the figure was down to just 95. So our cutting edge was blunted, and we were short of quality spinners as well, even though Neil Smith was developing impressively. With four-day cricket now the norm in the championship, we needed greater depth and variety in spin to make a serious challenge, a fact underlined when Middlesex outplayed us at Edgbaston on a wicket ideal for John Emburey and Phil Tufnell.

I was nervous the first time I led Warwickshire that season, because although I had captained the side a fair amount before that first game against Northants, this was the real thing: I couldn't shelter behind being just the stand-in. We beat Northants by eight wickets and I enjoyed an unbeaten 87, and then we went to Kent and beat them. So that was a good start against two of the strongest county sides. But it didn't last. We tailed away in the championship after Donald left for Sri Lanka, and injuries to key bowlers didn't help either. No one averaged more than 40 in the championship, only two got over a thousand runs and the young players were having to learn rapidly. But I was glad to get the likes of Trevor Penney, Neil Smith and Michael Bell playing, because they would learn more in the hard world of the first eleven, rather than chugging along in the seconds. Although we finished second bottom of the championship in my first season as captain, there were encouraging signs. We just needed to sharpen up our approach, be more influential in the spin bowling department, keep the seamers fit and get more from our batsmen. The competition for places was increasing, and the 'comfort zone' was being eliminated.

With half the season gone, it was clear to me that we needed a good run in the Nat West Trophy to give us confidence and an incentive for the rest of that 1993 season. We had gone out in the Benson and Hedges Cup in the first round, we were nowhere in the championship and struggling in the Sunday League. I decided to rest Munton and Small as they battled against injuries, and keep them fresh for the shorter games in the Nat West. Our semi-final win down at Taunton showed the kind of resilience I wanted. Somerset, a dangerous one-day side, must have fancied a target of 253 at just over four an over, especially when Gladstone Small limped off after bowling only five overs. He had already taken two key wickets by then, but I then had to fiddle some overs from bowlers who would possibly not have been used. Jason Ratcliffe and Roger Twose gave me six overs that only went for 24 as our tight fielding and overall discipline made up for the loss of Small. I was really pleased with that effort, and so we had got to Lord's after falling at the semi-final stage in the last two seasons.

Our remarkable win against Sussex in the Final was a triumph for positive thinking, a refusal to think we would lose. It's been called the greatest one-day Final, and it's hard to argue with that. We had to chase 322, the highest total yet in a Lord's Final, and we finally did it in the dark, playing with great heart and aggression. Our bowlers had been carted around by David Smith and Martin Speight and a lesser side would have been demoralised, especially after losing both openers at 18, and Dominic Ostler at 93/3. But everybody kept going, scoring at nearly a run a ball. Asif Din and I enjoyed a record partnership and Asif's hundred in as many balls was remarkable. Even then, when he was out in the penultimate over, we weren't fancied, but we won it off the last ball. It was a fantastic win, against the odds, with the lead coming from two of our most experienced players – Paul Smith and Asif. We won it without our overseas

COUNTY CAPTAIN　　　　　　　　　77

player, Allan Donald, and with our other two Test bowlers – Gladstone Small and Tim Munton – going for a lot of runs. Young players like Neil Smith and Roger Twose kept their heads, bowling very sensibly, while Roger faced the most important delivery of his life, getting the necessary run off the last ball of the match and the only delivery he faced. For me, there were heroes everywhere as I looked around that deliriously happy dressing-room at Lord's.

I'm not sure my joy was universally shared around Edgbaston, though. Soon after, one committee man said, 'Even though we've won a trophy, it's been a disappointing season.' I thought that harsh. We'd struggled with injuries, a team in transition, with a new captain and our star bowler away for the last six weeks of the season – yet we had pulled off a miraculous victory in a Lord's Final. I thought at the time it was a highly significant victory, a vindication of our positive approach and the collective strength of our team spirit. The players took enormous pride in that win, and you could see our confidence rise as a result. Next year, we created history by winning three trophies and coming second in the fourth. Brian Lara was with us then, and his fabulous batting meant a great deal to us – but the win we snatched at the death the previous September at Lord's was hugely significant. It allowed me as captain to justify our aggressive style of playing, it brought self-belief to the younger guys, and revitalised the older ones. We came to believe that no game was ever lost by us until the facts said otherwise. If we could beat Sussex in those circumstances, we could take on anybody. Only those who don't play modern first-class cricket underestimate the importance of self-confidence. It comes and goes, but the crucial thing is to hang on to it as long as you can, and if it's waning in an individual, you need supportive team-mates to revive it. I felt we were getting there at Edgbaston by the end of the 1993 season.

I found captaincy stimulating and satisfying, but it was difficult to switch off mentally. I tend to be very analytical and at the end of the day's play I like to dawdle in the dressing-room, mulling over the events out in the middle, wondering if I'd got it right. There are times when I don't want to talk cricket, as my

Mum sometimes finds when she stays with me for home games. Richard Illingworth had me caught at mid-off once, when I was trying to hit him over the top. That dismissal annoyed me, and when I got back home, I could see my mother wanted to discuss something with me as we sat having dinner. I asked her what was wrong and she said, 'I thought it was a bit early to try hitting him over the top.' I started to explain I was trying to push mid-off back, so I could pick up singles, that I just got too close to the ball, but then I told her, 'That's it! No more cricket talk tonight!' Yet sometimes I'll happily talk cricket with her or chat about it on the phone to my brothers. Normally, though, I prefer to switch off if I can, take in a movie with a huge box of popcorn or nip along to Ronnie Scott's Jazz Club in Birmingham and listen to some quality music. It's important to engage the brain because that shuts off cricket.

But it's not easy. I dream about cricket. Tactics actually come to me in my sleep! I also have nightmares that the boys won't follow my instructions when we're out in the field: that fine leg won't go out there, and the bowler shouts, 'Where's the fine leg gone?' I actually have a recurring dream that I can't put my pads on and it's my turn to bat! Cricket is such a dominant factor in my brain that I'll stop mid-sentence when I'm discussing something else if I've thought of something I should have done on the field. Sometimes it's impossible to get away from it.

Bob Woolmer was a constant support during my early period as captain. We'd adjourn regularly to T.G.I. Fridays restaurant in Birmingham, and while I chewed on my pasta, Bob would demolish a huge rack of lamb, polish off some red wine – and we'd talk cricket. He had such a passion for the game that we'd go into all sorts of areas, finding out different ways to motivate the players, to stretch them. Bob would tell me where I'd fallen down in the job, but always in a constructive, understanding manner.

My communication skills have sometimes let me down as captain. At times I've been in my own world, with my brain going at a hundred miles an hour – so that I've forgotten to talk to a player about something that was important. I really ought to have got into the habit of writing things down that need to be attended to, but I never get round to it. I don't always put in the necessary hours after close of play, because I feel I must get away from an atmosphere that can become claustrophobic. That's also selfishness on my part, I should be more thorough and professional in my dealings with players. Roger Twose, a forthright character and a man I respected, used to tell me that I ought to have more one-on-ones with the guys, rather than talking collectively. That's all very well, but there are only so many hours in the day, and I also had to think about my own game. I saw how John Barclay got ground down by all the minutiae of captaincy – the committee meetings, the gripes from players, the earbashers in the bar – so that he had to take a couple of games off by the end of the season. I didn't want that to happen to me, but I admit there have been occasions when I've been distracted and not told a player something important to him. When I first became captain, I told the guys that if someone was going to be left out, I wouldn't go into detail at the time. I'd tap the player on the shoulder half an hour before the start, tell him the score and say that we'd talk in detail later, or to go and see the coach for further explanation. I had to be hard-nosed about it on the first morning of the match, because I had my own preparations to organise, and also the rest of the team to consider. It sounds harsh, but the dropped player isn't much use to us at that stage, and the last thing I wanted was to have ranting and raving when I was trying to get everyone motivated for the match ahead. The players just had to accept that was to be the way of it, but I'm sure some were upset at the way things were done.

I've got a quick temper and at times I do lose it in front of the guys. It happened when I dropped Paul Taylor at slip off Tim Munton's bowling in that fantastic championship match against Northants in 1995. That was the best four-day game I ever played in, and with both sides locked at the top of the table, tensions were running high, when I dropped the ball. I felt awful, because runs were precious and that might have been an important miss. Straight away, Keith Piper told me, 'You're falling back', which really threw me. He was trying to give me coaching tips, ten seconds after I'd dropped the ball, instead of offering the usual encouragement I'd expect from a team-mate.

Keith and I are great mates – we used to share a house together – but he can flare up at the wrong times or say the wrong thing, and this was such an occasion.

Soon after that we came off at the end of the session, and as we walked into the dressing-room, I saw my helmet on the floor. I kicked out at it, it sailed across the room, and hit our coach, Phil Neale, on the back of the head. It must have looked very funny, but I shouted, 'Sorry, Phil!' and went straight into the showers area. I undressed, stood under the shower for a long time and cooled down. It was important for me to get away from the rest of the team and conceal how upset I was. At other times, I'd go into the kitchen and have a cup of coffee if I thought things were getting on top of me – just to get away from the players, to ensure harsh words weren't uttered in the heat of the moment.

Out on the field, I think I'm quite good on tactics. I like trying to be one jump ahead, to juggle the resources and keep our spirits up. I'm quite firm with the bowlers when they want a certain field and I disagree. Tim Munton likes to have a third man, but there are times on certain wickets when I'd rather have a fifth slip. You can see a bowler's disappointment when they don't get the field they want, but in the end the captain carries the can for results, so he should have what he thinks is best. I liked the players to express their views and play with aggression, but at times I needed to dampen things down. Keith Piper can be difficult to handle, but I liked his infectious, bubbly character on the pitch. Roger Twose was another challenge at times. I really admired Roger's approach to cricket – he was full of guts and passion, yet cool in a crisis, an absolute godsend. But he was very vocal and could get the red mists very easily. When he came on to bowl, he would often ask for a defensive field and if I overruled him, he'd say, 'You always get the field you want when you're bowling.' I'd have to point that I was the captain and he'd spit back, 'You're a crap captain', and then I'd say something like 'And you're a fat buffalo, Roger.' The cut and thrust of sophisticated debate!

In my early days, I noticed how strong-minded captains had to be if they were to be successful. Mike Gatting was very hard when he led the Middlesex side. It was sink or swim with him, if you were one of his players or an opponent. I've heard some amazing bust-ups on the field between Gatting and his two spinners, Phil Edmonds and John Emburey, especially when Gatt wouldn't give them the field they wanted. I once heard Embers tell him, 'Put someone there who's quicker than you – you can't run any more, you're too fat.' Gatt doesn't find it personal, even when we have a laugh at his expense on the field. It's no secret that Gatt likes his food, so whenever he's batting, and the interval is coming up, we'll start shouting, 'Come on fellas – it's getting near to lunch, Gatt's concentration's going', or 'Great line that, Allan – Gatt likes a nibble, he can't stop having a nibble.' Gatt is so competitive in everything he does that he won't let things like that bother him. I really admire the way he has kept up his standards over the years as captain. When I took the Warwickshire job, I asked his advice and he told me, 'Don't forget about your own game. If you're playing well, it'll help you in the job.' He was absolutely right, and on a personal level, our success in 1995 meant more to me than our historic season of '94, because I contributed more as a player.

Graham Gooch was another who set the highest personal standards to the rest of his side as captain. He came from a tough school at Essex, where he and Keith Fletcher made sure the players knew what was expected of them. However I felt Goochy's body language did let him down whenever a catch was dropped, or his bowlers didn't get the right line. That was because it meant so much to Goochy and he had difficulty understanding why others in the team lacked his dedication and desire to succeed. He was terrific to me when I played for him with England; I think he liked my bubbly attitude and I found him very supportive. He used to tell me to play the way I did for Warwickshire and I was impressed with the way he led by example and trained so hard. Goochy was quite right to say that times had changed, that you couldn't have a good night out and then expect to turn it on at full power next day in a vital game. He felt you had to treat your body like an engine, putting the best oil in it, with regular services. Goochy's image as the unsmiling Roundhead was a total travesty of the man. On my first England tour in 1992, to New Zealand and the World Cup, he was great company. He loved a laugh, enjoyed a drink at the right times and encouraged the players fully. Goochy was right to ignore those who didn't know him and just looked for the generalisation; he concentrated on his own self-esteem and won the respect of the players because of his self-discipline and professional standards.

Another hard captain was Allan Border. He was as tough as nails on the field, and happy to hand out the verbals. When Warwickshire played the Australians on the 1993 tour, he sledged me for playing the reverse sweep, asking me what kind of a (expletive deleted) shot that was. I was more impressed with his tactical grasp, though. When I batted against the off-spin of Tim May, he started off with a slip, short leg and silly point. After I'd got to 16, he had just one man round the bat at silly point, and he had sealed off all the gaps. He'd taken a good look at where I played the ball and I was stuck. I thought, 'Where the hell am I going to get a run?' and I just dried up. May had me caught at silly point for 23, but it was the shrewd captaincy of Border that did it for me.

Chris Cowdrey was chalk-and-cheese to Border, but I always admired the forceful way he led the Kent side. He was like John Barclay in the way he'd rush around the field, shouting 'Come on chaps', full of verve and encouragement. I warmed to him as a person and a captain and thought he was the kind of guy I'd love to play for. I thought about going to Kent when I left Sussex, and it was because of Chris Cowdrey. His achievement in taking Kent to within one point of the championship in 1988 was remarkable. Worcestershire had all the big guns – Botham, Dilley, Hick, plus some emerging England players – while Kent had no stars, yet missed out by a single point. They were a brilliant fielding side, with Cowdrey setting the perfect example.

Mike Brearley was a fantastic captain in his tactical awareness, with the knowledge of when to squeeze the opposition batsmen. When I first came to England as a teenager and joined the MCC groundstaff, I'd watch how he calmly manipulated his Middlesex bowlers and fielders while I was working the Lord's scoreboard. You always knew who was in charge, even though

Brearley would just wave a hand or clap quietly. His fielders looked towards him all the time, and he seemed to know the geometry of the field so well. I loved the way he used his spinners, Phil Edmonds and John Emburey. His two best fielders, Graham Barlow and Roland Butcher, would be at mid-wicket and extra cover, covering huge areas of ground between them, and then he'd have a short leg, a deep mid-wicket, a mid-on and silly point. It was an in-and-out field, so that the batsman couldn't go for the big hit because he had the man out at deep mid-wicket, and there were no quick singles to scamper with Barlow and Butcher on either side of the wicket. Brearley seemed to know just when a batsman was going to be positive, so he'd send a man out into the country, or if the batsman was being passive, he'd call up Clive Radley to silly point and often he'd snaffle one.

That Middlesex side under Brearley were streets ahead in terms of aggression and tactical skill on the field, and the captain pulled the strings so capably. No wonder he was such a great captain of England, especially with so many superb bowlers to choose from. All the talk about Brearley's supposed defects as a batsman seemed irrelevant to me. Middlesex and England won more games than most under his captaincy, and there was a common thread running through their confident performances: they had a masterful captain who knew how to get the best out of his players. Clearly he had thought deeply about the art of captaincy.

6

The Winning Habit

In the space of two years, and over three seasons, Warwickshire created cricket history by winning six trophies. We came to regard Lord's as our second home, winning three of the four Finals we appeared in. From a professional point of view, being the county champions in '94 and '95 gave us all the greatest pleasure and if I had to pick one trophy that pleased me most of all, it would be retaining the championship. My contribution was more satisfying than in '94 when I played in only eight championship matches, through injury and poor form: the following season, I averaged 34 with the bat and 17 with the ball, and I missed only two games. Above all, though, that title win in '95 was a fantastic achievement. There had been a lot of gripes around the county circuit and in the media that our first championship win stemmed from the brilliance of Brian Lara and the erratic Edgbaston wickets. Yet our batsmen all scored runs in 1994, and at a good speed, and the fact that we recorded more wins than any other county since 1979 surely indicated our all-round strength, home and away. Taking the title by a margin of 42 points didn't seem to cut much ice: it was far easier just to dub us 'Larashire'.

Next season, we were still undervalued even though our percentage of victories was the greatest in the history of the county championship, 14 out of 17. Of course, the long, hot summer helped, and it's daft to try to make comparisons with other sides from different eras, but surely Warwickshire deserved more praise than we got? Eventually, it came, grudgingly, in the face of some persuasive factual evidence on our behalf. Half our victories came away from home, on pitches that were prepared to draw the sting from Allan Donald, and the margin of those victories was very wide – three by an innings, two by ten wickets, one by nine wickets and the other by 111 runs. Yet we still had to face criticism that we won the title because the Edgbaston wickets favoured our seam attack. That might have been relevant if our three international seamers had operated together on those pitches, but Gladstone Small and Tim Munton suffered injuries, so that Donald, Small and Munton were in harness together for just one championship match that season – and that, at home, was drawn. With Brian Lara no longer with us, our allegedly weak batting seemed to get along, with six batsmen averaging over 40. Only Middlesex scored more batting bonus points than us, by a matter of two points.

Eventually, I found it rather amusing that so many so-called experts kept shaking their heads at the supremacy of a side with average players, and just one world-class performer – Lara in '94 and Donald in '95. With a bit of luck, we might have swept to the full hand of trophies in '94, when it could be argued that the toss of a coin thwarted us at the Nat West Final, forcing us to bat with the ball seaming all round the place. As we only lost the '95 Sunday League by run rate, after recovering from a bad start to post ten successive wins, we might have collected seven trophies in two seasons. Now that would have been a difficult one for our detractors to sort out!

We even seemed to take some of our fellow professionals by surprise. When I joined the England tour party in South Africa in 1995/96, I used to enjoy winding up some of the lads who still couldn't fathom out why we had been so successful. Darren Gough and Mark Ilott were particularly stubborn about our successes. Darren used to say, 'You're not the best team', and so the debate would begin in the team bus as we travelled somewhere. I'd point out the facts, yet he and Mark would keep saying, 'Lancashire are the best team, they've got the best players. I didn't need any invitation to stick up for my players, especially with so many Lancashire guys on the trip, who would be listening to me as we debated the issue. It was always good-humoured,

though, and Goughy made us all laugh with his dogmatic
stance, in the face of overwhelming statistical evidence. In the
end, he compromised – he said we didn't have the best players,
but we played best together as a team. Surely that was all any
county captain could ask for. I was quite happy with that grudg-
ing admission from Goughy and in fun told him, 'You and the
other lads are very welcome to come down to Edgbaston and
polish our trophies. If you're very good, we'll let you lift them
up!'

Others in the first-class game were more generous, though.
When Nick Knight, Dominic Ostler and Keith Piper toured
Pakistan with England 'A', the coach, John Emburey, made it
clear to his players that they had to approach their cricket like the
Warwickshire side. I was very pleased to be told this on the
grapevine, especially as Embers had been in the Middlesex team
that came second to us in our '95 championship win. He also
made some appreciative remarks in Wisden: 'They are now way
ahead of other clubs in terms of talking out a game plan and at
stretching their players, making a team of average players a
highly successful unit. Other clubs, note.' I do, however, disagree that we were a team made up of average players. Some of
Dominic Ostler's strokeplay was at times breathtaking and
Trevor Penney and Keith Piper have been quite excellent in the
field, better in my view than any other cricketers in the country
in their specialist positions. I could go on all day about the
aspects of individual brilliance possessed by each player in that
successful Warwickshire side – but let's say that 'average' isn't
the word to use. Mark Nicholas, the Hampshire captain, came
into our dressing-room after we had won the '94 title by beating his side and asked our secret. He later wrote about us in very
interesting terms, saying that he couldn't think of another team
who wanted each other to do so well, with no hint of rivalry.
Mark felt that the supportive environment that had been created
had allowed positive cricket to flow. He was right!

So what else was the secret of Warwickshire's success? Luck for
a start. Cricket is not an exact science, that's why it's so fascinating. I hear commentators say, 'You get out what you put in', but
I don't buy that. Devon Malcolm bowled his heart out for

England at Perth in '95, yet they kept dropping catches off him, and he took 2/198 in the match. Wasim Khan did very well for us in his first season in '95, yet he was dropped several times in his early innings. He ended up averaging 46 in the championship. Luck comes and goes at bewildering times in a cricketer's career, and you make the most of it when it comes. We were very lucky that Manoj Prabhakar's injured ankle meant we had to turn to Brian Lara to replace him in April 1994. When he scored 375 against England a few days after agreeing to join us, we felt even luckier. He then scored six championship hundreds in his first seven innings for us, including that amazing 501 not out against Durham, and we were on a roll. Brian's positive example only matched the way we were going to approach our cricket that season, but the speed at which he scored his runs was crucial. Throughout that season, he scored his championship runs at the rate of five and a half per six balls, an amazing performance. That rate gave our bowlers more time to bowl out the opposition twice, a vital asset in four-day cricket.

Apart from our great fortune in having Lara with us, our success owed much to planning and attitude. The seeds had been sown by Andy Lloyd and Bob Cottam in terms of attitude and getting in some good young players. That 1989 Nat West gave us some breathing space and I saw our 1993 triumph in the same competition as justification of the work put in by Bob Woolmer and the cricket management.

The first time I met Bob I told him I felt it was the cricket management's job to make sure the players at Edgbaston were better prepared than any other county – surely this would give us a better chance? Bob was receptive and I appreciated his honesty when in his first team chat he told us he was still learning as a coach. His efforts could not have been greater. He ensured we became better prepared than ever before. He brought in specialists – psychologists, doctors of nutrition and sports scientists – to help with the fitness. The truth is that Bob knew enough about all these areas of expertise to educate the team himself, but he realised that players pay more attention when it's being explained by outsiders with letters after their names. Bob was such an innovative coach and encouraged all the

players to communicate at team discussions. We had more meetings and fun when Bob arrived than in any other previous
season. It was important to sit down and discuss regularly how
we could improve, how we could surprise the opposition. It's a
common complaint from older cricketers that young players
don't talk enough cricket, they prefer to be off quickly after the
day has ended, but Bob Woolmer and I didn't want that. It was
very gratifying to see the young lads talking about the game in
the bar, in the dressing-room, or during the day when we were
batting. They became deep thinkers, ready to challenge the
views of the senior players, and that democratic atmosphere was
good for team spirit. Bob Woolmer had once told Andy Lloyd,
'You don't realise how important it is for the captain to set the
tone of the day', and I realised that it was up to me initially to
make sure we weren't going to be lethargic. A fair degree of
bluffing was needed at times – you can't always feel like cracking
jokes and smiling – but I think Bob Woolmer and I managed to
make our dressing-room sound chirpy and bubbly. The sound
of laughter does wonders for morale in any team environment.

We didn't go in for regimented things at Edgbaston, but
some matters are important, and I was very keen on communi-
cating my thoughts. At the start of each season, I would stand
up at the first big team meeting and emphasise the points that to
me were vital: 'You're not under any pressure to win a trophy. I
want you to enjoy it, above all. Get behind your team-mates, do
your best every ball and you can be proud of yourselves. Sorry,
guys, but I'm going to get a big philosophical and spiritual here.
Seriously, I don't care if we don't win anything this year. Fellas,
we chase a ball around a field for a job. We're not important. We
don't save lives. We're entertainers. In 20 years, no one's going
to really care how we did this year! Someone might be talking
about it around a dinner table, but you're not going to be there.
It's really not that important. Cricket will come and go in your
lives, so enjoy it while you're here. What you will have forever is
your self-esteem. Now winning games doesn't help that, but
doing your best every day does. Guys, let's really enjoy this year!'
It would then tend to be a bit quiet for a few seconds before
Roger Twose or Keith Piper would appear moved, and shout

something like, 'Yeah, let's do it!', and slap each other on the back. Roger's favourite saying was, 'I love you great guys,' and that would always get a laugh, but he was trying to show how much it meant to him to be part of a team that was giving a hundred per cent. I really meant it when I'd tell the players to forget about the pressure of winning trophies – that was the responsibility of the coach and the captain, they were the ones who had to get the best out of the players. I wanted them to feel as relaxed as possible, as I believe you play your best cricket when you're relaxed and confident. I was trying to take the pressure off them by making them realise it's just a game. I believe in total encouragement, enthusing about the most complex sport in the world, hopefully lifting spirits and motivating tired bodies if necessary.

I'm also quite keen on group communication before each session. Sometimes, it'll be a quick word along the lines of 'Come on fellas, that wicket's going to deteriorate, first innings runs would be nice.' If we'd been batting and we'd got to lunchtime, I'd question the batsmen who'd been in, and ask them to tell us about the pitch. What pace is it? Is there any turn? Most would elaborate and discuss particular strengths and weaknesses. Roger Twose used to be the most in-depth: he was a fine communicator as well as an intelligent cricketer. Dominic Ostler's descriptions of the condition of the wicket were always good for a laugh. In his early days, he would blush and shrug his shoulders, before stuttering a few words. He's such a nice bloke, and at times I felt sorry I had to put him on the spot, but I knew in the long run it would help his confidence. After a while, Dom would come up with comments that appeared to the point and arrogant like, 'It's flat, there's nothing going on, just smash it!' – as if he'd rehearsed his words. He has now matured into a very self-confident man, with a certain presence at the crease that shows his increased confidence and he communicates as well as anyone now in the dressing-room.

Team meetings can also be good fun. At times Roger Twose would go totally over the top, eyes bulging, veins in the neck throbbing, roaring out, 'Yeh! Let's go for them, come on!' You had to tell Roger that the bell hadn't sounded yet, and we still had five minutes to go! Then he would call me 'Big Ears' to take the attention away from himself and that would raise a laugh. The trick, I feel, is to blend information with informality. At the close of play, we might have a de-briefing as the players change. It depends on how the game has gone. If we've had a bad day or session, I'll keep the conversation to the minimum and leave it for the following morning. I'll make sure my voice is pitched in a positive fashion when I tell the lads not to worry about it tonight, because if the captain sounds depressed, that can be contagious. Time for a spot of bluffing.

Out in the middle, I like communication in a group at the fall of each wicket. I want to know what the ball is doing, how we feel the wicket is playing, what to do about the next batsman. I'm all for celebrating a wicket, but after that, I want us to use the precious few seconds constructively when the new chap is on his way out. It'll be something like, 'Right, boys, Gatt's in next. Now he likes to play his shots right away, but he's an lbw candidate going half forward. Try to get the ball to come into him, because he leaves an open gate. He loves spinners, so let's keep them away from him for a time. So Neil, you're coming off – Allan get loose.' If it's a bowler who can bat a bit, it'll be along the lines of, 'This bloke's a compulsive hooker. Let's put a man out for the hook. But it's a slow wicket, so let's do some double bluffing. Keep the ball pitched up all the time, we've got a mid-off and mid on. Keep looking at the man on the hook, but don't bounce him. Let's try and get him bowled or lbw, half forward, because he's expecting the short one. Right, good plan, let's go!'

I might be concerned about the lack of shine on the ball, that it's not swinging much, so I'll tell the guys to work harder on it. More spit and polish. Possibly the ball has started to reverse swing, so I'll tell the guys to watch for the signal. To help the reverse swing, players must keep their sweaty palms off the rough side and dampen the other side of the ball. The fielders will then know to leave the rough side alone, throw the ball to mid-off and let him do the work on the ball. I don't know the scientific reason why the ball goes into reverse swing, but it sure helps to get batsmen out. The ball will reach a certain condition and then late swing can be achieved. In the past, fast bowlers didn't like to bowl with an old ball, as they didn't realise the technique used to make the ball reverse swing. Watching the Pakistani pair of Wasim and Waqar destroy the England batting in 1992 has helped cricketers understand reverse swing and now most England bowlers can use the technique. Unfortunately, English bowlers are rarely as effective as this brilliant pair of Pakistanis because they don't have their pace.

I expect concentration when we're out in the field. We became one of the best fielding sides in the championship by hard work, imaginative practice sessions by Bob Woolmer and going for young lads who could field well. Trevor Penney's work in the covers has been remarkable in recent seasons. He can be classified as an all-rounder, because in addition to a career batting average of over 40, he saves around 15 to 20 runs in a normal innings, and runs out batsmen all the time. Yet that didn't happen overnight for Trevor. He practised day after day back home in Zimbabwe and his work before play starts every day is an object lesson in professionalism. Roger Twose and Dominic Ostler gave us great athleticism in the field, and Nick Knight's arrival in 1995 was another boost – he's a terrific catcher close in and very quick and athletic everywhere.

We have taken a high percentage of catches at slip, absolutely vital in both successful championship campaigns. It was a real challenge on some cold days when Allan Donald was motoring in – those snicks would really fly. We'd get the twelfth man to bring out hand-warmers, which would be kept in our pockets. You definitely stand a better chance of hanging onto the ball with warm hands. We'd feel jealous on a cold day that Keith Piper had his nice warm gloves on and we'd hope all the edges were thin and go to him. Some of his catches in recent seasons have been unbelievable, and they have turned tight games for us. Keith is particularly good at taking low snicks in front of him that wouldn't have carried to slip. I can't believe there is a keeper on the circuit who is more naturally gifted, and now that his concentration is improving, he is even more consistent. He sets the standard for the rest of the guys in the field.

There are times, though, when I have to remind some of the

guys about the need for concentration. Sundays can be a test for me as captain. It can get very noisy, and that's when you need your fielders to be looking in your direction all the time, because they can't hear you out on the boundary, with the crowd roaring in a tense finish. It's a club rule that the boys don't sign autographs when they're on the field in Sunday games, because they must be concentrating. Dominic Ostler can be very frustrating to captain in such situations. I like the fielders to bustle into position, keeping an eye on me for late changes of mind, but Dominic turns his back after ten yards and plods to his position out in the deep. It's very frustrating to have to wait for all your fielders to get into their positions, and Dominic is the worst offender. I know he thinks I pick on him, but he hasn't improved that area of his fielding. I want urgency on the field, for the opposition to think they just can't take liberties, and showing poor body language is more annoying to me than any technical deficiencies. I want all ten to shout 'Bad Luck!' if someone drops a catch, even at a crucial time, because that's the sort of thing which underlines a good team spirit, and the batsmen are reminded that there are 11 players out there, determined to get rid of him. You need to impose yourselves on the batsmen, to give them no peace at all.

For all his brilliance, Keith Piper needs to be given sharp reminders at times. Sometimes Keith is too keen and gets too vocal and I have to come out of the slips because he's saying too much. He won't skirt around the subject: 'Skip, he's bowling crap – take him off.' If a snick has gone between second slip and gully, he'll tut-tut and say, 'Third slip'. At times like that, I feel like throttling Keith, even if he is such a good mate. You always wish you had one more fielder, but you must go with your hunch and hope the team is going in the same direction and following your thought processes.

At Warwickshire we encouraged our batsmen to learn every shot in the book and then in matches choose the correct ones for the conditions. It's about having the right game plan. The best players in the world adapt their techniques to suit the conditions and the players were told to aspire to be the best, not to set attainable, moderate goals for the season, but aim for the top.

We tried to instil the right environment, where batsmen would-n't be castigated for getting out. If we were sitting watching our innings and a player made a mistake, you used to hear someone say, 'That's a bad shot – what's he doing?' so Bob Woolmer and I would turn it round and say, 'Just hang on – he's playing that shot for a reason. OK, poorly executed but the right idea'

I didn't want people talking negatively when they were watch-ing. It only puts the next batsman due in under pressure. He feels he will also be analysed by his team-mates and if he were to play a poor shot, you could be sure his mind would think back to the boys watching and then wonder what they'd be saying. Bob and I put a stop to any negatives being blurted out impul-sively and instead made the guys say things like, 'Bad luck, missed out on four there.'

We wanted the players to work things out, to think deeper about their game. In a Benson and Hedges Cup game, Asif Din got himself out against the off-spin of Surrey's James Boiling. The bowler had seven men in the ring, saving one and Asif was caught at mid-off. When he came in, he said, 'Sorry, Skip – bad shot', but I made a point of saying that it was only the execution that was wrong, the idea was good. The ball wasn't turning much, and Asif was trying to hit over the top, so that Boiling would then go on the defensive, putting men out in the deep. Then Asif would have been able to milk the bowling, playing him into the gaps, pushing it around for four or five an over. That would have been thoughtful cricket with little risk attached. It was the correct game plan, but he just got too close to the ball in executing the shot. If, on the other hand, a bats-man gets himself out by hitting into the wind, with two men out for the lofted shot, that is poor cricket, because he ought to know that the ball might hold up in the air, despite the power-ful execution of the shot. I would talk to him privately, perhaps the next day, after he's had time to cool down. He would know straight away that he'd made a mistake, otherwise he shouldn't be playing professional cricket. The important point is that he shouldn't be made to feel worse than he already does in front of his team-mates.

Dominic Ostler sometimes gets bored with just picking up the singles. He likes to play big shots, to dominate the bowler, and sometimes he chooses the wrong option, but I'd rather he erred on the side of being positive. Yet some days it's hard to play expansively on wickets that need more graft and attention, and this is where communication within the team is important. Before we bat, I'll say, 'I think this pitch will help the seam bowlers, so we might have to be a little careful. Make sure you're all watching, chat together out in the middle and tell us what's happening when you're out.' The trick is to settle for, say, 180 in a 40 overs game on a tricky pitch, but to avoid finding yourself 60 for 6 when you think you can get 260 by playing your shots all the time. It's a matter of judgement, of trusting your partner's view of things. Roger Twose was always great to bat with, because he was so confident and cool at the big times. He'd say, 'Skip, I'll go into positive mode now, you just knock it around, I'm ready for them.' I'd look at it a little more cautiously: 'Hang on Rog, this guy's only got one over left, then it's the off-spinner. I reckon I'll be able to sweep him to that short boundary because I've got the wind behind me', and we'd come to some sort of compromise. But I'd expect all my batters to keep looking at the options, and going for their shots when the situation was right.

You must think as a team, help each other and forget about individual statistics. How many times have you seen a player get to 99 in a limited overs match and start playing differently? That's bad cricket – he is wasting vital deliveries that ought to be adding to the team's score. If you've got to 99, there can't be much wrong with the way you've played that day, and you shouldn't alter, even for an over. You'd settle for 99 every time you went out to bat, wouldn't you? Even Nick Knight, a great team man, got sidetracked by his desire to get a hundred in his first season with us. He had played superbly for us, yet he narrowly missed his century at various stages of the season, and he started to tighten up whenever he got near to the three figures. But he should have been playing better in the nineties than in the early stages of his innings.

There are many statistics in the game of cricket, and you have to assess which ones are the most relevant. I think runs per ball faced is more important than if you have scored a hundred, rather than ninety, especially in limited overs matches. At Warwickshire, we try very hard to keep the game plan uppermost in the mind, rather than individual landmarks, and that was one of the reasons why my efforts with the bat pleased me so much in the 1995 championship season, after poor form the season before. Often when I came in, we were going for quick runs, after a good start and – following the necessary format for the four-day game – the need was to crack on to give us time to take the wickets. When we played Hampshire, I managed to get a few in the slot as we chased quick runs before the declaration. I'd made up my mind that I was going to try sweeping Kevin James, and although he had a lot of fielders around the boundary, I was hitting out, rather than picking up the singles that were available everywhere. I ended up 77 not out, and as I came into the dressing-room, Roger Twose said, 'Well played, Skip, nice innings. Great to see you not playing for the not out, but for the team.' I was pleased Roger had spotted I was going for the runs, that being not out was an incidental – and I was even more pleased that he had spoken about that in front of the rest of the side. That was exactly the sort of team spirit Bob Woolmer and I had been looking for since we came together in 1993.

Professional cricket can be a very selfish exercise unless the captain and coach nip that in the bud. You are, after all, dealing with people's livelihoods, and there is the temptation to play for yourself, to get to a level of competence. At Warwickshire, we expect that competence but we also look for unselfishness within the framework of efficiency. Neil Smith is the best example of the team man. In championship games, he can bat as low as number ten sometimes, and he'll play either sort of game, depending on the circumstances. In the one-day matches, we decided to open with him as a sort of wild card – they came to be known as 'pinch-hitters' after the 1996 World Cup. Neil took to the job straight away; he was happy to open his shoulders and play his shots right from the first over, because that was the best option for the team in those types of games. If he got out for nought early on, it didn't matter, because we knew the risks attached. Another player might have muttered about having to throw his wicket away, but not Neil. We call him 'The Iceman' because of his cool temperament; ask him to do anything with bat or ball and he'll try it without any fuss.

That unselfishness among the players was very heartening whenever one of them was injured. Every professional wants to play, rather than sit on the physiotherapist's couch, or do weeks of rehabilitatory work alone in the gym – wondering if you can get your career back on the line, and if the guy who has taken your place is now the automatic choice. Senior players like Tim Munton, Gladstone Small and Andy Moles were terrific in that respect. In the two seasons when we won so many trophies, all three of them had various worrying injuries, not the niggly type that soon clear up. All of them must have been concerned about their futures in the game, but they kept their concerns to themselves. They worked hard on their own and showed the right, positive attitude to the rest of the squad. In another team, the frustrations those guys must have felt could have become corrosive, but they gave all they could to the first team effort when not playing. They came on the away trips, for physio treatment and to give support, and they took all the mickey-taking in good heart, even from the younger guys who had taken their places. Andy Moles suffered a bad Achilles tendon injury, but he wasn't seen moping, even though he must have been desperately disappointed at missing out. Tim Munton had to have a back operation, a very serious setback for a fast bowler, yet he appeared cheerful when he surely wasn't. Gladstone had the assorted knee, calf and thigh injuries a fast bowler gets after a long time in the game, yet he and these senior players would talk to the younger players, offering advice and showing joy at their team-mate's successes. Gladstone also had to put up with Ostler and Twose bantering with him, calling him 'Grandad', and constantly pinching his backside, telling him he had the best bottom in the championship! Glad is brilliant for team morale!

It was terrific to captain Allan Donald during this period of success, not just because of his matchwinning ability, but the way he supported the rest of the guys. When he first came over from South Africa, he'd come straight out of national service and he hardly said a word. He wasn't all that fluent in the

English language – he's an Afrikaaner – and he'd sit in the corner of the dressing-room, taking it all in. He matured as a person, and marrying a local girl, then having a daughter helped put him on another level of maturity. Having grown up with most of the lads, Allan really wanted to do it for the team.

Before I became captain, I used to try motivating him with daft things like, 'Al, I was having a drink with this batsman last night and he said he was really looking forward to facing you – says he played against you in the second team a couple of years ago and doesn't reckon you're very quick,' but when I kept repeating it every game, Allan soon rumbled me! He never really needed motivating, though: he had his own high personal standards and his regard for the rest of the team. He's gone from being a nice, young lad who could bowl fast but erratically, to a great professional who wants his team-mates to do well. He's never arrogant when he's successful and didn't complain if he had to do something that might reduce his effectiveness – like bowling him into the wind in a one-day game. Allan realised he was harder to hit than a slower bowler therefore it was best for the team for Allan to bowl from the worst end. He was so focused in the 1995 season that I just needed to wind him up. Having missed out on the 1993 Nat West Final and the 1994 season because of his commitments with South Africa, Allan was hungry for success with us. He was also hurt that Warwickshire had decided to go with Brian Lara as the overseas player for the 1996 season, a decision I thought was wrong. Allan was determined to show they were making the wrong cricketing decision, and when he forecast that he would take a hundred championship wickets, I was delighted, because he is not given to boasts. He ended up with 88 championship wickets, getting one every six overs, a fantastic strike rate. If he hadn't missed three games because of a broken bone in his foot he surely would have got the hundred.

He was remarkably fast, accurate and consistent throughout the '95 season, but I shall never forget his spell on the third evening of our home match at Edgbaston against Derbyshire. It was the penultimate game and we had to win. There was rain about, and although our first innings lead of 118 was satisfactory,

we had to make early inroads on that third evening when
Derbyshire came out to bat. They lost three wickets in that final
40 minutes, all to Allan Donald in an awesome display of clini-
cal fast bowling. He knew what he had to do and he was
inspired. He said it was the fastest spell of his career and he was
so pumped up with adrenalin that even after the close of play he
sat in the dressing-room, eyes wide open, wanting more. He had
put so much in those six overs because he knew it was a vital
phase of the game. Derbyshire could have easily avoided defeat
on the final day, but due to Allan's inspiration we wrapped it up
and went to Canterbury to clinch the title. It was absolutely
right that Allan should get the final wicket to beat Kent and
bring us the title, and the emotion he showed at that moment
made us realise what it meant to him. I've seen some great overseas players in county cricket, but I can't believe there's been a
better professional and a greater team man than Allan Donald.
Warwickshire are very lucky that he's a big enough man to swallow his disappointment at being passed over in favour of Brian
Lara and come back as our fast bowling coach and fitness trainer.
Many other overseas stars would have sulked, then flounced off
to another lucrative county deal. I like to think the atmosphere
we've had in our dressing-room had something to do with Allan
staying with us.

Looking back on that amazing 1994 season, when we lost just
four out of 43 games in the four competitions, it's clear that we
did it by stealth. All the early headlines were dominated by Brian
Lara's arrival, then he continued to grab the attention for the
first two months of the season with his brilliant batting.
Meanwhile, we kept on winning cricket matches, and it stayed
that way. Brian Lara only managed five half-centuries in the one-
day competitions, but the other batsmen more than made up for
that with bold displays. We had kept quiet about our aims for
the '94 season, other than the usual platitudes about trying to
play attractive, winning cricket, but we were very bullish about
our prospects, even before we signed Lara. We took a lot of
strength from that historic win at Lord's the previous
September, our younger players were looking impressive, the fitness levels were excellent, and Roger Twose had come back from

New Zealand full of confidence after working on a couple of
weaknesses.

His 277 not out in the first championship match against
Glamorgan was overshadowed by Brian Lara's terrific hundred,
but it was more significant to me. Roger was to prove an
absolute rock over the next two seasons before he emigrated to
New Zealand to try to forge an international career. He was a
fantastic competitor, chockful of confidence – the sort of confidence that really annoys the opposition – with a cool brain in the
heat of battle. Roger was also invaluable to me in getting over
the message about how we should play spin. We both agreed
that our batsmen had been too orthodox in previous seasons
against the spinners and that we had to improvise more, play the
reverse sweep, the paddle, getting the ball where the fielders
weren't. We also believed these shots against the spinners should
be premeditated, and we hammered home to the players that
they'd be expected to extemporise. I believe our success in 1994
was more than any other reason down to our effectiveness
against spin. Bob Woolmer and I stressed the need to practise
the reverse sweep long and hard before trying it out in the
middle, and the results were very gratifying. In the Sunday
League and Nat West competitions in 1994, we got out just 24
times to the spinners, averaging 5.5 runs an over. We faced 8
overs of spin less than the opposition, scoring a staggering 238
runs more. In these competitions, the opposition only scored at
3.8 runs per over against Neil Smith and Richard Davis, losing a
wicket every 16 runs. We lost a wicket to spin every 44 runs and
scored at nearly 6 an over. Our success against seam bowlers was
no better than the opposition, in fact it was slightly inferior. We
scored at 4.6 runs per over against seam and pace bowling and
lost a wicket every 23 runs. Our seamers conceded 4.6 runs per
over, but only took a wicket every 26 runs. On those statistics,
you would finish mid-table in the Sunday League, but our superior batting against spin took us to nearly all three of the one-
day trophies in '94.

Before the 1994 season, Dominic Ostler and Trevor Penney
didn't want to play the reverse sweep, but Twose nagged away
at them. He was batting with Penney in a second eleven game

down at Taunton, and the off-spinner came on with a 6/3 field, with six fielders on the legside. Trevor wasn't keen on trying the reverse sweep, even though the field was open for the shot. He had practised it in the nets, and played it well, but he was wary about trying it out in the middle – the old syndrome of 'getting out in a bad way' I suppose. Roger Twose was having none of that. He marched down the pitch and simply ordered Penney to play the reverse sweep, saying, 'Look at the field, Trevor – do it, just do it!' He hit four off the first reverse sweep, then a couple more next ball. Trevor couldn't believe how easy he found it.

Soon after that, he was in a partnership with Twose against Yorkshire, and two spinners were in tandem. I saw Roger walk down to talk to Trevor and it was clear what advice he was giving him. He played the shot, scampered three and I could see how pleased he was. That was great; another dimension to Trevor Penney's batting. Earlier that season, he had played out a maiden at Guildford to James Boiling's off-spin and he told me that he hadn't thought about the reverse sweep, even though it was a 6/3 field. Yet Graeme Welch, in one of his early games for the first team, had come in and played it first ball! The young players in the second team were all playing it now, in contrast to a few years earlier when Neal Abberley, their coach, had told Roger Twose, 'Do that again and you're out of the net.' To be fair to Abbers, he had come to see the point of the shot and he was as keen as Woolmer and myself to see it practised, then played in a match whenever it was needed. When Phil Neale succeeded Bob Woolmer, he was staggered to hear us nominate where our batters would play the spinner – 'He won't do it now, he'll knock it square for one, because a man's there to block it. Hang on, it's there for him now, the bloke's been moved.' He was amazed that we knew each other's game so well. I took that as a great compliment.

I was very grateful to Roger Twose for banging on about the reverse sweep to the guys during the 1993 and '94 seasons. Roger's a highly intelligent, articulate chap and he would put the message over clearly in team nettings: 'Listen fellas, it's easy, you've just got to practise it. We should all be playing it, you'll get one run at the very least.' I was delighted my beliefs had rubbed off on another player and it became almost a mission to Roger. When we played Glamorgan, Matthew Maynard congratulated him on having the bottle to play the reverse sweep to the first ball Roger faced, and it was music to my ears when I heard the likes of Gladstone Small and Neil Smith say, 'That's great cricket' as they watched Roger play it, or premeditate a shot against the spinners. Neil and Gladstone had taken some persuading about the new way of playing the spinners from the time we had our team meeting in Trinidad, back in '91, and it was terrific to see they had been won over.

We kept stressing the importance of practising the reverse sweep before trying it out in the middle, though. In 1993, in a Sunday League game against Surrey, Jason Ratcliffe played it in desperation against James Boiling after he and Andy Moles had got stuck. We had needed a positive start from our two openers because we knew that Waqar Younis would come on late in the innings, and it would be very difficult to score at more than six an over off a world-class reverse-swing expert. But they couldn't get the ball away, and the asking rate escalated to ten an over eventually. We duly collapsed to 176 all out, losing by 18 runs, because of the poor start. Boiling got away with 2/40 in his ten overs. Everything I had asked for in our team meetings had gone out of the window and I was annoyed. I told Jason afterwards that it was poor cricket to play the reverse sweep when he had never practised it. I believe he took that on board and that he's a better player of spin these days than he was in 1993.

Nick Knight had the right attitude when he joined us in 1995. He said how impressed he had been by our batting in one-day games the year before, and that he wanted to broaden his range against the spinners. He came up to stay with me before the season started, I showed him a video I had compiled about batting against spin and we went into the indoor nets to practise. Phil Neale joined us, and he coached the reverse sweep for the first time that day. It was a good session, Nick was very receptive and adaptable as we worked on premeditated shots. He wore the helmet and grille, because you can easily get a top edge.

In the 1995 season, Nick played the spinners very well, and he ended up playing for England. He would play the slog/sweep in front of square and if that was blocked off, then he'd go for the reverse sweep or the paddle. He wanted to play those shots well and he worked very hard in the indoor nets. Nick has a very quick brain and fast hands: I saw him one day set himself for the sweep, notice the ball had been dropped short, change his mind at the last instant and go for the cut instead. Normally I would say, 'Don't cop out – once you're down there, you've got to go through with the shot', but Nick's reactions were so sharp he got away with it.

Despite our success at Warwickshire with premeditating spin, I think there is still a resistance against it in some circles. The England captain, Mike Atherton penned an interesting article for my benefit brochure, about our match against Lancashire, when they scored 305/2 and we fell short of the target. It was a Benson and Hedges game and we didn't play the reverse sweep well that day, with Trevor Penney eventually getting out playing the shot. That night I went to a supporters' forum and the first question I took was, 'Why did Trevor Penney play that ridiculous shot? It cost us the game.' So I got on my soapbox, gave him all the statistics and explained how valuable the reverse sweep and premeditating spin is in modern cricket and concluded that we simply had a bad day. He apologised profusely, I got a nice round of applause and there was no harm done.

Mike Atherton obviously felt the same way as that supporter. In his article for me, he called it a 'Get Out of Jail' shot, referred to Warwickshire's 'obsession' with the stroke and pointed out that Brian Lara never had to play it, nor wanted to. Well for a start Brian Lara is a genius, but even he was starting to play the paddle towards the end of his great season in '94. I also believe he would be an even more destructive player if he mixed up his shots against the spinners, because there were times when he got tied up by them in the Sunday League and indeed was regularly dismissed by spin. In fact, Brian Lara and Paul Smith were responsible for one third of our dismissals to spinners in the Sunday League and Nat West and both hardly ever premeditated. I don't expect Atherton to know that, he was usually fairly busy elsewhere on Sundays. It was nonsense, though, to suggest that great players like Lara don't need it in their locker.

Desmond Haynes played it regularly and he scored more hundreds in one-day internationals than anyone else. Mike Gatting, Ian Botham, Javed Miandad and many other top batsmen have played the reverse sweep productively. I'm fairly certain that Mike Atherton didn't score one-day runs as quickly as Roger Twose in '94 and '95, so perhaps he might think about broadening his range. As for it being a 'Get Out of Jail' stroke, I never wanted it to be played that way, as Jason Ratcliffe had found out two years earlier. In the vast majority of cases, our batsmen have played it safely and productively, and I was disappointed that the England captain seemed so rigid and orthodox in his thinking. In fact several of Atherton's Lancashire team-mates now play the shot, among them Graham Lloyd, who is one of the best players of spin in the country. At Warwickshire we see it as a safe, controlled stroke and it has helped us win trophies.

Our bold approach against the spinners also benefited us in championship matches, when we were on a run chase on the final day. In 1994, we won two games against the clock, when we were, in effect, into a one-day game, with the asking rate around six an over. At Northampton, we got 230 off 37 overs to win by four wickets, with Nick Cook's left-arm spin going for nearly six an over, and at Scarborough, we rattled along at five an over to beat Yorkshire by eight wickets, with Jeremy Batty and Richard Stemp taking some stick. I was delighted with Andy Moles that day. He had worked really hard with Bob Woolmer to widen his repertoire of strokes and he premeditated superbly, making 48 in as many balls. Because Andy was receptive to the new methods at an advanced stage of his career, he was now playing with far greater freedom than in his early days, when he was a little stodgy. He was now worth his place in a one-day side just as much as in the longer games.

Paul Smith was another senior player who eventually worked hard at the reverse sweep in the indoor nets, so that at the start of the 1995 season, he was playing it successfully against Leicestershire's Adrian Pierson. Poor Adrian was badly mauled by us in a Sunday League game later in the same year. Roger Twose initially reverse swept Pierson fine and when the fielder at backward point was moved to short third man, Roger then struck boundary after boundary with the reverse hit. Now the reverse hit is more complicated than its brother, the more conservative reverse sweep. In playing the reverse hit, you put your back foot forward, which turns your shoulders into a left hander's position (if you're a right-hander), and this allows a full swing of the bat. I actually came across this shot accidentally while coaching the Hong Kong side in 1993. I was trying to coach the reverse sweep to Stewart Brew, Hong Kong's premier all-rounder, but he kept putting the wrong leg forward and smacking the ball square on the offside. It looks a high-risk shot and is more difficult than the reverse sweep, but if practised properly, can be effective. I had shown it to Roger at the start of the 1994 season and he took to it immediately. Poor Adrian Pierson didn't know what to do that day at Leicester, eventually going for 1/79 in his eight overs. Afterwards, as we commiserated with our former team-mate, he asked where he had gone wrong. Roger replied, 'You did nothing wrong, mate – I just wouldn't have bowled you.' He wasn't trying to put Adrian down, just pointing out that Warwickshire's prowess against spinners is so good that we fancied ourselves against any of them.

I was absolutely delighted that we didn't stand still after our great season in '94, when we took everybody by surprise. We didn't lose anybody to the Test team in '94, only Keith Piper made it on one of the England tours that winter, and we had little national media coverage until the second half of the season, with the earlier focus on Brian Lara – so we just cruised along, enjoying the fact that not many rated us until we had won three out of four competitions. Then it was time to revise a few rigid opinions. The next season was even more satisfying, because we buried the myth of 'Larashire'. The team continued to evolve, with Neil Smith blossoming into an England player and young lads like Wasim Khan, Ashley Giles and Dougie Brown coming into the side and playing with great freedom and confidence. I was anxious to prove there was still some life left in me as a cricketer, after fitness and form worries reduced my effectiveness in the '94 championship, and I was pleased with my contribution. All through that '95 season, players from other counties were coming up to me, saying they would like to play at Edgbaston, which was a nice compliment. It was also flattering to see more county sides premeditating against spin in 1995 and I knew that most observant sides would eventually catch us up. In the 1996 season, Northants played our spinners brilliantly and one of their batsmen, Mal Loye told me afterwards that they'd had a team meeting in 1994 after losing to us in a Sunday League game. Their coach, Bob Carter had pointed out Warwickshire's superiority that day in playing spin and he suggested they copy our unorthodox methods.

In my time as captain, I was more than happy with the players available to me and was delighted that Nick Knight strengthened us in 1995. It meant a lot that he would choose to leave a successful outfit like Essex to join us. I had been impressed by a hundred by him against us in our first championship season and Nick told me that he liked the way we approached our cricket. He moved for the sake of his career, for ambition not for financial considerations, and he was impressive right from the start. He was hungry for success, a very bright, personable guy who spoke eloquently about the game and wanted to learn. He adapted very swiftly to the Warwickshire way of thinking, and reacted well to the encouragement. In his very first game he sidled up to me and said, 'Skip, do you think we might try a leg gully?' I liked the way he acknowledged the captain's authority, while at the same time showing his own independent style of thinking in a pleasant manner. Nick Knight has definite leadership qualities and he has proved a great signing for us.

It was a terrific feeling, sitting in the Lord's dressing-room in 1995, after another successful Final, to see the pleasure all the lads felt in each other's performances. There was Keith Piper hugging everyone, Roger Twose – in his last big match for us – singing loudly and tunelessly. That warm feeling of camaraderie can only be understood by a team that has gone through so much together, and getting a call from our former coach, Bob Woolmer, from Cape Town made it all the more sweet. Six trophies in 24 calendar months was the best possible answer to those outside the game who couldn't understand how a side lacking household names could be so supreme – and to those on the circuit who chose to ignore the facts and continue denigrating us. They kept harping about the pitches at Edgbaston, the unreliable bounce, the fact that we had a huge advantage with our seam attack. Mike Brearley, writing in the aftermath of the '95 Edgbaston Test, when England were overwhelmed by the West Indies, suggested that such pitches were the reason why we won championships. I was disappointed that a man of Brearley's stature hadn't bothered taking a deeper look than just one Test Match. For a start, Steve Rouse, our groundsman, is very much his own man and doesn't take too much notice of the observations of the coach or captain once the season starts. He has his own idea about what constitutes a good cricket wicket. Mike Brearley might also like to consider that in our first championship season, we were unbeaten away from home and next season lost one game on our travels and ended up winning as many matches away as at home. We can't have been that bad then! After a time, I decided to let the carping comments just slide away. I'd say to our players, 'Listen guys, in ten years' time, no one will talk about the quality of the pitches at Edgbaston, they'll talk about you making history. The public have short memories, and you're just a conversation piece around the dinner table or in the pub. The most important thing is that you do well for each other, and your very best as an individual. Focus on your own self-esteem. Ask yourself after each day's play if you did your best? If the answer is 'yes', that is good enough for me.

I tried to avoid a set routine in how I dealt with players individually, even though I'd look for a collective attitude. Some players get keyed up when a big game approaches. Keith Piper gets more nervous and vocal on the morning of a big match, and I have to tell him to relax and not to vary his preparations, just maintain his high standards. Sometimes, a flash of anger from Keith can be counter-productive. He showed his intense disappointment in a Sunday League game against Glamorgan that we had to win and looked like losing as we defended a small total. Neil Smith bowled five 'dot' balls at David Hemp, then gave him a really slow delivery that was swept to the boundary. Keith put his hands up in horror and said to me, 'What's he doing? That's stupid cricket!' and I then tried to calm him down. We soon got a wicket and as we gathered round, Keith had a go at Neil, saying things that were totally out of order. Luckily Neil's a calm character who knew that our keeper was just pumped up, but I had to pull Keith aside and have a strong word. He's a great lad, but can be a little combustible at times, so he has to be treated in a certain way.

Paul Smith has to be handled in the right fashion too. He's a maverick, a free spirit, and if you put your arm around him all the time, and be nice to him, you won't get what you want. In most situations, you want him to bowl with fire in his belly, and to achieve this I'll deliberately try to rile him. As he's walking back to his mark, I'll shout out, 'Come on Smithy, get your arm up, they're playing you off the front foot. You're bowling like a girl!' He's the one cricketer on the staff for whom I'll ignore my rule about not denigrating for cricketing reasons. He could lose his energy quickly because he'd lose his adrenalin and that would result in a reduction of pace and effectiveness. He did, however, respond well to the big occasion and was at his best when he bowled 'effort' balls, on a wicket of uneven bounce. In the 1994 Nat West semi-final against Kent, he bowled medium pace early on and he was treated dismissively. He slunk away to the boundary, disgusted with himself, showed poor body language, and didn't walk in with the bowler. The crowd suddenly woke up, the atmosphere suddenly galvanised Paul, and when I brought him back he bowled like a demon. He was almost as quick as Allan Donald that day, and with the crowd on his side, he helped win us a match that we really should have lost. He did it again that season, at Lord's in the Benson and Hedges Cup Final, when he picked up the Gold Award for a terrific all-round performance.

I think the right mental attitude is a very important ingredient in winning cricket matches. It's about fine tuning, getting yourself prepared in the way that suits you, so that when you start the serious business, you feel 'I'm looking forward to this, I'm ready.' Cricketers tend to look for excuses when they fail, so I don't want a regimented approach to the preparation for the day's play. I tell the guys to do what they want, as long as they're prepared to their own satisfaction. I don't see much point to all those throw-downs to the batsman on a slow outfield, where the surface is so different from the actual middle. I like to bowl on the edge of the square, at a single stump, rather than be enclosed in the nets. To me, the environment for practice must be similar to the actual match. Most of your technique has been ingrained in you as a teenager, and if you practise too much before the start of play, you can lose your edge, and your ability to maintain your concentration for the day can be impaired. These days, my preparation in the morning tends to be a shower, a cup of coffee, a session with the physio (to get loose), and a few catches thrown at me. It all depends on what's best for you. We are probably the only county that doesn't have a regimented warm-up. Routines can get monotonous and boredom makes you tired. You can get stiff after a warm-up and for me, the key time to be warm is when it's actually needed – out in the middle.

All I ask is that the players are mentally confident and physi-cally ready when they take the field, and I don't care how they've achieved that. I had to bite my tongue one day when Neil Smith was run out without facing a ball, going for the second run. Neil admitted when he came in that he wasn't quite loose enough, and he should have been. I once ran out Gladstone Small in a one-day game, and although it looked my fault, it wasn't, because Glad wasn't backing up properly. These little subtleties can change a game. Look at Dean Jones: he's terrific at backing up, and he turns so quickly for the second or third run. Cricketers should copy him. I expect my players to attend to details like that without needing to hammer home the point.

I'm fascinated at the variants you can encounter in a team game like cricket. It's an evolving sport, with so many new ideas coming through every season. It was significant to me that more opposition batsmen played the reverse sweep against our bowlers in 1995 than the year before. I like to think we were among the first to use a 'pinch-hitter' in Neil Smith to open the innings. We were also happy to be flexible in the middle order, putting bold strikers like Paul Smith and Dougie Brown in early for the one-day games and leaving a fine player like Trevor Penney till later in the innings, when he's so good at scampering singles and running twos to the fielders on the boundary. You

Top left: Dermot was winning trophies from an early age. Here he is in Kowloon, 1973, aged 10. *Top right:* Aged 7 months – already enjoying life. *Middle and bottom:* The four brothers (from the left) Philip, Mark, Dermot, Paul in 1967 and 1990.

Top: Dermot with his beloved daughter Emily and *(bottom)* with his mother on Boxing Day 1991.

Right: Dermot in his first season at Sussex in 1983, aged 20 and *(below)* making his first appearance for England as sub in the Texaco Trophy game against the West Indies at Old Trafford in 1991.

Monica Reeve

Roger Wootton

Batting against Kent whom Warwickshire beat in the Nat West semi-final in 1994, before losing in the final – one of only 4 games that they lost all season.

Reverse sweeping in the final AXA Equity & Law match against Gloucestershire in 1994 which won Warwickshire this trophy to add to their County Championship and B & H Cup.

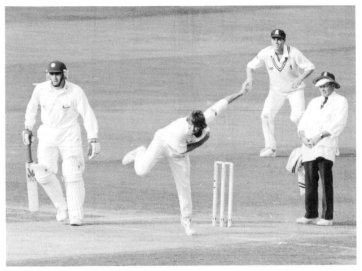

Bowling in the Nat West final at Lord's against Northants in 1995, which Warwickshire went on to win.

Taking a sharp catch to dismiss Vikram Solanki of Worcestershire off Neil Smith in 1995.

Victory celebrations after their Nat West Trophy win against Sussex in 1993.

With Tim Munton, the vice-captain, holding their three trophies for 1994, an unprecedented feat.

The boys celebrate winning yet another Lord's final to take the Nat West Trophy in 1995.

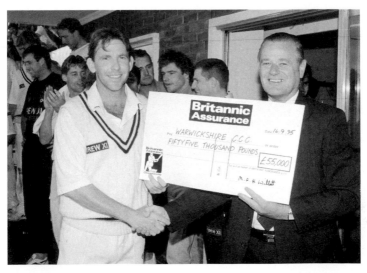

Receiving the winner's cheque after winning the Britannic Assurance County Championship in 1995 at Kent in Canterbury.

Dermot displaying his O.B.E. outside Buckingham Palace in March 1996 which he was awarded in the 1995 New Year's Honours list for his services to cricket and *(below)* unwinding at Lord's having won the Nat West Trophy in 1995.

don't have to hit boundaries to achieve a run rate as high as 7 an over, and Trevor knows this; often he saw us home with sensible, intelligent strokeplay. I'll also open the bowling with a spinner if it's justified. To me cricket is the art of the possible and you need to be flexible to stay on top. I like to think that Warwickshire have won so many trophies in recent years because they kept one jump ahead of the rest. Success didn't suddenly happen in 1994 as if by magic. We were creeping up on the rails, hoping no one would notice, but in the end they did. It may still be a mystery to Darren Gough, but our methods in winning so many trophies contained no dark secrets. It's amazing what you can achieve in a team sport when everyone feels relaxed and privileged to be out there, playing for each other.

Getting Up Noses

'I don't like you, Reeve. You get up my nose and if you come anywhere near me, I'll rearrange yours.' Not the usual after-match banter you experience in a committee room when the players of both sides mingle for a drink. But Lancashire's David Lloyd was in no mood for genial niceties when we gathered in the Old Trafford committee room in May 1995. Clearly, a few things had been festering with the Lancashire coach during this particular game, but he probably chose the wrong time and place to have a go at me. Lloyd's outburst was in front of some Lancashire committee including Chairman Bob Bennett. It was another indication that on the county circuit, there is no love lost between Lancashire and Warwickshire. And that incident was further proof of how I can get under people's skins – and sometimes I even mean to.

That bust-up with Lancashire had been on the cards for some time. We had known that some of their players and David Lloyd had resented our success, that we were making more of our assets than they were at Old Trafford, and Lloyd's early season comment of 'How can they win three trophies in a year with that side?' wasn't enjoyed in our dressing-room. Whenever we played them, you could see how important it was for them to take us down a peg or two, that they felt we were up ourselves and arrogant. We thought that was rich, coming from Lancashire. I thought both sets of players were very similar in approach, but clearly our continued success bothered David Lloyd. In his capacity as an excellent summariser for BBC Radio, David never missed a chance to have a dig at Warwickshire for the quality of pitches at Edgbaston and once, when he was covering a semi-final involving Warwickshire, he referred to us as 'strutters'.

The roots of that incident involving David and me had obviously been growing for some time. I know I had really annoyed Wasim Akram the year before with a daft remark that I instantly regretted. It was the summer when Imran Khan had admitted publicly that he had altered the condition of the ball with a bottle top when he played for Sussex. When Lancashire came to Edgbaston, Wasim was fielding down on the boundary and he signalled to his twelfth man for something. I was standing at the door to the players' entrance and shouted out, 'Bottle top?' As soon as I said it, I realised it was tactless and Wasim looked furious. It was a remark made in jest, to entertain our lads, but it was one of umpteen cases when my smart mouth was running away from my brain. Soon, half-truths were circulating around the circuit and it was being said that when I went out to bat, I brought on a bottle top and presented it to Wasim Akram. Not true, but I was told that Wasim was out to get me and I could understand why I wasn't the most popular opponent to the Lancashire lads.

Then, a week before the Old Trafford bust-up, Lancashire came to play us at Edgbaston in a Benson and Hedges Cup game. That led to David Lloyd alleging that I had tried to 'out-psych' him and his twelfth man in the viewing area when Warwickshire were batting. Lloyd thought I was deliberately trying to belittle his off-spinner Gary Yates by making derogatory remarks about his bowling, putting unfair pressure on Lloyd, who was sitting a few yards away with his twelfth man. That was rubbish. I was so involved in our efforts to match a big score of over 300 that I was babbling to the boys about how we had to get after the spinners. I blurted out, 'Come on fellas, we've got to take him for six an over.' I just blurted it out in front of the guys in the viewing area, because I knew the importance of getting at least a run a ball on such a good pitch against the spinners. We played spin so well in one-day games that I wanted to remind the lads who were due to bat that we simply had to get after Gary Yates. It wasn't meant to be derogatory at all to Yates, who is a fine all-round player in one-day cricket, or a slur on Lancashire cricket in any way, it was simply a gee-up to our boys – but David Lloyd saw hidden meanings. I also found out that David didn't like my impersonation of Lancashire accents. I have this habit of copying people's voices and at times walk around in my own world, babbling away, doing impressions. Now David's voice is very distinctive and when I hear it, I can't help myself and try to copy it. I can see how it could be construed as mickey-taking, but I have honestly never done anything like that off the field, to deliberately upset someone. I actually love listening to David Lloyd, I find his enthusiasm infectious on the radio or in after-dinner speeches, he is brilliant. Presumably, though, I must have been working on my Lancashire accent on the day that David heard me, and he must have concluded I was taking the mickey out of his part of the world.

All of that came to a head at Old Trafford when we played Lancashire in a championship and Sunday League match. The atmosphere had been highly competitive right from the start. On the Sunday, when John Crawley was given out caught by Neil Smith on the mid-wicket boundary, the lumpy stuff hit the fan. Crawley was walking back to the pavilion after ascertaining that it was a fair catch, when David Lloyd shouted from their balcony, 'Stay there, Creepy! He had his foot on the rope!' I went over to Neil Smith, and he told me that he took his foot off the rope before he took the catch and that it was fair. John Holder, the square leg umpire, saw the incident much more clearly than the Lancashire guys on their balcony and confirmed that Crawley was out. But the shouts from the Lancashire balcony incensed the crowd and Neil Smith and the rest of us got some real stick after that. Unfortunately for John Crawley, he bore the brunt of some anger. As he walked up the stairs to the Lancashire dressing-room, Gladstone Small, who was not playing that day, came out and gave him a mouthful. A few minutes later, as we got on with the game out in the middle, David Lloyd came downstairs and stated that none of our players were welcome upstairs. So, if any of our team got injured over the next two days, or wanted to use the gym, it was off limits. In the committee room after the game, I tried to have a word with David to explain that Neil Smith did have his foot on the rope, but lifted it off as the ball came his way. I was however annoyed that one of my players was being blatantly accused of cheating, but it probably wasn't the best time to try to talk it through. I had naively thought that David and I had got on well, so I was surprised at the volley of abuse that greeted my approach. The following day, Bob Bennett asked me to join him and David Lloyd in a meeting and that was when it became apparent to me that I had severely upset the Lancashire coach. We worked out our differences and I hope that David sees it now as a misunderstanding, rather than deliberate mind games.

In my early days at Sussex, I thought it was important to be liked and to be popular. I was over-sensitive to people's comments and tried hard to fit in. It's honestly not worth the effort! It's funny, but people I tend to warm to, and spend time with, are often categorised as arrogant or show-offs, a couple of allegations that are regularly thrown in my direction. It's water off a duck's back now! I focus on my own self-esteem and am more content now that I ever was when I made an effort to impress in the past. It's sad, but I'm not as trusting as I used to be, or as sociable. There are too many who dislike you because of petty jealousy. As soon as you are successful, people suddenly judge you, and some love to try knocking you down. I have made a few friends through cricket and shared fun times on the county circuit and England tours. It's not imperative, though, to be liked by people who don't really know me. I would far rather have the respect of my players and that of the opposition as a cricketer. I've seen a few sides full of so-called nice chaps that never won anything. I treasure Allan Donald's quote about me: 'I'd hate to play against Dermot Reeve, he must be a pain in the neck, but he's great to have in the side.' That's all that matters in the tough school of professional sport. I was also delighted by a comment Robin Smith made to me during our first England tour together in 1992. After a fortnight, he said to me, 'I have to apologise to you, Dermot. For years, I've thought you the biggest shit in county cricket, but now I've got to know you, you're okay.' It was nice to know that I had got under the skin of such a nice guy when we were in opposition, because I don't see it as my function to be nice to the opposition. I stand by the quote: 'You're out there to win matches, not friends.' On that tour of New Zealand, I got annoyed at Robin Smith indulging in genial chat with Mark Greatbatch as Robin was fielding at silly point. Now I know that's part of Robin's charming nature, but I had to tell him he should try to make Greatbatch feel uncomfortable at the crease, not ask him where he was dining out that night. If that meant some verbals, give it out.

I learned a lot about being mentally strong during my nine years of grade cricket in Western Australia. Out there, the Aussies don't even think about passing the time of day with opponents, and they rarely spend more than a few minutes together after the game, preferring to go back to their own club and drink as a unit. I learned to give it back if anyone had a go at me on the field, but I wish I could have come up with the kind of reply I heard one day from a guy called Peter Capes. Peter had played for Western Australia as a bowler who could also bat usefully, and one day in a grade match he came up against a typical, cocky young Aussie fast bowler, who clearly felt that sledging was a vital part of his armoury. After beating him with one good delivery, he shouted derisively at Peter, 'And you're a State player!' When he almost got him again with a good delivery, the lad got even more abusive. Peter looked down the pitch at the quickie and said, 'If you're going to have a verbal go at me, you'll win that battle, because you know who I am. But I haven't got a f***ing clue who you are!' That really brought the bowler down a peg or two, because the clever implication from Peter was that he was a nobody.

When the red mists descend out there on the field, there are times when I wish I could summon up a quip like Peter Capes managed that day. But it's more important not to be fazed by anything that's said out there, to show you won't be overwhelmed. It's a test of character, and that was hammered home to me right at the start of my career with Sussex. I was so happy to be playing county cricket that I was determined to enjoy it all the time, and hoped to be popular. But I soon realised it was a very hard school and your nerve and heart were tested as much as your skills. Early on, Mark Nicholas baited me as we were holding out for a draw against Hampshire. I was blocking successfully, so Nicholas shouted out in that familiar public school drawl, 'That's it, I've had enough – this chap can't bat. Come on, Macco, finish it off.' And with that, he threw the ball to the great Malcolm Marshall. Well, Nicholas' arrogant manner had succeeded in annoying me, and that made me even more determined to see it out. I held out for the draw and was very pleased to thwart Mark Nicholas. His subtle form of sledging hadn't worked and to cap a great moment for me, Malcolm Marshall said, 'Well played, lad' as we walked off.

I had an early run-in with Ian Botham in my first season that helped me. At that stage, I was totally in awe of Ian. He had been my hero when I was on the Lord's ground staff as I watched him take so many wickets for England with some brilliant swing bowling. I loved his confident, visual manner and thought him a fabulous advert for the English game. So when I first faced Ian in a county game, it was all I could do to stop myself asking for his autograph! I came in to bat just before lunch against Somerset and even I realised, naive as I was, that it would be a good idea if we faced as few deliveries as possible before the interval. In the last over before lunch, with Somerset trying to squeeze in another over, I kept pulling away from my crease, gesturing towards the sightscreen as some imaginary spectators walked past. Ian was standing at slip and knew what I was up to and he growled at the young sprog, 'Get on with it, I know what you're trying to do!' I almost blurted out, 'Yes, sir!' but calmed myself and stuttered: 'You'd do the same'. I thought I'd passed a little test in the great man's eyes.

A few years later, I was sufficiently self-confident to come off best in a sledging bout with Botham. It was an incident that has gained a lot of exaggerated mileage, so much so that various cricket magazines and newspaper articles over the years have maintained that I called Botham that day 'a fat has-been'. Not true. What is true is that I wouldn't be brow-beaten and intimidated by him and made that clear. The undercurrent to the flashpoint was that Ian was beginning to be under pressure for his all-rounder's spot in the England team by the time we had our spat in 1990. After his back operation, he hadn't made the England tour party to the West Indies in '89/'90 and that had hurt him. I was one of several players putting in decent performances in county cricket as an all-rounder and although none of us could compare with a great player like Botham in his prime, he was still having to rack up some performances to get back in the England side – and he knew it. His pride was hurt by the England selectors, he knew his body was beginning to let him down and he was eyeing up the pretenders to his crown. His magnificent competitive instinct wouldn't allow him to acknowledge those rivals to his England spot and I'm sure he didn't think much of me.

So when I came in to bat at Edgbaston against Worcestershire in May 1990 I'm sure Ian wanted to blow away this upstart with the annoying manner. Although I was batting well, he kept telling me how lucky I was and I took that as a compliment, because I must have been getting to him. Ian kept throwing his arms up, going through the complete repertoire of hard-luck stories and histrionics (I could recognise them all, because I did the same stuff when I was bowling), until he got me out. Or rather, he prevailed on umpire Nigel Plews to confirm an optimistic lbw shout. I'd taken a big stride forward, got an inside edge on to the pad when the appeal bellowed out of Botham. I was given out, and as I walked away disappointedly, Botham shouted at me, 'F*** off!' I turned back, stared at him and was rewarded with, 'Go on, f*** off!' All the Worcestershire players then joined in as they gathered round Botham and I stopped ten yards from them and said to Botham, 'Pick your dummy up and put it back in your mouth.' Botham roared at me, 'I'll ram it down your face!' and after walking a few yards back to the pavilion, I turned and said to him, 'You've had your day, mate.' With that, I was off. Afterwards my captain, Andy Lloyd told me, 'Beefy's after you, he wants to fill you in. What did you say to him?' I wasn't bothered at all by the incident, it was a moment that should have stayed on the field, not for public consumption. Somehow my remarks to Botham were picked up and recycled though. It's still printed that I called him a 'fat has-been'. For all my faults, I've rarely had a go at a fellow cricketer about his physical shape – and all I did was to show to Ian Botham that I wouldn't be intimidated by anyone on the field. I think he respected that, because we had a chat about my alleged remark some time later and we got on fine when I first toured with him for England in 1992.

If you took all the cricketers I've annoyed out in the middle, you'd have a pretty handy team. Curtley Ambrose would take the new ball for a start. I hope he wouldn't bowl beamers, though – as he did at me in 1990. That match at Northampton was memorable for me because I made the highest score of my career – 202 not out – and because Ambrose decided the way to get rid of me was with a beamer. The trouble started just after I reached my hundred, when I played forward to Mark Robinson. I hit the pad with the inside edge of my bat, the ball went through to the wicket-keeper and all the slips went up for the catch. I was given not out and Greg Thomas, a fiery character, came up from second slip and gave me a real mouthful. The umpire, Don Oslear, was quick to intervene and said, 'Greg, he never hit it, the bat hit the pad, go back to slip and shut up.' Well Greg bowled the next over and I hit him for a couple of boundaries. The last ball was a well-placed beamer and I got out of the way just in time. Thomas said, 'Sorry, it slipped', a likely story from someone good enough to bowl for England.

Thomas came off and I continued to enjoy myself on a beautiful batting pitch. Ambrose came on and I hooked a bouncer past square leg to the boundary. I stood there watching the ball go to the fence, enjoying the moment, and when I turned round, there was Curtley towering over me. He stared at me and said, 'Be careful.' Through my grille I started back, but never said a word. I honestly wasn't fazed. It was such a slow wicket that I was looking forward to facing probably another bouncer. The next ball I never saw – because it didn't bounce. Curtley had beamed me. He then bowled me another two and somehow I stayed calm, telling myself to keep on batting. Although it wasn't the end of the over, I wasn't going to carry on batting without a chest and arm guard so I called for the protection as Barry Duddleston, the umpire at Curtley's end, seemed stunned by it all. Geoff Humpage came on with a chest pad for me, pausing only to give Ambrose a piece of his mind. I thought, 'Gee, thanks Geoff – I've still got to bat against this bloke!' After the over, Ambrose left the field.

At the close of play, I sat in the dressing-room and got angry. Those beamers could have killed me. It doesn't matter that the Northants guys believed I was out: what Ambrose did was inexcusable. What disciplinary action would be taken? I found out next morning, when I was asked into the office of Northants' chief executive, Steve Coverdale. There was my captain, Andy Lloyd, his opposite number, Allan Lamb – and Curtley Ambrose. Lamby had missed the incident – he wasn't playing through injury – but opened up by saying, 'Honestly, Dermot – I've got to believe that Curtley didn't mean it, because he's a great bowler and the beamers missed you.' I was trying to work that one out when Lamby brushed it aside: 'It doesn't matter, because Curtley wants to apologise. Curtley, say you're sorry.' And Curtley uttered his one word of that meeting: 'Sorry'. Lamby ushered him out of the office: 'Okay, Curtley, go off and warm up now', and closed the door. He then turned to me and said, 'Don't worry, the bloody wanker bowled me two in the West Indies, as well'. With that, Lamby donned his sunglasses, ready to walk out. I was dumbfounded. It was hardly a fulsome apology. Lamby also added, 'What do you expect, running down the wicket to fast bowlers?' I had done no such thing and the myth also grew that I had gone down on one knee to sweep Ambrose for six, and that had got his dander up. Has anyone ever seen Curtley Ambrose swept for six by a batsman on one knee? Strange how these rumours grow and become truths in the eyes of people who weren't actually there.

I do seem to have this ability to annoy West Indian fast bowlers, as Winston Benjamin would surely agree. He bowled me two beamers one day at Hinckley after a close lbw decision went against him. I could see he was angry at Merv Kitchen's decision and he bowled me two bouncers in a row. The first I hooked for four with a proper stroke, the next was mishooked over the wicketkeeper. Next ball was a fast, accurate beamer and I saw it just in time, getting the ball on the splice of my bat in front of my face. It could have killed me, and it wasn't pleasant to turn round and see all the slips laughing. Next ball was the same and Merv Kitchen thankfully took action and said, 'That's it, captain, have a word with your player', and David Gower did the necessary. Next ball – a bouncer. Benjamin was then warned for intimidation and he then threw all his toys out of the cot as he finished the over off three steps. After I took a single, Geoff Humpage played the last ball of the over back to the bowler. As it bobbled back to him, Benjamin hoofed the ball over cover point's head and third man had to chase after it. 'Yes, run,' I shouted at Humpage and we got three extra runs from his pique. I thought that was very funny, which I'm sure didn't endear me to the fielders or Winston Benjamin.

There is a fine line between justifiable needle and unfair behaviour on the field and I wouldn't want anyone to think I'm blameless. I admit I have transgressed sometimes. Even though I deplore the use of beamers, I admit I bowled one at Gehan Mendis once. We were playing at Old Trafford against Lancashire and Mendis, my old team-mate at Sussex, had given me some fearful stick, fielding at silly point when I batted. That didn't worry me, all part and parcel of the game. When I bowled at Mendis and Graeme Fowler, my first delivery swung prodigiously and I said, 'Oh, great – it's swinging' and Mendo then gave me some more verbals from the non-striker's end. It then dawned on me that Mendo had worked it all out. He was trying to rile me, to get me to drop it short in my anger, rather than pitch it up, looking for late swing. Mendo was a great cutter and puller and he was looking to pick me off if I tried to bang it in. Anyway, his constant sledging finally got to me and I proceeded to bowl some attempted beamers. The first was a knee-high full toss, the next a waist-high full toss and the third a beamer at head height that Mendo avoided. My next ball led to a big shout for lbw from me; the umpire, Dickie Bird, shouted 'Not out' instantly, threw my sweater at me and walked away. It was the end of the over and Dickie was quite right to show his displeasure at me. I had lost my rag for once and he let me know it wasn't to happen again, in the right way. That's the only time I've ever tried to bowl beamers.

I know the reputation about me that's grown on the county circuit and how it seeps into the media, and I only worry about the factual inaccuracies, rather than the general image, which, I think, is one of a guy who wants to win, who will try hard to stay on the legitimate side of the game's spirit, but will push the opposition as hard as possible. So it's felt that I'm always spoiling for a set-to on the field and that there are certain players looking out for me. Kevin Curran and I often have a laugh at people's expense in that sense. He and I are similar types on the field and whenever Northants play Warwickshire, we try to live up to the myth that we can't stand each other, that it wouldn't take much for us to come to blows on the field. At times one of us will give the other a little shoulder barge if either is in the way, or one will point the bat at the other if he's hit a boundary. It's become a laugh with Kevin and me and we try to see if the press reports will pick up the next day on alleged hostility towards each other. I have tremendous respect for Kevin as a cricketer, and we get along fine socially, but it's funny when I hear that commentators have said, 'There's no love lost between Curran and Reeve on and off the field.' How do they know?

The worst verbals I've encountered on a cricket field came from the New Zealander Mark Greatbatch, and I admit I was amused at how easily I managed to wind him up. He's known as 'Paddy' by his team-mates because he easily loses his temper and gets in a 'paddy', and I got him going during a one-day international at Dunedin in 1992. It was a very slow pitch, a low-scoring game, and when I came in to bat the game was anyone's and tensions were bubbling nicely. Greatbatch wasn't happy with me at all: I'd got him out in the previous one-dayer, caught at deep square leg, and in this game, taken behind by Alec Stewart, a decision that did not please our 'Paddy'. When I came in, I started trying to extemporise on the slow wicket, using the slog sweep to try to break free of some accurate bowling. I was trying to put pressure on the fielders with my partner, Chris Lewis. The ball would go to Greatbatch in the short extra cover and short mid-wicket regions and I'd be skipping down the pitch, daring him to throw at my stumps, hoping for some overthrows. That was annoying him, so I said, 'Go on, then, try it', and he started swearing at me, giving me a right earful. I found it very funny, and proceeded to ask him how many he had scored. It proved a red rag to this particular Kiwi bull and the air was blue.

By now, I was really pumped up, loving the tight situation and that I was getting under the opposition's skins. I hit Rod Latham for two boundaries to relieve the pressure, each time shouting 'Yes!' in exhilaration, and that really annoyed Greatbatch and his captain, Martin Crowe. Crowe snarled at me, 'I don't know why you're laughing, let's see how you are when you lose.' For a time, it looked as if we might. Greatbatch caught Lewis, he showed the ball to me in triumph and Crowe shouted at me, 'Just f*** off.' Tempers were fraying as Derek Pringle came in, and he worked the ball around superbly to bring us victory in the last over with five balls to spare. I had the satisfaction of hitting the winning runs and as I walked off the field with a huge smile on my face, Martin Crowe came over, shook my hand and said, 'Well played.' I considered that the gesture of a true sportsman, despite what went on between us a few minutes earlier. To me, that's how the game ought to be played – give nothing to the opposition, try all legitimate ways to unsettle them, and forget about it when the game is done.

My problem is that my mouth runs away from me sometimes, and I can see how that can really annoy opponents. And umpires, too. John Hampshire stopped play once against Essex, because he took exception to something I shouted from gully. I'd just got back from grade cricket in Australia, so I was still full of all that breezy cockiness you expect from Australian cricketers. When Allan Donald was about to bowl, I shouted, 'Come on Al! Let him have one!' John Hampshire walked over and told me I was over the top. I said I was only trying to sow seeds of doubt in the batsman's mind, so that he might go back to a ball that proved to be pitched up. John thought it was against the spirit of the game, but to me there was nothing wrong with encouraging our strike bowler, and getting the batsman thinking.

On the whole, I think we get on well with umpires, because at least we play with spirit at Warwickshire and don't moan at them. I'm sure they have to turn a deaf ear sometimes to some of the things we say on the field. For some reason, the chemistry between Kent and Warwickshire has never been right during my time at Edgbaston, and I dare say I've contributed to that. In one match, Allan Donald fired out Neil Taylor second ball, and as the batsman walked slowly away, our captain, Andy Lloyd, shouted, 'That's good enough for that ****' That set the tone for the game, which was hardly cucumber sandwiches and strawberry jam in spirit. When I batted, Richard Ellison stuck out his foot and tried to trip me up as I looked for a second run, and when I bowled, my mouth got the better of me again. Matthew Fleming was batting, a player who likes to play his shots and does in a very positive manner. Well I made a great fuss about setting a fielder out for the hook on the backward square leg boundary – and Fleming fell for it. As he passed me on the way to the pavilion, I said loudly, 'What a bloody idiot!' A daft thing to say, I know, but you get carried away in the heat of battle, and my self-confidence that borders at times on obnoxiousness does me no favours.

We really enjoy putting one over on Kent, particularly when the adrenalin flows. We've had more verbal battles with them than any other side in recent years and we had great fun down at Canterbury in the last weekend of the 1995 season. On the Saturday, we had wrapped up the championship by an innings and our celebration must have stuck in their throats in the adjoining dressing-room. That defeat meant they were bottom of the table for the first time this century, so they really had to pick themselves up for the Sunday League game next day. Kent were favourites to win the title, and at best we could be level on points, but sadly lost out on run rate. Worcestershire could still win the title but unfortunately for them, their game was abandoned due to rain. Midway through our innings the news spread through the packed Canterbury crowd that Kent had won the league. It was their first trophy since 1978 and the players were quite rightly celebrating on the field. I knew that I'd get some stick from the Kent players when I batted but, I was determined they weren't going to win this game. I wanted to ensure that their Sunday League title would be theirs only on a faster run rate, with Warwickshire runners up. If you're going to relinquish your title, do it with style, I thought. I knew that if our game the previous week hadn't been abandoned with Warwickshire in a great position, we would have retained the title. As far as I was concerned, all that adrenalin out in the middle galvanised me. As I walked towards the stumps, Graham Cowdrey stayed at the crease, and shouted to his fast bowler, Martin McCague, 'It's Reeve, Martin – come on, knock his head off.' That was all I needed to get me going. I bellowed loudly at Cowdrey, 'F*** off, you stupid prick!' and that really pumped me up. My partner, Roger Twose – who never needed a second bidding to get stuck in – joined me in the middle and shouted, 'Yeh, come on – let's get aggressive!' Roger loved situations like that, even though we were in a tight spot. He loved to goad the opposition, and Kent got the full works from him. As we got nearer to victory, he shouted to me, 'Remind me, Skip – what was our bonus for winning three trophies last year?' and then an over later, 'Come on, Skip – you've been in this situation before – like when we won the Nat West a few days ago!' It would be fair to say that Roger used to go over the top occasionally and in his last match for Warwickshire, he was more vocal than usual. With 25 runs still required for victory, Dean Headley asked the umpire to save him a stump. I shouted over, 'Don't worry, Deano – I'll save you a stump!' He said, 'Thanks,' before he realised I was taking the mickey by insinuating that I'd still be there at the finish. I was determined to see the job home, and enjoyed handing that stump over. That night, we left Kent's supporters to their celebrations at the ground, and went off for our own fun, enjoying the memories of six trophies from September '93 to September '95.

I know that Warwickshire aren't a popular side under my captaincy. This despite having some really nice guys on the staff in recent years, who were very well liked on the circuit, but as veterans like Asif Din and Gladstone Small will confirm, we were winning nothing for years with a popular bunch of players. I'm employed to get the best out of the players and I enjoy my cricket more if I'm aggressive. I know there are many people in the game who don't like me and that we are seen as a brash side, over-confident to the point of cockiness. Honestly that doesn't bother me, as I've been employed to get the best out of the team and believe this is helped by our boisterous attitude. Just before the start of our historic season in 1994, I attended a captains' meeting and a few umpires were present. One of them said that the game was becoming too noisy and vocal out in the middle, and he cited Warwickshire as the worst offenders. I replied that in my opinion English cricket was in danger of being too soft, that we needed a sharp, competitive edge, that we're too friendly to the opposition out in the middle.

Before every season, I tell my players what's expected when we're in the field. I want them to be positively vocal, to address their comments about an opposition batsman to each other. The tone of comment is crucial, it mustn't be half-hearted. I want the boys to be positive and upbeat in their encouragement. There is a fine line between strong vocal encouragement and the kind of sledging that questions a batsman's parentage or mocks his physical shape, and although we all fall from grace sometimes, I insist the boys don't get personal. I think it's fair enough if a guy plays an unconvincing shot against Allan Donald that I shout out from the slips, 'I'm not convinced, Al' or 'He's not happy against you, Al.' That's encouraging your bowler, letting the batsman know that we think he's on borrowed time. I don't think that's sledging. I tell my players that it's a war out there, to forget any friendships with opposition players until close of play. I want the opposition to feel uncomfortable against us, that it's our turf they're on – even when we're playing away – and that the odds are eleven of us, against two of them when we're fielding.

You can make a batsman lose his composure by letting him think he shouldn't be out there. When Nick Knight joined us from Essex, I liked his attitude right from the start in the field. He'd stand at silly point, staring at the batsman, and shout to our spinner, Neil Smith, 'Come on, bring me in the game. You and me, Neil, you and me!' In other words, 'I'm not afraid of being in here, I'll take the knocks. Are you up to it?' Nick claps his hands loudly and puts pressure on the batsman, something he obviously learned at the hard Essex school, where many trophies were won under Keith Fletcher and Graham Gooch. Such vocals can inhibit a batsman. I've seen their hands shake or their feet twitch when I've been close in. It's a tough game, and provided those things are kept under control, I see no harm in putting psychological pressure on the batsmen.

Our games against Worcestershire are always red-blooded

affairs, and not just because they are local derbies and both sides have jostled each other for trophies in recent years, but because they've got some tough characters on their side as well. Richard Illingworth and Steve Rhodes always bait me, and I've had a few four-letter words flung in my direction when they've got me out, but it's forgotten when the boundary line is crossed and the pavilion gate closed behind me. The important thing to me is that you shouldn't show that you are bothered by all the vocal stuff. That was Tim Curtis' mistake.

Now Tim's a cricketer of the old school, and a very charming bloke, but he got exasperated at us when he was batting one day. I stopped a ball, the rest of the side shouted, 'Great stop, Derm!' and there was a lot of hollering, designed to gee us all up. Tim stopped batting, tut-tutted and said, 'It's just like a zoo out here.' That did it. I performed my best sea-lion impression and some of the other lads joined in.

Sometimes we have gone too far on the field. No one's perfect and I'm certainly no angel – but Roger Twose has been a real thorn in the flesh of some opponents. Next to me, Roger must have been the most unpopular Warwickshire player in the opposition's eyes, because he can appear so bumptious, arrogant and over-aggressive. One day, Alec Stewart said to me, 'That Twose is a pain in the neck, isn't he?' I said, 'Actually, Alec, he's a really nice guy. He's intelligent, sensitive, cares about the outside world – and he's a hell of a guy to have on your side because of his aggression. I'm glad he's in my team.' I thought that was an interesting comment from Alec, bearing in mind that he also played a lot of grade cricket in Western Australia, and has the reputation of occasionally getting up people's noses on the field, but I let that one pass.

I agree that Roger can go over the top, though. I had to speak to him when we played England 'A' early in the '95 season. Paul Nixon, the opposition wicket-keeper, had broken his hand, but he was brave enough to carry on batting, although in obvious pain. I was well aware at the start of that season that we had picked up a certain reputation for verbals and that we were being closely monitored by the umpires. Allan Donald bowled one that beat Nixon for pace, as he went for the hook. It passed harmlessly down the legside as Nixon played far too late. Roger Twose at mid-on just burst out laughing and shouted at Nixon, 'Nico, what are you doing?' I thought that was a little disrespectful of Roger, because Nixon was battling away with a broken hand, showing a lot of guts. A quiet word did the trick afterwards, but that didn't stop Roger getting stuck in when he felt the need. He and Kevin Curran had an interesting conversation later that season, which alerted the umpires, but those two could look after themselves.

I'm sure that one of the reasons why I get up some people's noses is because I don't conform to the stereotype of an English cricketer. Having lived in Hong Kong, played so many years in Australia and enjoyed travelling all my life, I suppose I see life and my career in colonial, rather than typically English terms. I'm not all that sentimental about the public school attitude to cricket – all that 'for the good of the game' stuff, and that false modesty. I don't care about looking stylish on the field, I'm more bothered about effectiveness and succeeding. Because I'm hyperactive and talk quickly, I do blurt out some tactless remarks at times and I have upset some people. I'm an extrovert who enjoys life, who likes to party, who makes no pretence at shyness. I have developed a thick skin, and become more selfish with my time. I'll make an effort to be with those I'm interested in, but walk away from anything that doesn't appeal to me.

I suppose I'm vain, although I still dress like a student, and don't bother about buying expensive clothes. I don't gel or blow-dry my hair, unlike many, but the general feeling about me is that I'm very keen on myself. I've been headbutted in a night club just because I was Dermot Reeve, with a fairly high profile in the Birmingham area, and I've also received death threats. I've heard the rumour that I once said to a friend in a night club, 'Come on, let's get out of here – nobody recognises me.' That's a total fabrication, laughable.

I took more seriously the gossip item in a Birmingham newspaper that I walked into a Birmingham night club wearing my England World Cup shirt with 'Reeve' on the back of it, so that everybody would know who I was. The truth is much more mundane. One Sunday lunchtime, my brother and his family came up to Birmingham and we went out to lunch at one of my favourite restaurants, T.G.I. Fridays. In my usual panic to find something clean to wear, I pulled out a pair of jeans and the cleanest T-shirt I could find. It was one of the powder blue polo shirts we were issued with for the tour to New Zealand in 1992, with the word 'England' on the chest, and nothing on the back. Someone mentioned this to the local press and the next thing the public read is that I'm prancing around a night spot one evening, with my name on the back of the shirt I wore in the World Cup Final. I managed to get a retraction from the paper the following week, but that didn't stop the lie appearing later in the *Cricketer* magazine. I mentioned it in conversation to the England captain, Graham Gooch, who said in his dry way, 'Yeah, Derm, I heard about it – but didn't you have your phone number under your name?' It was nice to have a laugh about something that had got under my skin.

I find it amazing how these myths get recycled – like the 'fat has-been' one about Ian Botham, the brush I had with Brian Lara at Northampton, and this nonsense about my World Cup shirt. Is it because the journalists just wade through the cuttings and don't bother checking the revised facts, or is it the case that an image needs to be consolidated?

I suppose everyone who is successful in some profession has to put up with it. I'm only a minor sporting celebrity in one area of England, but I wouldn't want to be any higher in profile. I worked it out that as long as I'm happy with myself, I won't worry too much. I've got some very good friends with whom I clicked straight away, who understand my idiosyncrasies. T.G.I. Fridays and Ronnie Scott's Jazz Club in Birmingham are second homes to me, where I can hang out with people who don't care about how I'm doing on the cricket field. My loving, supportive family are even more important to me, we're always there for each other, taking a keen interest in our respective careers. As for those players I have annoyed on the cricket field, I admit I must be a pain to play against, but hopefully the guys I've played with have always found me supportive.

8

One-Day Cricket

I've been categorised as the ideal one-day cricketer, full of ingenuity and cheek, pulling the strings in the field and smashing a few runs in the hectic final stages to sweep my side to victory. All very flattering, I suppose, and there have been times when I've got it right. I'm also pigeonholed as a 'bits and pieces cricketer', someone who isn't outstanding in any one particular discipline, a handy man to have in your side, they say. Now I accept many people get carried away by statistics, and that it appears I make a more important contribution in one-day games for Warwickshire than in first-class cricket – but I believe my record in the longer form of cricket isn't as ordinary as many believe.

When I arrived at Edgbaston from Sussex in 1988, I averaged 25 in first-class cricket with the bat and 28 with the ball: since then it's 38 with the bat and 24 with the ball. Just to take some other all-rounders' records in first-class cricket around the same time: with Derek Pringle it was 28 with the bat and 26 with the ball, Kevin Curran a highly impressive 36 and 27, David Capel 30 and almost 32, Chris Lewis 31 and 29, Phillip DeFreitas 22 and 28 and Craig White 30 and 30. My career first-class batting average stands at 34.8 and 26.8 with the ball. So I don't think that in the longer games I have been inferior to other key all-rounders in county cricket. It's just convenient to label me a one-day player.

When I finally started to make some impression as an all-rounder at Edgbaston, it was inevitable that I would be built up as a rival to Ian Botham, as a potential England all-rounder. That was just a good line for the press, because Botham had been a great performer for England, one of the most charismatic and successful players we ever had. Anyone who stepped into his shoes in the national side would dread the comparison with such a great player and hope the media would lay off him, just judging him on his own merits. It didn't really bother me when my name was mentioned as a potential Botham in the late eighties and early nineties. I knew he was in decline after some serious injuries, but he was still a dangerous player. It brought out the competitive streak in me though, and I always relished our Midland derbies against Worcestershire, when I'd try to get one over Ian on a personal level. For a four-year period, during which Ian came back from his back operation and then played his last Test, I was quite happy with our comparative figures in championship cricket:

1989: Botham: 276 runs at 16, 51 wickets at 22.
       Reeve: 581 runs at 44, 11 wickets at 14.
1990: Botham: 576 runs at 36, 17 wickets at 32.
       Reeve: 1,265 runs at 55, 28 wickets at 27.
1991: Botham: 567 runs at 37, 38 wickets at 23.
       Reeve: 1,260 runs at 48, 45 wickets at 21.
1992: Botham: 705 runs at 33, 24 wickets at 42.
       Reeve: 833 runs at 34, 13 wickets at 48.

So in that four year period, Botham averaged 30 with the bat and 27 with the ball, compared to mine of 45 with the bat and 25, when I bowled.

I couldn't be mentioned in the same breath as Ian Botham, but he wasn't the only one troubled by injuries in that period, with three of those seasons featuring only fitful bowling from me in first-class cricket. But I was happy that my record in that time didn't lose out in comparison to the legend.

So is Dermot Reeve more valuable in one-day cricket than in the longer game? That's for others to decide. I like all forms of cricket, especially if I'm winning and the team are right behind me. I suppose the generalisation about me comes from all those Lord's Finals, most of them successful, with three Man of the

Match Awards coming my way. I've been so fortunate to play in six Finals, and three of them have involved fantastic finishes. There's no doubt I play better when the adrenalin's pumping. For some reason, I can actually see the ball better when I'm batting in one-day games than in the championship. The game is there to be won or lost in a couple of overs, and you've simply got to get cracking and pump yourself up. Sometimes when I walk out to bat in a tense one-day situation, I'm looking for something or someone to galvanise me. It may be an opponent's remark, which will force me to rap back a waspish comment, or perhaps my team-mate will get me going. Roger Twose used to be terrific at that, with comments like, 'Come on Skip, let's show them how it's done – enjoy the pressure!'

It's hard for many to change their game when batting in a Sunday League game during the middle of a championship match. You go out there on a Sunday and there's little time to scratch around. I've sometimes let the ball go through and suddenly thought to myself, 'What am I doing? This is a Sunday game.' If my adrenalin is surging, though, I seem to be pain-free, quick on my feet and see the ball well. I'll look to nudge the ball around early on, getting used to the conditions, the pace and bounce of the pitch. I'll always look for that productive shot between the wicket-keeper and slip, that would get you out in a four-day match. I don't play in a wide area like someone such as Neil Fairbrother, because I lack his expansive range of strokes, so I'll concentrate on areas that have worked for me – the sweep/slog on one knee, the paddle, and of course, the reverse sweep. I go for the slog/sweep off the faster bowlers because I don't drive all that successfully. I don't hit well through the line of the ball unless I've been able to use my feet and swing my arms. Perhaps it's my grip on the bat, but I don't usually back myself to clear mid-off or mid-on, a distance of around 35 yards. On the legside, the square leg fielder is only 20 yards away, so I can clear him easier with my dominant bottom hand. It's a percentage shot that I have practised, but bowlers have been getting wise to me. They move the fielder from deep backward square leg to forward square leg to block my slog/sweep, so I have to look elsewhere for a safe, attacking shot. Bob Woolmer helped improve my driving and I scored runs in different areas in my last couple of seasons which was both satisfying and enjoyable. You can never stand still in one-day cricket.

Things happen so quickly in one-day cricket, that you can be out of the game in a couple of overs. We have a couple of sayings in our dressing-room that we use to keep us concentrating – 'Every Ball's an Event' and 'Control the Controllables'. In other words, leave the captaincy to the guy in charge and make sure your own game is up to scratch on the day. Input is welcomed by the captain, but the frenetic nature of these games – especially on Sundays – means there is little time for extended thought and group discussion while out on the pitch. The captain has to keep his eye on the scoreboard much more than in four-day cricket. Generally you are more defensive in the field, balancing the needs of getting early wickets with the necessity to save runs. When do you put the sweepers back and take out those two slips? Your fielders must be in the exact place when the bowler is running in, you simply cannot afford doziness, when a guy strays. Every single ball is crucial. You can't afford any looseners from your bowlers. That is permissible in a four-day game, because sensible looseners from your bowlers mean they've got a better chance of avoiding injury. In a one-day game, a loosener is often a four-ball, and no gifts are encouraged.

In some ways, one-day cricket is harder than Test cricket. You're under the spotlight in one-dayers, you can't get away with a wayward spell or block it at the crease. If you're patient in a Test, you get praised for a responsible innings, but that's bad batting in the one-day context. The 'dot' ball is a godsend to the captain in one-day cricket, whereas the Test batsman easily keeps that out and just waits for the bad ball. Of course, Test cricket is mentally draining, but all that scampering around in the field and high-adrenalin drama of one dayers is also demanding. A routine Test Match day lasts just 90 overs, but a one-day game can take up 120 overs and not be finished until around eleven hours after you've arrived at the ground. Fatigue sweeps over you very quickly once you slump in the dressing-room and the adrenalin ebbs away as quickly as it appeared.

Many people seem to think I experiment all the time when I bowl in one-day games. They see my very slow, looping delivery and say, 'There he goes again, old Dermot – every ball's different, isn't it?' Not true. In my early days at Sussex, we had a lot of strike bowlers who traded wickets for runs, and my coach, Stewart Storey, told me, 'Your job's to bowl maidens.' That's what I've always tried to do. In the 1995 Nat West final I attempted to bowl every ball the same way and in the same area. It wasn't a great surface to bat on, so runs had to be chiselled out. There was no justification for much experiment, and the ball wasn't swinging, so for 60 deliveries I tried a stock ball – full up to the batsman, on a tight line, bowling to my field. That was a case of using my experience, adapting to the conditions, but there are times when you have to mix it up.

Since my shoulder operation in 1988, I've lost a yard of speed, so I had to think about varying my pace. That's when I discovered my slower ball that proved effective for a long time in one-day cricket. When I was playing grade cricket in Western Australia, I saw Simon O'Donnell and Steve Waugh bowling a slower delivery out of the back of the hand in a one-day series against New Zealand. I remember a great delivery from O'Donnell that completely foxed John Bracewell, the ball hitting the leg stump as Bracewell ducked to avoid the looping, slower ball. I decided to work on that. I had built a net in my back garden in Perth and practised bowling with the back of my hand facing the batsman. I tried it out in the nets at my club, and I had batsmen ducking into what they thought was a beamer. In our next match, I got two wickets with the slower ball, one of them an lbw when the guy ducked away and the ball plopped on his foot. When I came back to Warwickshire, I got wickets with it in one-day games straight away, including Viv Richards when he whacked it straight up in the air. All four of my wickets in a Sunday League game against Derbyshire were from deliveries out of the back of my hand and I found it was particularly effective on a loose surface that helped the spinner. I found that even if the batsman spotted it was the slower ball and allowed it to pitch, it might hold up on him if he went for the big shot and the ball would occasionally go up in the air. For a while, it had great surprise value, but after a time batsmen were waiting for it, so I had to conceal it and work on other slower ball variations. It's a constant guessing game. Adam Hollioake possesses the best slower ball I have faced and showed in two one-day internationals against Pakistan how crucial it is. To be honest, without it Adam is a pretty average seamer but its value is so great that Adam could play a vital role for England in one-day cricket for a long time. He is a fine, hard-hitting batsman, a brilliant fielder and he should have been in the England squad for the 1996 World Cup. I would have picked him before any other all-rounder for that tour.

Bowling at my speed, which has reduced every year, its vital to swing the ball.

I used to watch closely a swing bowler like Terry Alderman who was so dangerous with those little outswingers that would tempt the batsmen into the nicked off-drive. Then he would bowl straighter and quicker and skid one through for the lbw. Ian Botham was very good at that as well. You have to have some ingenuity to bowl well in cricket, because a good batsman wants to get into a rhythm, he likes batting against a medium-pacer who is the same speed every delivery. On a flat wicket against someone like Graeme Hick, my stock delivery would probably go for four, so I'll look to mix up my line and speed. Perhaps I'll bowl an over of blatantly slow deliveries, with a quicker one slipped in that might scuttle through for the lbw.

In four-day cricket the condition of the wicket is the deciding factor as to how to bowl. If it's got pace in it, I'll bowl more 'effort' balls, in shorter spells, with a third man. If it's a slow pitch, that generally suits my bowling, I can get the wicket-keeper up, looking for the legside stumping and inhibiting the batsman from skipping out of his crease. I'll bring the third man up into the ring, and bowl a full length, with a couple of slips in for the outswinger. In one-day cricket, I'd rarely have more than one slip. You're always testing the batsman's technique, because he has to hit the ball harder to get pace on to the slower deliveries to pierce the inner ring of fielders. Because I'm bowling slow-medium floaters, some batsmen feel they have to get after me, as I look so innocuous. That suits me, because there's always a chance then that they'll slog it up in the air or get lbw playing across the line. In one-day cricket, the onus is on the batsman to play shots, so I just try not to go for runs. In four-day cricket I enjoy tempting a batsman, trying to bore him out particularly when the wicket is low and slow. It's a matter of adapting to the conditions as quickly as possible. Some bowlers are very clever at concealing their intentions. They cover the ball as they run in, so it's impossible to see which way the ball will swing, or indeed if a slower ball is on the way.

One day at the Oval, Bob Woolmer's attention to detail had us in stitches at his suggestion for coping with Waqar's reverse swing. Bob thought he would sit in the stand behind the bowler, with a green and a red flag. He said that he would be able to spot which way the ball would be swinging when Waqar placed the ball in his hand before turning to run in. Green flag for the outswinger, red flag for the other way. Bob was partly serious about it, until it was pointed out that it wasn't really on!

Another hilarious moment with a slower ball came in a match against Hampshire when Michael Bell was running up to bowl. The non-striker, Adrian Aymes, spotted Keith Piper walking up to the stumps and shouted, 'Slower ball!' to his partner. We all stopped and I asked David Shepherd if Adrian was allowed to do that. A compromise was struck – no shouting from Adrian, but a loud cough when he saw Piper move in. I told Piper to walk forward then back, going for the double bluff. Adrian coughed loudly just as Michael bowled it, and it turned out to be a quick seamer, rather than a slower ball. Piper just got to it and we all saw the funny side of the incident.

Many dismiss me as a lucky cricketer, especially in one-day games, because of the way I get batsmen out. It appears a fluke as they hit me straight up in the air off what looked like a very ordinary delivery, or I bluff them out with a change of pace. They used to say the same about a far greater all-rounder, Ian Botham, without giving him the credit for the self-confidence to try something different, to unsettle the batsman. Branding you 'lucky' tends to ignore the hard work that goes into dismissals. You can't just run up and bowl a slower ball against good bats-men, you need to work at it for hours and hours in the nets. The same applies to the reverse sweep or any other shot that enables you to get the ball through the field. Style is an irrelevance in one-day cricket, especially when the gaps seem very small and the fielders are choking the run rate.

It's attitude that's more important than style in one-day cricket and it was that never-say-die spirit which won us the Nat West Trophy in 1993 against Sussex, as we chased 321 in 60 overs. David Smith and Martin Speight batted marvellously for Sussex and some of our bowlers took a real pasting, but strangely enough, we took strength from that as we sat in the dressing-room before our innings. It was a case of breaking down the run rate, and forgetting we'd make history if we got there. It was simply five runs an over. We lost our openers for 18, but they hadn't used up many overs and the reaction from one of our openers was very encouraging. Jason Ratcliffe was, of course, disappointed at getting out, but soon he rallied and said to us, 'That wicket is a belter, the best I've ever batted on! We'll get these, lads, come on!' That was great to hear, and typical of our team spirit. Paul Smith and Dominic Ostler carried on playing positively, and we just had the feeling that it was going to be our day. We didn't subscribe to the theory that wickets in hand were vital, because bowlers have got better at bowling the death overs, they vary the pace more imaginatively. The field placings are more professional now, and the standard of fielding generally is vastly improved. So it was a case of going at the rate of five an over, and expecting to dominate the spinner, Ian Salisbury. He went for five-and-a-half an over, but when I joined Asif Din at 164/4, the rate required was now above a run a ball. Asif then played the innings of his life, the fastest hundred in a Lord's Final. He had a wonderful eye, and improvised marvellously that day – stepping back to carve over backward point. As the chase was really on, I was full of adrenalin, shouting instructions to Asif. Asif kept touching the little bag he carried round his neck that reflects his Muslim faith, and looking skywards for inspiration. We let the required rate get up to beyond eight an over, but were confident we could still win. We kept talking about having one big over, which would get us back on track – just one over that would get us around fifteen and it was ours for the taking. But we never managed to do it, and we needed 20 off the last two overs. Ed Giddins bowled a fine over for Sussex, giving away just five runs – and he also dismissed Asif. It was up to me, now; you couldn't expect Roger Twose, our new batsman, to pick up the pace just like that in the gathering gloom. In that over from Giddins, I was looking to get him away with the sweep/slog, but he bowled a very good full length. I dug out an excellent yorker fifth ball, then squeezed out another for a single off the last ball. I was dejected, while the reaction of Giddins made it clear he thought Sussex had won. So we had to get 15 off the final over, to be bowled by Franklyn Stephenson, an experienced fast bowler with a deadly slower ball and the hostility and accuracy to restrict any batsman if he got his radar right. At that moment, Roger Twose was fantastic. He marched down the wicket, shook me out of my disappointment and shouted, 'Come on Skip – we can do it!' Roger was always very vocal at the crease, and I needed his support then.

As Franklyn ran up to bowl at the start of that final over, I can clearly remember thinking, 'What am I going to do? He's got one of the best slower balls in the world. Will I see it?' He had fine leg up and long-on and long-off out, so I thought there was a good chance he'd bowl the slower one. I just told myself to look hard and I managed somehow to club a fast ball straight back over his head for four. The next I struck out to long-on and I should have been run out, but Peter Moores' throw from behind the stumps missed. The third ball was a yorker, dug out to short extra cover, and Bill Athey's misfield brought us two more to long-off. Eight off the first three balls: a good start. Roger roared at me: 'Wherever you hit it, we're coming back for two!' 'OK!' I bellowed back, amid the noise of the crowd. He was right. I was the man in, seeing the ball well considering the darkness that was closing in. Roger's vocal encouragement was proving to be an essential boost to me keeping the adrenalin flowing. The fourth ball amazed me – a sweet shot through the covers, a stroke I rarely play. Franklyn was astonished and afterwards, in the bar, he still couldn't get over it. I don't know where that shot came from to this day.

At that stage, Franklyn had bowled all quick deliveries, and no sign of the dreaded slower ball. The fifth was the slower ball and

I picked it up late, got an inside edge to fine leg and we scrambled a single. To this day, I wish I'd set myself to hit him for four, but I made the mistake of concentrating on getting a bat on it, rather than swinging my arms. That left Roger on strike for the last ball of the match. We needed one to win, provided we didn't lose a wicket, because they had lost six and we were five down at that stage. Two runs would be even better, making it a clear victory. By now it's almost dark and we're both breathing heavily. Alan Wells rearranges his field, the crowd is hoarse, the lights on the scoreboard are very bright indeed, and Roger and I are trying to make sense of it all. I told him, 'Their wicketkeeper is standing up. I think that means he'll bowl a slower ball because he won't risk a quicker one with the keeper up. If he bowls you a quicker one, get the bat on it and we'll run through. But look for the slower ball.' I've watched that final ball so many times on the video and sure enough it was the slower ball. Roger spotted it, slowed down his bat swing, waited for the ball and then hit in the air. For a moment, I thought he was going to be caught by Neil Lenham at third man, up in the ring, but it squirted away. We sprinted the first and ran the second, just to make sure the scorers hadn't made a mistake, all the while yelling our heads off. I grabbed a couple of stumps for souvenirs and raced off to the pavilion. I wanted to stand there and savour the moment, but no chance. Someone ripped the helmet off my head, Franklyn said, 'Give me your bat' and he then too raced off the field. I felt for Franklyn afterwards – 19 times out of 20, you would have expected a bowler of his class to defend an asking rate of 15 in the final over.

I was so high on adrenalin at the time, and then for a time afterwards, until the enormity of that win sunk in and I felt very tired. Those surges of adrenalin out in the middle had got me through, helping me see the ball so clearly and swing my arms freely. I was so proud for the team, for the aggressive way we had pursued that target, at the refusal to give in. I still get the shivers watching it again on the video.

Two years later, we were in another cliffhanger at Lord's and Roger and I were at the centre of the final stages. It was one of those games that ebbed and flowed, but Northants would probably have won it but for a slice of luck that came my way. Well, a large slice of luck, actually. We were struggling on a slow pitch to get 201 to win, with their Indian leg-spinner, Anil Kumble, bowling magnificently. When I joined Roger, we were 122/5 and Kumble still had plenty of overs left. Early in my innings, he did me for pace as I played a sweep and the ball hit my back leg. Dickie Bird gave me 'not out' to the inevitable lbw appeal and I could have kissed him. Kumble and his fielders couldn't believe it, and after watching the video, neither could I. It was a straight, full delivery on the line of middle stump, and just a foot or two ahead of the stump. I don't know how I got away with that one. I know Dickie is known as a 'not outer', but he must have had a mental block for that ball. I finished 37 not out, and, with a tight bowling spell, I picked up another Man of the Match award, but it could so easily have gone to Anil Kumble instead. I got all the favourable publicity – all that 'Captain Marvel' stuff – but I enjoyed the one thing that is a variable in tight one-day finishes: luck.

We weren't at our best in that Final. Injuries had robbed us of Gladstone Small and Tim Munton, and we had to trust in the inexperienced Dougie Brown and Michael Bell. Dougie came into the game with a cracked hand, and Nick Knight was carrying a broken finger and they were two early casualties against some excellent new ball bowling by Paul Taylor and Kevin Curran. A score of 28/3 with 17 overs gone already was hardly the victory platform on a slow pitch with some variable bounce. Then Kumble came on and he bowled Dominic Ostler with one that hurried on straight: a disappointing dismissal that one, because we had talked before the game about not going back to Kumble's quicker ball. He is so fast off the pitch that it's a major risk to step back and try to cut him; he had picked up so many wickets that way in county cricket that season.

I know the TV cameras picked us out on the balcony, looking cheery at the time of our batting crisis. I was next man in, and I didn't feel lucky, but we all put up the bold front when the cameras were on us. Bob Woolmer rang up at that stage from Cape Town to wish us well, and I shouted 'Hello!' to him across the dressing-room. I don't know if Bob had detected some uncharacteristic tension, but he would have been pretty dense if he hadn't. We were in trouble, and Kumble was winning the game for Northants. Eventually when I joined Twose, it wasn't just a case of seeing off the danger man, we had to get runs off Kumble as well. With Paul Smith next man in, a player more comfortable against the seamers than Kumble, I gave Roger the reassuring viewpoint: 'If you get out now, we'll struggle.'

Roger was dropped twice, I escaped thanks to Dickie Bird, and it was very hairy. I had told Roger I was going to try sweeping Kumble, but I mistimed the shots because of his pace. Roger would tell me, 'I'm going big this over, Skip' and I'd tell him: 'Fine, but don't get out.' I tried the sweep again, but only got one leg-bye off Kumble to the short boundary, and I remember thinking, 'How am I going to get a run here?' By then, Kumble just had to go for runs, otherwise we would probably lose. I noticed Allan Lamb put a man finer on the offside for the reverse sweep, but I still decided to try it off Kumble. I got down at the right time, played it correctly and it went very fine, to beat the fielder. That was a nice moment. So Lamby moved the fielder even finer and I decided not to try the shot again. If Kumble had bowled it slower and I'd got a top edge going for the reverse sweep, it would have been a routine catch to that fielder who had been placed finer. So I settled for playing Kumble square for a single or two and we ended up taking eight off his final over. I suppose that boundary was decisive, but we never got on top of him. He's a fabulous bowler, and his figures of 1/29 off 12 overs didn't do him any justice at all.

So Kumble was off at last, and we had four wickets in hand. Roger was then run out on his call to the keeper after we had put on 54 at four an over. Kevin Curran came on. He's a bowler I've enjoyed jousting with over the years, a guy I get on very well with off the field, but we strike sparks off each other when we're out there in the middle. I knew Kevin's strong competitive instinct would have him fired up for this battle against me, and with 20 needed off the last three overs, this one was going to be decisive. For the first ball, mid-on was up for the single and the wicket-keeper back, which suited me. On that slow pitch, I would have had to slog from the crease if the keeper had stood up. I would have been more vulnerable then, instead of being able to come down the crease and hit through the line of the ball. Four runs.

After that boundary, the keeper still stayed back and I was delighted. The next three balls went to extra cover, stopped by Allan Lamb and finally another boundary over mid off. With four leg-byes also coming in the over, we got 12, leaving us eight for the last two overs. We got home with seven balls to spare, but it was far closer than that. If Kumble had enjoyed more luck, and Curran had insisted on calling up the keeper to keep me in the crease, it may have been Northants' day. Again I was amazed at the way the surges of adrenalin had helped me think clearly and see the ball well, but I knew what a hard-earned victory that was. Only in our fielding were we clearly superior to Northants, as the tension got to them in the final overs. For me, the biggest pleasure in that win was that we hadn't played all that well, but still came through with grit and guts.

We had been much more impressive on our way to Lord's that year. In the quarter-final at Derby, we bounced back the day after losing that dramatic championship game against Northants by seven runs – a draining, tension-filled match spread over four days that left the players on both sides shattered. It was the best game of its type I had ever played in and our defeat meant Northants had overtaken us at the head of the championship table. A less resilient side would have faded away in the last six weeks of the season, but we put it right the very next day. We lost Neil Smith in the first over, but good batting all the way down the order brought us to 290/6. We then swept away Derbyshire, with Allan Donald blasting out the later batsmen after the stranglehold applied by superb fielding and nagging bowling by Tim Munton.

The semi-final at Cardiff was an even better team performance than at Derby. Glamorgan really fancied their chances that day, and I couldn't blame them. They had some fine stroke players, an excellent bunch of fielders and bowlers ideally suited to the home conditions. They won the toss on a slow pitch that was certain to deteriorate for batting. It would turn and bounce, and in Robert Croft and Steve Barwick, they had potential match-winners. A score of around 200 would be a tall order, and with the ground absolutely packed with noisy Welshmen, it seemed as if we were playing a country, as well as a county.

When they went out to bat, their home supporters looked forward to the day with understandable optimism. At lunch they were 80/8 and the game was effectively over. Tim Munton had bowled unchanged to take 2/18 in his 12 overs and Trevor Penney's glorious fielding had been underestimated yet again. Trevor is a marvellous athlete, so quick to the ball, so swift at releasing it – but we had felt for a time that he ought to be hitting the stumps more with his throws. Phil Neale worked hard with him before the Cardiff match, and the result was the direct hit that pinged out Matthew Maynard's middle stump as he struggled to get back. Getting the dangerous Maynard like that is as good as bowling him with an absolute beauty, and Trevor followed that up with a great piece of fielding to get David Hemp run out.

That demoralised Glamorgan, and as lunch approached, they stopped looking for runs. I crept in at silly point as they blocked it, and snaffled Colin Metson to make them eight down. Soon they were all out for 86 and we had won by eight wickets in the 25th over. It was a comprehensive thrashing, a fantastic all-round performance that contained all the ingredients we had looked for in recent years, but I was amazed at Glamorgan's passive approach as we got among their wickets. We wouldn't have played for lunch, as the wickets fell. Our attitude would have been, 'Come on boys, someone will get runs. If one of us gets 50 and the rest chip in, that gets us to 200, and they'll struggle to get them.'

You must always believe you can win a match, and that self-belief has got us out of so many tight situations in one-day cricket. That was the reason why we got through against Kent in the 1994 Nat West semi-final at Edgbaston. Kent really ought to have won that at a canter. We made 265/8 in our 60 overs, and on a good batting wicket that was about 30 short. They started well and I had to use up most of the available overs from Tim Munton and Gladstone Small as we searched for wickets. On such a good pitch, I knew that we needed to bowl them out because otherwise they'd get the runs. It didn't work for a long time, though, and at 183/2, with Neil Taylor and Carl Hooper established, they needed only 83 with 14 overs left. Nine times out of ten, that would have been a stroll for the batting side. Then Dominic Ostler took a great catch on the square-leg boundary to get Taylor and Kent began to panic. Graham Cowdrey went to a stunning catch behind the stumps by Keith Piper, leaping high to claw the edge down with one glove, and that inspired us. We kept Hooper away from the strike, he got frustrated and got himself out. We nagged away at the rest of the Kent batting and they buckled. The crowd really got behind us when we needed lifting, and we wouldn't let go. They lost by eight runs in a game that typified the crazy, unpredictable nature of one-day cricket.

If you sat down and analysed the various ways in which you can throw away a one-day game, you'd probably shrivel and underachieve. That's why I tell our guys to strip the game down to its bare essentials and don't think about how easily it can all go horribly wrong. I find the mental demands of one-day cricket fascinating, with the need to keep several overs ahead in the field uppermost in my mind. I believe your best one-day sides possess six reliable bowlers. Look how important it was for England in the second Texaco Trophy international against Pakistan to be able to call on Adam Hollioake after Ronnie Irani had started badly. You need options. All-rounders in quantity are very valuable, and we have been lucky to have the Smiths, Dougie Brown, Graeme Welch, Roger Twose and myself to call on, so that we bat a long way down and our main batters aren't compromised by the need to be cautious. They have licence to play their shots and extemporise as much as they want.

It's fascinating to see how much the one-day game is evolving, though. Every season, there seems to be a new train of thought that overturns the established conventions – like starting carefully, having wickets in hand for the last ten overs, using your fastest bowlers at the death, putting the spinner on during a quiet period. All those ideas have been challenged in recent years and I like that. You need to keep thinking ahead, coming up with new ways of turning a game in a few minutes. Every ball really must be an event.

9

Captaincy Hassles

I nearly resigned the Warwickshire captaincy during our second marvellous season during a row. It came at the end of June 1995, at a time when I felt I was not getting the full backing of some players and the management. For a time I felt very low and it needed some give-and-take on all sides to get us back on an even keel. By the time the rumours leaked out of the Warwickshire camp and found their way into the press, we were all pulling again in the same direction, but for a few weeks in the month of June, I was close to packing it in. The background to it just underlines the hassles involved in being a county captain when some players start to doubt you, and you don't get the full backing of the management. The irony at that time was that we were again near the top of the championship table, rolling over sides ruthlessly and looking good for another great year. On the face of it, we must have appeared our usual bouncy selves. However, the problems had been building up for some months.

I had been very unhappy at the lack of support given to me over Brian Lara's behaviour in the previous season. I will continue to stress that he is the greatest batsman I have ever seen, and that he did wonders for our performances – but he was a pain to captain. Dennis Amiss and Bob Woolmer just wanted to let it slide, get through that 1994 season without any undue fall-out, and take a breather. I went along with that, even though it rankled that the captain had received less than adequate support. So it was doubly galling to me when it was announced by the club the following February that Lara, not Allan Donald, would be our overseas player from 1996 onwards. To make matters worse, Lara would be on a three-year contract. I had not been consulted on the matter during any of the negotiations, I just had the *fait accompli*. Surely the club captain ought to have had some say in the decision, especially as our relationship had been rocky for most of the previous season? It was also terribly hard on Allan, a true professional, a 100 per cent Warwickshire man. Brian Lara didn't give English domestic cricket much respect, he saw it as a chore, too easy for him. Allan Donald was never like that, despite being a top Test player. A great supporter of his team-mates, he would sense when one of the younger bowlers was a bit down, and he'd suggest they had a bowl to get some confidence back. He would ask us for support in the field, shouting, 'It's gone quiet out here – get behind me!' Allan was as motivated playing for us as he ever was with South Africa.

I was still brooding about the Lara decision when we went to Cape Town on our 1995 pre-season tour. A chat with Allan Donald reassured me of his motivation for the coming season, which might have been his last for the club, with Lara signed up for the next three. So I had no worries in the short-term about our overseas player, but I was concerned about our general preparation for the new season. I knew we would be there to be shot at, after our record-breaking season, and yet I sensed a level of complacency in Cape Town. Apart from Dougie Brown, the fitness levels for every player were down. That indicated a lack of commitment during the winter, and it meant we would be wasting valuable time trying to get properly fit, rather than working on skills.

Bob Woolmer was with us for his swansong during that Cape Town fortnight. Bob had joined the South African national side as their director of coaching and I knew we would miss him, but it was time for his successor, Phil Neale, to make his presence felt. It was an uneasy period of transition and difficult for Phil, who sensibly took a back seat, watched how Bob worked with the players and monitored their response.

During that period in Cape Town, Bob didn't really handle things in his usual genial manner. He was upset at our general lack of fitness, felt we were sloppy in the field, and was very hurt

when we lost badly to Western Province at Newlands. I realised
that Bob desperately wanted Warwickshire to look impressive in
front of the South Africans, because it would reflect well on his
methods, and also because he had praised us highly. He's still a
proud Englishman, despite living in Cape Town, and he wanted
the locals to see a top unit in action. We let him down, but that
was partly due to the fact that we were getting ready for a long
season and bound to be rusty, in addition to some complacency.
Perhaps Bob was comparing us with his South African national
squad which was unfair as most of our guys hadn't played for
months, or for that matter, weren't international cricketers.

I knew that Bob wanted to give some home truths to several
of our players in those last few days, to get things off his chest
that he had been storing up at Edgbaston over the years, and
that led to friction. He really gave Paul Smith a rocket about his
fielding and I could tell that Bob had wanted to say that for
some time. Then Trevor Penney talked back to Bob in the Cape
Town dressing-room after a remark about his batting. A couple
of years earlier, Bob had spoken sharply to Trevor about the way
he had batted against Martin McCague and clearly Trevor
hadn't forgotten, so he came back with a volley, in front of all
the players. I felt a little sorry for Phil Neale and our new signing, Nick Knight, that some players were wading into Bob, and
vice versa. We had prided ourselves on the open environment,
where everyone was encouraged to speak their mind, but now
there was back-chat all over the place. The spirit just wasn't right
in Cape Town and I had some negative vibes about our season
as the start loomed.

In our opening first-class match, we were hammered by an
innings by England 'A' and within a month we had lost our first
three Sunday League games, and were out of the Benson and
Hedges Cup. So two of the four trophies on offer seemed to
have slipped away from us before we could blink. We weren't
right in our approach and although other sides were successfully
raising their game against us, that should have been an incentive
to players with pride and professionalism – the qualities we normally show. As captain, I was struggling as well. I didn't feel I
had the support of all the players, an impression confirmed when

we played at Durham in the middle of May and a couple of players talked back to me on the field. Now I know that some things are said out there between team-mates in the heat of the moment, but this was different. Richard Davis, our left-arm spinner, was disappointed that he only bowled two overs in the Durham match, but the pitch was helping the seamers. Richard gave me some lip on the field, and Paul Smith also weighed in. Phil Neale, who was easing himself into his new job, was just observing the situation in his early weeks, and I told him that the spirit wasn't right, that we weren't all as together as usual. We had a team meeting at Durham after the game and I said that some of the team were judging me as a cricketer and I didn't feel supported. We weren't encouraging each other enough, techniques were being criticised behind players' backs – and it had to stop. I wasn't enjoying the captaincy and said we must pull together. It was difficult to tell how effective my words had been. Incidentally, we beat Durham comfortably in the four-day match.

I still believed I could cut it as a player, even though others might think otherwise. In the 1994 season, I hadn't done well in first-class cricket, although my one-day record was arguably better than any previous season. Because of a series of injuries, I only played in nine first-class matches. Tim Munton deputised ably for me as captain, winning eight of the nine championship games under his leadership. I decided to save myself for the one-day games in July and August as we chased trophies on all fronts, and the side kept going for the championship without me. It wasn't a blow to my ego at all. I'd had a bellyful of Brian Lara, so let Tim and Bob handle him in their own way. I felt it vital for the team that Tim had the same freedom to captain as I'd been given. I'd learned from when I led the side occasionally when Andy Lloyd was injured, finding it easier without the club captain at my shoulder. As we came down the home straight, I was fit again for the championshi games, but I stayed out of the side by choice. Young Graeme Welch was making a good impression as an all-rounder, and it was better for the team that he stayed in, and I continued to rest up for the one-dayers. When we won the championship at home to Hampshire, a lot was made of my gesture to Tim Munton, insisting that he should be presented with the championship trophy. It was just obvious to me that it was only right that Tim should be pushed to the front. He hadn't missed a championship game, had taken 81 wickets and led the side successfully for half the matches.

What I hadn't bargained for was a change in attitude to me as a player by Dennis Amiss, though. Our chief executive dropped a heavy hint before the start of the 1995 season. Dennis said that I should consider dropping myself in favour of Tim in championship cricket if my form wasn't good. A ball hadn't been bowled! Surely he should have been encouraging me and wishing me well as captain and player in all four competitions. I was hurt and angry. I pointed out to Dennis that 1994 had been my best season in one-day cricket, only to be told, 'That's not the real cricket, though.' Try telling that to the members who packed out Edgbaston on Sundays, and who celebrated three one-day trophies in just 12 months!

So I didn't feel I had the right support of the chief executive at the start of the next season, when I wanted to crack down on the players. After all, he hadn't consulted me when they decided to sign up Brian Lara for another spell, and he clearly thought my best days as a county cricketer were behind me. As for the players, I honestly felt some wanted me out of the side. There was a definite clique within the team – comprising Neil Smith, Andy Moles, Richard Davis and Tim Munton – who I'm sure would have preferred Tim to be club captain. There will always be personality problems within a team and that is understandable. You don't need to be everyone's best mate, but you should respect and support your team-mates in cricketing matters. On captaincy, Tim's style in 1994 was different to mine, but this was 1995, and a decision had been made by the club that I was to be captain in all four competitions. It was ironic that Tim wasn't even fit to play until we took on Sussex early in June, as he was still recovering from a back operation in the winter. To confuse matters, I missed a couple of championship games through back and rib injuries, and I could sense the clique were more bubbly and vocal with me on the sidelines. The freedom of expression these players had enjoyed in the past meant that some were speaking out, at times undermining my status as captain. The atmosphere was unhealthy, even though we had won five of our first seven championship matches.

I felt we had recovered a good deal of momentum after a complacent start, and was personally happy with my own game. I was averaging 30 with the bat and 28 with the ball by the time we came to Ilford to play Essex at the end of June. Before the match Tim Munton, Phil Neale and I looked at the pitch, and discussed what our final 11 would be. Phil and Tim wanted to play our spinner, Richard Davis, because they were sure the ball would turn and Essex would no doubt be playing their two spinners – John Childs and Peter Such. They wanted to leave out Dougie Brown, a seamer. Yet Dougie had just taken eight wickets in the previous championship match against Yorkshire and 24 wickets in only 5 championship games. As far as I was concerned, he played in front of a few players at the moment. I wasn't sure that Tim was a hundred per cent right after his serious back operation. He had played in the last two championship games and he still looked to be feeling his way into his action and proper follow-through, which is understandable when you've had a major back problem and you're a seam bowler, who thrives on hard work. There was a possibility in my mind that Tim might sit out this Essex game, but looking at the wicket, I thought it would be abrasive and help the ball reverse swing. Tim and Dougie both bowl well when the ball is in this mode. The ball was definitely going to spin, but I felt it would turn slowly, without the helpful bounce spinners love. I was happy to leave out Richard Davis because of this and play just the one spinner, Neil Smith.

It was then suggested that we play both spinners and leave out a batsman, young Wasim Khan, but I wasn't happy at weakening the batting. For me, Dougie Brown had to play, not just because he was in good form with the ball but his batting would be important. So we talked round and round the subject till Phil asked if I had thought about dropping myself. He said, 'If we were playing at Edgbaston, there'd be a strong case for you dropping yourself, but you're a good player of spinners, so on balance you ought to play here.'

I had never considered there might be a thought about me

standing down, and my brain started to race in all directions. Tim said nothing, just shrugging his shoulders, which made me feel slightly betrayed. Surely a supportive vice-captain would have insisted I played? The three of us sat out in the middle while the others practised and we were getting nowhere. Phil was adamant about two spinners, I was insistent that Brown played, while at the same time shocked that the possibility had been raised about dropping me. If I had felt it right for the team, I would have dropped out for the Ilford match, but I didn't. I felt my form and fitness were decent and that I deserved to be backed. In the end, Tim came down on my side and we made Richard Davis twelfth man. When we batted, I dropped myself down to number seven in the order and asked Phil Neale to walk around the ground with me. I was seriously thinking about resigning the captaincy and I wanted Phil's honest opinion: was he voicing what the players were saying? Was Dennis Amiss interfering? As a former county captain himself, he needed to understand why I felt let down. I told him I was gutted and needed to talk this thing through. 'Imagine, Phil, that you're back at Worcester as captain, with five wins out of five under your belt. Imagine that you're averaging in the mid-30s with the bat in the championship. How would you feel if the new coach suggested that someone like David Leatherdale came in to replace you as a player?' I hadn't lost respect for Phil as a person: he was expressing an honest opinion on the way he saw how the squad should best be utilised. However it was obvious he didn't feel it was vital who was captain. Phil's response to my question was sympathetic but cagey. I was on a real downer at Ilford, keeping myself apart from the players, sitting in my hotel room, just playing my guitar, wondering exactly where I stood. The only spontaneous support came from Allan Donald, when I told him I was thinking about jacking in the captaincy: 'I want you to stay on. I've got total respect for you as skipper and I'm right behind you. If you resign, you'll play into their hands.' That was inspirational at a bad time for me, and I shan't ever forget Allan for that. I decided to carry on.

I also felt vindicated in the team selection at Ilford, and the ball did reverse swing. Donald picked up six wickets and I took

3/37 in the first innings. Munton got three wickets in the match and Neil Smith took seven. There was turn, but it was never unplayable. Peter Such took 2/122 in the game and John Childs 2/104. Dougie Brown scored an invaluable 85 as we built a big lead, and we won impressively by ten wickets. So we prepared for the trip to Leicester. Before I left, Dennis Amiss deflated me again, when he said: 'It might turn there, perhaps you shouldn't play yourself.' I know that at that stage, Richard Davis had been in to see Dennis about not being in the side, but I did think I might have had more support from the man in charge, especially as he had played the game long enough, and knew the various interests and factions involved. Surely the captain has to be supported, especially when the side's winning every game? Yet the Warwickshire team spirit that had impressed so many in recent years wasn't 100 per cent. I was determined to get it sorted out at Leicester. I called for a meeting and said, 'Listen fellas, we talk about helping each other along when we're tired and a bit down. That's what we need now. You may have heard a few rumours about me at Ilford, but don't worry about it. I'm not jacking in the captaincy, I'm totally motivated and on the field, I'll be my normal self. So just concentrate on your own game. Let's get it back to where we were.' I didn't want to know who was for or against me. The players must have realised that I was looking for extra support. I had seen it happen to John Barclay at Sussex, when his form declined because of injuries, and the players started to question him as captain. I was going to dig in and see it through.

We beat Leicestershire inside two days by an innings, and I had match figures of 33.4-17-47-6. Surely Amiss and any other detractors would take notice? I got runs and wickets in the Sunday League match as well and started to feel more confident. Then a vital game a couple of days later, one of the turning points of the season. We beat Kent by ten runs in the second round of the Nat West after a hard struggle. We made 262, and with dangerous players like Aravinda De Silva, Trevor Ward, Graham Cowdrey, Matthew Fleming and Mark Ealham in their team that day, Kent must have been favourites to get through at just over four runs an over on a good batting surface. But we raised our game superbly, operated as a tight unit again and our big-match experience saved the day. At last I felt the whole team was pulling together again and supporting me. The atmosphere was brilliant in the dressing room afterwards.

After that Kent game, we got on a roll and played brilliantly for the next two months in all three competitions. We lost just two games – by seven runs to Northants in the championship and by two runs to Worcestershire in the Sunday League. We steamrollered opponents and the season got better and better for me as the weeks progressed. I was absolutely chuffed to take 5/30 in the final championship game at Canterbury when we clinched the title. All season, the ball felt pretty good coming out of my hand and I backed a hunch and decided to open the bowling that day.

The week leading up to Canterbury had been the longest of my career. We thought we had the title won after rolling over Derbyshire, thanks to Allan Donald's magnificent bowling. All we had to do was endure a couple of hours while Leicestershire managed to get a draw down at Uxbridge against our closest challengers, Middlesex. Rain had affected that game badly, but Leicestershire still had a chance for prize money, so they were very keen on victory as well. So when Mike Gatting declared after some friendly bowling, he knew that Leicestershire would go for the target of 251 in two sessions, a very generous rate for the batters. At 131/2, it looked as if Middlesex would lose, but I couldn't stay any longer at the ground. After agreeing that we'd all be back at Edgbaston at 5.30 for the victory celebrations if Middlesex hadn't won, I went home.

I lay on the sofa, picking at my guitar, wondering what was happening at Uxbridge. Our supporters stayed at the ground, watching in agony as the latest Uxbridge score was updated after each over on Teletext in the members' bar. A friend rang me at tea-time and said, 'They're six down.' So Gatt had manipulated it, he'd thrown the bait out to Leicestershire and they'd swallowed the hook. I went back to the dressing-room, sat in a hot bath and Keith Piper said to me, 'Parsons is out – they're eight down.' That was it, I thought, there are too many overs left, they won't hold out against Tufnell and Emburey. Adrian Pierson, our old team-mate, was now in, but there were 12 overs to go. I phoned the Uxbridge ground and a guy told me there were only seven overs to go and still eight wickets down. Come on, Adrian, do it for us mate! Then another wicket fell and Adrian had just Alan Mullally left. It seemed to take an eternity for the Teletext pages to change at the end of each over: three overs left, 12 needed, one wicket to fall. By now our physio, Stuart Nottingham, had found the commentary on the radio, on BBC Five Live. We stood in the physio's small room, listening to Henry Blofeld talking down the overs. It came down to two runs for victory and we're hanging on to each other for dear life. A draw or a tie would give us the title, so one run would be enough – not much to ask! We're starting to bounce up and down together in the room, as Blofeld said, 'Tufnell comes in to bowl, and Mullally hits it.' We had our arms up in the air, with our mouths open, just waiting to roar and then we hear, 'It's in the air, it might be caught – Emburey's caught it. Middlesex have won by one run!'

We had gone from elation to despair in one instant. We looked at each other and everyone started cursing Mullally – why couldn't he leave it to Adrian, why go for death or glory? I started to laugh hysterically, saying, 'Why couldn't they lose by 30? Why just by one?' I suddenly felt totally drained. Gladstone Small said, 'All we do now is go down to Canterbury and win it properly, without relying on anybody else', and Allan Donald said, 'We've proved people wrong all season, all we have to do is win one more time!'

Great reactions from two senior players and of course they were right, but I felt inconsolable that night. At home, I plugged in my electric guitar and hit the strings full bore: it must have been a terrible row! I didn't go to the Professional Cricketers' Association dinner that week in London, because that would have meant seeing Mullally, and Gatt's gloating face. As a joke I wrote a song about Mullally in the style of a Sex Pistols' number and the lyrics were very uncomplimentary. At least it got a laugh out of the boys on a practice day. All week I kept thinking, 'We've won 13 out of 16 and that would win the title easily in any other year. We're going to start nicking a few sometime, and dropping some in the slips, it's the law of averages. We can't keep winning, can we? I was waking up in the middle of the night, with Henry Blofeld's radio commentary ringing in my ears, convinced that Middlesex had lost by one wicket. Then I remembered.

On that first morning at Canterbury, I was more stressed out than at any time of my life. I just didn't know what to do if I won the toss, I was so worried I'd make the wrong decision. There was a bit of moisture on the surface, but it looked a decent wicket, so it would be best to bat first. The pitch would get worse, we could play two spinners and they would use the rough against the Kent batsmen. Supporting Neil Smith's off-spin was Ashley Giles, who had replaced Richard Davis in mid-July and looked a fine cricketer, totally at ease in the first team. We had won so many matches by winning the toss, putting the opposition in, bowling them out cheaply, then controlling the game. Tim Munton, Phil Neale and I agreed we'd bowl if I won the toss: it seemed the easier option. Fifteen minutes later, when I went out for the toss, I felt the wicket. It felt dryer, so I decided to go with my gut feeling. Be positive, bat first. When I came back after calling correctly, I told the guys, 'It looks a good batting wicket, there's a bit of moisture, so it may do a bit early on. Get over the new ball, fellas, and we'll see you at lunchtime!'

It was all a big act from me, I was terrified in that first half-hour. Tim gave me a sideways look and I said, 'I just hope it doesn't go all over the place off the seam.' We both laughed nervously. I sat on the balcony willing Wasim Khan and Nick Knight to a large partnership and they did us proud. Nick got a big hundred and by the end of the first day, I could relax – especially at the news that Middlesex hadn't got onto the pitch at Taunton, because of rain.

We beat Kent by an innings with a day to spare and we had a brilliant party that Saturday night in Canterbury. The wives and girlfriends came down to celebrate, we took over a restaurant and all the players had to do a party piece to keep the fun going. Wasim Khan's impersonation of Dennis Amiss was a particular hit and we chanted 'You Bears! You Bears!' as the drink flowed. Just as well we had a late start the next day for the final Sunday

League game. We had no chance of retaining our title, even if we beat Kent, as they had a far superior run rate. We had played on some poor one-day wickets on Sundays, particularly at Durham and Worcester, where scores of 132 and 152 proved beyond us. Coincidentally, we didn't face any spinners in those matches. We beat Kent by five wickets, which was very satisfying, and left us in no doubt that we were the superior side. If rain hadn't wiped out our match the previous weekend when we had Derbyshire 81/5, we would probably have retained the Sunday League title. As it was we finished level on points, runners-up.

That was a brilliant weekend at Canterbury and I felt very happy at how the season had turned out. I felt I had vindicated myself as a cricketer, finishing second in the first-class bowling averages behind Allan Donald, and ending up with an average of 36 with the bat. That was hugely satisfying after my poor figures in '94. I also felt I had the team behind me again, after a bad couple of months. All 14 championship victories came under my captaincy, including eight in a row, but I was pleased that I could still hold my own place down in the side as a cricketer, irrespective of my captaincy. No one was suggesting any more that I should stand down for the good of the team.

Captaining Warwickshire has given me great fulfilment but there have been times when I've wondered if it was worth the aggravation. I know the best aspect of my captaincy was when I was out on the field, that I wasn't the best at working behind the scenes, within a committee structure. That's partly my fault because I have a restless nature and get frustrated when I cannot win a proposal around a committee table. For example, on several occasions, I brought up in the cricket committee a recommendation to help get our players fitter and better-prepared for the county season. Players at Warwickshire aren't paid anything during October-April, yet are expected to report fit for pre-season. I suggested a financial reward if a player registered a certain level in a fitness assessment when he reported back. The players resent that they should train in the winter and practise in the nets for no financial gain. I wanted that pre-season period to be spent on fine-tuning cricket skills, rather than getting the players properly fit. Your technique suffers when you are tired and I thought that just a few hundred pounds would have been one way to motivate their attitude to fitness. Ideally, I believe players should be on eight-month contracts, reporting back on February 1, and over the next two months, they would then become fitter and more athletic under supervision. That way, they'd be more likely to meet the demands of the over-loaded fixture list. This would cost the club more than £100,000 in extra wages, so I believed my suggestion of a few hundred pounds a player was more realistic. I never got anywhere with that idea in cricket committee. In fact, one committee member suggested that, instead of an incentive, we fine the players if they reported back, unable to reach the necessary level on the fitness assessment. The committee didn't seem to realise that most players don't like training unless they have to, that it's difficult for the captain to bite his tongue when we reassemble, if three or four aren't fully fit. for a few weeks, and you're losing valuable preparation time. So the captain goes into important early matches in a season unsure about some of his players' fitness, and that's something which shouldn't be allowed in the modern game. This despite all the cash pouring into the game from the TV deal with B Sky B, and the increased revenue from marketing such a successful club.

I found my influence as club captain at committee level to be peripheral and frustrating. Yet they say the captain's input is vital. So why did no one consult me about hiring Brian Lara for another three years, after our disagreements had been well documented? I got a large say in picking the eleven for the next match, but not in terms of future development of the staff, or consultation about the next overseas player. In the end, the most important thing for the captain is to maintain your form as a player: otherwise you're really on the back foot. Mike Gatting's advice to me when I took the job about keeping up your playing standards is so true. Those doubts nearly saw my demise during a season when we won two more trophies. Is it any wonder that experienced county captains get worn down by it all?

10

Playing for England

My England career lasted almost five years – from my debut at Lord's in a one-day international in 1991, to that sad day in March 1996 when we slunk out of the World Cup, thrashed by Sri Lanka. We didn't deserve anything from that tournament: one-day cricket at that level had passed us by. Our management team of Ray Illingworth and Michael Atherton must take the bulk of the blame for that. They were way off the pace in terms of preparation, tactical flexibility and man-management. It may sound as if I have an axe to grind, having been treated dismissive in South Africa at the start of 1996, then originally missing out on the World Cup party, but that would have been a complete irrelevance to me if England had looked the part on those two trips. But we didn't. Above all, I wanted England to compete properly, to look fresh and businesslike and tactically innovative. Those few months certainly knocked on the head any arrogant ideas that, having started one-day cricket 30-odd years earlier, we still knew best how to play it. We had been left behind. The quality of management by Illingworth and Atherton was also streets behind the leadership of Graham Gooch, Mickey Stewart and Keith Fletcher when I first played for England.

The break-up of my marriage in 1990 had something to do with me becoming an England cricketer. It's sad, I know, but I turned to fitness training as a sort of therapy to get over it, and I became a fitness fanatic in the winter of 1990/91. So the 1991 season saw me raring to go, fitter than ever before, and I probably played the best all-round cricket of my career. Fortunately, I had that bit of luck you need and was selected for England. Julie and I had been married for four years when we split up, and she took my two-year-old daughter, Emily, back to Australia at the end of the 1990 season. With hindsight, I probably didn't work hard enough at my marriage, but I was still shattered when it ended. For the next year, I hated going back to an empty house. Early on, I'd sit there, unnerved by the silence, staring at the photos of my daughter, bashing the phone, trying to catch family and friends if they were at home, and then talking to them for ages. I was an emotional wreck. I had to snap out of it.

For therapy, I went to the gym. In the end, I became addicted and unless I did some vigorous exercise every day, I would feel tense and uneasy. Exercise was the one thing during that time that made me feel content and after a workout I could face the empty house and the silence. I met a sports scientist called Karen Rodkin, who was tremendously helpful to me. She taught me about the physiological side of training, how you should best prepare yourself for your sport. Karen told me that cricketers need to train anaerobically, rather than aerobically because cricket is all about bursts of energy. She said a cricketer should train like a sprinter, rather than a marathon runner, because it's all about short bursts. So on a training run, I wouldn't go for the long slog, to build up stamina: I'd do a 100-metre sprint, then walk 100 metres, then back to sprinting. In the pool, I'd swim sprints – 50 metres as fast as I could, then rest for 30 seconds, then repeat the process. Eventually I got up to 20 50-metre sprints in the pool, followed by 20 seconds' rest. I read all the books and really got into the subject. The greater your capacity to produce energy anaerobically, the less lactic acid and therefore stiffness you will get. Many cricketers are stiff before they bowl and that produces injuries. Before this fitness regime, I used to feel stiff when batting after bowling 20 overs, and I realised I wasn't properly fit for the all-rounder's responsibilities. I really pushed myself in that gym, to blot out for a few hours the pain I was feeling at the absence of my daughter. I deliberately didn't have a night in alone for a year. I would either arrange an evening out or stay at the gym until 10 o'clock. I became addicted to the endorphins produced after hard exercise. You feel as if you're floating – I'm told you feel that way after a narcotic, like opium. It got me through a very emotional period.

So I had more time to focus on my dream of playing for England. I hadn't forgotten the scepticism of Alan Wells when I voiced my ambitions in my early days at Sussex and his conservative attitude shared by some others only fired my ambition all the more. My form at the start of the 1991 season was good, and I got into the one-day squad at the expense of Ian Botham, who had torn a hamstring at Edgbaston in the first match. I was playing down at Chelmsford at the time, and I just flew up the motorway to Old Trafford. I was amazingly exhilarated, thinking that I'd surely get one game out of the two remaining ones, even though perhaps not tomorrow. That's how it turned out, although I got on the field as substitute fielder. That was great fun: a big crowd, with England doing well and the ball coming to me a lot at backward point. Gus Logie kept me busy there and I eventually caught Carl Hooper. It was great to be on the field at the finish, wearing the England gear. Mum was there to watch me and I met the Prime Minister, John Major, who popped into our dressing-room for a chat. It's a different world playing for England!

Off down to London then for the third game in the one-day series, with me desperately hoping to play at Lord's. I nearly didn't make it after a car crash on the M6 that saw me narrowly miss a concrete bridge as I slammed on the brakes and went backwards down the motorway. Despite whiplash in my neck, I slept well and waited for the result of Allan Lamb's fitness test on his bruised instep. As we warmed up, I saw our physio, Lawrie Brown, working on Lamby and he soon shook his head. The captain, Graham Gooch, came over to me and said, 'Dermot, you're playing. Congratulations – good luck and well done.' The adrenalin just shot up from my toes – I was playing for England! I didn't get a bat but I bowled 12 efficient overs, including a good shout for lbw against Brian Lara and a maiden at Viv Richards. As I sat on the balcony, waiting to go in to bat, I noticed the field that the off-spinner Carl Hooper was using.

It was a 6/3 field to the right-hander and I said to the coach, Mickey Stewart: 'If he bowls at me with this field, I'm going to reverse sweep him first ball. Is that OK?' Mickey's answer was very reassuring: 'You've got this far playing that way for Warwickshire. Don't change your approach just because you're now playing for England.' That was a great attitude and Mickey encouraged me to think that way all the time we were on England duty together.

I didn't want that day at Lord's to end. We won by seven wickets and I didn't get in for a bat, but I loved it all. Rory Bremner came in for a natter, and it was relaxing to hear him do some impersonations. When the game was over, I was still on a high and wanted to party. When Goochy said, 'That's it, boys, well done – see you at the First Test', I felt deflated. I didn't want to leave the England dressing-room, it was such a fantastic pleasure to be part of it all. I didn't get the call for the first couple of Tests, but my form held up and I kept hoping. I was called into the 13 for the Trent Bridge Test but the balance of the side, with Jack Russell keeping wicket, meant I couldn't break through once they had decided to play the spinner, Richard Illingworth. So off I went to Portsmouth to play against Hampshire, with hopes of playing at Edgbaston. I took eight wickets in the championship game and felt good about my all-round form. On the Sunday morning, Graham Gooch called me at the ground to say, 'Bad luck, Dermot. You've done nothing wrong, but we know what side we want, and we're only going in with 12 for Edgbaston.' They had actually gone back to Chris Lewis as the all-rounder. That was the worst moment of my career so far, and I was inconsolable for a while. I had gone from euphoria to despondency in a fortnight and now thought my chance might have gone for good. Bob Woolmer stood over me and said, 'Let it out, boy – I know how you feel, it happened to me as well.' That just made it worse and, covering my head, I lost it for a moment or two. Everyone had told me I had done nothing wrong, that I had impressed them, but all I had to show for it was a single appearance in a one-day game. That wasn't the same as playing in a Test Match.

With Ian Botham on his way back to full fitness, our rivalry was now being built up in the press. With England now 2/1 down in the series, it was felt the team needed to sacrifice Jack Russell, play Alec Stewart as the wicket-keeper, leaving the side with four front-line bowlers plus an all-rounder. We played Worcestershire in a championship game just before the Oval squad was announced and Ian and I both did well. He got 81 on the first day, I made 97 the day after, and Ian got the nod on the Sunday. To celebrate his recall, he took 7/54 to beat us by an innings. England won that Oval Test, and Both's presence undoubtedly helped raise the side's morale, but all I could think of was that it could have been me there. The boys tried to cheer me up by making a positive out of a negative, that I might have missed out on the tour that winter if I had failed at the Oval – but all I wanted was that sweater with the lions on it.

More disappointment came when I was left out of the senior tour to New Zealand with the consolation prize of going to the West Indies with England 'A'. That was more than I could have expected 12 months earlier, but I felt disappointed that I had come so near, and yet I hadn't made that final vital leap. Still, I was put on stand-by for the senior tour, because there were doubts about the fitness of Angus Fraser, who had a hip problem. I thought it strange that an all-rounder would be a possible swap for a seam bowler, but there you go. In the end, I got on the trip to New Zealand and to the World Cup, because Angus couldn't make it. It was a fantastic experience to play in front of 87,000 spectators in the World Cup Final, even if we did lose it, and to play in all three Tests in New Zealand was a huge thrill; but before we left England, I incurred an injury that had serious consequences for the next couple of years.

We were training at the National Sports Centre at Lilleshall before flying out to New Zealand and I was fired up to do well and impress Graham Gooch. After my fitness regime, I had never felt so strong, my all-round record for the 1991 season was good, and I wanted the captain to know how keen I was. I bowled for an hour and half on the first day and Goochie said, 'Derm, well done – you're bowling with a bit of zip,' which was a big boost to me. Next morning, I could barely move. Every joint in my body ached and all I did at the gym was have a massage, sauna and light swim. I was in agony. The next day was more nets and I could barely carry my bag to the dressing-room. Phillip DeFreitas and David Lawrence were already changed and I told them how I felt. They said they felt exactly the same after Tuesday's bowling session. Chris Lewis listened to that and said, 'I bowled here last year and ended up with a stress fracture of the back. There's no way I'm doing the same thing. I'm coming in off four paces.' The pain didn't go away. We mentioned it to Mickey Stewart and he arranged for us to have a different set of training shoes to absorb the impact of the hard surface. We eventually found out what caused the pain; it seems the shock pads where the bowlers land had been taken out because it affected the bias when indoor bowls was played. So the surface was similar to concrete and England bowlers were damaging their bodies, just so that a game of bowls could be played properly! We just couldn't absorb the pressure satisfactorily when we landed. Chris Lewis had the right idea, although I think our management felt he was just coasting. Poor David Lawrence, who only knew how to bowl flat out, was in agony as he charged in on that hard, unyielding surface. I've often wondered whether Lilleshall contributed to the terrible injury that ended his career, when he broke his left kneecap soon afterwards in New Zealand. It was, after all, his left knee that caused him a lot of pain during those training sessions.

By this stage, with three weeks before we left for New Zealand, I had a pain in my buttock. It was there when I did the sprints and a deep rub from the physio and anti-inflammatory tablets didn't really help. When we got to New Zealand the pain got worse and I struggled to bowl with any pace. I was just trotting in, concentrating on moving the ball sideways. I was lucky that the pitches out there were so slow, that my lack of pace wasn't exposed. In the World Cup, I wasn't able to bowl the odd quicker ball, so I lacked variety. I collapsed in pain in the match against South Africa and got through by popping pills and on the adrenalin from playing in such a fabulous atmosphere. I bowled three overs in the World Cup Final and, basically, I was in varying degrees of pain for most of the time.

When I got back to England in the spring of '92, the injury

was finally diagnosed: a stress fracture of the pelvis. No wonder it had been so sore. Rest was the only cure and I didn't really bowl with consistent conviction for the next three years. It was funny that Ian Botham was fit at the start of the '92 season and I wasn't, yet I had attended the pre tour Lilleshall sessions whilst he did his pantomime. Late in '92, when I was picked to go on the England tour to India and Sri Lanka, I trained at Lilleshall in the way recommended by Chris Lewis, taking it easy off a few paces when bowling. By then, a large foam sponge area had been laid down to absorb the pressure on landing, but that was a little late for me – and for poor old David Lawrence.

Apart from that injury, though, those three months at the start of 1992 were a wonderful experience for me. I shall never forget the moment I was told I was going to play for England at last in a Test Match. We were at Christchurch and Graham Gooch called my room, asking me to go and see him. I knocked on Goochy's door, walked in and he was in the bath. He stuck out a hand through the foam and said, 'You're playing tomorrow, we haven't told anyone else yet, so keep it quiet. I know you'll do well.' I raced back to my room, beaming from ear to ear, and my room-mate, Chris Lewis, said, 'Well?' I just jumped up and down on my bed, nodding. Chris put his hand out and said 'Congrats.' I shook it fiercely then said, 'But you can't say anything, Lewie.' I couldn't keep it all to myself and that night I saw Mum and whispered the good news to her. She'd taken the first available plane out when there was a chance of me playing after a good performance in the first of the one-day internationals and I was really happy for her when I broke the good news. I saw her eyes start to water and I felt the same.

We batted first and by the time I came in at number seven we had a lot of runs in the book. I got off the mark first ball, blocking a good-length delivery from Danny Morrison to square leg, shouting 'Yes!' and racing in. I kept thinking, 'I've got a run for England!' and then started to look for more as the declaration came near. Chris Lewis played a top knock and I started to club a few blows on the slow pitch. I got to 50 by smacking one from Dipak Patel to the mid-wicket boundary and I immediately pointed my bat to Mum in the area where I knew she was sitting.

That was a fabulous moment, making all the waiting a few months earlier that much sweeter.

We won that Test and I celebrated with the boys after climbing out of my sick bed. I had gone down with food poisoning after a pasta marinara caught me out, but when it looked as if we would win, I caught a cab and presented my green face to the dressing-room. I wasn't going to miss that on my Test debut! I was struck by the level of intensity in the dressing-room during a Test, compared to a county game. Robin Smith got out for 90-odd and he was really annoyed at missing out on his hundred. Over the years it's seemed to me that guys play more for themselves than in county cricket, which I guess is understandable, but can be a problem when you need everyone to give it their all in a tight situation. That was never the case on this tour. In this series, we were clearly the better side as New Zealand struggled to come to terms with the retirement of Sir Richard Hadlee and John Bracewell.

There was an air of confidence in our team, and I was in the thick of it at short leg or silly point, shouting encouragement to our bowlers. I even gave Phil Tufnell a volley in the dressing-room when it appeared to me that he was worried about Chris Cairns' bowling. It was the second Test at Auckland, and we had been sent in on a damp pitch of uneven bounce. Something around 200 would have been a handy score in such conditions, and as we clawed our way past 150, Tuffers said to me, 'How fast is Cairns, Derm?' I said, 'Tuffers, you're going out there to bat for your country and we need runs. It's a slow wicket. Get behind every ball.' When he went out to join Derek Pringle, I was thinking, 'Don't back away!' as Cairns ran in to bowl. There was a slight movement to leg as he played the first one, but then he played a short delivery quite well and you could see his confidence rise. He and Pringle added over 30 and Tuffers came in at the end of the innings full of himself: 'Yeh, it wasn't that bad, Derm!' Tuffers and I got on straight away on that tour. He's a fun guy, with a fast bowler's temperament, who really wants to do well for the side. We had a lot of laughs together on that tour and he took my verbal attack on him that day very well.

We won the first two Tests and drew the third, and that was

the end of my Test career. My last Test innings was a first-baller: bowled around my legs by Murphy Su'a. So my Test career began with 59 and ended with a first-ball duck. Cricket is a great leveller. As far as I was concerned, anything in Test cricket after that first appearance in Christchurch was a bonus for me. My lifetime's ambition had been achieved and I hadn't felt out of my depth as we won the series convincingly.

A week or so later, and we were deep into the World Cup. It was a marvellous experience, playing in so many high-pressure games all over Australia. To see my daughter again was a major plus and the atmosphere in the day/night games was wonderful. If you couldn't motivate yourself for those matches, you were in the wrong profession. It was fantastic to beat Australia at Sydney and at one stage, as I sat watching us bat, I thought, 'Great, we're going to hammer the Aussies!' I felt like a spectator at that point and our confidence was sky-high. I enjoyed smashing Allan Donald for 17 in the last over of our innings in the semi-final, but I was never fully fit as a bowler because of my pelvic injury. I was fortunate to be bowled at some good times, and not relied on to always bowl a full quota of ten overs. With far better bowlers than me in the competition it was an injustice to finish top of the World Cup bowling averages. I played in all but one of the games, took some good slip catches and did enough with bat and ball, but I wasn't at my best. It didn't matter so much, though, because we had a lot of all-rounders and the spirit was terrific.

It was a major blow to lose the Final to Pakistan, but they were the better side on the day. It's been said we ran out of steam, but I think it was more a case of brilliant bowling by Wasim Akram. The two deliveries that bowled Allan Lamb and Chris Lewis were beauties, and before I went into bat, one or two of our guys said, 'Derm, when you go in, ask the umpires to have a look at the ball.' I faced an over from Aqib Javed that featured deliveries which swung very late and I carried out the instructions, but Brian Aldridge could see nothing wrong with the condition of the ball. I wasn't convinced the ball had been tampered with. I think we ought to give them credit for some brilliant bowling, and don't forget they were without the injured Waqar Younis.

And give credit also to their leg-spinner Mushtaq Ahmed, who bowled superbly. I couldn't get after him and he got me finally caught at mid-off.

It was the last chance to win the World Cup for a lot of our players like Ian Botham, Graham Gooch and Allan Lamb, but it was only when we walked around the boundary afterwards to thank our supporters that I realised the enormity of the occasion. A massive wave of people greeted us in the South Stand, which has a greater capacity than the whole of Lord's. I suppose it was like the World Cup Final at Wembley in 1966 – except that, sadly, we didn't have our version of Geoff Hurst.

A year later, I toured India and Sri Lanka, with hopes of playing in Tests as well as one-dayers, but it was not to be. It was more memorable for my Mum, who came out for the tour, staying in backpackers' accommodation, travelling everywhere second class, but loving the experience. When she ended up as England's official scorer for the last three Tests of the tour after Clem Driver's illness, she was in her element. Although Mum was happy to experience all aspects of life in India, I was glad that she was upgraded into the air-conditioned, five-star hotels that are one of the plusses of a cricket tour to that country. Unfortunately, she didn't get much chance to record great deeds by her son. I played in all eight of the one-day internationals, but missed out on all four Tests. It might have been different if Alec Stewart had kept wicket in all of the Tests, because that might have made room for me, but he wasn't that keen on the job on that tour, so I ended up doing a lot of net bowling and drinks carrying. There was always the chance of getting a late call-up for a Test, though, because of the usual stomach upsets you associate with touring those parts, but it was not to be.

It's certainly different touring India, and I mean no disrespect when I say that. The crowds are unbelievably keen on their cricket, and I was more recognised in a Madras street than in Birmingham. Some of the crowds were very hostile and excitable, preferring to throw rocks than garlands of flowers. If you fielded at third man in some of the one-dayers, you couldn't hear your captain's instructions because of the noise from firecrackers. Transport difficulties were huge on the tour. Indian Airlines were on strike and some of the pilots flying our planes had been bought out of retirement. One flight into Delhi was particularly hair-raising, as we came to a juddering stop just 40 yards from a fence and the co-pilot gasped over the intercom, 'Oh, it's only through the grace of God that we have landed safely, we've had total hydraulic failure!' It all added to the fun of the proceedings! I took a video camera on the tour, taking shots of the odd rat and Phil Tufnell throwing a wobbler about the umpires.

Yes, the umpires: their interpretation of the lbw law did us no favours. The Indians would just put their bat behind their front pad and literally kick the ball away. It was so obvious there was no attempt to play a shot but countless appeals were always turned down. They didn't play the sweep shot and when I was given out lbw on the sweep and asked why, I was told, 'Bad cricket – sweep shot not good. Play straight, good cricket.' So the laws of the game didn't seem to apply. Eventually the likes of Alec Stewart and Neil Fairbrother would just stick their pads down the wicket and play no stroke, a style that was foreign to them. The Indians didn't even appeal, it was bizarre! If you missed a sweep shot and the ball struck your pad a foot outside the line of off stump everyone appealed. It was a nightmare. Kumble in particular troubled us with his extra bounce, but that tour convinced me of the need to have neutral umpires. We were outplayed, though.

That tour wasn't frustrating just for me. Several of our guys didn't get the breaks and it told against them in the future. Paul Jarvis bowled his heart out, and he came back with a lot of credit, but he never played another Test for England. He got in for the first two one-day internationals against the Australians, but didn't make the First Test and faded away. I thought he was very unlucky. Chris Lewis bowled the quickest spell of the tour at Colombo in the Sri Lanka Test, taking the new ball ahead of Devon Malcolm, and yet England haven't used him properly in his time in the side. He shouldn't be viewed as a stock bowler in the medium-fast mould of Angus Fraser; he should be thrown the new ball, told he's going to operate in six-over bursts and bowl quick. Bowling is hard work and I don't think Chris has seen himself as a fast bowler: he is too attuned to 20 overs a day, so he paces himself. In doing that, he has let the management believe he isn't really giving it his all, and I don't believe that's fair to him. He needed his ego to be boosted, to be told he's a top player. I think Chris felt a bit of an outcast and that he wasn't with a group of mates when he played for England around that period, but he's such a talented cricketer that we were in danger of wasting his talents. Phil Tufnell is another misunderstood cricketer. Because he cares so much about doing well for England, he gets carried away, but that aggression, if it is channelled in the right way, is good for him and the team. I think he has been the most talented slow left-arm bowler in the country for some years now: he has the variations, the loop, the flight and he turns it just enough. Perhaps it's been a combination of poor man-management and Tuffers' own defects that has contributed to his spell in the wilderness, but he should have played more times for England.

I suppose David Gower's non-selection for that 1993 tour summed up the English attitude to individuals. There was a huge fuss from his supporters, and Graham Gooch was pilloried for picking Mike Gatting ahead of David. Well I thought Gooch was right to go for Gatting, even though he had a disappointing tour. To me the basis on which a batsman gets picked for England is that he performs in county cricket. A top batter ought to be churning out the runs if he's committed and focused and there was a question mark there against Gower. Gatting was still the best batsman in county cricket, a record far superior to that of Gower. David hadn't done that much in the last few seasons in county cricket, even though he had performed against the Pakistanis in 1992 in the Tests, but you can't keep other batsmen out who have staked a claim with consistent runs. It's different for a fast bowler, because of the heavy workload, and in that case you go for the guy you believe will get the best players out and will keep running in for you in the Tests.

I didn't buy all this garbage about Graham Gooch being the Roundhead to David Gower's Cavalier. As a batsman myself, I've seen Gooch play with so much flair for so many years, dancing down the pitch to smash the spinners through extra cover, getting after them with the slog/sweep over mid-wicket. When I watched him bat in the one-day international against Pakistan at Old Trafford in 1992, I was amazed when he was bowled by Aamir Sohail, giving himself room to play on the off-side. This was after he had swept Aamir for a couple of twos and he was really motoring. I couldn't believe Goochy changed his game plan after milking the bowler with the sweep. I bided my time till he was relaxed after his dismissal and then asked him why he didn't just carry on sweeping Sohail. He said: 'I could only get two for that, I wanted to hit him for four!' More Cavalier than Roundhead, I think. Goochy was a deceptive bloke with a great, dry sense of humour, despite that solemn demeanour. I had total respect for him as player and captain and for the way he treated me. I agreed with his attitude to full commitment and intensive training and I relished the way he encouraged me to play my own way. Mickey Stewart's successor as coach, Keith Fletcher, was just as supportive. He told me that he liked the fact that I could adapt my game to the state of the match, that I should always follow my instincts and treat playing for England in the same way as with Warwickshire. I appreciate some England players of my period had some problems with the England hierarchy in terms of man-management and attitude to their responsibilities, but I can't speak highly enough of the way I was treated by Gooch, Stewart and Fletcher.

I'm sure I would have had a fairer crack of the whip if Mike Atherton and Ray Illingworth hadn't been in charge of England for the South Africa tour and the World Cup of 1996. During that depressing period, I found myself comparing the support and encouragement I'd had in those two World Cups, and the Atherton/Illingworth combination didn't come out of it very well. Now that's just on a personal level and my gripes would have been a complete irrelevance if we had done ourselves justice in South Africa, then in the World Cup – but we didn't and the hierarchy have to take a fair degree of blame for that. Atherton gave no real indication of having a feel for captaining a side in one-day cricket. He had made no secret in the past that he prefers Test cricket, that the one-dayers aren't as important. As a result, his captaincy lacked drive, purpose and flair. Add to that his passive body language and you're struggling when the team is up against it, when the ball is flying all over the place. I felt he was quite physically and mentally drained by the end of that South African tour, and there was a case for having a different captain for the World Cup.

I was very flattered to be mentioned as the possible captain for the World Cup, but that was never on, because it had been made clear to me that my face didn't fit with the management, but there were other contenders – Alec Stewart, for instance, who has always struck me as a very positive leader, full of ideas and receptive to others thoughts. English cricket is so orthodox in its thinking that no one would take the brave step of suggesting to Atherton that he should stand down for the World Cup, and re-charge his batteries for the cricket in which he excels – Test Matches. It's not as if he would have been picked on merit for the World Cup games after tailing away badly in South Africa. Apart from runs in the one-dayer at Bloemfontein, he had failed in the other internationals and his form hardly picked up in the World Cup. He scored one half-century in six innings in the tournament, and that would have justified him being dropped unless he was captain. So did Mike Atherton waste a place? On his recent one-day record, was he one of our best five batters? Did he not gum up the run flow when he opened the innings, when more progressive sides were flourishing with the new con-cept of the pinch-hitter?

It was Illingworth who proved the biggest problem, though. He was too negative, far too dogmatic and he lacked any aware-ness of how much the game had changed. I kept hearing that he'd watched all of England's home games for the last decade in his capacity as a TV commentator, and had a brilliant cricket brain, but I saw no evidence of this. I had approached Ray the winter before in Australia whilst I was working as a commenta-tor, to see if he was interested in watching a video I had made on Warwickshire's success and premeditating against spin. That might sound arrogant but I had done my homework and England weren't performing as well as their opposition against spin in one day cricket. I had researched the figures and at the time of showing the video to Ray, they stood like this: Englands last 21 one day Internationals going back as far as the India tour of 1993.

England Run Rate against spin – 4.1
Opposition Run Rate against England's Spinners – 4.6

England Spin bowlers average – 42 runs per wicket
Opposition Spin bowlers average – 30 runs per wicket

Those differences are quite substantial and, with a World Cup in the subcontinent a year away, they needed to change it if England were to have success. I eventually managed to show Ray the video, and all he could say was, "I could tell when a player was going to sweep, because I could see him grip the bat tighter. So then I bowled the ball faster". Now any decent player of the reverse sweep or paddle would tell you that it helps when a bowler puts more pace on the ball, because you just have to deflect the ball, using the pace, thus giving you more chance of a boundary.

What could I say! Ray then changed the subject and talked about England selection, justifying to me the omission of Angus Fraser from the original tour party, and the video of spin was discussed no further.

As we slunk out early from the World Cup, we were all aware of the various inquests flying around back home in the media, but I knew the real problem. The management hadn't got the best out of the players they had selected. The players couldn't speak out because their tour contracts wouldn't allow it. There was an urgent need to be cheery and upbeat on that tour, but from the moment he got on the team bus every morning, our Raymond was moaning – about the traffic, the weather, the hotel, the breakfast – it was all so negative. Our team meetings, on both tours, were in general a joke. Neil Smith and I couldn't believe how little we talked about the opposition in our team meetings. We had come from the Edgbaston environment, where things would be thrashed out in detail, where every player had his own personal video to examine specifics in his technique.

Usually, England's meetings on the eve of the game were super-ficial, prefaced by the captain saying, 'Right, shan't keep you very long, lads.' But we ought to have been kept there longer, talking in detail, discussing gameplans, and oppositions' strengths and weaknesses. Not because we were losing, but because it should be a prerequisite at this level. It was exasperat-ing that we talked so little cricket. As Neil Smith said to me, 'The lads won't believe it when we tell them we are far more profes-sional than the England set up.' My mind went back to the first team meeting I had attended under the Atherton/Illingworth colours. When we played a one-dayer against New Zealand in 1994, we never talked about Chris Pringle's slower ball, where Martin Crowe likes to hit the ball, or that Bryan Young likes to play a forcing shot off the back foot on the offside that goes in the air. When I was out in the field, I remember thinking that Darren Gough needed a deep gully and backward point rather than two slips – and sure enough, Young played the ball at catch-able height through the backward point area. We lacked atten-tion to detail. Every side should have detailed videos of the opposition. We got one on Anil Kumble before we played him in the Nat West Final and it was invaluable for those who hadn't faced him before. England didn't seem to think such matters important, almost as if it was a confession of weakness to talk about the opposition.

Of course, it could be concluded that I have an axe to grind. I was only picked for two of the seven one-day internationals in South Africa, but I honestly wouldn't have minded missing out, or being in a losing side, if I felt we had prepared properly. I was so frustrated at the lack of intensity given to gameplans and the laid-back attitude. Not being originally selected for the World Cup was the biggest blow of my career. I was only chosen for the World Cup once the competition had started, to replace Craig White who had picked up a rib injury, and although I only played in the last two games, it was still terrific to be out there, representing my country. I had no thoughts at all about making myself unavailable, not just because of the honour, but also because I so desperately wanted us to go one better than the 1992 World Cup Final. In retrospect, we didn't stand a chance, because other countries had passed us by in their tactics and approach.

I feared the worst for my own prospects before I got out to South Africa just after Christmas. Having returned from Australia to England, I read that Craig White had been summoned from the 'A' tour of Pakistan – where he hadn't fared all that well – to join up with the squad in South Africa. Now Craig and I are good friends, we roomed happily together on that tour and I rate him highly as a cricketer – but I was the one picked in September as stand-by for the South African tour, and to fly out for the one-dayers in January. So here was Craig being slipped in by two selectors – Atherton and Illingworth – after four – those two plus David Graveney and Brian Bolus – had chosen the squad in September. It's well known that Illy rates Craig very highly, but I was baffled to know what had happened in the intervening three months to push me down the pecking order. When I later heard that Phillip DeFreitas had been asked by Illingworth at the end of November if he fancied going to the World Cup, the outlook for me got even bleaker. Daffy was playing out in South Africa for Boland and after a lively game against us, Illy popped the question. Good for Daffy, another cricketer I rate highly, especially in one-day cricket, but our squad seemed to be picking up all sorts of players in December purely on the whim of the manager. I wondered what Bolus and Graveney subsequently thought about the validity of their opinions at the September tour selection meeting.

In my first net, at Port Elizabeth, I had another hint that perhaps I wasn't an automatic choice for the World Cup. Illingworth watched me ease myself gently into my bowling, making sure that I wasn't going to tweak anything after just getting off a long flight from London. He said to me, 'At that pace, you must bowl with the keeper up.' I resisted the temptation to answer, 'Well, actually I'm just getting loose, but it normally depends on the pace of the wicket, and Keith Piper actually stood back in last year's Nat West final. Did you watch that game?'

After drawing the Port Elizabeth Test, we moved on to Cape Town for what we all thought would be the decisive game in the five-match series. Everybody was weighing in with their opinions about the pitch, what side we should play and how we should approach the game. Experts like Ian Botham and Geoffrey Boycott were saying we had to play the wild card, Devon Malcolm, and risk dropping a batsman, to go for broke. I felt at the time that our batting would be a bit thin if we dropped one in favour of another bowler and I looked at the South African line-up, noticing that they were going in with only four front-line bowlers. Criag Matthews was dropped for a batsman – Jacques Kallis – who bowled a bit. They were backing the main bowlers to bowl us out twice and I thought that significant.

We lost the Cape Town Test badly, and Devon Malcolm took the brunt of the management's anger, which I thought was out of order: when you get bowled out for 150 on the first day, you are in trouble, whatever your erratic fast bowler does. Devon got the blame for failing to clean up young Paul Adams when he joined Dave Richardson for a vital last-wicket stand when they weren't all that far ahead. Fair enough, Devon's radar wasn't at its best, but he was rusty after playing hardly any cricket the previous month, and wasn't there a bowler at the other end? As we sat dejectedly in the dressing-room after we lost, Illingworth flipped and told Dev that he had lost us the Test. That was very hard but Atherton made it worse by pointing the finger at Dev in his press conference. Such thoughts should be kept in-house, and in any event, the batters should have shared the responsibility, having been bowled out cheaply twice. Illingworth also had a go at Graham Thorpe after he got himself out in the first innings. Thorpey was undone by a ball that went late across him, and was caught behind. As he sat on the physio's couch, brooding about it, Illy came in and said, 'It was a bit wide, wasn't it, you should have let it go.' Thorpey had only been out five minutes earlier and I could tell he was put out by Illy's comment, so I tried to smooth it over. 'It looked like a good ball to me, I thought it went late off the wicket,' I said. I was trying to be constructive and avoid Illingworth belittling a disappointed player at the wrong time; perhaps Illy put the black spot on me for disagreeing with him?

So we started the one-day internationals after losing the Test series. There were seven games to be played in a hectic period of

12 days and then the World Cup party of 14 would be picked. We started off with a day/night friendly at Newlands against Western Province, which we lost. It wasn't looking good. John Barclay, the assistant tour manager, had said, 'Dermot, we don't talk enough cricket. It would be wrong if you didn't speak up at team meetings, you're a successful county captain and you're entitled to have your say.' I respected John Barclay's honesty and when Illingworth asked to have a chat with myself, the captain and vice-captain before the first one-dayer at Cape Town I was delighted. We fixed the meeting for three o'clock the next afternoon and I wrote a lot of thoughts down, ready for a detailed discussion. I got to Illingworth's room five minutes early. He told me the side for tomorrow and I was in it. He asked if Allan Donald was likely to open the bowling against us; I told him he didn't like the white ball when it was new and preferred operating with it first change. He asked if I thought Richard Snell would open the batting for them as the pinch-hitter; I said I wasn't sure because Dave Richardson had opened in recent one-dayers. The four of us then talked generally for a few minutes but time was slipping by: the coach was due to leave at 3.30 for practice under the lights. I was looking for an intensive discussion about bowling options, where we should have our best fielders, my feeling that Alec Stewart ought to keep wicket and that Phil DeFreitas or Neil Smith should be the pinch-hitters rather than waste them at numbers 9 or 10. Illy then said, 'Right, let's get on the bus' and that was it.

It was the only time I was invited into a closed meeting with the management on that tour. Perhaps Illy was just being political by suggesting it that day, so he could turn round and say, 'We did ask Reeve for his thoughts', but he hadn't really. He and the captain had just skated over the subject. After our practice session under the lights, Atherton said a few words, then launched into DeFreitas, saying, 'That was a dreadful shot you played against Meyrick Pringle the other night. You've played a lot of one-day cricket, you should know better.' I couldn't believe he would be so tactless and insensitive as to single out a player like that in front of the others. DeFreitas is at his best as a batsman by being positive, but we all knew there was a personality conflict between the two of them, dating back to their days together at Lancashire. Daffy said afterwards 'It's started already'.

We lost the Cape Town one-dayer narrowly and if Shaun Pollock hadn't been so inspirational, we would have won it easily. There was no cause for alarm and I said so at the next meeting when we were asked for our views. I pointed out that Dave Richardson likes to drive straight, so we needed mid-on to be straighter, while Jonty Rhodes likes to clip it through mid-wicket, closing the face and scampering quick singles, so we needed to block that shot. I said that we were the better side for 80 per cent of the game and that we were a little rusty. Graham Thorpe had played splendidly in that game, but got out at a bad time when we needed him to nail down the win. I made a point of saying what a top knock he had played and then suggested that he used his feet more to the medium pacers, Kallis and Cronje when the wicket keeper is standing back. When I bowled that was Bob Woolmer's idea to get after me in the last game, because he knew it disconcerted me. I told the squad that if a batsman skips down to my bowling when the wicket keeper is standing back it's very unsettling. You have to make the decision of whether or not to bring the wicket keeper up to the stumps. If you do it puts pressure on the keeper and usually results in more extras. If you don't bring him up to the stumps it's always in your mind that the batsman might advance down the track, and turn a length ball into a half volley.

I continued that with mid off and mid on up, if the ball's in the right spot you can play it over the top and probably get mid off or mid on back. If the ball's not in the right spot, you can just defend it and you'd be surprised at how many captains will still immediately put a fielder on the boundary, giving you more gaps for singles. I also pointed out that Kallis and Cronje bowled lots of slower deliveries to Thorpey and Neil Fairbrother. Thorpey took the advice well, and I felt I expressed my views articulately and constructively enough. I hadn't blundered in, I'd waited till we were all asked if we had any thoughts. Robin Smith came over to me after the meeting, saying it was good to hear my thoughts. And he was impressed with how quickly I picked things up. Atherton and Illingworth appeared to be happy with my contribution, but I couldn't believe how Illingworth ended the meeting. He said, 'Oh yes, you tailenders, you didn't look like you could hit a one, never mind a four. I want you to have some batting practice, work at your batting.' So the meeting had ended on a big negative! Neil Smith was one of those tailenders who didn't have a bat in the nets the day before, because we ran out of time and bowlers. The wicket was excellent on the side of the Newlands square, but I had to ask if I could have a bat and by that time, the enthusiasm had waned. I faced Neil Smith, Graeme Hick, Darren Gough (off a short run, and he was wearing rubbers), and the physio Wayne Morton. After about ten minutes, Hicky shouted, 'Last round!' as he had bowled enough and the wives were waiting back at the hotel. I had to hold in my anger. I really felt for Neil Smith and the others who weren't offered a bat yet criticised by Illingworth in the meeting the next day. We won the next game at Bloemfontein to square the series.

Off to Johannesburg for the third and fourth games over the same weekend and Atherton began the team meeting with, 'I don't want to keep you long. Good win at Bloemfontein, we're back on the winning track. Anyone got anything to say – Dermot?' It was the way that Atherton said 'Dermot?' that stung me a little. He hadn't teed me up beforehand that he was going to call on me, and I thought he sounded a little sarcastic, as if I had said rather too much after the Cape Town defeat. I felt he was having a dig at me, but I recovered to say: 'You've caught me out a bit, Skip, but now you ask me – yes, I think we can learn from the South Africans' mistake at Bloemfontein. They were too expansive in the second half of their innings because of their good start. Too many batsmen went for big shots early in their innings and they ended up getting only 60 in their last ten overs, rather than 80 or 90. They should have milked us more, and gone really big, with wickets in hand in the last five overs.' I still felt we ought to be having precise discussions about our game and the opposition, but clearly Atherton, at that stage of the tour, didn't.

I played the next day at Johannesburg, a game that we lost. I suffered a slight tweak in the groin while chasing a ball in the field, and was worried I might not be fit for selection for the match at Centurion Park the following day. I thought I should inform the chairman that I might be a doubtful starter. When we arrived back at the hotel I asked Ray Illingworth if I could have five minutes with him. He said 'I'm going for a shower and then I'm playing bridge. We'll talk tomorrow'.

I was gobsmacked! I iced the groin and hoped it would be just a twinge that would not prevent me from playing. I informed Michael Atherton the next morning at breakfast that the groin felt sore and I would need a fitness test when we got to the ground. I went through a detailed fitness test and satisfied myself that I was fit enough to get through the day, the groin was no worse than a little pre-season twinge, something you could play with. I told Atherton I was fit and available, and he replied, 'We're playing Craig White today.' That was another big hint that I was going to miss out on the World Cup. I felt I was being marginalised; time was running out for me to impress Atherton and Illingworth, but I was bound to play at Durban, where the ball swings. In the nets at Durban, I bowled well at the captain, beating him several times, with Illingworth looking on. I told them I was fit, but they didn't pick me. I couldn't believe it, I was the only one of the fast bowlers to miss out, in conditions that were absolutely right for swing bowling.

When we were in the field at Durban, I had first-hand experience of Illingworth's knocking attitude to the players. We weren't fielding well, and the last straw came when Phillip DeFreitas dropped a difficult catch, but one that this excellent fielder would usually take. Illingworth stood up in the dressing-room and shouted, 'You f****** stupid w******!' in front of the lads who weren't playing. I'm not saying Illy was the only person to ever swear in the dressing room, of course he wasn't and he's entitled to let off steam and have a blast at a player if he wants to. I just believe it's not the way of getting the best out of your team, in fact it's detrimental. Players in the dressing room who heard the outburst may play the next game or field as sub-stitute if there was an injury. If that player then mis-fielded you could be sure his mind would flash back to the dressing room and he would wonder how much stick he was getting from the chairman. He probably wouldn't want the ball to come to him in the field. The old 'Fear of Failure Syndrome'. Illingworth's outburst was bound to get around the whole team. When we lost at Durban, Atherton stormed into our dressing-room, threw his hat into a corner and shouted, 'Bloody fielding!' So again the finger was being pointed at certain individuals, rather than a cool appraisal of how the fielding could be improved. Later that night, in a bar in Durban, I told Atherton to his face that he needed to talk to his players about their own game, to lift their spirits. I said that communication with the players was poor and that Illingworth was now a laughing stock, that not many in the squad took any notice of him, and laughed behind his back. Atherton seemed to take it well enough, but maybe that was the final nail in my coffin.

So we were 4–1 down in the series, with two to go, and I realised clearly that I must play in the last couple of games; otherwise I was out of the World Cup. I felt that the pitches at both East London and Port Elizabeth were slow enough to suit my type of bowling, so that I might get picked. Dominic Cork and Darren Gough were particularly supportive at that stage, and so was Alec Stewart, who has been a good mate for years. It was nice to have the support of the vice-captain

Clearly Alec's support for me wasn't relevant because when Illingworth read out the 13 players for the East London game, my name wasn't amongst them. I was shattered, and when Atherton started talking about our running between the wickets, I had to bite my tongue. I had felt all along we were terrible in this department, with us not backing up far enough, but I was so choked I couldn't speak. I wanted to, but I would have cracked up if I'd tried. After that team meeting, Alec Stewart was very sympathetic to me, saying that we were going round in circles in team meetings. Neil Fairbrother agreed, saying that we had got the balance of the side wrong all along, that we should have tried to win the series at the start with our best one-day side, then experimented. In short, we were a shambles, lacking in direction and leadership. No wonder the South Africans thrashed us.

Deep down, I knew my fate but I wanted to force it out into the open, to make Atherton face me and tell me what was going on. During our innings at East London, he was on his own in the dressing-room and I asked him what were my chances for a game at Port Elizabeth and for the World Cup. He said, 'I don't think it looks hopeful.' He asked me where I thought I could fit in. I said that one of Peter Martin, Phil DeFreitas, Neil Smith and myself would probably miss out, if they were going to take Jack Russell. I asked if England were likely to play Richard Illingworth and Neil Smith together or would they use Hick as the second spinner. I was clutching at straws. Atherton said he was concerned about my fielding and overall fitness. I pointed out that I had missed just a couple of games last season, that when I arrived in South Africa I had won the fitness test organised by our physio, Wayne Morton, that featured Neil Smith, Neil Fairbrother, Devon Malcolm, Darren Gough and myself. I agreed that I had slightly strained my groin at Johannesburg, but it was only a niggle that had now cleared up. As for my fielding, I said that he was putting me out of position. I hadn't been mid-on or mid-off consistently for almost ten years, that at Warwickshire I did short extra cover or short mid-wicket, and when necessary, slip. I believed I had good hands and added the information that in the 1992 World Cup, I had caught very well at slip. As for batting, I should ideally be the last of the batters, at number seven, and one of six bowlers in the side. He listened patiently to all that, and I left thinking that although I had little, if any, chance, it was good to get a few things off my chest.

When we got to Port Elizabeth, Atherton came to my room and asked my room-mate, Craig White, for some privacy. The conversation was short. I wasn't going to the World Cup, because of my fielding and fitness. I shook his hand, saying, 'Good luck, Mike'. I sat on my bed fuming, then stood in the shower for half an hour, to cool down. Craig White returned and was very understanding. He's a great guy and I wished him well. He knew that Illingworth's regular public support for him was a bit of a millstone around his neck and he had his own fitness problems. Craig had been carrying a hamstring strain for a few games and he nearly pulled out of the Durban game. I overheard our physio tell him, 'If you don't play here, you might miss out on the World Cup.' So Craig played.

Actually, I never saw it as a straight fight between me and

Craig for one place. I would have taken us both, because you can't have too many all-rounders, as we proved in the 1992 World Cup. If one of them fails as a bowler there are always options. I wouldn't have taken Jack Russell, because I think he lacks the power of stroke to do well in one-dayers, on slow wickets. Jack is a brilliant keeper and you couldn't ask for a better team man but for balance in one-dayers I would keep with Alec Stewart. Illingworth kept going on about the left-hander doing well against leg-spinners like Shane Warne and Mushtaq Ahmed, but Jack's forte is in the longer games. His steadfast effort to help Mike Atherton save the Johannesburg Test was a wonderful effort, full of courage and character – but that was an innings to save a match, not win it. Yet I believe Jack was told soon after that he was going to the World Cup, as a reward. Alec Stewart ought to have kept wicket and opened the batting, because if he has a weakness, it is going in and having to face spin immediately. If he's opened the innings and has runs on the board, he's more likely to collect runs in his orthodox manner when a spinner is introduced into the attack.

That night in Port Elizabeth, I went out for a few drinks with Mike Watkinson, Darren Gough and Wayne Morton and ended up on my own, talking with some Afrikaaners, which nearly got me into trouble. I woke up next morning, with all my clothes still on, with a furious hangover. I got more and more annoyed as the day wore on, because I felt I hadn't been given a fair crack of the whip. I'd heard some TV commentators saying, 'Is Dermot Reeve past it?', but they hadn't said that three months earlier when I was playing well for Warwickshire. I was simply a bit rusty in that first one-dayer at Cape Town and I had been given hardly any chance to shake off that rustiness in the next ten days. How do you find form when you don't play? Perhaps I was never going to be picked for the World Cup, and it took too long for it to dawn on me.

At Port Elizabeth, I bumped into Illingworth in the lift and he had to speak to me. 'Bad luck, kid, someone had to miss out,' was all he managed. I thought of giving him a mouthful, but there was no point. From early on, he and Atherton had pushed me sideways. My emotions were blurred, of course, but I remember thinking at the end of that series that it would have been a travesty of justice if we had beaten South Africa. We would only have beaten them because of the talent of our players, rather than any planning, or attention to detail. I felt for Atherton because Illingworth kept chiming in with negative comments in our team meetings. Perhaps that's why Mike tried to keep the discussions short. Mike probably felt there was very little he could do about it. John Barclay and Wayne Morton did their best to be upbeat and positive, and I know John Barclay was desperate for us to talk in more detail on gameplans and tactics.

On the day the South African tour ended, I gave an interview to BBC Radio, admitting my disappointment and saying that I was upset and angry. I thought I spoke reasonably, pointing out the facts, that I had hardly played, that I still felt rusty and that it was difficult for me to stake a claim to the World Cup when I'm not being picked. I agreed it was the lowest point of my career but made a particular point of wishing the lads well, sincerely wishing them to come back with the World Cup. I believe it was a dignified interview in the circumstances, and I could have said a lot more that would have really made people sit up. The tabloids picked up the interview off the radio, turned the quotes around, and the banner headlines were there for us all to read when we flew into Heathrow. The headlines didn't do justice to the tone of the interview but never mind – some England boys were delighted. Over breakfast, some said, 'Well done, Dermot, give Illy more of that, he deserves it.' They wanted him out, and were fed up with his carping.

His back-up coaches weren't that popular either. John Edrich, the batting coach and Peter Lever, who looked after the bowlers, had been with England for the first part of the tour. Most of the lads were upset at the way that Devon Malcolm had been singled out by Lever, who described him as 'a cricketing nonentity'. That was out of order, guaranteed to demoralise a guy like Devon. It was certainly an opinion not shared by the South African batsmen who were very wary of Devon after his sensational bowling at the Oval in '94. I didn't blame Devon for getting back at Illingworth and Lever when he went back home, early in January. He gave a long interview to the *Daily Express*, which was printed over three days and it was faxed to us in the hotel at Durban, making interesting reading. I thought he was right to hit back.

As for Devon's suggestion that there might have been a racial element behind his treatment, I'm not sure. All I can say is that Illy referred to Devon as a 'Nig-nog' in the nets at Port Elizabeth at Christmas. It came after Devon had bowled out of turn. It wasn't directed at Devon, but I heard Illingworth utter the word in exasperation. That may appear a racist comment when set down on paper, but possibly Illingworth didn't realise the significance of what he was saying. He is not a subtle man. A month earlier, at East London, John Edrich was helping to supervise some practice, and there was no sign of Devon. Edrich was heard to say, 'Where's the black boy?' Again, that may well have been Edrich's style of address, without thinking of the deeper ramifications. If so, it was still insensitive. We are all products of our environment and the era in which we played cricket, and when Edrich was an England regular, black players didn't feature in the England set-up. In blurting out the words 'black boy' he may have meant no harm, but it was heard by a couple of the England squad, it did nothing for team morale. That remark confirmed to some players that Illingworth and his lieutenants didn't understand the psyche of modern England cricketers. The game, and the society in which it was played, had moved on from their day.

A few days after we got back from South Africa, Illingworth went on television to defend himself and had a go at me over my mildly critical radio interview. He showed a strange grasp of the facts in the process. He said that I hadn't been fit for a couple of one-day matches, so I rang him up and challenged him about that. I reminded him that I had told him to his face that I was fit for Durban, and that, after a vigorous fitness test at Centurion Park, I was available for that as well. In other words I was fit for all seven of the games, even though I was only picked twice. I suggested he should talk to the press to clear the air about that issue, but he said he was fed up with the press, though he conceded my point.

He must have thought he had got shot of me, but then Craig

White injured his rib and I was flown out to join the World Cup squad. When I first saw Illingworth, I told him I was absolutely delighted to be there, that our difference of opinion was water under the bridge, and that I'd be doing my utmost to help the team. Illy said he didn't like me using the word 'angry', but I felt he would have expected a player with any pride to be angry at missing out on the World Cup. If you don't feel any passion about playing for your country, should you be considered in the first place? Anyway, we patched it up. He didn't say another word to me for the next ten days, even after I got 80-odd in as many balls in a warm-up match. Then, at the last moment, as I walked on the pitch for the game against Pakistan, he patted me on the back and said, 'Good luck, kid.' I mentioned this to Robin Smith who said, 'That's nothing, Dermot. He barely said two words to me on the whole South African tour.'

Robin felt Illy had been unfair to go on the record to the press, saying that he and Alec Stewart had to prove themselves all over again after the South African trip. He believed that batting with the tail in South Africa meant that it was hard to get big scores when you have to play shots as others are getting out at the other end. That's the problem when you're at number six – you need someone to stay there with you, but the lads kept getting rolled over in the lower middle order. It was hard to see how Robin could get hundreds in those circumstances. He had also suggested to Illingworth that a sports psychologist would help some of the England players, let them talk out their tensions and relate to a sympathetic person, but Illingworth was having none of that. It didn't matter that the South Africans used such innovative methods, Illy felt if you were good enough to play for England, you had to sort it out for yourself.

In Robin's opinion, Illingworth had instilled a fear of failure. In the World Cup he felt the batters were all determined to get a score, no matter how long it took, because it was down there in the scorebook and they would be picked again. It didn't seem to matter that those runs weren't coming at a run a ball. Illingworth's negative vibes were making the guys play for themselves, not the team interest. Just because Mike Atherton averages over 40 in one-day internationals doesn't mean he's the ideal opener, because his ratio of runs per ball in his career is slow for this type of cricket. We would talk briefly about getting off to a quick start and making use of the field restrictions in the first 15 overs but I bet our openers let more balls go through to the keeper than any other team. The Sri Lankans were successful in the 1996 World Cup because they were positive throughout. They lost two wickets in their first over against India, but that didn't faze them. They still got to 251 in their 50 overs, playing with great style and courage. This in the semi-final of the World Cup, against the home side, in Calcutta. How would England have approached such early setbacks? In the quarter-final against Sri Lanka, with only two fielders outside the inner ring for the first 15 overs, we managed 35 in the first ten overs.

Our team meeting before that quarter-final match against Sri Lanka showed we hadn't advanced our thinking all that much since South Africa. Sanath Jayasuriya, their opener, was an obvious danger man to us. The left-handed opener had smashed a few attacks early in the tournament and I was looking forward to hearing how our think-tank was going to combat him. Atherton said he wanted Peter Martin to bowl to Jayasuriya with a 6/3 field. Pete looked shocked at the news, and I don't blame him. The six fielders were to be on the offside, with just three patrolling an area where Jayasuriya is so strong – he loves to flick the ball over mid-wicket or mid-on and there was to be no-one on the leg-side boundary. Atherton told Pete he had to bowl straight, because Jayasuriya loved width but this ignored Jayasuriya's knack of hitting straight balls over mid-wicket. Now Pete's a swing bowler, with the ability to bring the ball back into the left-hander for the lbw or to be bowled through the gate: surely he needed his legside to be strengthened?

I spoke up at the meeting: 'Can I just clarify this? You want Pete to have no one back on the legside at all? You want him to give Jayasuriya no room at all? Personally I'd find it hard to bowl with that field.' Pete said, 'I'm worried about that, I thought I'd have a split field.' What disturbed me was Peter Martin was told this on the eve of the quarter-final, when we had been netting at Karachi for days, and no one had spoken about such a ploy. Pete could have had time to work on the idea at left-handers in the nets, but instead it was sprung on him the night before. He would be going to bed worrying about where he'd been told to bowl and what the field was. I really felt for Pete. The captain also said we would be swapping the bowling around in the first 15 or so overs. He clearly believed that was tactically flexible, but it wasn't. I got the impression he feared there would be a lot of stick flying around in those early overs, and that the burden would need to be shared around – but what if someone is bowling well? Do you take him off after a couple of overs because it had been discussed the night before? Wasn't there just a chance that England's bowlers might do well the next day? That suggestion hardly built up the confidence of the bowlers.

Next day it all went predictably wrong. We were too slow at the start of our innings and we finished at least 40 short, with 235. Jayasuriya plundered us for 82 off 44 balls, until I had him stumped during my marathon stint of four overs. We lost with ten overs to spare and we slunk deservedly out of the competition. It was our tenth defeat in succession by a Test-playing country in one-day matches. There were no excuses, we had been caught up and overtaken in this type of cricket by so many other countries. We had been complacent and unimaginative, thinking we could just turn on good performances like a tap.

Raymond Illingworth's contribution in the team meetings had been a little more muted than in South Africa, possibly because it had dawned on him that he wasn't getting through to the players. He did provide us with one comic gem, though. After South Africa had beaten us comfortably at Rawalpindi, Illy made the relevant point at a team meeting that we mustn't let bowlers tie us down with line and length. If the wicket-keeper is back, we have to use our feet and get down to the pitch of the ball, even against the quicker bowlers. He was right to point out that the South Africans had mid-on and mid-off straight, and so they were difficult to beat. All we were getting was scrambled singles to them, there was no chance of getting twos. So we had to use our feet and clear their heads. That was good advice, but surely better off before the match or during the innings. Anyhow he suggested we practice this method the next day at nets.

So we're in the nets at Karachi and Neil Fairbrother is twinkling down the pitch and depositing the ball for six as if it had been a match. It's going well, this new strategy, isn't it? Well no, actually – Illingworth is tearing his hair out, saying, 'What's he doing, the bloody idiot? He'll lose the balls if he hits straight!' In the end, Fairbrother got fed up of Illy's nagging and said, 'That's it, I'm not batting', and walked out of the net. Illy had discovered that we were down to our last batch of balls, and we couldn't afford to lose any of them. So there we were, practising a desirable discipline in our attempts to progress in the World Cup – and we had to stop it because we had run short of cricket balls! And we're supposed to be a professional outfit. We were in hysterics as the manager back-tracked on his suggestion of the night before.

On the flight home, the players agreed among themselves that we were still none the wiser about what was our best one-day side. We had been too complacent. Before the Sri Lanka game, our physio Wayne Morton gave a good, upbeat pep-talk to us. The gist of it was, 'We're better than this lot, lads', but I sat there thinking, 'No we're not. It all depends on the day.' Wayne is an excellent physio and a good motivator, but it was odd that the captain wasn't giving that upbeat message. The Sri Lankans were obviously a top side. When I was in Australia, I'd seen them at first hand. They had limited success there, but you could see how useful they would be on the sub-continent. Batsmen like De Silva and Jayasuriya would be doubly useful because their bowling would be effective on slow wickets. That meant they would have two all-rounders in the first four of the batting order and a keeper opening the batting. I always think there is less pressure on all-rounders or keepers in one-day cricket when they bat, because of the extra chance with their other speciality and so this gives them more freedom when they are at the crease. The Sri Lankans also looked good in the field. Their batsmen would struggle when the wicket had bounce in it, but they were unlikely to come across this surface in the World Cup. They played all their group matches at home and odds of 20/1 before the tournament didn't do them justice. I told my brother to stick some pounds on them and he celebrated the night Ranatunga lifted the trophy. Our think-tank hadn't seemed to have grasped what was needed from us in the World Cup. We ought to have looked at our record against spinners. It's not good in recent years. The opposition spinners turn the ball more than ours, and on those slow pitches in Pakistan, we may face around 30 of the allotted 50 overs against spin. Yet no one seemed to have talked through a strategy of playing the spinners with flair and boldness.

I didn't think that Atherton saw any of this as his area of responsibility. He concentrates very much on his own game and expects others to have their techniques in good shape. He is a terrific Test batsman and as courageous as they come. He is very hard on himself and expects a certain level of intensity from the players. At times I felt Mike's 'hard man' image and visual commitment would go over the top. At fielding practice, he would get very aggressive, snarling and shouting if he, or anyone else, fumbled a pick-up. I felt if he lightened up a little, he might find that the guys would field better, because they too would relax. There were times I was afraid to say, 'Bad luck, well tried!' in the dressing-room in an attempt to keep up morale. It was as though you had to show severe disappointment for a time and Mike certainly did – but at times I wished he had been consoling his team and lifting their spirits for the next day.

His ability to motivate is suspect. He finds it hard to avoid showing disappointment when a catch is dropped. The captain should be the first to shout out, 'Bad luck, never mind!', because the other players take the lead from their skipper at such times. If you show negative body language, you are then motivating by intimidation, there's a fear of failure. To get the best out of a team, you need to be bubbly and chirpy and make them feel it's their efforts that are important.

I had to bite my lip so many times under Atherton and Illingworth. Significantly, after the World Cup, Mike Gatting said on television that Atherton would learn the ropes of captaincy more if he did the Lancashire job. He said, 'It would be good practice.' I believe Gatt is right. I mean no disrespect to Mike Watkinson, who does a fine job at Lancashire, but Atherton needs to learn more about man-management, and how to react quickly out on the field. He is by no means a bad tactician on the field, and it wasn't any captaincy weaknesses on the park that resulted in England's poor performances in South Africa and the World Cup – more the planning behind the scenes and handling of players.

On a personal note, I've no idea how I stand with Mike now! Perhaps I got his back up by speaking too openly at team meetings in South Africa, but I had been asked to do so by the assistant manager, John Barclay and I always tried to sound constructive. I believe Mike and I have got on OK socially, and we seem to have enjoyed a good laugh from time to time.

One thing about Ray Illingworth: he contributed some amusing moments. After we had crashed out of the World Cup, we were driving through Lahore in a team bus and Robin Smith asked Illy if he had ever previously toured Pakistan. Illy didn't realise Robin knew the answer, and launched into a monologue. 'No, I was picked, but made myself unavailable. It wasn't like it is now, no nice hotels. We would have had to stay in places like that' – pointing out of the bus at some shacks on the roadside. 'Anyhow, I had started up a business selling Christmas cards and I could make more money in a week in Scotland than I would playing for England. I mean, you can get someone else to work for you, but they never work as hard as you, do they?' I couldn't believe my ears and couldn't resist saying, 'Actually, I had to cancel a dozen dinners to come out here, and it's cost me money, but I never gave it a second thought. you don't when it's for your country.' Graham Thorpe had to choke back the laughter and we had a big chuckle about it later.

I wouldn't have recounted this anecdote if it wasn't for what I read when I returned to England. Illy had sounded off in the *News of the World* about how money-conscious modern English players were. The gist of his whinge was that current players didn't seem to love the game as much as he did. He had come back and played for Yorkshire at the age of 51 and would have chopped off his little finger to play county cricket! Strange this from a bloke who would rather sell Christmas cards in Scotland than play for his country!

Is Cricket Dying?

At the end of England's tour to South Africa, the boss of their cricket, Dr Ali Bacher, said to me: 'You know, we're not just representing our country, Dermot – we're selling the game worldwide.' I thought that was a great attitude, very much in tune with the modern demands of the entertainment industry. Dr Bacher realised that cricket is now in a fiercely competitive market place, that it must adapt to new ideas and reach out to a base that hasn't really been tapped yet. The same is so true of cricket in England.

We must ensure the game appeals to youngsters in England and break the hold that football has on their affections. County membership in general caters for a clientele that's getting older, that likes the game just as it is, with a few reservations. That's all very well, and I do respect some traditions of English cricket, but not a great deal is being done to sell it to the generation that's coming through. Unless you have dedicated parents, or a club that caters for youngsters, the Bothams of tomorrow will lack positive encouragement. You can't look to their schools to provide that inspiration, unless they're lucky enough to go to fee-paying schools with excellent facilities or get coached by unselfish teachers prepared to give up their spare time.

In Australia, the future for cricket is much brighter because they have worked out the market. Kerry Packer was tremendously important to Australian cricket, even though many diehards didn't think so at the time. He glamorised it with top-class camerawork and extra razzamatazz, so that the punters thought they'd be missing something if they didn't go to the games or watch them at home. Night cricket was a fantastic innovation, it's so exciting to watch or play. The slow motion replays conveyed the drama of the occasion, to see the passion that goes into playing the game at such a high level of intensity. It's not about strawberries and cream when you're playing for your country, it's about a bowler desperate to get you out and the resulting triumph for batsman or bowler makes for great theatre if it can be conveyed to the public. That's what Packer achieved. For me, there'll always be room for the sedate, village green atmosphere of cream teas and genteel behaviour, but that doesn't inspire youngsters to play above themselves. You need passion, a rock 'n' roll atmosphere to get the kids into the ground. Cricket has to compete these days with more sports encroaching on the season. Football seems to start earlier than ever, in mid-August, and the World Cup and European Championships come along every two years. Rugby league is now a summer game and major athletics tournaments – like the Olympics and the World Championships – are staged during an English summer. I can't imagine that many youngsters turning on the television in 1996 were turned on by England's cricketers. We need colour, noise and excitement to grab their attention and get them hooked on this great game. Hopefully, they'll then become as addicted to cricket as I was when I started at school, and graduate to loving the longer game – Test cricket.

In English professional cricket, the crowds sit there for six or seven hours and go quietly off in the early evening, without being entertained all that much. That is often the fault of the players or the regulations by which we have to play, so why not have a competition whose sole aim is to entertain? We could have a 20 or 25 overs a side competition in midsummer, when the light is still good in mid-evening, and the game wouldn't need to start until around five o'clock. The bowlers would be limited to four or five overs and the object of the exercise would be entertainment. Risks would be taken, the fielding would be sharp and, because the overs are few, you would surely get a lot of close finishes. There is nothing as tedious as a one-day game over 60 overs that is cut and dried fairly early or goes into a second day.

With these shorter games, admission would be very cheap and you could get a live band in to jazz it up. Every time a wicket falls, let's have some loud music celebrating the fact, youngsters love all that. You could turn up at the ground after work or school and it would all be over by about eight o'clock. The atmosphere often takes a long time to warm up in one-day games – I prefer to watch it on TV for that reason – so let's warm it up right away. So many people think that cricket is boring, so if we take steps to broaden its appeal, we are halfway to getting kids interested. For too many, cricket is a very long game and football and rugby attract them for their brevity. If we shorten the game and make it a spectacle, with live counter-attractions, you've got a chance with the next generation.

To stage that midsummer competition, the amount of championship cricket would have to be reduced. A total of 17 county matches, plus three other one-day competitions, means you have tired players, unable to perform consistently with the type of verve and commitment you need to sell the game. The championship should consist of only 14 four-day games per county, which would mean you would miss out on playing three counties per year but that's less important than the rest players need.

In a championship match, we are supposed to bowl just a handful of overs less than in a five-day Test, with the rate in a county game set at 18½ an hour, compared to 15 an hour in Tests. At times I'm bored stiff watching Test cricket, when nothing seems to be happening and the players get away with 12 overs an hour. If I'm bored, and I'm in the profession, what about the uncommitted? They should be made to bowl the same amount in Tests as in championship cricket, but the county quota should be reduced to 17 an hour. Before this season you had county players having to rush around in championship games, in order to bowl the required 18½ overs per hour are unable to perform to their full potential as a result. I know that counties want their members to be happy, but I'm sure that the members would rather see top quality cricket. It makes professional sense to bowl the seamers on a pitch that favours them, rather than the spinner, and that means you're out on the field till after 7, because the seamers take longer to bowl their overs. Yet you see people leave the ground at six o'clock because they've got better things to do. So we end up performing for a public that's not even there any more.

A friend of mine attended the 1993 Nat West Final that we won in breathless fashion in semi-darkness, and was amazed to hear a chap say to his wife with four overs to go, 'Come on, dear, it's time we left.' He had the MCC tie on, clearly a lover of cricket, and he and his wife had sat there all day with their hamper and wine – but the game had gone on too late for them because the over rate had been understandably slow. One of the great finishes in one-day history and they walk out! That's the kind of traditionalist thinking that we are up against in English cricket. It's time the game was marketed more vigorously to give alternative forms of cricketing entertainment to those who would see it in a different way to that couple.

I know it's a constant gripe among English professionals, but we do play too much. We need a more balanced programme that allows more time for rest, with more qualified people to treat us. It's ridiculous that each county has just one physiotherapist who ends up having to treat too many players within half an hour of the game starting. You tend to go to the physio when you're injured, but what about getting advice on how to avoid injuries? In American football, the players have to come in on a rest day to get rub-downs to stop potential injuries from occurring, and it's the same in Australian rules football – but we're years behind. Every county should have a rubber, as well as physio – someone whose job is to work on the vulnerable areas, to massage deeply to get rid of general stiffness and potential injuries. I spend around £1,000 a summer getting that kind of specialised treatment at health centres away from Edgbaston, because the club's physio just doesn't have the time to give me the sort of attention I need. It's like giving your car a general service. The public don't realise the level of fitness that's needed, and bowlers will tell you that batsmen don't either. They'll say, 'Come and have a bowl at me in the nets' without realising how stiff and tired you are. Some players give up the game simply because they can't run up and bowl any more, nothing to do with age.

Experience does help get you through the physical demands. You tend to rely on adrenalin. I'll hobble in to the ground in the morning, convinced I won't be able to bowl, put my boots on and just hope for the best. But once you get the blood going, it feels like a different body, and if someone hits you for four, that really pumps you up. But it isn't a great idea just to rely on adrenalin to get you through as a bowler. I believe that there are too many county clubs who are over-keen to push cortisone into you, to disguise the injury. Over the years, such injections take their toll: why not find out why there's an inflammation in the first place?

There isn't a professional cricketer who doesn't worry about injuries and their effect on his career. Batsmen don't realise what a bowler has to go through in a season. One year, I couldn't bowl much because of injury and played as a batsman. It was like a holiday compared to being an all-rounder, and that experience only increased my admiration for the sheer will and strength of Ian Botham, who had to bowl so many overs for so many years. The strain on a fast bowler is incredible. I was out in Australia for the 1994/5 Ashes series and I marvelled at the way Craig McDermott kept running in. It was calculated that during the Adelaide Test, McDermott had run more than a half-marathon over five days, in terms of approaching the wicket, following through and returning to his bowling mark – and that ignores the physical strain of actually bowling the thing. McDermott had two days off after Adelaide and then it was off to Perth for the next Test. He injured his back there in the nets, as he hunched over in his stance having a bat. I'm not surprised, that was surely the after effects of Adelaide. He still bowled at Perth, taking six wickets in the second innings. In effect, he was being asked to run a second half-marathon within a couple of days. Just how advisable was that?

The science of getting fit for cricket and then maintaining that fitness is in its infancy in England. That's why I was so disappointed that Warwickshire wouldn't go with my suggestion to pay our players a couple of hundred pounds if they excelled in a fitness assessment at the start of pre-season. Ideally they could come in around mid-January for training and lectures on nutrition, the science of the body, the prevention of injuries – as well as practice in the indoor nets – they would be better cricketers because they'd be fitter. Then in April they could work hard on their technique, rather than playing catch-up on their fitness. The players need an incentive to get fit during the winter, because if they're not getting paid for it, they'll concentrate on their job, to pay the mortgage. I was happy for them to be fined if they weren't fit enough, provided the club gave them a financial carrot, but they wouldn't agree. The club seemed to feel that it was the players' own responsibility, but they just didn't understand the thinking of the players. Those still in England in the winter are expected to be on call to do the public relations tasks, going around local cricket clubs, handing over cheques, etc etc – all for nothing, for the honour of representing Warwickshire. But those appearances don't pay the bills. In 1994, the Warwickshire players created history by winning three domestic trophies, and being second in the fourth – yet an Aston Villa footballer earns more in a week than we picked up for our bonus that season.

The club's attitude, in common with other counties, is 'If you don't like it, someone else will take your place.' They have you over a barrel because of the benefit system. It's semi-feudal and archaic and it allows the county club to dictate a good deal of your career. It was because I was hoping eventually for a benefit that I bit the bullet over Brian Lara in 1994. The best batsman in the world was not setting the right example to the rest of the team, the captain who wished to have him disciplined was not getting enough support from the management – and I knew I was the expendable one, not Lara. I thought of my daughter out in Perth, aware that a successful benefit would allow me to see her more often, and then I picked up the phone and offered the olive branch to Lara. If it hadn't been for the prospect of a benefit – which was later confirmed for 1996 – I would have refused and gone public. The promise of a benefit ties you to a club, and they don't have to pay you your market value. Some shrewd cricketers are realising that now, and are leaving for more money and banking on a benefit eventually with their second county. I don't blame them. If a player backs his own ability, he should just sign a one-year contract because he's then in a stronger bargaining position when he's a free agent. The clubs prefer a two-year deal, wait till there's a year to go, then add on another year. They don't like long-term contracts, because they then doubt a player's commitment. It's becoming a game within itself. There's more talk now among players about salaries than I can remember. The grapevine tells you how much can be made elsewhere, so that when a player kicks up a fuss about money, the club that doesn't want to lose him usually finds some extra cash from somewhere, unless of course he's waiting for a benefit – in which case nine times out of ten he will stay put and not kick up a fuss.

I honestly feel players should be allowed to move freely between counties without ever being contested. At the moment, if a player's existing club offers him a contract when his previous one has ended, that player would be put on list one and considered a contested player if he moved. A county can only sign two List One players in five years. I can only deduce that the reason is that it prevents a wealthy county from buying all the best players. If they could, then these players would be earning their market value and probably wouldn't need a benefit year.

You can have a situation at the moment where a talented youngster cannot get into his county first team and plays all year in the second eleven. If he could move to a new county and play first-class cricket immediately he may wish to, but if his present county don't want him to leave, he becomes a List One player. It could be that the county willing to offer the youngster terms has already used up two List One signings or that they may not wish to use one up on a second eleven player. So the player would remain at his present county to play second eleven cricket and perhaps be frustrated by the system. If that isn't restraint of trade, what is?

The whole category of Lists One and Two should be abolished immediately and counties made to work harder to keep players happy and loyal. We must also attempt to get talented young sportsmen aspiring to play cricket, rather than football, and if wages weren't so far apart that would help.

Good luck to the younger players who are now flexing their muscles and manage to move on. I think of David Smith, who was sacked by Warwickshire after nine years as a capped player and didn't get a benefit. The club holds all the aces in those circumstances. They know that young players won't go out on strike over money because they'll just get dumped by the clubs, so it's up to the star players to flex their muscles and ensure all the English players are treated with more respect. I also believe that overseas stars earn too much from the English game. Some get touted around for as much as £100,000 a season by their agents and I know that certain counties have been willing to accommodate such demands. I think that's extortionate, when you consider how little some do for the club, apart from on the field, and that's only if they are fully committed. They're not all like Allan Donald. I'm all for having one overseas player on a county's books, but even the best of them shouldn't be paid more than £50,000 a season. That's more than enough for about five months' work – they are rarely there for the pre-season work in the cold of early April.

English cricket is stuck in an administrative time warp. How many innovations have come from England, rather than Australia and South Africa? I can think of one-day cricket, back in 1963, but it was Australia who staged the first one-day international back in 1971. That was because a Test match in the Ashes series had been washed out and the Aussie administrators were quick to see that a one-day game would bring in some money and entertain the public who had been frustrated at missing out on the Test match. Would our administrators have reacted so swiftly, or would they have set up a committee to investigate the feasibility of such a game in the future? Innovations like night cricket, the white ball, names on shirts, coloured clothing, logos on the outfield, electronic scoreboards and TV replays have all come out of Australia and South Africa. We ought to play more one-day internationals in England, and in coloured clothing because that would attract youngsters and bring more money into the game for the players, but the traditionalists at Lord's mutter about the sanctity of Test cricket. Of course, it's the best form of cricket, but many people can't afford to give much time and attention to such a long form of cricket. It's fine for senior citizens or those with a lot of leisure time and patience, but we have to look at ways of spreading interest in cricket. The Test and County Cricket Board need to understand that the customer base for Test cricket and the four-day game is getting older, and the vacuum needs to be acknowledged and filled.

Coaching is also still very traditional in English professional cricket. The MCC Coaching Book is too venerated, in my opinion. In Australia, they talk about getting a good technical base, but they concentrate on scoring runs, not just staying in. Rod Marsh, who runs their Academy, tells the players that they simply must look to score at four an over minimum, whereas we coach lads to hit the bad ball and defend the good ones. Sometimes you just have to take risks, though. The MCC manual says that if the ball is pitched outside the off-stump, you hit it through the offside – but what if all the fielders are on the offside? Why not take a middle and off guard and smack it through the deserted legside area? Is there anything wrong with premeditating a shot against the spinner, or is the object of the exercise to be technically correct, not to get out and hope for some loose deliveries? Coaching in England isn't innovative enough: there's a feeling that you've got to look the part. Yet Steve Waugh doesn't care what he looks like and he has a fantastic record at the highest level. Allan Border stands out more in my mind than any other player for effectiveness rather than elegance. Everyone would like to bat like Mark Waugh, but it's just not possible. Strength of mind is vital. That's why Ian Botham was so great, he tried everything with the ball, he wanted to entertain and always approached the task with boldness, despite the conformists huffing and puffing.

Now that I've finished playing, I would love to make a video about how to play the modern game. It would be an alternative to the MCC manual and I'll hammer home the need for enjoyment, for effectiveness, working out your plus points, going for results not style. And the reverse sweep would be in the video. I'm glad to say that a short video I compiled on playing spinners has been shown around some Birmingham schools by Andy

Moles, when he spent a winter spreading the gospel of cricket. Andy told me that the reverse sweep seemed very popular. Gordon Lord, one of the regional coaches for the National Cricket Association, also asked to see that video, so perhaps at last the old conservative notions are being challenged. Not before time.

It seems to me that English cricketers need to be more positive in their attitude. Perhaps we are short of heroes at the moment. In Australia and South Africa, the youngsters look up to the likes of Warne, Slater, Rhodes and Donald because they project themselves impressively and the game is marketed so well. In England, we are crying out for new heroes to replace people such as Botham and Gower. In Australia, their best young players are taught how to deal with the media early on, and that can help open commercial avenues for the players, as well as selling the game. I remember hearing a radio interview with Justin Langer about his pleasure at being picked to go to the West Indies with the senior Australian squad. Langer was just a young player, who would probably have been earmarked as a reserve batsman unless something went wrong with injuries or form with the established choices, but he wasn't bothered about that. He said, 'I'm really looking forward to it, I'm sure I'll do well.' He wasn't being bombastic, it was said in a pleasant, matter-of-fact tone that underlined his quiet confidence. In similar circumstances, a young English player would mutter a platitude like, 'They're a very good side, but we'll go out there to do our best and hopefully we'll do well.'

Our players are too worried about how they are perceived by fellow professionals, that they might be accused of being too full of themselves if they spoke positively and said what was really on their mind. I'm sure that's one of the many reasons why some in the English game have never taken to me, because I'm a positive guy who makes no apologies for it. Warwickshire as a side have become unpopular on the circuit because we are confident and successful, as well as being led by a captain who doesn't care about being popular, so there's been a backlash against us. That doesn't bother me or the players, as long as we keep annoying people by winning trophies. If Dominic Cork was in our side we would be hated even more, because many see Dominic as obnoxiously full of himself and irritating. I hope he takes that as a compliment: it means people take notice of him, because he is a success. He feels good about his game, he has that spark of self-confidence that helps your game when you're up against tough opponents. I'm not a great believer in this false modesty that seems so typically English. I know that my job is fairly irrelevant, chasing a small red ball around the field. I don't help save lives, but I do help bring pleasure to some people by leading ten other guys to success. So if I'm asked what I do by others who don't know me, I'll tell them that I played cricket, and captained Warwickshire. Why be shy about it?

Professional cricket has always been hard, I'm sure, but I believe the attitudes out in the middle are tougher now than when I started in 1983, and that's not a bad thing. At least that is closer to the kind of atmosphere you get in a Test Match, so that a young player is less likely to freeze when he plays for his country. I'm quite happy to look for a verbal confrontation on the field if my mind isn't sharp enough that day. I find that igniting my adrenalin gets my legs moving more freely and helps me see the ball better. Paul Allott used to hand out some major verbals when he was bowling for Lancashire because that helped him get through any pain. I have seen him get a wicket through abusing my team-mate Alan Green, who stood there for 15 seconds before he walked. Afterwards he said that he hadn't hit the ball, but that Allott went on about it so much that he thought the bowler had to be right. That wasn't cheating by the bowler just competitiveness to the extreme, and it happens a fair amount. Bowlers appeal when the ball has gone down the leg-side and they know the batter hasn't touched it. They hope the umpire has heard a sound, that's all. I don't blame the batsman for thinking, 'I've hit that, but they've been trying to cheat me, so I'll do them'; but if I know he's nicked it, and he knows I know, he'll get some verbals. Then again, if I get verbals for not walking, I'll turn around and say, 'Oh you walk do you?' or 'I'm so very sorry' in a sarcastic tone.

There are times when you nick it and no one appeals and other times when you've hit the ground or your pad and been given out. I've stood beside Keith Piper at slip and been convinced there was a nick, but he's said, 'He got nowhere near it.' There are swings and roundabouts and a fine line between supporting the bowler and cheating. It's cheating when the ball hasn't carried and you appeal for the catch, but if you're not sure that's simply giving your bowler the support he deserves. You're out when the umpire says so, not the opposition. I've seen guys in Australia who have stood their ground after hitting the ball to cover, hoping to get away with a bump'ball decision. That's cheating.

Mind you, players are getting more sophisticated about bluffing the umpire. Roger Twose gave me a masterclass one day after he had made a fuss about being given out caught behind in a 2nd XI match. He didn't look at the umpire, stood hand on hip, disgusted at the wicket-keeper's appeal, marked out his guard again at the crease, finally looked up at the umpire's raised finger, and looked astonished that he was given out. He shook his head as he stalked back to the pavilion and we all sympathised when he stomped into the dressing-room. 'Bad luck, Roger – you didn't hit that then,' I said and he answered, 'Oh yes I did – I used to do acting at school. I did a good Julius Caesar.' He then went through the whole performance for us, after I told him I could never get away with that because I always look guilty. He went on and on for ages, about looking scathingly at the slips and the keeper, ignoring the umpire, and all that rigmarole. Eventually, I had to tell him we were pulling his leg, that I'd done the same thing – but it was an interesting insight into the way that some young players are now approaching the game. Doing the umpire no favours is the norm these days.

It's not easy for modern umpires. There's more pressure on them, but I do think the standard has improved since I started. All I look for in a good umpire is consistency. Dickie Bird is not the kind of umpire you want at your end when you're bowling, because his natural reaction seems to be 'not out', but at least he's the same when you're batting, as I happily discovered when Anul Kumble had me plumb lbw and Dickie let me off in the 1995 Nat West final. Good umpires like John Holder, David Shepherd and the Palmer brothers don't chop and change their views on what constitutes a dismissal, and that gives confidence to the players. There are some daft rules, though. The one about one bouncer per over protects batsmen unduly. If he has a weakness against the short ball, he ought to be peppered with it, it's part of the fast bowler's tactical armoury. If the umpire is strong enough, and understands the nature of the individual contest, he will judge it accordingly and the captains wouldn't complain if he told the fast bowler to ease up. Just because a number eleven batsman is grafting away, that doesn't mean we have to be nice to him and pitch the ball up. The bowler has to get him out before too many runs are scored, but this rule protects the tailender. You're trying to get him out, rather than hit him, but the sentimentalists say, 'Oh, it looks awful to see a tail-ender getting bouncers' – but the professionals have to get results. We are the ones who have to contend with the huge gap between aesthetics and reality.

Another rule that does bowlers no favours is the one-day rule about wides and no-balls. Now I think it's right that a beamer above waist height is called a no-ball, but what if it's a slow full toss? That's not intimidatory, and as Franklyn Stephenson used to prove with his slower ball, it is a subtle ploy that surprised batsmen. Calling that a no-ball is robbing a bowler of a skilful tactic and just making life easier for the umpires. The readiness to call wides in one-day games is a problem, too; there seems little margin for error, and interpretation seems to vary from umpire to umpire. So you end up bowling more overs because of this inclination to call wides, yet the game's rulers keep banging on about the slow over rates. It seems to me that there are too many former batsmen on the committees at Lord's who formulate the laws. Not many favours seem to be done for bowlers.

I think cricket in England from a supporter's point of view is different from other countries because they don't mind all that much if the national side loses. Of course, ignominious performances like that in the '96 World Cup lead to knee-jerk reactions in the media and the usual rash of phone-ins calling for the resignation of everybody, but that only happens when the England team has played particularly poorly. Admittedly, such events aren't as rare as they used to be! I believe that the typical

English cricket fan isn't desperate for us to win at all costs and is happy if there has been attractive cricket to watch, from whatever side. That's fine if you are a genuine cricket lover, who admires individual skill and doesn't expect your national side to win most of its games. It's not an attitude that's all that common in other countries. Effigies of unsuccessful captains get burned in India and Pakistan, their personal lives are made a misery, and politicians get involved, demanding public debates. In South Africa and Australia, you get sacked from the job, because their culture is all about winning. The quality of the opposition is not a matter to dwell on, you are expected to beat them. That's why they have an enlightened attitude to their top players. They don't believe in over-working them, by making them play in low-key games for their State side. Their national boards of control have the power to pull a player out of any game to ensure he is fresh for the time when he represents his country.

That's not the case in England, and it should be. Raymond Illingworth was quite right to lobby for this, and it was shortsighted to deny him the wisdom of his argument. Look at the experience of Robin Smith in the 1995 season. His heroic batting in the Edgbaston Test, when he was battered around the body by the West Indian fast bowlers, was a terrific display of guts. His reward? He had to drive down to Southampton to play for Hampshire in a Sunday League game because the Test had ended on the Saturday and his county said he had to play. Robin was exhausted by that working-over at Edgbaston and the delayed reaction hit him over the next few days as he answered his county's call. Then his cheekbone was fractured in the next Test at Old Trafford and that's his season over and he becomes a borderline case for the tour to South Africa. Robin finally made that trip, but he would have probably been in a better shape to face the West Indian fast bowlers at Old Trafford if he hadn't had to play straight away for Hampshire. He needed rest, and time for the psychological scars to heal. If he had been contracted to England, rather than Hampshire, Ray Illingworth would have ensured he was in a proper frame of mind and his body refreshed before he next played for England.

So England supporters must realise that our national side will only succeed despite the system rather than because of it. I don't think the professional game is dying in England. Greater media exposure and more money for the players have helped, but the interests of the counties and the need to cater for the member-ships at those counties mean the progress of professional cricket as a major spectator sport is being checked. The game needs to be more vibrant, the competitions should be streamlined, and the players must be faced with a programme that galvanises them sufficiently to make the paying customer want to see the entertainment in the flesh. Traditions in cricket are all very well, but that doesn't mean some of our administrators have to live in the past.

A Sad Farewell

I played my last game for Warwickshire on Monday, June 17 at Headingley, where we lost to Yorkshire by ten wickets. Of course, I didn't know that at the time, but the hip injury which had bothered me for some time was to prove more serious than I realised. I had been limping around like an old man for a week or two and I was embarrassed when I saw my discomfort in the field whenever I watched us on television. In the end, the decision was made for me a month later, that I had to retire on medical grounds: there was a lot of arthritis in the hip joint. The hip would never be normal and if I tried to play any more continuous cricket, the quality of my life in the future would be a problem. I was quite philosophical after my initial feelings of shock and disappointment. I was aware that many professional cricketers have their careers ended prematurely on the say-so of someone else – the captain or members of the cricket committee – and that they often feel frustrated and unfairly treated. For me, there could be no complaints, the matter was out of anyone's hands. I had exceeded my expectations as a professional cricketer and had a great deal of fun along the way. The captaincy of Warwickshire had helped me stretch myself as a person as well as a leader, but now I had to think positively about other matters. It was more important to ensure that I could be fit enough to walk around a golf course without much pain for the next 20 years, and to be able to kick a football with my future offspring. My life now had to take another course.

So there was no fairy tale ending to my final season.

Warwickshire didn't consolidate on its success of recent years and the captain didn't go out in a blaze of glory. Yet we had no divine right to keep winning trophies, even though we were very confident at the start of the 1996 season. We'd enjoyed an excellent pre-season tour in South Africa and I was particularly pleased with my batting. I was hitting the ball better than at any stage in my career and my good form with the bat carried through to the start of the season, when I scored a big hundred against Sussex and we won that championship match easily. It all looked set up for us, with Shaun Pollock settling in very well as the replacement for Allan Donald. Yet it all slid away. It was galling to myself and Phil Neale, because we were determined to avoid a repeat of the complacency at the start of the '95 season, which took some time to eradicate and cost us the Sunday League. I can't put my finger on the main reason why we didn't repeat our triumphs in the '96 season. Although I just had the occasional feeling that some of the players weren't giving me their total concentration in team talks. Now it's understandable that players are tempted to switch off when they hear the same old things from the captain in team meetings and I think it became a bit of a yawn at times to some of the players as I continued to drum home the familiar points that had helped us to our high status. I do believe that true motivation must come from within that player, but it's also up to the captain to ignite that spark. So perhaps I wasn't as inspirational in motivation as I should have been.

You only need to be a little off-centre in your preparation and approach to start missing out and that's what happened to Warwickshire. Forget all the injuries – we had surmounted those handsomely in the '95 season. We began to lose out in close finishes, when we would normally get through with a combination of determination, boldness and high morale. It was a blow to lose the Benson and Hedges Cup semi-final at Northampton, when we had gone a long way to winning the game.

Northants won through in the manner of Warwickshire, pulling their innings round after a bad start, then fielding brilliantly and bowling to a plan. Opposition sides were more switched on to our strengths and many had caught us up in terms of attention to detail. No longer were there gaps for the paddle and reverse sweep when we faced spinners and we had to work harder for runs. I was impressed by the overall standard of fielding and most counties were approaching their cricket in a positive manner. Warwickshire didn't have the copyright on success and it was up to us to keep trying innovations. We were there to be shot at and we were victims of the Manchester United syndrome: opposition teams were raising their game when we played them. That's the way it should be, and if we had won the 1996 championship, that would have been a great achievement, because of the fresh challenges to us from many revived sides. But it wasn't to be and there's no point in moaning about it.

I suppose my preoccupation with my injured hip didn't help my captaincy on the field. It's hard to be upbeat when you're carrying your right leg and can't follow through on delivering the ball. I'm sure my body language on the field during that last month of my career wasn't very dynamic. I had been mulling over extending my career when my contract ran out at the end of the '96 season and I had been optimistic about having perhaps another two years left. But the hip had bothered me since a warm-up game at Karachi during the World Cup. I thought it was just a strain in the groin or lower back and put it down to stiffness in the morning: anyway, you bite the bullet when you're hoping to play for your country in the World Cup. When I came home, I had an X-ray, and although there was some abnormality in the hip, I was advised to keep playing and hope it would go away. It didn't, though. I would wake up with an ache on my right hip, as if someone had put an ice pack on it. In my final game, against Yorkshire, I set off to walk from slip to the other end and I had a curious sensation in my hip. It was locking as I walked, and I had to drag it along. I was worried now. I had a scan, then saw a doctor in Cambridge who had treated Angus Fraser and Dean Headley for hip problems. I had an injection into the hip joint in the hope of getting me through the season, but still was unable to bowl or sprint. Finally, we accepted an arthroscopy would be the next step, but that would put me out for the season. After the operation, Dr Villas informed me there had been a lot of soft tissue damage in the joint, which he had hopefully cleared up, but the arthritis was a major worry. He recommended I give up for good.

The following day I dealt with the media enquiries about my retirement and met up with Dennis Amiss and Mike Smith at Edgbaston to talk through the implications. They told me that I was still club captain, and therefore would still have a say in team selection. They wanted me to stay close to the side, which was nice of them. I made it clear that my replacement as captain, Tim Munton, should now be the one that led team meetings and ran the show. I would offer my thoughts if pressed, but Tim was now in control and the transition had to be handled smoothly and quickly. It was good of Dennis and Mike to insist I could still make a contribution when my morale was rather low, but there were still conflicting emotions as I cleaned out my locker that day in the dressing-room and put everything into a black bin-bag. Things I had accumulated over nine seasons at Edgbaston were shoved into that bag, but it would be some time before I'd be able to sit down and wade through it all.

But it wasn't all anti-climax and personal trauma in my final season. There were still plenty of laughs to be had – sometimes at the expense of other players. When we played Leicestershire at Edgbaston, I enjoyed jousting with their players out in the middle as we blocked it out for the draw. Leicestershire had made a good start to the season and they were full of themselves when they played us. They are one of the most vocal sides – a match for Warwickshire in that department, and we're not exactly a sullen lot – and as they scented victory, they were doing a lot of yapping. Alan Mullally bowled superbly, putting in one spell that was as good as anything I had come across in all my years of county cricket – and didn't he know it. As I tried to bat out for a draw, he kept chipping away at me and my partner Keith Piper, so I answered back: 'You've been getting a few wickets then, Alan – the mouth's coming along with it.' Then their wicket-keeper, Paul Nixon started to shout, 'Come on Larashire! Come on Donaldshire! Let's get them out, they've only ever had one player!' Mullally got more and more frustrated and said to me, 'You're hopeless, you blokes – you won't win anything this year.' Now I hadn't forgotten how Mullally had given away that game to Middlesex at Uxbridge last September, so I said, 'If that's the case, Al, we'll have to re-name ourselves Leicestershire.' That brought a high-five from my delighted batting partner, Keith Piper and extra satisfaction when we held out for a draw. Those words have come back to haunt me, but I am sincerely happy for James Whittaker and Leicester for their success this year. It was particularly nice to hear James say that they had learnt a lot from Warwickshire.

So, despite struggling physically out on the field, I hadn't lost my ability to get under the skin of some opposition players. I was still getting the blame for certain flashpoints, though, which were none of my doing. Take the game at Northampton in June. On the first day of that championship match, the press box was full of most of the luminaries in the cricket press. Ours was the most attractive championship game on offer, and with England places there for the taking between the first and second Tests, there were a few players keen to make an impression. The first day's play was great value, with Northants batting well early on, then we hit back after tea and bowled them out. I managed to pick up five wickets, but that all seemed an irrelevance judging by the following morning's papers. Once again, I had been allegedly involved in an ugly spat on the field with David Capel, as I stuck up for Keith Piper. We had the sight of players squaring up to each other, the umpires having to mediate and Reeve right in the middle of it all, stirring up trouble. The press dusted off the game six years earlier, when Curtley Ambrose beamed me, they revived the old cliché about there being friction between the two sides in recent years, and just blew the whole thing up, just to make a few cheap headlines. The implication was that it was my fault. The truth was easy to discover if the reporters had been bothered to look for it.

This time, I was actually the mediator, trying to calm things down. Gladstone Small bowled one at David Capel, and although I heard no noise there appeared to be a deflection as Keith Piper dived in front of me to take the ball. I shouted, 'Howzat?', umpire Tony Clarkson said, 'Not out' and that was the end of it as far as I was concerned. But Capes turned round, glared at me, and abused me for daring to appeal. Calmly, but sarcastically, I said, 'David – you bat, I'll field and we'll let the umpires do the umpiring. OK?' Piper, as is his wont, joined in and shouted, 'Yeh! Shut up Capes!' At the end of the over, as Keith and I walked past David, I said to the other umpire, Trevor Jesty, 'Trev, I'm allowed to appeal, you know,' and as Keith chipped in again, Trevor told him to stay out of it. As Keith passed Capes, he gave our wicket-keeper a pointed stare. Keith said to him, 'I'm not allowed to say anything,' and Capel shouted back aggressively, 'What did you say?' Keith replied, 'I can't say anything, I'll tell you later.' Capel shot back: 'You want to fight me later?' It was a total misunderstanding but Piper then changed his direction, walking towards Capel, as he raised his bat at him. I was walking towards slip and I heard Keith say, 'You're ugly'. Capes replied, 'I'm not as ugly as you' and by now it was all getting very silly. The pair of them were like a couple of rutting stags and I was finding it hard not to laugh at the puerile level of abuse they were hurling at each other. Capes shouted to me, 'You're always having a go at me, you're past masters at this. Just leave me alone,' Trevor Jesty had to tell Capel to calm down and get on with the game. When it had calmed down, I reminded Trevor, 'Just to confirm one point with you Trevor. This wouldn't have happened if Capes hadn't complained about me appealing for that catch. It's not always Warwickshire who start it, you know.' That night, I told the press my side of the story, but they still fingered me the next morning. They chose to ignore my version and beat up the line about Warwickshire and Northants having another go at each other, and my provocative part in past spats, as well as this latest one. It was a classic case of reporters deciding on their line and refusing to budge from it, in the face of contrary evidence. As for supposed hostility between both sides – David Capel phoned me up in sympathy when I announced my retirement and Kevin Curran suggested that he and I should stage a mock fight on the field during the Sunday League game, because he knew it was being covered by television. Kevin thought it would be a great laugh to have us wrestling on the ground, then get pulled apart by the umpires and fielders. After all, didn't many reporters and commentators state as a fact that Kevin and I didn't get on? Therefore it must be true! I thought that was a very funny idea, but in the end, we agreed it might not look very pleasant, even though it would only be a leg-pull.

There's never been any problem with my relationship with Kevin Curran, but sadly Michael Atherton made it clear in my final season that he had little time for me. He had agreed to turn out in a major benefit match -Warwickshire v. The Rest of the World, alongside top players like Aravinda DeSilva, Merv Hughes, Richie Richardson and Gary Kirsten. A fortnight before the game, Atherton told me he was pulling out because he disapproved of remarks I had made about him on television a few weeks earlier. I had been a guest on *Sport in Question*, hosted by Ian St John and Jimmy Greaves, and I responded honestly to a question about Atherton's quality as a player to be in England's best one-day side. I made some mild criticisms about his batting in one-day matches, coming to the conclusion that I would have a different strategy and balance for the side and not pick Michael for one-dayers. I said that guys like Alastair Brown and Adam Holioake ought to get preference, but I went on to say what a top Test batsman Atherton was, praising his courage and his stickability. In the end, though, I maintained that one-day cricket required a different format and players: I also felt that a lot of players in the county game felt the same way about Atherton. I didn't feel I had been unfair to Atherton, but when we met up at Edgbaston, he said he didn't like to be criticised by England team-mates and that he wouldn't be playing for me on the third of August. I said, 'Would you rather I'd lied about you?' but he clearly felt that I ought to have been aware I'd be asked a question like that and ought to have been ready with some vague answer. But I didn't feel I had been pushed into a corner on the programme: I thought he was being over-sensitive and told him so. After all, I had still invited him to play in the game, even though he had earlier dropped me from the original World Cup Squad and criticised my fielding. Atherton then said that days off in the English season are precious and he wasn't now going to give up this one on the third of August – but when he agreed to play, he presumably had thought days off were precious. He then paused for a moment and said he'd made up his mind and was sticking to his decision. Some may feel that's a noble attitude, while others would just say that Mike was being stubborn. It was clear to me he thought less of me after my public comments, but I wasn't bothered. I'd answer the question just as honestly and comprehensively if it's put to me again.

So I'd got under the skin of the England captain and I also upset the game's most traditional body, the M.C.C. in my final season. Here again I plead innocent. During our championship game in May against Hampshire, we were battling to get a draw on the last afternoon. The left-arm spinner, Rajesh Maru was trying to get me out by pitching the ball outside of the leg stump into the rough, looking for sharp turn. Now I had seen John Emburey combat this tactic before, by throwing his bat away and thrusting his left leg down the pitch. This had the double advantage of nullifying an appeal for lbw and avoiding a catch because the law states that a batsman can only be caught off the glove provided the appropriate hand is still on the bat. Embers had got away with it, and I thought that was a good method to eliminate getting bowled, lbw or caught. It was then up to Maru to try a different tactic. I threw my bat away in the direction of silly point fifteen times and eventually Maru had to change his line of attack to me. But I was in the clear under Law 32. If Maru had brought in a couple more close fielders on the offside, he could have appealed under law 37 – obstructing the field – or the umpires could have told me to stop throwing my bat away, because I was endangering the fielders. But he didn't do that, so I was within my rights under the laws of cricket.

That wasn't the end of the matter, though. The M.C.C. rumbled into majestic action and advised the Test and County Cricket Board that I could have been reported by the umpires for unfair play, or given out on appeal for obstructing the field, or even for the 'wilful' act of handling the ball if it had struck the glove. The T.C.C.B. then ruled that any repeat of my actions would be deemed 'unacceptable' and that umpires and players had been informed that the M.C.C. was now expecting them to abide more stringently to the interpretation of such laws. I had found a grey area, and the administrators felt it wasn't in the spirit of the game. It seemed to me that they were ruling against an innovative tactic, one that might have forced left-arm spinners to attack more, rather than relying on attritional bowling outside the leg-stump. I was then invited to attend an M.C.C. cricket committee meeting by Sir Colin Cowdrey to explain my actions. I wasn't sure whether I was going to get my wrist slapped or if the M.C.C. were genuinely interested in debating the matter. I am happy to say the meeting was stimulating and illuminating. It seemed Sir Colin and others were fed up with the negative tactic of pitching the ball outside leg stump, to stop batsmen scoring. Rajesh Maru was however bowling in a semi-attacking mode and I pointed out if the words 'holding the bat' were removed from Law 32, then a player wouldn't drop his bat in future. I admitted it doesn't look too good to drop the bat, but I had to ask the question why the words 'holding the bat' were there in the first place.

I then suggested that, to combat captains instructing spinners to bowl negatively outside the line of the leg stump, a law should be introduced, allowing a maximum of five fielders on the leg-side. At present in first-class cricket, you can have as many fielders as you want on either side of the wicket, but a captain only puts six on the legside when he is being defensive and negative. It wouldn't totally stop the tactic of bowling outside leg into the rough, but at least there would be a gap somewhere for the batsman to exploit and you would get far less kicking off of the ball. It was a pleasure to give my views to the M.C.C. cricket committee, and hopefully some good will come out of the whole bat-throwing saga.

There was another amusing sideshow during the 1996 season in England and it lasted for two and a half weeks in the High Court. That libel action involving Imran Khan, Ian Botham and Allan Lamb was followed closely on the county circuit but not taken too seriously. Much was said in court about ball-tampering, with fingers being pointed in various directions and certain former players making righteous denials about ever tampering with the ball. Well I agreed with Geoffrey Boycott who took the witness stand to confirm that it's all a matter of degree. Most bowlers I know in the game have helped themselves by tampering with the ball or its seam. Of course, that is cheating, but what's the difference between that and the batsman refusing to walk when he has nicked the ball, and he gets away with it? Either both are right or both are wrong. It's such a grey area that much is open to interpretation. Most spinners walking back to their mark grip some dust from the turf to enable them to hold the ball better: is all that dust finally removed from the ball when he spins it? Isn't that a case of bending the letter of the law, because outside elements are allowing the spinner to be better at his job? When Asif Din played for Warwickshire, he was acknowledged to be our best shiner of the ball. Was that because he worked harder with the ball on his trousers or was it because he sucked Extra Strong Mints? Some of our lads believed that the sugar from the mint when mixed with saliva was a better polishing agent than pure saliva. I've heard that chewing gum is equally useful in that direction. Now you'll find a few of the Warwickshire boys climbing into the Extra Strong Mints on the field as they polish the ball. Is that paying attention to detail, so that the ball will shine up strongly, or is it cheating? I recall a New Zealand swing bowler telling me that he took out a bottle top when bowling in a Test and he turned in wonderful figures. The umpire knew something was going on and told him, 'Oh, the game is fair now – both sides are cheating.' That remark underlines the fact that professional cricketers will try to get away with a lot if they can. It's a fact of life, and we ought to be aware that sharp practice goes on in all areas of society. Why should modern cricket be immune from it? The bowler tries to maximise his qualities to get results because of a fear of failure. He must retain his place in the side – and therefore his job – on the basis of results, just like a salesman. His employers usually assess him on figures, and so the pressure is put on the bowler to produce results, rather than just go out there to enjoy it. It's no wonder that a bowler will try to get any advantage because he's playing for his livelihood. Geoffrey Boycott was right when he said in the High Court that few motorists stick to the speed limit, that they'll only abide by it if they suspect there's a police car in the vicinity. It's the same with modern professional cricket: what can you get away with? Is there a grey area to exploit?

So what now for Dermot Reeve and Warwickshire, the most successful county side in recent years? I think the club has to think long and hard about my successor as captain for the 1997 season. Tim Munton took over from me for the rest of the '96 season, and he did a good job in '94 when he took us to the championship. But that was before Tim had his serious back operation and I'm not sure he's still the bowler he was. I believe Tim has lost a bit of nip which is so important to a bowler of his type. If Tim's back can stand up to the further rigours, and he is confident that it won't affect his captaincy, then he would have my vote – but he has to be an automatic selection, with no injury worries long-term. There are other candidates. Nick Knight will make a very good captain, but I think for now he ought to concentrate on his own game, and cement his place in the England side. He'd make an excellent vice-captain over the next year or so. Andy Moles will be inevitably distracted by his benefit year in 1997, and he too has had injury problems over the last couple of seasons. I think Allan Donald would be an excellent choice as captain if Munton wasn't certain of his prolonged fitness. Allan certainly has the respect of all the players, he would be highly motivated by the honour and I don't believe it would affect his bowling. He is so impressive in his pride of performance, his attitude to the team effort and his personal maturity that he would thrive under the responsibility. Allan Donald has never been one to duck out of responsibility and Courtney Walsh at Gloucestershire has shown there is no reason why an overseas fast bowler can't captain a county side, as long as the commitment is there.

As for me, I'm at a personal and professional crossroads. I'm getting married next year, to Donna Nelmes, a sports lover who I met at the start of the '96 season. Although my first marriage failed, I'm still enough of a romantic to think it can work again for me, and I'd love to be a father again. As for work, I'm now looking for fresh challenges. Three days after my retirement was announced, I sat in front of the television and it suddenly dawned on me that I wasn't going to be able to play cricket for a living again. I started to ask myself questions: what am I going to do for the rest of my life? I would love to throw my knowledge of the game into coaching and it was nice to have the phones ringing and counties asking my plans for the future. But I don't want to just coach a county exclusively. I'd like to put my ideas into practice with youngsters and perhaps hold seminars for current club coaches. I'd also like to work in the cricket media, because I find that very enjoyable. As I sat at home, mulling over my future, I realised that my own self-esteem is fuelled by giving a hundred per cent to challenges. It won't be enough for me to coast, to speak at a few dinners and play a lot of golf. I must set myself new goals, giving all my effort to things that will tax me. Although I am sad my playing days are over, I genuinely feel excited about the future.

Career Statistics

Dermot Alexander Reeve
Born Kowloon, Hong Kong 2nd April 1963.
Educ. King George V School, Kowloon.
Inventive middle order right handed Batsman
Right arm fast medium swing bowler. Lively fielder.
Inspirational captain of Warwickshire since 1993.
Played for Hong Kong in the 1982 ICC Trophy.
Three test matches for England 1991-92.
Test record 124 runs in 5 innings, av. 24.80
HS 59 v New Zealand, Christchurch on Test debut 1991-92.
2 wickets for 60 runs. 1 catch.
29 Limited overs Internationals for England. 291 runs in 21 innings. 9 not outs, av. 24.25. HS 35
20 wickets in 191.1 overs, for 820 runs, av. 41.00. BB 3-20. Econ rate – 4.29.
First-class career record 241 matches, 322 innings, 77 not out, 8541 runs, average 34.86. 7 centuries, Highest score 202* Warks v Northants., Northampton 1990. 1000 runs or more in season twice – 1412 in 1990 best. 200 catches; 456 wickets for 12232 runs, av. 26.82. BB 7-37 Sussex v Lancs., Lytham 1986. Played Sussex 1983-87; Warwickshire 1988-96. Captain of Warwickshire 1993-96

Dermot Reeve for Warwickshire in First-Class Cricket
Against each Team

Cty	Mch	Inn	no	Runs	H.S.	Av'ge	C	F	Ct	Overs	mdns	Runs	Wts	Av'ge
Dby	6	9	0	327	67	36.33	–	4	7	105	33	205	9	22.77
Dur	3	3	1	95	47	47.50	–	–	3	64	27	125	7	18.85
Ess	7	11	4	335	97*	47.85	–	2	6	102.4	27	272	5	54.40
Glm	11	14	3	519	79	47.18	–	4	14	145.1	48	314	14	22.42
Glo	7	11	3	311	86*	38.87	–	2	10	129.5	35	316	15	21.06
Hts	7	10	2	226	77*	28.25	–	1	7	178	60	359	18	19.94
Knt	8	12	3	378	72*	42.00	–	4	10	159	50	380	20	19.00
Lan	6	8	4	411	121*	102.75	1	2	–	51	16	101	1	–
Lei	8	13	0	279	67	21.46	–	2	8	156.2	57	317	17	18.64
Msx	7	12	2	155	41	15.50	–	–	10	109	28	273	6	45.50
Nth	13	21	4	831	202*	48.88	2	4	12	256.3	77	560	29	19.31
Nts	7	8	1	180	70*	25.71	–	1	6	79.3	24	172	5	34.40
Som	9	13	5	461	82	57.62	–	5	7	132.2	33	338	7	48.28
Sur	6	12	1	172	53	15.63	–	1	3	100.2	33	242	10	24.20
Sus	5	8	3	414	168*	82.80	1	2	8	76.4	24	165	7	23.57
Wor	11	18	1	502	97	29.52	–	1	11	150	52	358	10	35.80
Yks	12	16	4	551	99*	45.91	–	4	13	178.5	64	374	14	26.71
CTY	133	199	41	6147	202*	38.90	4	39	135	2174.2	688	4871	194	25.10
OU	1	1	0	7	7	–	–	–	–	6	4	9	2	4.50
CU	1	1	1	102	102*	–	1	–	3	25	10	43	3	14.33
Aus	1	1	0	23	23	–	–	–	–	23	5	55	2	27.50
SL	1	2	0	6	5	3.00	–	–	–	20	4	75	2	37.50
EnA	1	2	1	77	77*	–	–	1	1	18.2	5	41	2	20.50
Bor	2	2	0	120	107	60.00	1	–	6	27	10	56	2	28.00
Mad	1	1	0	2	2	–	–	–	1	9	2	27	2	13.50
T	141	209	43	6484	202*	39.06	6	40	146	2302.4	728	5177	209	24.77

Key; CTY = County Championship; T = Total, all first-class Warwicks matches; Aus = Australian XI; SL = Sri Lankan XI; EnA = England "A"; Bor = Border; Mad = Mashonaland.

Season-by-Season Record for Warwickshire – First-Class

	Mch	Inn	no	Runs	h.s.	Av'ge	C	F	Ct	Overs	Mns	Runs	Wts	Av'ge
1988	16	23	3	431	103	21.55	1	–	11	292	71	750	24	31.25
1989	14	17	4	581	97*	44.69	–	4	13	97.4	35	163	11	14.81
1990	24	37	12	1373	202*	54.92	3	5	26	364.4	108	900	33	27.27
1991	20	33	7	1260	99*	48.46	–	14	10	402.1	117	957	45	21.26
1992	17	28	4	·833	79	34.70	–	7	15	267	80	632	13	48.61
92/3	1	1	0	13	13	—	–	–	2	21	9	34	2	17.00
1993	17	28	7	765	87*	36.42	–	5	22	284.1	108	528	22	24.00
93/4	1	1	0	2	2	—	–	–	1	9	2	27	2	13.50
1994	9	10	1	116	33	12.88	–	–	18	144	48	308	10	30.80
94/5	1	1	0	107	107	—	1	–	4	6	1	22	0	—
1995	16	22	4	652	77*	36.22	–	5	17	312	117	661	38	17.39
1996	5	8	1	351	168*	50.14	1	–	7	103	32	195	9	21.66
T	141	209	43	6484	202*	39.06	6	40	146	2302.4	728	5177	209	24.77

Dermot Reeve for Sussex in First-Class Cricket
Against each team

Cty	Mch	Inn	no	Runs	h.s.	Av'ge	C	F	Ct	Overs	Mns	Runs	Wts	Av'ge
Dby	6	7	3	59	26	14.75	–	–	5	192.2	43	581	18	32.27
Ess	5	9	0	110	51	12.22	–	1	5	104.3	27	270	12	22.50
Glm	6	5	3	68	52	34.00	–	1	1	138	44	316	14	22.57
Glo	4	4	1	91	32*	30.33	–	–	2	70.2	11	213	6	35.50
Hts	7	10	3	206	65	29.42	–	1	3	187.4	48	599	12	49.91
Knt	8	9	4	148	87*	29.60	–	1	10	215.5	63	498	17	29.29
Lan	4	7	2	145	64	29.00	–	1	1	136.3	38	315	13	24.23
Lei	6	9	1	80	25	10.00	–	–	6	165	39	418	16	26.12
Mdx	7	8	3	228	57*	45.60	–	3	4	202	48	597	22	27.13
Nth	5	5	2	92	56*	30.66	–	1	3	142.1	40	421	14	30.07
Nts	3	5	1	29	12*	7.25	–	–	2	91.1	19	250	9	27.77
Som	3	3	2	43	16*	—	–	–	–	101.3	24	265	10	26.50
Sur	9	7	1	285	119	47.50	1	2	4	240.2	59	698	27	25.85
Wks	5	4	2	60	30	30.00	–	–	1	148	44	411	14	29.35
Wor	4	5	2	41	28*	13.66	–	–	–	119.2	26	330	13	25.38
Yks	4	3	1	46	35*	23.00	–	–	2	121	39	280	11	25.45
CTY	86	100	31	1731	119	25.08	1	11	48	2375.4	612	6462	228	28.34
CU	2	–	–	–	–	—	–	–	1	59.5	23	92	8	11.50
SL	1	–	–	–	–	—	–	–	1	21	8	36	1	—
NZ	1	–	–	–	–	—	–	–	1	17	0	43	1	—
Pak	1	1	0	30	30	—	–	–	–	23	5	95	1	—
T	91	101	31	1761	119	25.15	1	11	51	2496.3	648	6728	239	28.15

Season-by-Season Record for Sussex – First-Class

Year	Mch	In	no	Runs	H.S.	Av'ge	C	F	Ct	Overs	Mdns	Runs	Wts	Av'ge
1983	17	20	5	192	42*	12.80	–	–	7	472.1	131	1233	42	29.35
1984	21	22	4	486	119	27.00	1	3	14	572.4	175	1420	55	25.81
1985	17	15	5	170	56	17.00	–	1	6	475.5	107	1424	48	29.66
1986	19	21	9	307	51	25.58	–	1	10	525.5	127	1411	52	27.13
1987	17	23	8	606	87*	40.40	–	6	14	450	108	1240	42	29.52
T	91	101	31	1761	119	25.15	1	11	51	2496.3	648	6728	239	28.15

Total First-Class County Career Record 1983-96

Mch	In	no	Runs	H.S.	Av'ge	C	F	Ct	Overs	Mdns	Runs	Wts	Av'ge
232	310	74	8245	202*	34.93	7	51	197	4799.1	1376	11905	448	26.57

Dermot Reeve in Limited Overs Cricket
Nat West Trophy

For	Mch	In	no	Runs	H.S.	Av'ge	C	F	Ct	Overs	Runs	wts	Av'ge	5	B/B
Wks	31	26	7	721	81*	37.94	–	4	12	284.5	892	33	27.03	–	4/54
Sus	12	7	5	63	26*	31.50	–	–	4	123.5	355	16	22.18	–	4/20
T	43	33	12	784	81*	37.33	–	4	15	408.4	1247	49	25.44	–	4/20

Benson & Hedges Cup

For	Mch	In	no	Runs	H.S.	Av'ge	C	F	Ct	Overs	Runs	wts	Av'ge	5	B/B
Wks	29	25	9	464	80	29.00	–	1	15	254.1	979	39	25.10	–	4/23
Sus	15	10	4	103	30*	17.16	–	–	1	127.4	569	16	35.56	–	4/42
T	44	35	13	567	80	25.77	–	1	16	381.5	1448	55	26.32	–	4/23

The Sunday League

For	Mch	In	no	Runs	H.S.	Av'ge	C	F	Ct	Overs	Runs	wts	Av'ge	5	B/B
Wks	112	99	23	2172	100*	28.57	1	9	32	617.5	2667	95	28.07	1	5/23
Sus	55	24	9	170	21	11.33	–	–	17	393	1855	69	26.88	–	4/22
T	167	123	32	2342	100*	25.73	1	9	49	1010.5	4522	164	27.57	1	5/23

Dermot Reeve in Test Cricket

Mtch	Inn	n.o.	Runs	h.s.	Av'ge	50s.	ct	Overs	Mdns	Runs	Wts	Av'ge	B/B
3	5	0	124	59	24.80	1	1	24.5	8	60	2	30.00	1/4

Reeve's three Test matches were all against New Zealand in 1991. His best score came on his debut, 59 on the second day (Jan 19) in the 1st Test at Christchurch. The innings occupied 160 minutes, lasted 125 balls, and included 5 fours. Batting no. 7, Reeve added 76 for the 6th wicket with AJ Lamb, and 78 for the 7th with CC Lewis. Reeve's Test wickets were those of CL Cairns, with the 8th ball of his first Test, and AH Jones in the 2nd innings of his third Test when he finished with figures of 4.5

overs, 2 maidens, 1 wicket for 4 runs.

Dermot Reeve in Limited Overs Cricket

Mch	Inn	n.o.	Runs	h.s.	Av'ge	50s	ct	Overs	Runs	Wkts	Av'ge	B/B
29	21	9	291	35	24.25	–	12	191.1	820	20	41.00	3/20

Reeve's first Limited overs International for England was against West Indies at Lord's in 1991. His best bowling performance was 3-20 against New Zealand at Auckland in 1991/92 and he won the man-of-the-match award. His best score of 35 came in 34 balls against Sri Lanka at Faisalabad in England's final and unsuccessful match of the 1996 World Cup. Batting No.8, Reeve added 62 in 57 balls for the 8th wicket with D Gough.

Dermot Reeve as Warwickshire Captain

Reeve first led Warwickshire in a first-class match against Cambridge University on Fenner's ground 26-28 April 1990. Reeve scored 102 not out before Lunch on the second day, but rain destroyed hopes of a result. Before being officially appointed for the 1993 season Reeve had led the county in nine first-class matches, winning 1, losing 3. As official captain Reeve won 24 out of 50 first-class matches, with 11 defeats. 17 of Warwickshire's final 22 first-class games under his leadership were won.

With Reeve as official captain, 1993-95 and the first part of 1996 Warwickshire twice won the County Championship, won the Nat West Trophy twice, and were beaten finalists once. The Benson & Hedges was won once and the Sunday League saw one top spot and one runners-up placing in 1995. When Reeve resigned through injury in 1996 Warwickshire were well placed in the County Championship and Sunday League. The winning of 5 Trophies in 2 seasons (1994–95) by one county is unprecedented in County Cricket history. No captain has equalled Reeve's 14 victories in the 15 Nat West Trophy games in which he led the side.

Robert Brooke.

PENGUIN POPULAR CLASSICS

THE ADVENTURES OF TOM SAWYER

MARK TWAIN

PENGUIN BOOKS
A PENGUIN/GODFREY CAVE EDITION

PENGUIN BOOKS

Published by the Penguin Group
Penguin Books Ltd, 27 Wrights Lane, London w8 5tz, England
Penguin Books USA Inc., 375 Hudson Street, New York, New York 10014, USA
Penguin Books Australia Ltd, Ringwood, Victoria, Australia
Penguin Books Canada Ltd, 10 Alcorn Avenue, Toronto, Ontario, Canada m4v 3b2
Penguin Books (NZ) Ltd, 182–190 Wairau Road, Auckland 10, New Zealand

Penguin Books Ltd, Registered Offices: Harmondsworth, Middlesex, England

First published 1876
Published in Penguin Popular Classics 1994
1 3 5 7 9 10 8 6 4 2

Printed in England by Clays Ltd, St Ives plc
Set in Monotype Baskerville

Preface

MOST of the adventures recorded in this book really occurred; one or two were experiences of my own, the rest of those boys who were schoolmates of mine. Huck Finn is drawn from life; Tom Sawyer also, but not from an individual; he is a combination of the characteristics of three boys whom I knew, and therefore belongs to the composite order of architecture.

The odd superstitions touched upon were all prevalent among children and slaves in the West at the period of this story; that is to say, thirty or forty years ago.

Although my book is intended mainly for the entertainment of boys and girls, I hope it will not be shunned by men and women on that account, for part of my plan has been to try pleasantly to remind adults of what they once were themselves, and of how they felt and thought and talked, and what queer enterprises they sometimes engaged in.

Hartford, 1876

THE AUTHOR

CHAPTER I

'TOM!'

No answer.

'Tom!'

No answer.

'What's gone with that boy, I wonder? You Tom!'

The old lady pulled her spectacles down and looked over them, about the room; then she put them up and looked out under them. She seldom or never looked *through* them for so small a thing as a boy, for they were her state pair, the pride of her heart, and were built for 'style' not service; she could have seen through a pair of stove lids as well. She looked perplexed a moment and said, not fiercely, but still loud enough for the furniture to hear, 'Well, I lay if I get hold of you, I'll – '

She did not finish, for by this time she was bending down and punching under the bed with the broom – and so she needed breath to punctuate the punches with. She resurrected nothing but the cat.

'I never did see the beat of that boy!'

She went to the open door and stood in it, and looked out among the tomato vines and 'jimpson' weeds that constituted the garden. No Tom. So she lifted up her voice, at an angle calculated for distance, and shouted:

'Y-o-u-u- *Tom!*'

There was a slight noise behind her, and she turned just in time to seize a small boy by the slack of his roundabout and arrest his flight. 'There! I might 'a thought of that closet. What you been doing in there?'

'Nothing.'

'Nothing! Look at your hands, and look at your mouth. What *is* that truck?'

'*I* don't know, Aunt.'

'Well, *I* know. It's jam, that's what it is. Forty times I've said if you didn't let that jam alone I'd skin you. Hand me that switch.'

The switch hovered in the air. The peril was desperate.

'My! Look behind you, Aunt!'

The old lady whirled around and snatched her skirts out of danger, and the lad fled, on the instant, scrambled up the high board fence, and disappeared over it. His Aunt Polly stood surprised a moment, and then broke into a gentle laugh.

'Hang the boy, can't I ever learn anything? Ain't he played me tricks enough like that for me to be looking out for him by this time? But old fools is the biggest fools there is. Can't learn any old dog new tricks, as the saying is. But, my goodness, he never plays them alike two days, and how is a body to know what's coming? He 'pears to know just how long he can torment me before I get my dander up, and he knows if he can make out to put me off for a minute, or make me laugh, it's all down again, and I can't hit him a lick. I ain't doing my duty by that boy, and that's the Lord's truth, goodness knows. Spare the rod and spile the child, as the good book says. I'm a-laying up sin and suffering for us both, *I* know. He's full of the old scratch, but laws-a-me! he's my own dead sister's boy, poor thing, and I ain't got the heart to lash him somehow. Every time I let him off my conscience does hurt me so; and every time I hit him my old heart 'most breaks. Well-a-well, man that is born of a woman is of few days and full of trouble, as the Scripture says, and I reckon it's so. He'll play hookey this evening,* and I'll just be obliged to make him work tomorrow, to punish him. It's mighty hard to make him work Saturdays, when all the boys is having a holiday, but he hates work more than he hates anything else, and I've got to do some of my duty by him, or I'll be the ruination of the child.'

Tom did play hookey, and he had a very good time. He got back home barely in season to help Jim, the small col-

*South-western for 'afternoon'.

8

oured boy, saw next day's wood, and split the kindlings before supper – at least he was there in time to tell his adventures to Jim while Jim did three-fourths of the work. Tom's younger brother (or rather half-brother) Sid was already through with his part of the work (picking up chips), for he was a quiet boy, and had no adventurous, troublesome ways. While Tom was eating his supper and stealing sugar as opportunity offered, Aunt Polly asked him questions that were full of guile, and very deep – for she wanted to trap him into damaging reyealments. Like many other simple-hearted souls, it was her pet vanity to believe she was endowed with a talent for dark and mysterious diplomacy, and she loved to contemplate her most transparent devices as marvels of low cunning. Said she, 'Tom, it was middling warm in school, warn't it?'

'Yes, 'm.'

'Powerful warm, warn't it?'

'Yes, 'm.'

'Didn't you want to go in a swimming, Tom?'

A bit of a scare shot through Tom – a touch of uncomfortable suspicion. He searched Aunt Polly's face, but it told him nothing. So he said:

'No, 'm – well, not very much.'

The old lady reached out her hand and felt Tom's shirt, and said:

'But you ain't too warm now, though.'

And it flattered her to reflect that she had discovered that the shirt was dry without anybody knowing that that was what she had in her mind. But in spite of her Tom knew where the wind lay now. So he forestalled what might be the next move.

'Some of us pumped on our heads – mine's damp yet. See?'

Aunt Polly was vexed to think she had overlooked that bit of circumstantial evidence and missed a trick. Then she had a new inspiration:

9

'Tom, you didn't have to undo your shirt collar where I sewed it to pump on your head, did you? Unbutton your jacket!'

The trouble vanished out of Tom's face. He opened his jacket. His shirt collar was securely sewed.

'Bother! Well, go 'long with you. I made sure you'd played hookey and been a swimming. But I forgive ye, Tom, I reckon you're a kind of a singed cat, as the saying is — better'n you look, *this* time.'

She was half sorry her sagacity had miscarried, and half glad that Tom had stumbled into obedient conduct for once.

But Sidney said:

'Well, now, if I didn't think you sewed his collar with white thread, but it's black.'

'Why, I did sew it with white! Tom!'

But Tom did not wait for the rest. As he went out of the door, he said:

'Siddy, I'll lick you for that.'

In a safe place Tom examined two large needles which were thrust into the lapels of his jacket — and had thread bound about them — one needle carried white thread and the other black. He said:

'She'd never noticed if it hadn't been for Sid. Confound it, sometimes she sews it with white and sometimes she sews it with black. I wish to geeminy she'd stick to one or t'other — *I* can't keep the run of 'em. But I bet you I'll lam Sid for that. If I don't, blame my cats.'

He was not the model boy of the village. He knew the model boy very well, though, and loathed him.

Within two minutes, or even less, he had forgotten all his troubles. Not because his troubles were one whit less heavy and bitter to him than a man's are to a man, but because a new and powerful interest bore them down and drove them out of his mind for the time; just as men's misfortunes are forgotten in the excitement of new enterprises. This new interest was a valued novelty in whistling, which he had just acquired from a Negro, and he was suffering to practise it undisturbed. It consisted in a peculiar bird-like turn, a sort of liquid warble, produced by touching the tongue to the roof of the mouth at short intervals in the midst of the music. The reader probably remembers how to do it if he has ever been a boy. Diligence and attention soon gave him the knack of it, and he strode down the street with his mouth full of harmony and his soul full of gratitude. He felt much as an astronomer feels who has discovered a new planet. No doubt as far as strong, deep, unalloyed pleasure is concerned, the advantage was with the boy, not the astronomer.

The summer evenings were long. It was not dark yet. Presently Tom checked his whistle. A stranger was before him; a boy a shade larger than himself. A new-comer of any age or either sex was an impressive curiosity in the poor little village of St Petersburg. This boy was well dressed, too – well dressed on a week-day. This was simply astounding. His cap was a dainty thing, his close-buttoned blue-cloth roundabout was new and natty, and so were his pantaloons. He had shoes on, and yet it was only Friday. He even wore a neck-tie, a bright bit of ribbon. He had a citified air about him that ate into Tom's vitals. The more Tom stared at the splendid marvel, the higher he turned up his nose at his finery, and the shabbier and shabbier his own outfit seemed to him to grow. Neither boy spoke. If one moved the other moved – but only sidewise, in a circle. They kept face to face and eye to eye all the time. Finally, Tom said:

'I can lick you!'

'I'd like to see you try it.'

'Well, I can do it.'

'No you can't, either.'

'Yes I can.'

'No you can't.'

'I can.'

'You can't.'

'Can.'

'Can't.'

An uncomfortable pause. Then Tom said:

'What's your name?'

''Tisn't any of your business, maybe.'

'Well, I 'low I'll *make* it my business.'

'Well, why don't you?'

'If you say much I will.'

'Much – much – much! There, now.'

'Oh, you think you're mighty smart, *don't* you? I could lick you with one hand tied behind me, if I wanted to.'

'Well, why don't you *do* it? You *say* you can do it.'

'Well, *I will*, if you fool with me.'

'Oh, yes – I've seen whole families in the same fix.'

'Smarty! you think you're *some* now, *don't* you?'

'Oh, what a hat!'

'You can lump that hat if you don't like it. I dare you to knock it off; and anybody that'll take a dare will suck eggs.'

'You're a liar!'

'You're another.'

'You're a fighting liar, and darn't take it up.'

'Aw – take a walk!'

'Say – if you give me much more of your sass, I'll take and bounce a rock off'n your head.'

'Oh, of *course* you will.'

'Well, I *will*.'

'Well, why don't you *do* it, then? What do you keep *saying* you will for? Why don't you *do* it? It's because you're afraid.'

'I *ain't* afraid.'

'You are.'

'I ain't.'

'You are.'

Another pause, and more eyeing and sidling around each other. Presently they were shoulder to shoulder. Tom said:

'Get away from here!'

12

'Get away yourself!'

'I won't.'

'*I* won't, either.'

So they stood, each with a foot placed at an angle as a brace, and both shoving with might and main, and glowering at each other with hate. But neither could get an advantage. After struggling till both were hot and flushed, each relaxed his strain with watchful caution, and Tom said:

'You're a coward and a pup. I'll tell my big brother on you, and he can lam you with his little finger, and I'll make him do it, too.'

'What do I care for your big brother? I've got a brother that's bigger than he is; and, what's more, he can throw him over that fence, too.' (Both brothers were imaginary.)

'That's a lie.'

'*Your* saying so don't make it so.'

Tom drew a line in the dust with his big toe, and said:

'I dare you to step over that, and I'll lick you till you can't stand up. Anybody that'll take a dare will steal a sheep.'

The new boy stepped over promptly, and said:

'Now you said you'd do it, now let's see you do it.'

'Don't you crowd me, now; you'd better look out.'

'Well, you *said* you'd do it – why don't you do it?'

'By jingoes, for two cents I *will* do it.'

The new boy took two broad coppers out of his pocket and held them out with derision.

Tom struck them to the ground.

In an instant both boys were rolling and tumbling in the dirt, gripped together like cats; and for the space of a minute they tugged and tore at each other's hair and clothes, punched and scratched each other's noses, and covered themselves with dust and glory. Presently the confusion took form, and through the fog of battle Tom appeared, seated astride the new boy, and pounding him with his fists.

'Holler 'nuff!' said he.

The boy only struggled to free himself. He was crying, mainly from rage.

'Holler 'nuff!' and the pounding went on.

At last the stranger got out a smothered ''nuff!' and Tom let him up, and said, 'Now that'll learn you. Better look out who you're fooling with next time.'

The new boy went off brushing the dust from his clothes, sobbing, snuffling, and occasionally looking back and shaking his head, and threatening what he would do to Tom the 'next time he caught him out'. To which Tom responded with jeers, and started off in high feather; and as soon as his back was turned the new boy snatched up a stone, threw it, and hit him between the shoulders, and then turned tail and ran like an antelope. Tom chased the traitor home, and thus found out where he lived. He then held a position at the gate for some time, daring the enemy to come outside; but the enemy only made faces at him through the window, and declined. At last the enemy's mother appeared, and called Tom a bad, vicious, vulgar child, and ordered him away. So he went away, but he said he ''lowed' to 'lag' for that boy.

He got home pretty late that night, and when he climbed cautiously in at the window he uncovered an ambuscade in the person of his aunt; and when she saw the state his clothes were in, her resolution to turn his Saturday holiday into captivity at hard labour became adamantine in its firmness.

CHAPTER II

SATURDAY morning was come, and all the summer world was bright and fresh, and brimming with life. There was a song in every heart; and if the heart was young the music issued at the lips. There was cheer in every face, and a spring in every step. The locust trees were in bloom, and the fragrance of the blossoms filled the air.

Cardiff Hill, beyond the village and above it, was green with vegetation, and it lay just far enough away to seem a Delectable Land, dreamy, reposeful, and inviting.

Tom appeared on the side-walk with a bucket of whitewash and a long-handled brush. He surveyed the fence, and the gladness went out of nature, and a deep melancholy settled down upon his spirit. Thirty yards of broad fence nine feet high! It seemed to him that life was hollow, and existence but a burden. Sighing he dipped his brush and passed it along the topmost plank; repeated the operation; did it again; compared the insignificant whitewashed streak with the far-reaching continent of unwhitewashed fence, and sat down on a tree-box discouraged. Jim came skipping out at the gate with a tin pail, and singing *Buffalo Gals*. Bringing water from the town pump had always been hateful work in Tom's eyes before, but now it did not strike him so. He remembered that there was company at the pump. White, mulatto, and Negro boys and girls were always there waiting their turns, resting, trading playthings, quarrelling, fighting, skylarking. And he remembered that although the pump was only a hundred and fifty yards off Jim never got back with a bucket of water under an hour; and even then somebody generally had to go after him. Tom said:

'Say, Jim; I'll fetch the water if you'll whitewash some.'

Jim shook his head, and said:

'Can't, Mar's Tom. Ole missis she tole me I got to go an' git dis water an' not stop foolin' 'roun' wid anybody. She say she spec' Ma'rs Tom gwyne to ax me to whitewash, an' so she tole me go 'long an' 'tend to my own business – she 'lowed *she'd* 'tend to de whitewashin'.'

'Oh, never you mind what she said, Jim. That's the way she always talks. Gimme the bucket – I won't be gone only a minute. *She* won't ever know.'

'Oh, I dasn't, Ma'rs Tom. Ole missis she'd take an' tar de head off'n me. 'Deed she would.'

'*She!* she never licks anybody – whacks 'em over the head with her thimble, and who cares for that, I'd like to know? She talks awful, but talk don't hurt – anyways, it don't if she don't cry. Jim, I'll give you a marble. I'll give you a white alley!'

Jim began to waver.

'White alley, Jim; and it's a bully tow.'

'My; dat's a mighty gay marvel, *I* tell you. But, Ma'rs Tom, I's powerful 'fraid ole missis.'

But Jim was only human – this attention was too much for him. He put down his pail, took the white alley. In another minute he was flying down the street with his pail and a tingling rear, Tom was whitewashing with vigour, and Aunt Polly was retiring from the field with a slipper in her hand and triumph in her eye.

But Tom's energy did not last. He began to think of the fun he had planned for this day, and his sorrows multiplied. Soon the free boys would come tripping along on all sorts of delicious expeditions, and they would make a world of fun of him for having to work – the very thought of it burnt him like fire. He got out his worldly wealth and examined it – bits of toys, marbles, and trash; enough to buy an exchange of work maybe, but not enough to buy so much as half an hour of pure freedom. So he returned his straitened means to his pocket, and gave up the idea of trying to buy the boys. At this dark and hopeless moment an inspiration burst upon him. Nothing less than a great, magnificent inspiration. He took up his brush and went tranquilly to work. Ben Rogers hove in sight presently; the very boy of all boys whose ridicule he had been dreading. Ben's gait was the hop, skip, and jump – proof enough that his heart was light and his anticipations high. He was eating an apple, and giving a long melodious whoop at intervals, followed by a deep-toned ding dong dong, ding dong dong, for he was personating a steamboat! As he drew near he slackened speed, took the middle of the street, leaned far over to starboard, and rounded-to ponderously, and with laborious pomp and circumstance, for he was personating the *Big Missouri*, and considered himself to be drawing nine feet of water. He was boat, and captain, and engine-bells combined, so he had to imagine himself standing on his own hurricane-deck giving the orders and executing them.

'Stop her, sir! Ling-a-ling-ling.' The headway ran almost out, and he drew up slowly towards the side-walk. 'Ship up to back! Ling-a-ling-ling!' His arms straightened and stiffened down his sides. 'Set her back on the stabboard! Ling-a-ling-ling! Chow! ch-chow-wow-chow!' his right hand meantime describing stately circles, for it was representing a forty-foot wheel. 'Let her go back on the labboard! Ling-a-ling-ling! Chow-ch-chow-chow!' The left hand began to describe circles.

'Stop the stabboard! Ling-a-ling-ling! Stop the labboard! Come ahead on the stabboard! Stop her! Let your outside turn over slow! Ling-a-ling-ling! Chow-ow-ow! Get out that head-line! Lively, now! Come – out with your spring-line – what're you about there? Take a turn round that stump with the bight of it! Stand by that stage now – let her go! Done with the engines, sir! Ling-a-ling-ling!'

'Sht! s'sht! sht!' (Trying the gauge-cocks.)

Tom went on whitewashing – paid no attention to the steamer. Ben stared a moment, and then said:

'Hi-yi! You're up a stump, ain't you!'

No answer. Tom surveyed his last touch with the eye of an artist; then he gave his brush another gentle sweep, and surveyed the result as before. Ben ranged up alongside of him. Tom's mouth watered for the apple, but he stuck to his work. Ben said:

'Hello, old chap; you got to work, hey?'

'Why, it's you, Ben! I warn't noticing.'

'Say, I'm going in a swimming, I am. Don't you wish you

17

could? But of course, you'd druther work, wouldn't you? 'Course you would!'

Tom contemplated the boy a bit, and said:

'What do you call work?'

'Why, ain't that work?'

Tom resumed his whitewashing, and answered carelessly:

'Well, maybe it is, and maybe it ain't. All I know is, it suits Tom Sawyer.'

'Oh, come now, you don't mean to let on that you like it?'

The brush continued to move.

'Like it? Well, I don't see why I oughtn't to like it. Does a boy get a chance to whitewash a fence every day?'

That put the thing in a new light. Ben stopped nibbling his apple. Tom swept his brush daintily back and forth – stepped back to note the effect – added a touch here and there – criticized the effect again, Ben watching every move, and getting more and more interested, more and more absorbed. Presently he said:

'Say, Tom, let me whitewash a little.'

Tom considered; was about to consent; but he altered his mind: 'No, no; I reckon it wouldn't hardly do, Ben. You see, Aunt Polly's awful particular about this fence – right here on the street, you know – but if it was the back fence I wouldn't mind, and she wouldn't. Yes, she's awful particular about this fence; it's got to be done very careful; I reckon there ain't one boy in a thousand, maybe two thousand, that can do it the way it's got to be done.'

'No – is that so? Oh, come now; lemme just try, only just a little. I'd let you, if you was me, Tom.'

'Ben, I'd like to, honest injun; but Aunt Polly – well, Jim wanted to do it, but she wouldn't let him. Sid wanted to do it, but she wouldn't let Sid. Now, don't you see how I am fixed? If you was to tackle this fence, and anything was to happen to it –'

'Oh, shucks; I'll be just as careful. Now lemme try. Say – I'll give you the core of my apple.'

'Well, here. No, Ben; now don't; I'm afeard – '

'I'll give you all of it!'

Tom gave up the brush with reluctance in his face, but alacrity in his heart. And while the late steamer *Big Missouri* worked and sweated in the sun, the retired artist sat on a barrel in the shade close by, dangled his legs, munched his apple, and planned the slaughter of more innocents. There was no lack of material; boys happened along every little while; they came to jeer, but remained to whitewash. By the time Ben was fagged out, Tom had traded the next chance to Billy Fisher for a kite in good repair; and when he played out, Johnny Miller bought in for a dead rat and a string to swing it with; and so on, and so on, hour after hour. And when the middle of the afternoon came, from being a poor poverty-stricken boy in the morning Tom was literally rolling in wealth. He had, besides the things I have mentioned, twelve marbles, part of a jew's harp, a piece of blue bottle-glass to look through, a spool-cannon, a key that wouldn't unlock anything, a fragment of chalk, a glass stopper of a decanter, a tin soldier, a couple of tadpoles, six fire-crackers, a kitten with only one eye, a brass door-knob, a dog-collar – but no dog – the handle of a knife, four pieces of orange-peel, and a dilapidated old window-sash. He had had a nice, good, idle time all the while – plenty of company – and the fence had three coats of whitewash on it! If he hadn't run out of whitewash he would have bankrupted every boy in the village.

Tom said to himself that it was not such a hollow world after all. He had discovered a great law of human action, without knowing it, namely, that, in order to make a man or a boy covet a thing, it is only necessary to make the thing difficult to attain. If he had been a great and wise philosopher, like the writer of this book, he would now have comprehended that work consists of whatever a body is obliged to do, and that play consists of whatever a body is not obliged to do. And this would help him to understand why constructing artificial flowers, or performing on a tread-mill, is work, whilst rolling nine-pins or climbing Mont Blanc is only amusement. There are wealthy gentlemen in England who drive four-horse passenger-coaches twenty or thirty miles on a daily line, in the summer, because the privilege costs them considerable money; but if they were offered wages for the service that would turn it into work, then they would resign.

CHAPTER III

TOM presented himself before Aunt Polly, who was sitting by an open window in a pleasant rearward apartment which was bed-room, breakfast-room, dining-room, and library combined. The balmy summer air, the restful quiet, the odour of the flowers, and the drowsing murmur of the bees had had their effect, and she was nodding over her knitting – for she had no company but the cat, and it was asleep in her lap. Her spectacles were propped up on her grey head for safety. She had thought that of course Tom had deserted long ago, and she wondered to see him place himself in her power again in this intrepid way. He said:

'Mayn't I go and play now, Aunt?'

'What, a'ready? How much have you done?'

'It's all done, Aunt.'

'Tom, don't lie to me. I can't bear it.'

'I ain't, Aunt; it *is* all done.'

Aunt Polly placed small trust in such evidence. She went out to see for herself; and she would have been content to find twenty per cent of Tom's statement true. When she found the entire fence whitewashed, and not only white-washed but elaborately coated and recoated, and even a streak added to the ground, her astonishment was almost unspeakable. She said:

'Well, I never! There's no getting around it; you *can* work when you're a mind to, Tom.' And then she diluted the compliment by adding, 'But it's powerful seldom you're a mind to, I'm bound to say. Well, go 'long and play; but mind you get back some time in a week, or I'll tan you.'

She was so overcome by the splendour of his achievement that she took him into the closet and selected a choice apple, and delivered it to him, along with an improving lecture upon the added value and flavour a treat took to itself when it came without sin through virtuous effort. And while she closed with a happy Scriptural flourish, he 'hooked' a doughnut.

Then he skipped out, and saw Sid just starting up the outside stairway that led to the back rooms on the second floor. Clods were handy, and the air was full of them in a twinkling. They raged around Sid like a hailstorm; and before Aunt Polly could collect her surprised faculties and rally to the rescue, six or seven clods had taken personal effect, and Tom was over the fence and gone. There was a gate, but as a general thing he was too crowded for time to make use of it. His soul was at peace now that he had settled with Sid for calling attention to his black thread and getting him into trouble.

Tom skirted the block and came around into a muddy alley that led by the back of his aunt's cow-stable. He presently got safely beyond the reach of capture and punishment, and wended towards the public square of the village, where two 'military' companies of boys had met for conflict, according to previous appointment. Tom was general of one of these armies, Joe Harper (a bosom friend) general of the other. These two great commanders did not condescend to fight in person – that being better suited to the smaller fry – but sat together on an eminence and conducted the field operations by order delivered through aides-de-camp.

Tom's army won a great victory, after a long and hard-fought battle. Then the dead were counted, prisoners exchanged, the terms of the next disagreement agreed upon, and the day for the necessary battle appointed; after which the armies fell into line and marched away, and Tom turned homeward alone.

As he was passing by the house where Jeff Thatcher lived, he saw a new girl in the garden – a lovely little blue-eyed creature with yellow hair plaited into two long tails, white summer frock, and embroidered pantalettes. The fresh-crowned hero fell without firing a shot. A certain Amy Lawrence vanished out of his heart, and left not even a memory of herself behind. He had thought he loved her to distraction; he had regarded his passion as adoration; and behold it was only a poor little evanescent partiality. He had been months winning her, she had confessed hardly a week ago; he had been the happiest and the proudest boy in the world only seven short days, and here, in one instant of time, she had gone out of his heart like a casual stranger whose visit is done.

He worshipped this new angel with furtive eye, till he saw that she had discovered him; then he pretended he did not know she was present, and began to 'show off' in all sorts of absurd boyish ways in order to win her admiration. He kept up this grotesque foolishness for some little time; but by-and-by, while he was in the midst of some dangerous gymnastic performances, he glanced aside, and saw that the little girl was wending towards the house. Tom came up to the fence, and leaned on it, grieving, and hoping she would tarry yet a while longer. She halted a moment on the steps, and then moved towards the door. Tom heaved a great sigh as she put her foot on the threshold, but his face lit up, right away, for she tossed a pansy over the fence a moment before she disappeared. The boy ran around and stopped within a foot or two of the flower, and then shaded his eyes with his hand, and began to look down street as if he had discovered something of interest going on in that direction. Presently he picked up a straw and began trying to balance it on his nose, with his head tilted far back; and as he moved from side to side in his efforts he edged nearer and nearer towards the pansy; finally his bare foot rested upon it, his pliant toes closed upon it, and he hopped away with his treasure, and disappeared around the corner. But only for a minute – only while he could button the flower inside his jacket, next his heart, or next his stomach possibly, for he was not much posted in anatomy and not hypercritical anyway.

He returned now and hung about the fence till night-fall, 'showing off' as before; but the girl never exhibited herself again, though Tom comforted himself a little with the hope that she had been near some window meantime, and been aware of his attentions. Finally, he went home reluctantly with his poor head full of visions.

All through supper his spirits were so high that his aunt wondered 'what had got into the child'. He took a good scolding about clodding Sid, and did not seem to mind it in the least. He tried to steal sugar under his aunt's very nose, and got his knuckles rapped for it. He said:

'Aunt, you don't whack Sid when he takes it.'

'Well, Sid don't torment a body the way you do. You'd be always into that sugar if I warn't watching you.'

Presently she stepped into the kitchen, and Sid, happy in his immunity, reached for the sugar-bowl, a sort of glorying over Tom which was well-nigh unbearable. But Sid's fingers slipped, and the bowl dropped and broke. Tom was in ecstasies – in such ecstasies that he even controlled his tongue and was silent. He said to himself that he would not speak a word, even when his aunt came in, but would sit perfectly still till she asked who did the mischief; and then he would tell, and there would be nothing so good in the world as to see that pet model 'catch it'. He was so brim-full of exultation that he could hardly hold himself when the old lady came back and stood above the wreck discharging lightnings of wrath from over her spectacles. He said to himself, 'Now it's coming!' And the next instant he was sprawling on the floor! The potent palm was uplifted to strike again, when Tom cried out:

'Hold on, now, what're you belting *me* for? Sid broke it!'

Aunt Polly paused perplexed, and Tom looked for healing pity. But when she got her tongue again she only said:

'Umph! Well, you didn't get a lick amiss, I reckon. You'd been into some other owdacious mischief when I wasn't around, like enough.'

Then her conscience reproached her, and she yearned to say something kind and loving; but she judged that this would be construed into a confession that she had been in the wrong, and discipline forbade that. So she kept silence, and went about her affairs with a troubled heart. Tom sulked in a corner, and exalted his woes. He knew that in her heart his aunt was on her knees to him, and he was morosely gratified by the consciousness of it. He would hang out no signals, he would take notice of none. He knew that a yearning glance fell upon him, now and then, through a film of tears, but he refused recognition of it. He pictured himself lying sick unto death and his aunt bending over him, beseeching one little forgiving word, but he would turn his face to the wall, and die with that word unsaid. Ah, how would she feel then? And he pictured himself brought home from the river, dead, with his curls all wet, and his poor hands still for ever, and his sore heart at rest. How she would throw herself upon him, and how her tears would fall like rain, and her lips pray God to give her back her boy, and she would never, never, abuse him any more! But he would lie there cold and white and make no sign – a poor little sufferer whose griefs were at an end. He so worked upon his feelings with the pathos of these dreams that he had to keep swallowing – he was so like to choke; and his eyes swam in a blur of water, which overflowed when he winked,

24

and ran down and trickled from the end of his nose. And
such a luxury to him was this petting of his sorrows that he
could not bear to have any worldly cheeriness or any
grating delight intrude upon it; it was too sacred for such
contact; and so presently, when his cousin Mary danced in,
all alive with the joy of seeing home again after an age-long
visit of one week to the country, he got up and moved in
clouds and darkness out at one door as she brought song and
sunshine in at the other. He wandered far away from the
accustomed haunts of boys, and sought desolate places that
were in harmony with his spirit. A log raft in the river
invited him, and he seated himself on its outer edge, and
contemplated the dreary vastness of the stream, wishing the
while that he could only be drowned all at once and unconsciously, without undergoing the uncomfortable routine
devised by nature. Then he thought of his flower. He got it
out, rumpled and wilted, and it mightily increased his dismal felicity. He wondered if *she* would pity him if she knew!
Would she cry, and wish that she had a right to put her arms
around his neck and comfort him? Or would she turn coldly
away like all the hollow world? This picture brought such
an agony of pleasurable suffering that he worked it over and
over again in his mind and set it up in new and varied lights
till he wore it threadbare. At last he rose up sighing and
departed in the darkness. About half past nine or ten o'clock
he came along the deserted street to where the adored unknown lived; he paused a moment, no sound fell upon his
listening ear; a candle was casting a dull glow upon the
curtain of a second-story window. Was the sacred presence
there? He climbed the fence, threaded his stealthy way
through the plants, till he stood under that window; he
looked up at it long, and with emotion; then he laid him
down on the ground under it, disposing himself upon his
back, with his hands clasped upon his breast, and holding
his poor wilted flower. And thus he would die – out in the
cold world with no shelter over his homeless head, no

friendly hand to wipe the death-damps from his brow, no loving face to bend pityingly over him when the great agony came. And thus *she* would see him when she looked out upon the glad morning – and oh, would she drop one tear upon his poor lifeless form, would she heave one little sigh to see a bright young life so rudely blighted, so untimely cut down?

The window went up; a maid-servant's discordant voice profaned the holy calm, and a deluge of water drenched the prone martyr's remains!

The strangling hero sprang up with a relieving snort; there was a whiz as of a missile in the air, mingled with the murmur of a curse, a sound as of shivering glass followed, and a small vague form went over the fence and shot away in the gloom.

Not long after, as Tom, all undressed for bed, was surveying his drenched garments by the light of a tallow dip, Sid woke up; but if he had any dim idea of making 'references to allusions', he thought better of it, and held his peace – for there was danger in Tom's eye. Tom turned in without the added vexation of prayers, and Sid made mental note of the omission.

CHAPTER IV

THE sun rose upon a tranquil world, and beamed down upon the peaceful village like a benediction. Breakfast over, Aunt Polly had family worship; it began with a prayer built from the ground up of solid courses of scriptural quotations wedded together with a thin mortar of originality; and from the summit of this she delivered a grim chapter of the Mosaic Law, as from Sinai.

Then Tom girded up his loins, so to speak, and went to work to 'get his verses'. Sid had learned his lesson days before. Tom bent all his energies to the memorizing of five verses; and he chose part of the Sermon on the Mount, because he could find no verses that were shorter.

At the end of half an hour Tom had a vague general idea of his lesson, but no more, for his mind was traversing the whole field of human thought, and his hands were busy with distracting recreations. Mary took his book to hear him recite, and he tried to find his way through the fog.

'Blessed are the – a – a – '

'Poor – '

'Yes – poor; blessed are the poor – a – a – '

'In spirit – '

'In spirit; blessed are the poor in spirit, for they – they – '

'Theirs – '

'For theirs. Blessed are the poor in spirit, for theirs – is the kingdom of Heaven. Blessed are they that mourn, for they – they – '

'Sh – '

'For they – a – '

'S-H-A – '

'For they S-H – Oh, I don't know what it is!'

'Shall!'

'Oh, shall! for they shall – for they shall – a – a – shall mourn – a – a – blessed are they that shall – they that – a – they that shall mourn, for they shall – a – shall what? Why don't you tell me, Mary? What do you want to be so mean for?'

'Oh, Tom, you poor thick-headed thing, I'm not teasing you. I wouldn't do that. You must go and learn it again. Don't you be discouraged, Tom, you'll manage it – and if you do, I'll give you something ever so nice! There, now, that's a good boy.'

'All right! What is it, Mary? Tell me what it is.'

'Never you mind, Tom. You know if I say it's nice, it is nice.'

'You bet you that's so, Mary. All right, I'll tackle it again.'

And he did 'tackle it again'; and under the double pressure of curiosity and prospective gain, he did it with such spirit that he accomplished a shining success.

Mary gave him a brand-new 'Barlow' knife, worth twelve and a half cents; and the convulsion of delight that swept his system shook him to his foundations. True, the knife would not cut anything, but it was a 'sure-enough' Barlow, and there was inconceivable grandeur in that – though where the western boys ever got the idea that such a weapon could possibly be counterfeited to its injury is an imposing mystery, and will always remain so, perhaps. Tom contrived to scarify the cupboard with it and was arranging to begin on the bureau, when he was called off to dress for Sunday-school.

Mary gave him a tin basin of water and a piece of soap, and he went outside the door and set the basin on a little bench there; then he dipped the soap in the water and laid it down; turned up his sleeves; poured out the water on the ground gently, and then entered the kitchen, and began to wipe his face diligently on the towel behind the door. But Mary removed the towel and said:

'Now ain't you ashamed, Tom? You mustn't be so bad. Water won't hurt you.'

Tom was a trifle disconcerted. The basin was refilled, and this time he stood over it a little while, gathering resolution; took in a big breath and began. When he entered the kitchen presently, with both eyes shut, and groping for the towel with his hands, an honourable testimony of suds and water was dripping from his face. But when he emerged from the towel, he was not yet satisfactory; for the clean territory stopped short at his chin and his jaws like a mask; below and beyond this line there was a dark expanse of unirrigated soil that spread downward in front and backward around his neck. Mary took him in hand, and when she was done with him he was a man and a brother, without distinction of colour, and his saturated hair was neatly brushed, and its short curls wrought into a dainty and symmetrical general effect. (He privately smoothed out the curls, with labour and difficulty, and plastered his hair close down to his head; for he held curls to be effeminate, and his own filled his life with bitterness.) Then Mary got out a suit of his clothing that had been used only on Sundays during two years – they were simply called his 'other clothes' – and so by that we know the size of his wardrobe. The girl 'put him to rights' after he had dressed himself; she buttoned his neat round-about up to his chin, turned his vast shirt-collar down over his shoulders, brushed him off and crowned him with his speckled straw hat. He now looked exceedingly improved and uncomfortable; and he was fully as uncomfortable as he looked; for there was a restraint about whole clothes and cleanliness that galled him. He hoped that Mary would forget his shoes, but the hope was blighted; she coated them thoroughly with tallow, as was the custom, and brought them out. He lost his temper, and said he was always being made to do everything he didn't want to do. But Mary said persuasively:

'Please, Tom – that's a good boy.'

So he got into his shoes, snarling. Mary was soon ready, and the three children set out for Sunday-school, a place that Tom hated with his whole heart; but Sid and Mary were fond of it.

Sabbath-school hours were from nine to half past ten; and then church service. Two of the children always remained for the sermon voluntarily; and the other always remained too, for stronger reasons. The church's high-backed uncushioned pews would seat about three hundred persons; the edifice was but a small, plain affair, with a sort of pine-board tree-box on top of it for a steeple. At the door Tom dropped back a step and accosted a Sunday-dressed comrade:

'Say, Bill, got a yaller ticket?'

'Yes.'

'What'll you take for her?'

'What'll you give?'

'Piece of lickrish and a fish-hook.'

'Less see 'em.'

Tom exhibited. They were satisfactory, and the property changed hands. Then Tom traded a couple of white alleys for three red tickets, and some small trifle or other for a couple of blue ones. He waylaid other boys as they came, and went on buying tickets of various colours ten or fifteen minutes longer. He entered the church, now, with a swarm of clean and noisy boys and girls, proceeded to his seat and started a quarrel with the first boy that came handy. The teacher, a grave, elderly man, interfered; then turned his back a moment, and Tom pulled a boy's hair in the next bench, and was absorbed in his book when the boy turned around; stuck a pin in another boy, presently, in order to hear him say 'Ouch!' and got a new reprimand from his teacher. Tom's whole class were of a pattern – restless, noisy, and troublesome. When they came to recite their lessons, not one of them knew his verses perfectly, but had to be prompted all along. However, they worried through, and each got his reward in small blue tickets, each with a passage of Scripture on it; each blue ticket was pay for two verses of the recitation. Ten blue tickets equalled a red one, and could be exchanged for it; ten red tickets equalled a yellow one; for ten yellow tickets the Superintendent gave a very plainly bound Bible (worth forty cents in those easy times) to the pupil. How many of my readers would have the industry and the application to memorize two thousand verses, even for a Doré Bible? And yet Mary had acquired two Bibles in this way; it was the patient work of two years: and a boy of German parentage had won four or five. He once recited three thousand verses without stopping; but the strain upon his mental faculties was too great, and he was little better than an idiot from that day forth – a grievous misfortune for the school, for on great occasions before company the Superintendent (as Tom expressed it) had always made this boy come out and 'spread himself'. Only the older pupils managed to keep their tickets and stick to their tedious work long enough to get a Bible, and so the delivery of one of these prizes was a rare and noteworthy circumstance; the successful pupil was so great and conspicuous for that day that on the spot every scholar's breast was fired with a fresh ambition that often lasted a couple of weeks. It is possible that Tom's mental stomach had never really hungered for one of those prizes, but unquestionably his entire being had for many a day longed for the glory and the *élat* that came with it.

In due course the Superintendent stood up in front of the pulpit, with a closed hymn-book in his hand and his fore-finger inserted between its leaves, and commanded attention. When a Sunday-school superintendent makes his customary little speech, a hymn-book in the hand is as necessary as is the inevitable sheet of music in the hand of a singer who stands forward on the platform and sings a solo at a concert – though why is a mystery; for neither the hymn-book nor the sheet of music is ever referred to by the sufferer. This Superintendent was a slim creature of thirty-five, with a sandy goatee, and short sandy hair; he wore a stiff standing-collar whose upper edge almost reached his ears, and whose sharp points curved forward abreast the corners of his mouth – a fence that compelled a straight look-out ahead, and a turning of the whole body when a side view was required. His chin was propped on a spreading cravat, which was as broad and as long as a bank-note, and had fringed ends; his boot toes were turned sharply up, in the fashion of the day, like sleigh-runners – an effect patiently and laboriously produced by the young men by sitting with their toes pressed against a wall for hours together. Mr Walters was very earnest of mien, and very sincere and honest at heart; and he held sacred things and places in such reverence, and so separated them from worldly matters, that unconsciously to himself his Sunday-school voice had acquired a peculiar intonation which was wholly absent on weekdays. He began after this fashion:

'Now, children, I want you all to sit up just as straight and pretty as you can, and give me all your attention for a minute or two. There, that is it. That is the way good little boys and girls should do. I see one little girl who is looking out of the window – I am afraid she thinks I am out there somewhere – perhaps up in one of the trees making a speech to the little birds. [Applausive titter.] I want to tell you how good it makes me feel to see so many bright, clean little faces assembled in a place like this, learning to do right and be good.'

And so forth, and so on. It is not necessary to set down the rest of the oration. It was of a pattern which does not vary, and so it is familiar to us all.

The latter third of the speech was marred by the resumption of fights and other recreations among certain of the bad boys, and by fidgetings and whisperings that extended far and wide, washing even to the bases of isolated and incorruptible rocks like Sid and Mary. But now every sound ceased suddenly with the subsidence of Mr Walter's voice, and the conclusion of the speech was received with a burst of silent gratitude.

A good part of the whispering had been occasioned by an event which was more or less rare – the entrance of visitors; Lawyer Thatcher, accompanied by a very feeble and aged man, a fine, portly, middle-aged gentleman with iron-grey hair, and a dignified lady who was doubtless the latter's wife. The lady was leading a child. Tom had been restless and full of chafings and repinings, conscience-smitten, too – he could not meet Amy Lawrence's eye, he could not brook her loving gaze. But when he saw this small new-comer his soul was all ablaze with bliss in a moment. The next moment he was 'showing off' with all his might – cuffing boys, pulling hair, making faces, in a word, using every art that seemed

32

likely to fascinate a girl, and win her applause. His exultation had but one alloy – the memory of his humiliation in this angel's garden; and that record in sand was fast washing out under the waves of happiness that were sweeping over it now. The visitors were given the highest seat of honour, and as soon as Mr Walters's speech was finished he introduced them to the school. The middle-aged man turned out to be a prodigious personage; no less a one than the county judge – altogether the most august creation these children had ever looked upon; and they wondered what kind of material he was made of; and they half wanted to hear him roar, and were half afraid he might, too. He was from Constantinople, twelve miles away – so he had travelled and seen the world – these very eyes had looked upon the County Court House, which was said to have a tin roof. The awe which these reflections inspired was attested by the impressive silence and the ranks of staring eyes. This was the great Judge Thatcher, brother of their own lawyer. Jeff Thatcher immediately went forward to be familiar with the great man and be envied by the school. It would have been music to his soul to hear the whisperings.

'Look at him, Jim! he's a going up there. Say, look! he's a going to shake hands with him; he *is* a shaking hands with him. By jinks, don't you wish you was Jeff?'

Mr Walters fell to 'showing off' with all sorts of official bustlings and activities, giving orders, delivering judgements, discharging directions here, there, and everywhere that he could find a target. The librarian 'showed off', running hither and thither with his arms full of books and making a deal of the splutter and fuss that insect authority delights in. The young lady teachers 'showed off' – bending sweetly over pupils that were lately being boxed, lifting pretty warning fingers at bad little boys and patting good ones lovingly. The young gentleman teachers 'showed off' with small scoldings and other little displays of authority and fine attention to discipline; and most of the teachers, of both sexes, found

33

business up at the library by the pulpit; and it was business that frequently had to be done over again two or three times (with much seeming vexation). The little girls 'showed off' in various ways, and the little boys 'showed off' with such diligence that the air was thick with paper wads and the murmur of scufflings. And above it all the great man sat and beamed a majestic judicial smile upon all the house, and warmed himself in the sun of his own grandeur, for he was 'showing off' too. There was only one thing wanting to make Mr Walters's ecstasy complete, and that was a chance to deliver a Bible-prize and exhibit a prodigy. Several pupils had a few yellow tickets, but none had enough – he had been around among the star pupils inquiring. He would have given worlds, now, to have that German lad back again with a sound mind.

And now at this moment, when hope was dead, Tom Sawyer came forward with nine yellow tickets, nine red tickets, and ten blue ones, and demanded a Bible! This was a thunderbolt out of a clear sky. Walters was not expecting an application from this source for the next ten years. But there was no getting around it – here were the certified checks, and they were good for their face. Tom was therefore elevated to a place with the Judge and the other elect, and the great news was announced from headquarters. It was the most stunning surprise of the decade; and so profound was the sensation that it lifted the new hero up to the judicial one's altitude, and the school had two marvels to gaze upon in place of one. The boys were all eaten up with envy; but those that suffered the bitterest pangs were those who perceived too late that they themselves had contributed to this hated splendour by trading tickets to Tom for the wealth he had amassed in selling whitewashing privileges. These despised themselves, as being the dupes of a wily fraud, a guileful snake in the grass.

The prize was delivered to Tom with as much effusion as the Superintendent could pump up under the circumstances; but it lacked somewhat of the true gush, for the poor fellow's instinct taught him that there was a mystery here that could not well bear the light, perhaps; it was simply preposterous that *this* boy had warehoused two thousand sheaves of Scriptural wisdom on his premises – a dozen would strain his capacity, without a doubt. Amy Lawrence was proud and glad, and she tried to make Tom see it in her face; but he wouldn't look. She wondered; then she was just a grain troubled; next a dim suspicion came and went – came again; she watched; a furtive glance told her worlds – and then her heart broke, and she was jealous, and angry, and the tears came and she hated everybody; Tom most of all, she thought.

Tom was introduced to the Judge; but his tongue was tied, his breath would hardly come, his heart quaked – partly because of the awful greatness of the man, but mainly because he was *her* parent. He would have liked to fall down and worship him, if it were in the dark. The Judge put his hand on Tom's head and called him a fine little man, and asked him what his name was. The boy stammered, gasped, and got it out.

'Tom.'

'Oh, no, not Tom – it is – '

'Thomas.'

'Ah, that's it. I thought there was more to it, maybe. That's very well. But you've another one, I dare say, and you'll tell it to me, won't you?'

'Tell the gentleman your other name, Thomas,' said Walters, 'and say *sir*. You mustn't forget your manners.'

'Thomas Sawyer – sir.'

'That's it! that's a good boy. Fine boy. Fine, manly little fellow. Two thousand verses is a great many – very, very great many. And you never can be sorry for the trouble you took to learn them; for knowledge is worth more than anything there is in the world; it's what makes great men and good men; you'll be a great man and a good man yourself some day, Thomas, and then you'll look back and say, It's all owing to the precious Sunday-school privileges of my boyhood; it's all owing to my dear teachers that taught me to learn; it's all owing to the good Superintendent, who encouraged me and watched over me, and gave me a beautiful Bible, a splendid, elegant Bible, to keep and have it all for my own, always; it's all owing to right bringing up! That is what you will say, Thomas; and you wouldn't take any money for those two thousand verses, then – no, indeed you wouldn't. And now you wouldn't mind telling me and this lady some of the things you've learned – no, I know you wouldn't – for we are proud of little boys that learn. Now no doubt you know the names of all the twelve disciples. Won't you tell us the names of the first two that were appointed?'

Tom was tugging at a button and looking sheepish. He blushed, now, and his eyes fell. Mr Walters's heart sank within him. He said to himself, It is not possible that the boy can answer the simplest question – why *did* the Judge ask him? Yet he felt obliged to speak up and say:

'Answer the gentleman, Thomas – don't be afraid.'

Tom still hung fire.

'Now I know you'll tell *me*,' said the lady. 'The names of the first two disciples were – '

'DAVID AND GOLIATH!'

Let us draw the curtain of charity over the rest of the scene.

CHAPTER V

ABOUT half past ten the cracked bell of the small church began to ring, and presently the people began to gather for the morning sermon. The Sunday-school children distributed themselves about the house, and occupied pews with their parents, so as to be under supervision. Aunt Polly came, and Tom, and Sid and Mary sat with her, Tom being placed next the aisle, in order that he might be as far away from the open window and the seductive outside summer scenes as possible. The crowd filed up the aisle; the aged and needy postmaster, who had seen better days; the mayor and his wife – for they had a mayor there, among other unnecessaries; the justice of the peace; the widow Douglas, fair, smart, and forty, a generous, good-hearted soul and well-to-do, her hill mansion the only palace in the town, and the most hospitable and much the most lavish in the matter of festivities that St Petersburg could boast; the bent and venerable mayor and Mrs Ward; Lawyer Riverson, the new notable from a distance; next the belle of the village, followed by a troop of lawn-clad and ribbon-decked young heart-breakers; then all the young clerks in town in a body – for they had stood in the vestibule sucking their cane-heads, a circling wall of oiled and simpering admirers, till the last girl had run their gauntlet; and last of all came the model boy, Willie Mufferson, taking as heedful care of his mother as if she were cut glass. He always brought his mother to church, and was the pride of all the matrons. The boys all hated him, he was so good; and besides, he had been 'thrown up to them' so much. His white handkerchief was hanging out of his pocket behind, as usual on Sundays – accidentally. Tom had no handkerchief and he looked upon boys who had as snobs. The congregation being fully assembled now, the bell rang once more, to warn laggards and stragglers, and then a solemn hush fell upon the church, which was only broken by the tittering and whispering of the choir in the gallery. The choir always tittered and whispered all through service. There was once a church choir that was not ill-bred, but I have forgotten where it was, now. It was a great many years ago, and I can scarcely remember anything about it, but I think it was in some foreign country.

The minister gave out the hymn, and read it through

with a relish, in a peculiar style which was much admired in that part of the country. His voice began on a medium key, and climbed steadily up till it reached a certain point, where it bore with strong emphasis upon the topmost word, and then plunged down as if from a spring-board.

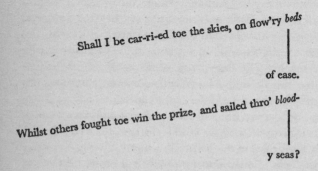

Shall I be car-ri-ed toe the skies, on flow'ry *beds*

of ease.

Whilst others fought toe win the prize, and sailed thro' *blood-*

y seas?

He was regarded as a wonderful reader. At church 'sociables' he was always called upon to read poetry; and when he was through, the ladies would lift up their hands and let them fall helplessly in their laps, and 'wall' their eyes, and shake their heads, as much as to say, 'Words cannot express it; it is too beautiful, *too* beautiful for this mortal earth.'

After the hymn had been sung, the Rev Mr Sprague turned himself into a bulletin board and read off 'notices' of meetings and societies and things till it seemed that the list would stretch out to the crack of doom – a queer custom which is still kept up in America, even in cities, away here in this age of abundant newspapers. Often the less there is to justify a traditional custom, the harder it is to get rid of it.

And now the minister prayed. A good, generous prayer

it was, and went into details; it pleaded for the Church, and the little children of the Church; for the other churches of the village; for the village itself; for the county; for the State; for the State officers; for the United States; for the churches of the United States; for Congress; for the President; for the officers of the Government; for poor sailors, tossed by stormy seas; for the oppressed millions groaning under the heel of European monarchies and Oriental despotisms; for such as have the light and the good tidings, and yet have no eyes to see nor ears to hear withal; for the heathen in the far islands of the sea; and closed with a supplication that the words he was about to speak might find grace and favour, and be as seed sown in fertile ground, yielding in time a grateful harvest of good. Amen.

There was a rustling of dresses, and the standing congregation sat down. The boy whose history this book relates did not enjoy the prayer, he only endured it – if he even did that much. He was restive all through it; he kept tally of the details of the prayer, unconsciously – for he was not listening, but he knew the ground of old and the clergyman's regular route over it – and when a little trifle of new matter was interlarded, his ear detected it and his whole nature resented it; he considered additions unfair, and scoundrelly. In the midst of the prayer a fly had lit on the back of the pew in front of him, and tortured his spirit by calmly rubbing its hands together; embracing its head with its arms and polishing it so vigorously that it seemed to almost part company with the body, and the slender thread of a neck was exposed to view; scraping its wings with its hind legs and smoothing them to its body as if they had been coattails; going through its whole toilet as tranquilly as if it knew it was perfectly safe. As indeed it was; for as sorely as Tom's hands itched to grab for it they did not dare – he believed his soul would be instantly destroyed if he did such a thing while the prayer was going on. But with the closing sentence his hand began to curve and steal forward; and the instant the 'Amen' was out, the fly was a prisoner of war. His aunt detected the act, and made him let it go.

The minister gave out his text and droned along monotonously through an argument that was so prosy that many a head by-and-by began to nod – and yet it was an argument that dealt in limitless fire and brimstone, and thinned the predestined elect down to a company so small as to be hardly worth the saving. Tom counted the pages of the sermon; after church he always knew how many pages there had been, but he seldom knew anything else about the discourse. However, this time he was really interested for a little while. The minister made a grand and moving picture of the assembling together of the world's hosts at the millennium when the lion and the lamb should lie down together and a little child should lead them. But the pathos, the lesson, the moral of the great spectacle were lost upon the boy; he only thought of the conspicuousness of the principal character before the onlooking nations; his face lit up with the thought, and he said to himself that he wished he could be that child, if it was a tame lion.

Now he lapsed into suffering again as the dry argument was resumed. Presently he bethought himself of a treasure he had, and got it out. It was a large black beetle with formidable jaws – a 'pinch-bug', he called it. It was in a percussion-cap box. The first thing the beetle did was to take him by the finger. A natural fillip followed, the beetle went floundering into the aisle, and lit on its back, and the hurt finger went into the boy's mouth. The beetle lay there working its helpless legs, unable to turn over. Tom eyed it, and longed for it, but it was safe out of his reach. Other people, uninterested in the sermon, found relief in the beetle, and they eyed it too.

Presently a vagrant poodle dog came idling along, sad at heart, lazy with the summer softness and the quiet, weary of captivity, sighing for change. He spied the beetle; the drooping tail lifted and wagged. He surveyed the prize;

walked around it; smelt of it from a safe distance; walked around it again; grew bolder, and took a closer smell; then lifted his lips, and made a gingerly snatch at it, just missing it; made another, and another; began to enjoy the diversion; subsided to his stomach with the beetle between his paws, and continued his experiments; grew weary at last, and then indifferent and absent-minded. His head nodded, and little by little his chin descended and touched the enemy, who seized it. There was a sharp yelp, a flirt of the poodle's head and the beetle fell a couple of yards away, and lit on its back once more. The neighbouring spectators shook with a gentle inward joy, several faces went behind fans and handkerchiefs, and Tom was entirely happy. The dog looked foolish, and probably felt so; but there was resentment in his heart, too, and a craving for revenge. So he went to the beetle and began a wary attack on it again; jumping at it from every point of a circle, lighting with his forepaws within an inch of the creature, making even closer snatches at it with his teeth, and jerking his head till his ears flapped again. But he grew tired once more, after a while; tried to amuse himself with a fly, but found no relief; followed an ant around, with his nose close to the floor, and quickly wearied of that; yawned, sighed, forgot the beetle entirely, and sat down on it! Then there was a wild yelp of agony, and the poodle went sailing up the aisle; the yelps continued, and so did the dog; he crossed the house in front of the altar, he flew down the other aisle; he crossed before the doors; he clamoured up the home-stretch; his anguish grew with his progress, till presently he was but a woolly comet moving in its orbit with the gleam and the speed of light. At last the frantic sufferer sheered from its course and sprang into its master's lap; he flung it out of the window, and the voice of distress quickly thinned away and died in the distance.

By this time the whole church was red-faced and suffocating with suppressed laughter, and the sermon had come to a dead standstill. The discourse was resumed presently, but it went lame and halting, all possibility of impressiveness being at an end; for even the gravest sentiments were constantly being received with a smothered burst of unholy mirth, under cover of some remote pew-back, as if the poor parson had said a rarely facetious thing. It was a genuine relief to the whole congregation when the ordeal was over and the benediction pronounced.

Tom Sawyer went home quite cheerful, thinking to himself that there was some satisfaction about divine service when there was a bit of variety in it. He had but one marring thought; he was willing that the dog should play with his pinch-bug, but he did not think it was upright in him to carry it off.

CHAPTER VI

MONDAY morning found Tom Sawyer miserable. Monday morning always found him so, because it began another week's slow suffering in school. He generally began that day with wishing he had had no intervening holiday, it made the going into captivity and fetters again so much more odious.

Tom lay thinking. Presently it occurred to him that he wished he was sick; then he could stay home from school. Here was a vague possibility. He canvassed his system. No ailment was found, and he investigated again. This time he thought he could detect colicky symptoms, and he began to encourage them with considerable hope. But they soon grew feeble and presently died wholly away. He reflected further. Suddenly he discovered something. One of his upper teeth was loose. This was lucky; he was about to begin to groan, as a 'starter', as he called it, when it occurred to him that if he came into court with that argument his aunt would pull it out, and that would hurt. So he thought he would hold the tooth in reserve for the present, and seek further. Nothing offered for some little time, and then he remembered hearing the doctor tell about a certain thing that laid up a patient for two or three weeks and threatened to make him lose a finger. So the boy eagerly drew his sore toe from under the sheet and held it up for inspection. But now he did not know the necessary symptoms. However, it seemed well worth while to chance it, so he fell to groaning with considerable spirit.

But Sid slept on, unconscious.

Tom groaned louder, and fancied that he began to feel pain in the toe.

No result from Sid.

Tom was panting with his exertions by this time. He took a rest and then swelled himself up and fetched a succession of admirable groans.

Sid snored on.

Tom was aggravated. He said, 'Sid, Sid!' and shook him. This course worked well, and Tom began to groan again. Sid yawned, stretched, then brought himself up on his elbow with a snort, and began to stare at Tom. Tom went on groaning. Sid said:

'Tom! say, Tom!'

No response.

'Here, Tom! Tom! What is the matter, Tom?' And he shook him, and looked in his face anxiously.

Tom moaned out:

'Oh, don't, Sid. Don't joggle me.'

'Why, what's the matter, Tom? I must call Auntie.'

'No, never mind. It'll be over by and by, maybe. Don't call anybody.'

'But I must! Don't groan so, Tom, it's awful. How long you been this way?'

'Hours. Ouch! Oh, don't stir so, Sid. You'll kill me.'

'Tom, why didn't you wake me sooner? Oh, Tom, don't!

43

It makes my flesh crawl to hear you. Tom, what is the matter?'

'I forgive you everything, Sid. [Groan.] Everything you've ever done to me. When I'm gone – '

'Oh, Tom, you ain't dying, are you? Don't, Tom. Oh, don't. Maybe – '

'I forgive everybody, Sid. [Groan.] Tell 'em so, Sid. And, Sid, you give my window-sash, and my cat with one eye to that new girl that's come to town, and tell her – '

But Sid had snatched his clothes and gone. Tom was suffering in reality now, so handsomely was his imagination working, and so his groans had gathered quite a genuine tone.

Sid flew downstairs and said:

'Oh, Aunt Polly, come! Tom's dying!'

'Dying!'

'Yes'm. Don't wait, come quick!'

'Rubbage! I don't believe it!'

But she fled upstairs nevertheless, with Sid and Mary at her heels. And her face grew white, too, and her lips trembled. When she reached the bedside she gasped out:

'You Tom! Tom, what's the matter with you?'

'Oh, Auntie, I'm – '

'What's the matter with you – what *is* the matter with you, child?'

'Oh, Auntie, my sore toe's mortified!'

The old lady sank down into a chair and laughed a little, then cried a little, then did both together. This restored her, and she said:

'Tom, what a turn you did give me. Now you shut up that nonsense and climb out of this.'

The groans ceased, and the pain vanished from the toe. The boy felt a little foolish, and he said:

'Aunt Polly, it *seemed* mortified, and it hurt so I never minded my tooth at all.'

'Your tooth, indeed! What's the matter with your tooth?'

'One of them's loose, and it aches perfectly awful.'

'There, there now, don't begin that groaning again. Open your mouth. Well, your tooth *is* loose, but you're not going to die about that. Mary, get me a silk thread, and a chunk of fire out of the kitchen.'

Tom said:

'Oh, please, Auntie, don't pull it out, it don't hurt any more. I wish I may never stir if it does. Please don't, Auntie, *I* don't want to stay home from school.'

'Oh, you don't, don't you? So all this row was because you thought you'd get to stay home from school and go a fishing? Tom, Tom, I love you so, and you seem to try every way you can to break my old heart with your outrageousness.'

By this time the dental instruments were ready. The old lady made one end of the silk thread fast to Tom's tooth with a loop and tied the other to the bed-post. Then she seized the chunk of fire and suddenly thrust it almost into the boy's face. The tooth hung dangling by the bed-post, now.

But all trials bring their compensations. As Tom wended to school after breakfast, he was the envy of every boy he met because the gap in his upper row of teeth enabled him to expectorate in a new and admirable way. He gathered quite a following of lads interested in the exhibition; and one that had cut his finger and had been a centre of fascination and homage up to this time, now found himself suddenly without an adherent, and shorn of his glory. His heart was heavy, and he said with a disdain which he did not feel, that it wasn't anything to spit like Tom Sawyer; but another boy said 'Sour grapes!' and he wandered away a dismantled hero.

Shortly Tom came upon the juvenile pariah of the village, Huckleberry Finn, son of the town drunkard. Huckleberry was cordially hated and dreaded by all the mothers of the town because he was idle, and lawless, and vulgar, and bad

– and because all their children admired him so, and delighted in his forbidden society, and wished they dared to be like him. Tom was like the rest of the respectable boys in that he envied Huckleberry his gaudy outcast condition, and was under strict orders not to play with him. So he played with him every time he got a chance. Huckleberry was always dressed in the cast-off clothes of full-grown men, and they were in perennial bloom and fluttering with rags. His hat was a vast ruin with a wide crescent lopped out of its brim; his coat, when he wore one, hung nearly to his heels, and had the rearward buttons far down the back; but one suspender supported his trousers; the seat of the trousers bagged low and contained nothing; the fringed legs dragged in the dirt when not rolled up. Huckleberry came and went at his own free will. He slept on door-steps in fine weather, and in empty hogsheads in wet; he did not have to go to school or to church, or call any being master, or obey anybody; he could go fishing or swimming when and where he chose, and stay as long as it suited him; nobody forbade him to fight; he could sit up as late as he pleased; he was always the first boy that went barefoot in the spring and the last to resume leather in the fall; he never had to wash, nor put on clean clothes; he could swear wonderfully. In a word, everything that goes to make life precious, that boy had. So thought every harassed, hampered, respectable boy in St Petersburg. Tom hailed the romantic outcast:

'Hello, Huckleberry!'

'Hello yourself, and see how you like it.'

'What's that you got?'

'Dead cat.'

'Lemme see him, Huck. My, he's pretty stiff. Where'd you get him?'

'Bought him off'm a boy.'

'What did you give?'

'I give a blue ticket and a bladder that I got at the slaughter-house.'

'Where'd you get the blue ticket?'

'Bought it off'n Ben Rogers two weeks ago for a hoop-stick.'

'Say – what is dead cats good for, Huck?'

'Good for? Cure warts with.'

'No? Is that so? I know something that's better.'

'I bet you don't. What is it?'

'Why, spunk-water.'

'Spunk-water! I wouldn't give a dern for spunk-water.'

'You wouldn't, wouldn't you? D'you ever try it?'

'No, I hain't. But Bob Tanner did.'

'Who told you so?'

'Why, he told Jeff Thatcher, and Jeff told Johnny Baker, and Johnny told Jim Hollis, and Jim told Ben Rogers, and Ben told a nigger, and the nigger told me. There now!'

'Well, what of it? They'll all lie. Leastaways all but the nigger, I don't know *him*. But I never see a nigger that *wouldn't* lie. Shucks! Now you tell me how Bob Tanner done it, Huck.'

'Why, he took and dipped his hand in a rotten stump where the rain-water was.'

'In the daytime?'

'Certainly.'

'With his face to the stump?'

'Yes. Least I reckon so.'

'Did he *say* anything?'

'I don't reckon he did, I don't know.'

'Aha! Talk about trying to cure warts with spunk-water such a blame fool way as that! Why, that ain't a going to do any good. You got to go by yourself to the middle of the woods, where you know there's a spunk-water stump, and just as it's midnight you back up against the stump and jam your hand in and say:

> Barley-corn, barley-corn, injun-meal shorts,
> Spunk-water, spunk-water, swaller these warts,

and then walk away quick, eleven steps, with your eyes shut, and then turn around three times and walk home without speaking to anybody. Because if you speak the charm's busted.'

'Well, that sounds like a good way; but that ain't the way Bob Tanner done.'

'No, sir, you can bet he didn't; becuz he's the wartiest boy in this town; and he wouldn't have a wart on him if he'd knowed how to work spunk-water. I've took off thousands of warts off of my hands that way, Huck. I play with frogs so much that I've always got considerable many warts. Sometimes I take 'em off with a bean.'

'Yes, bean's good. I've done that.'

'Have you? What's your way?'

'You take and split the bean, and cut the wart so as to get some blood, and then you put the blood on one piece of the bean, and take and dig a hole and bury it 'bout midnight at the cross-roads in the dark of the moon, and then you burn up the rest of the bean. You see that piece that's got the blood on it will keep drawing and drawing, trying to fitch the other piece to it, and so that helps the blood to draw the wart, and pretty soon off she comes.'

'Yes, that's it, Huck – that's it; though, when you're burying it, if you say, "Down bean, off wart; come no more to bother me!" it's better. That's the way Joe Harper does, and he's ben nearly to Coonville, and most everywhere. But say – how do you cure 'em with dead cats?'

'Why, you take your cat and go and get in the graveyard, long about midnight, where somebody that was wicked has been buried; and when it's midnight a devil will come, or maybe two or three, but you can't see 'em, you can only hear something like the wind, or maybe hear 'em talk; and when they're taking that feller away, you heave your cat after 'em and say, "Devil follow corpse, cat follow devil, warts follow cat. *I'm* done with ye!" That'll fetch *any* wart.'

Sounds right. D'you ever try it, Huck?'

'No, but old Mother Hopkins told me.'

'Well, I reckon it's so, then, becuz they say she's a witch.'

'*Say!* Why, Tom, I *know* she is. She witched pap. Pap says so his own self. He came along one day, and he see she was a witching him, so he took up a rock, and if she hadn't dodged he'd a got her. Well, that very night he rolled off'n a shed wher' he was a layin' drunk, and broke his arm.'

'Why, that's awful. How did he know she was a witching him?'

'Lord, Pap can tell, easy. Pap says when they keep looking at you right stiddy, they're a witching you, specially if they mumble. Becuz when they mumble they're a saying the Lords' Prayer backards.'

'Say, Hucky, when you going to try the cat?'

'Tonight. I reckon they'll come after old Hoss Williams tonight.'

'But they buried him Saturday, Huck. Didn't they get him Saturday night?'

'Why, how you talk! How could their charms work till midnight? and then it's Sunday. Devils don't slosh around much of a Sunday, I don't reckon.'

'I never thought of that. That's so. Lemme go with you?'

'Of course – if you ain't afeard.'

'Afeard! 'Tain't likely. Will you meow?'

'Yes, and you meow back if you get a chance. Last time you kep' me a meowing around till old Hays went to throwing rocks at me, and says, "Dern that cat!" So I hove a brick through his window – but don't you tell.'

'I won't. I couldn't meow that night becuz Auntie was watching me; but I'll meow this time. Say, Huck, what's that?'

'Nothing but a tick.'

'Where'd you get him?'

'Out in the woods.'

'What'll you take for him?'

'I don't know. I don't want to sell him.'

'All right. It's a mighty small tick, anyway.'

'Oh, anybody can run a tick down that don't belong to them. I'm satisfied with it. It's a good enough tick for me.'

'Sho, there's ticks a plenty. I could have a thousand of 'em if I wanted to.'

'Well, why don't you? Becuz you know mighty well you can't. This is a pretty early tick, I reckon. It's the first one I've seen this year.'

'Say, Huck, I'll give you my tooth for him.'

'Less see it.'

Tom got out a bit of paper and carefully unrolled it. Huckleberry viewed it wistfully. The temptation was very strong. At last he said:

'Is it genuwyne?'

Tom lifted his lip and showed the vacancy.

'Well, all right,' said Huckleberry; 'it's a trade.'

Tom enclosed the tick in the percussion-cap box that had lately been the pinch-bug's prison, and the boys separated, each feeling wealthier than before.

When Tom reached the little isolated frame school-house, he strode in briskly, with the manner of one who had come with all honest speed. He hung his hat on a peg, and flung himself into his seat with businesslike alacrity. The master, throned on high in his great splint-bottom armchair, was dozing, lulled by the frowsy hum of study. The interruption roused him:

'Thomas Sawyer!'

Tom knew that when his name was pronounced in full, it meant trouble.

'Sir!'

'Come up here. Now, sir, why are you late again, as usual?'

Tom was about to take refuge in a lie, when he saw two long tails of yellow hair hanging down a back that he recognized by the electric sympathy of love; and by that form was *the only vacant place* on the girls' side of the school-house. He instantly said:

'I STOPPED TO TALK WITH HUCKLEBERRY FINN!'

The master's pulse stood still, and he stared helplessly. The buzz of study ceased; the pupils wondered if this fool-hardy boy had lost his mind. The master said:

'You – you did what?'

'Stopped to talk with Huckleberry Finn.'

There was no mistaking the words.

'Thomas Sawyer, this is the most astounding confession I have ever listened to; no mere ferule will answer for this offence. Take off your jacket.'

The master's arm performed until it was tired, and the stock of switches notably diminished. Then the order followed:

'Now, sir, go and sit with the *girls!* And let this be a warning to you.'

The titter that rippled around the room appeared to abash the boy, but in reality that result was caused rather more by his worshipful awe of his unknown idol and the dread pleasure that lay in his high good fortune. He sat down upon the end of the pine bench, and the girl hitched herself away from him with a toss of the head. Nudges and winks and whispers traversed the room, but Tom sat still, with his arms upon the long, low desk before him, and seemed to study his book. By and by attention ceased from him, and the accustomed school murmur rose upon the dull air once more. Presently the boy began to steal furtive glances at the girl. She observed it, 'made a mouth' at him, and gave him the back of her head for the space of a minute. When she cautiously faced around again, a peach lay before her. She thrust it away; Tom gently put it back; she thrust it away again, but with less animosity. Tom patiently returned it to its place; then she let it remain. Tom scrawled on his slate, 'Please take it – I got more.' The girl glanced at

51

the words, but made no sign. Now the boy began to draw something on the slate, hiding his work with his left hand. For a time the girl refused to notice; but her human curiosity presently began to manifest itself by hardly perceptible signs. The boy worked on, apparently unconscious. The girl made a sort of non-committal attempt to see, but the boy did not betray that he was aware of it. At last she gave in, and hesitatingly whispered:

'Let me see it.'

Tom partly uncovered a dismal caricature of a house with two gable ends to it and a cork-screw of smoke issuing from the chimney. Then the girl's interest began to fasten itself upon the work, and she forgot everything else. When it was finished, she gazed a moment, then whispered:

'It's nice – make a man.'

The artist erected a man in the front yard, that resembled a derrick. He could have stepped over the house; but the girl was not hypercritical; she was satisfied with the monster, and whispered:

'It's a beautiful man – now make me coming along.'

Tom drew an hourglass, with a full moon and straw limbs to it, and armed the spreading fingers with a portentous fan. The girl said:

'It's ever so nice – I wish I could draw.'

'It's easy,' whispered Tom. 'I'll learn you.'

'Oh, will you? When?'

'At noon. Do you go home to dinner?'

'I'll stay if you will.'

'Good – that's a go.'

'What's your name?'

'Becky Thatcher.'

'What's yours? Oh, I know. It's Thomas Sawyer.'

'That's the name they lick me by. I'm Tom when I'm good. You call me Tom, will you?'

'Yes.'

Now Tom began to scrawl something on the slate, hiding

the words from the girl. But she was not backward this time.
She begged to see. Tom said:

'Oh, it ain't anything.'

'Yes it is.'

'No it ain't; you don't want to see.'

'Yes I do, indeed I do. Please let me.'

'You'll tell.'

'No I won't – deed and deed and double deed I won't.'

'You won't tell anybody at all? Ever as long as you live?'

'No, I won't ever tell anybody. Now let me.'

'Oh, *you* don't want to see!'

'Now that you treat me so I *will* see, Tom' – and she put
her small hand on his, and a little scuffle ensued. Tom pretending to resist in earnest, but letting his hand slip by
degrees till these words were revealed: '*I love you.*'

'Oh, you bad thing!' And she hit his hand a smart rap,
but reddened and looked pleased nevertheless.

Just at this juncture the boy felt a slow fateful grip closing
on his ear, and a steady lifting impulse. In that vice he was
borne across the house and deposited in his own seat, under
a peppering fire of giggles from the whole school. Then the
master stood over him during a few awful moments, and
finally moved away to his throne without saying a word.
But although Tom's ear tingled, his heart was jubilant.

As the school quieted down, Tom made an honest effort
to study, but the turmoil within him was too great. In turn
he took his place in the reading class and made a botch of
it, then in the geography class and turned lakes into mountains, mountains into rivers, and rivers into continents, till
chaos was come again; then in the spelling class, and got
'turned down' by a succession of mere baby words till he
brought up at the foot and yielded up the pewter medal
which he had worn with ostentation for months.

CHAPTER VII

THE harder Tom tried to fasten his mind on his book, the more his ideas wandered. So at last, with a sign and a yawn, he gave it up. It seemed to him that the noon recess would never come. The air was utterly dead. There was not a breath stirring. It was the sleepiest of sleepy days. The drowsing murmur of the five-and-twenty studying scholars soothed the soul like the spell that is in the murmur of bees. Away off in the flaming sunshine Cardiff Hill lifted its soft green sides through a shimmering veil of heat tinted with the purple of distance; a few birds floated on lazy wing high in the air; no other living thing was visible but some cows, and they were asleep.

Tom's heart ached to be free, or else to have something of interest to do to pass the dreary time. His hand wandered into his pocket, and his face lit up with a glow of gratitude that was prayer, though he did not know it. Then furtively the percussion-cap box came out. He released the tick, and put him on the long flat desk. The creature probably glowed with a gratitude that amounted to prayer, too, at this moment, but it was premature; for when he started thankfully to travel off, Tom turned him aside with a pin, and made him take a new direction.

Tom's bosom friend sat next him, suffering just as Tom had been, and now he was deeply and gratefully interested in this entertainment in an instant. This bosom friend was Joe Harper. The two boys were sworn friends all the week, and embattled enemies on Saturdays. Joe took a pin out of his lapel, and began to assist in exercising the prisoner. The sport grew in interest momently. Soon Tom said that they were interfering with each other, and neither getting the fullest benefit of the tick. So he put Joe's slate on the desk and drew a line down the middle of it from top to bottom.

'Now,' said he, 'as long as he is on your side you can stir

him up and I'll let him alone: but if you let him get away and get on my side, you're to leave him alone as long as I can keep him from crossing over.'

'All right, go ahead – start him up.'

The tick escaped from Tom, presently, and crossed the equator. Joe harassed him awhile, and then he got away and crossed back again. This change of base occurred often. While one boy was worrying the tick with absorbing interest, the other would look on with interest as strong, the two heads bowed together over the slate and the two souls dead to all things else. At last luck seemed to settle and abide with Joe. The tick tried this, that, and the other course, and got as excited and as anxious as the boys themselves, but time and again, just as he would have victory in his very grasp, so to speak, and Tom's fingers would be twitching to begin, Joe's pin would deftly head him off and keep possession. At last Tom could stand it no longer. The temptation was too strong. So he reached out and lent a hand with his pin. Joe was angry in a moment. Said he:

'Tom, you let him alone.'

'I only just want to stir him up a little, Joe.'

'No, sir, it ain't fair; you just let him alone.'

'Blame it, I ain't going to stir him much.'

'Let him alone, I tell you!'

'I won't!'

'You shall – he's on my side of the line.'

'Look here, Joe Harper, whose is that tick?'

'*I* don't care whose tick he is – he's on my side of the line, and you shan't touch him.'

'Well, I'll just bet I will, though. He's my tick, and I'll do what I blame please with him, or die!'

A tremendous whack came down on Tom's shoulders, and its duplicate on Joe's; and for the space of two minutes the dust continued to fly from the two jackets and the whole school to enjoy it. The boys had been too absorbed to notice the hush that had stolen upon the school a while

55

before when the master came tiptoeing down the room and stood over them. He had contemplated a good part of the performance before he contributed his bit of variety to it. When school broke up at noon, Tom flew to Becky Thatcher, and whispered in her ear.

'Put on your bonnet and let on you're going home; and when you get to the corner, give the rest of 'em the slip, and turn down through the lane and come back. I'll go the other way, and come it over 'em the same way.'

So the one went off with one group of scholars, and the other with another. In a little while the two met at the bottom of the lane, and when they reached the school they had it all to themselves. Then they sat together, with a slate before them, and Tom gave Becky the pencil and held her hand in his, guiding it, and so created another surprising house. When the interest in art began to wane, the two fell to talking. Tom was swimming in bliss. He said:

'Do you love rats?'

'No, I hate them!'

'Well, I do too – live ones. But I mean dead ones, to swing around your head with a string.'

'No, I don't care for rats much, anyway. What *I* like is chewing gum!'

'Oh, I should say so! I wish I had some now!'

'Do you? I've got some. I'll let you chew it awhile, but you must give it back to me.'

That was agreeable, so they chewed it turn about, and dangled their legs against the bench in excess of contentment.

'Was you ever at a circus?' said Tom.

'Yes, and my pa's going to take me again sometime, if I'm good.'

'I been to the circus three or four times – lots of times. Church ain't shucks to a circus. There's things going on at a circus all the time. I'm going to be a clown in a circus when I grow up.'

'Oh, are you? That will be nice. They're so lovely all spotted up.'

'Yes, that's so. And they get slathers of money – most a dollar a day, Ben Rogers says. Say, Becky, was you ever engaged?'

'What's that?'

'Why, engaged to be married.'

'No.'

'Would you like to?'

'I reckon so. I don't know. What is it like?'

'Like? Why it ain't like anything. You only just tell a boy you won't ever have anybody but him, ever ever *ever*, and then you kiss, and that's all. Anybody can do it.'

'Kiss? What do you kiss for?'

'Why that, you know, is to – well, they always do that.'

'Everybody?'

'Why, yes, everybody that's in love with each other. Do you remember what I wrote on the slate?'

'Ye – yes.'

'What was it?'

'I shan't tell you.'

'Shall I tell *you?*'

'Ye – yes – but some other time.'

'No, now.'

'No, not now – tomorrow.'

'Oh, no, *now*, please, Becky. I'll whisper it, I'll whisper it ever so easy.'

Becky hesitating, Tom took silence for consent, and passed his arm about her waist and whispered the tale ever so softly, with his mouth close to her ear. And then he added:

'Now you whisper it to me – just the same.'

She resisted for a while, and then said:

'You turn your face away, so you can't see, and then I will. But you mustn't ever tell anybody – *will* you, Tom? Now you won't – *will* you?'

'No, indeed, indeed I won't. Now, Becky.'

He turned his face away. She bent timidly around till her breath stirred his curls, and whispered, 'I love you!'

Then she sprang away and ran around and around the desks and benches, with Tom after her, and took refuge in a corner at last, with her little white apron to her face. Tom clasped her about her neck and pleaded.

'Now, Becky, it's all over – all over but the kiss. Don't you be afraid of that – it ain't anything at all. Please, Becky.'

And he tugged at the apron and the hands.

By-and-by she gave up and let her hands drop; her face, all glowing with the struggle, came up and submitted. Tom kissed the red lips and said:

'Now it's all done, Becky. And always after this, you know, you ain't ever to love anybody but me, and you ain't ever to marry anybody but me, never never and for ever. Will you?'

'No, I'll never love anybody but you, Tom, and I'll never marry anybody but you, and you ain't to ever marry anybody but me, either.'

'Certainly. Of course. That's *part* of it. And always, coming to school, or when we're going home, you're to walk with me, when there ain't anybody looking – and you choose me and I choose you at parties, because that's the way you do when you're engaged.'

'It's so nice. I never heard of it before.'

'Oh, it's ever so jolly! Why me and Amy Lawrence – '

The big eyes told Tom his blunder, and he stopped, confused.

'Oh, Tom! Then I ain't the first you've ever been engaged to!'

The child began to cry. Tom said:

'Oh, don't cry, Becky. I don't care for her any more.'

'Yes you do, Tom – you know you do.'

Tom tried to put his arm about her neck, but she pushed him away and turned her face to the wall, and went on crying. Tom tried again, with soothing words in his mouth, and was repulsed again. Then his pride was up, and he strode away and went outside. He stood about, restless and uneasy, for a while, glancing at the door every now and then, hoping she would repent and come to find him. But she did not. Then he began to feel badly, and fear that he was in the wrong. It was a hard struggle with him to make new advances now, but he nerved himself to it and entered: She was still standing back there in the corner, sobbing with her face to the wall. Tom's heart smote him. He went to her and stood a moment, not knowing exactly how to proceed. Then he said, hesitatingly:

'Becky, I – I don't care for anybody but you.'

No reply – but sobs.

'Becky,' pleadingly.

'Becky, won't you say something?'

More sobs.

Tom got out his chiefest jewel, a brass knob from the top of an andiron, and passed it around her so that she could see it, and said:

'Please, Becky, won't you take it?'

She struck it to the floor. Then Tom marched out of the house and over the hills and far away, to return to school no more that day. Presently Becky began to suspect. She ran to the door; he was not in sight; she flew around to the play-yard; he was not there. Then she called:

'Tom! Come back, Tom!'

She listened intently, but there was no answer. She had no companions but silence and loneliness. So she sat down to cry again and upbraid herself, and by this time the scholars began to gather again, and she had to hide her grief and still her broken heart, and take up the cross of a long dreary aching afternoon with none among the strangers about her to exchange sorrows with.

CHAPTER VIII

Tom dodged hither and thither through lanes until he was well out of the track of returning scholars, and then fell into a moody jog. He crossed a small 'branch' two or three times, because of a prevailing juvenile superstition that to cross water baffled pursuit. Half an hour later he was disappearing behind the Douglas mansion on the summit of Cardiff Hill, and the school-house was hardly distinguishable away off in the valley behind him. He entered a dense wood, picked his pathless way to the centre of it, and sat down on a mossy spot under a spreading oak. There was not even a zephyr stirring; the dead noonday heat had even stilled the songs of the birds; nature lay in a trance that was broken by no sound but the occasional far-off hammering of a woodpecker, and this seemed to render the pervading silence and sense of loneliness the more profound. The boy's soul was steeped in melancholy; his feelings were in happy accord with his surroundings. He sat long with his elbows on his knees and his chin in his hands, meditating. It seemed to him that life was but a trouble at best, and he more than half envied Jimmy Hodges, so lately released. It must be very peaceful, he thought, to lie and slumber and dream for ever and ever, with the wind whispering through the trees and caressing the grass and the flowers of the grave, and nothing to bother and grieve about, ever any more. If he only had a clean Sunday-school record he could be willing to go, and be done with it all. Now as to this girl. What had he done? Nothing. He had meant the best in the world and been treated like a dog – like a very dog. She would be sorry some day – maybe when it was too late. Ah, if he could only die *temporarily!*

But the elastic heart of youth cannot be kept compressed into one constrained shape long at a time. Tom presently began to drift insensibly back into the concerns of this life again. What if he turned his back, now, and disappeared mysteriously? What if he went away – ever so far away, into unknown countries beyond the seas – and never came back any more! How would she feel then? The idea of being a clown recurred to him now, only to fill him with disgust. For frivolity and jokes, and spotted tights, were an offence when they intruded themselves upon a spirit that was exalted into the vague, august realm of the romantic. No, he would be a soldier, and return after long years, all war-worn and illustrious. No, better still, he would join the Indians and hunt buffaloes, and go on the war-path in the mountain ranges and the trackless great plains of the Far West, and away in the future come back a great chief, bristling with feathers, hideous with paint, and prance into Sunday-school, some drowsy summer morning, with a blood-curdling war-whoop, and sear the eyeballs of all his companions with unappeasable envy. But no, there was something grander even than this. He would be a pirate! That was it! *Now* his future lay plain before him, and glowing with unimaginable splendour. How his name would fill the world, and make people shudder! How gloriously he would go ploughing the dancing seas, in his long, low, black racer, the *Spirit of the Storm*, with his grisly flag flying at the fore! And, at the zenith of his fame, how he would suddenly appear at the old village and stalk into church all brown and weather-beaten, in his black velvet doublet and trunks, his great jack-boots, his crimson sash, his belt bristling with horse-pistols, his crime-rusted cutlass at his side, his slouch hat with waving plumes, his black flag unfurled with the skull and crossbones on it, and hear with swelling ecstasy the whisperings: 'It's Tom Sawyer the Priate! the Black Avenger of the Spanish Main!'

Yes, it was settled; his career was determined. He would run away from home and enter upon it. He would start the very next morning. Therefore he must now begin to get ready. He would collect his resources together. He went to a rotten log near at hand, and began to dig under one end of it with his Barlow knife. He soon struck wood that sounded hollow. He put his hand there, and uttered this incantation impressively:

'What hasn't come here, *come!* What's here, *stay* here!'

Then he scraped away the dirt, and exposed a pine shingle. He took it up and disclosed a shapely little treasure-house whose bottom and sides were of shingles. In it lay a marble. Tom's astonishment was boundless! He scratched his head with a perplexed air, and said:

'Well, that beats anything!'

Then he tossed the marble away pettishly, and stood cogitating. The truth was that a superstition of his had failed here, which he and all his comrades had always looked upon as infallible. If you buried a marble with certain necessary incantations, and left it alone a fortnight, and then opened the place with the incantation he had just used, you would find that all the marbles you had ever lost had gathered themselves together there, meantime, no matter how widely they had been separated. But now this thing had actually and unquestionably failed. Tom's whole structure of faith was shaken to its foundations. He had many a time heard of this thing succeeding, but never of its failing before. It did not occur to him that he had tried it several times before, himself, but could never find the hiding-place afterwards. He puzzled over the matter some time, and finally decided that some witch had interfered and broken the charm. He thought he would satisfy himself on that point, so he searched around till he found a small sandy spot with a little funnel-shaped depression in it. He laid himself down and put his mouth close to this depression and called:

Doodle-bug, doodle-bug, tell me what I want to know!

Doodle-bug, doodle,bug, tell me what I want to know!

The sand began to work, and presently a small black bug appeared for a second, and then darted under again in a fright.

'He dasn't tell! So it *was* a witch that done it. I just knowed it.'

He well knew the futility of trying to contend against witches, so he gave up, discouraged. But it occurred to him that he might as well have the marble he had just thrown away, and therefore he went and made a patient search for it. But he could not find it. Now he went back to his treasure-house, and carefully placed himself just as he had been standing when he tossed the marble away; then he took another marble from his pocket, and tossed it in the same way, saying:

'Brother, go find your brother!'

He watched where it stopped, and went there and looked. But it must have fallen short or gone too far, so he tried twice more. The last repetition was successful. The two marbles lay within a foot of each other.

Just here the blast of a toy tin trumpet came faintly down the green aisles of the forest. Tom flung off his jacket and trousers, turned a suspender into a belt, raked away some brush behind the rotten log, disclosing a rude bow and arrow, a lath sword, and a tin trumpet, and in a moment had seized these things, and bounded away, barelegged, with fluttering shirt. He presently halted under a great elm, blew an answering blast, and then began to tip-toe and look warily out, this way and that. He said cautiously – to an imaginary company:

'Hold, my merry men! Keep hid till I blow.'

Now appeared Joe Harper, as airily clad and elaborately armed as Tom. Tom called:

'Hold! Who comes here into Sherwood Forest without my pass?'

'Guy of Guisborne wants no man's pass! Who art thou that – that – '

'Dares to hold such language,' said Tom, prompting, for they talked 'by the book', from memory.

'Who art thou that dares to hold such language?'

'I, indeed! I am Robin Hood, as thy caitiff carcase soon shall know.'

'Then art thou indeed that famous outlaw? Right gladly will I dispute with thee the passes of the merry wood. Have at thee!'

They took their lath swords, dumped their other traps on the ground, struck a fencing attitude, foot to foot, and began a grave, careful combat, 'two up and two down'. Presently Tom said:

'Now if you've got the hang, go it lively!'

So they 'went it lively', panting and perspiring with the work. By-and-by Tom shouted:

'Fall! fall! Why don't you fall?'

'I sha'n't! Why don't you fall yourself? You're getting the worst of it.'

'Why, that ain't anything. *I* can't fall. That ain't the way it is in the book. The book says, "Then with one back-handed stroke he slew poor Guy of Guisborne!" You're to turn around and let me hit you in the back.'

There was no getting around the authorities, so Joe turned, received the whack, and fell.

'Now,' said Joe, getting up, 'you got to let me kill you. That's fair.'

'Why, I can't do that. It ain't in the book.'

'Well, it's blamed mean. That's all.'

'Well, say, Joe, you can be Friar Tuck, or Much the Miller's son, and lam me with a quarter-staff; or I'll be the Sheriff of Nottingham, and you be Robin Hood a little while, and kill me.'

This was satisfactory, and so these adventures were carried out. Then Tom became Robin Hood again, and was allowed by the treacherous nun to bleed his strength away through his neglected wound. And at last Joe, representing a whole tribe of weeping outlaws, dragged him sadly forth, gave his bow into his feeble hands, and Tom said, 'Where this arrow falls, there bury poor Robin Hood under the greenwood tree.' Then he shot the arrow, and fell back, and would have died; but he lit on a nettle, and sprang up too gaily for a corpse.

The boys dressed themselves, hid their accoutrements, and went off grieving that there were no outlaws any more, and wondering what modern civilization could claim to have done to compensate for their loss. They said they would rather be outlaws a year in Sherwood Forest than President of the United States for ever.

CHAPTER IX

AT half past nine that night, Tom and Sid were sent to bed as usual. They said their prayers, and Sid was soon asleep. Tom lay awake and waited in restless impatience. When it seemed to him that it must be nearly daylight, he heard the clock strike ten! This was despair. He would have tossed and fidgeted, as his nerves demanded, but he was afraid he might wake Sid. So he lay still and stared up into the dark. Everything was dismally still. By-and-by, out of the stillness little scarcely perceptible noises began to emphasize themselves. The ticking of the clock began to bring itself into notice. Old beams began to crack mysteriously. The stairs creaked faintly. Evidently spirits were abroad. A measured, muffled snore issued from Aunt Polly's chamber. And now the tiresome chirping of a cricket that no human ingenuity could locate began. Next the ghastly ticking of a death-watch in the wall at the bed's head made Tom shudder – it meant that somebody's days were numbered. Then the howl of a far-off dog rose on the night air and was answered by a fainter howl from a remoter distance. Tom was in an agony. At last he was satisfied that time had ceased and eternity begun; he began to doze in spite of himself; the clock chimed eleven, but he did not hear it. And then there

came, mingling with his half-formed dreams, a most melancholy caterwauling. The raising of a neighbouring window
disturbed him. A cry of 'Scat! you devil!' and the crash of
an empty bottle against the back of his aunt's wood-shed
brought him wide awake, and a single minute later he was
dressed and out of the window and creeping along the roof
of the 'ell' on all fours. He 'meow'd' with caution once or
twice as he went; then jumped to the roof of the wood-shed,
and thence to the ground. Huckleberry Finn was there, with
his dead cat. The boys moved off and disappeared in the
gloom. At the end of half an hour they were wading
through the tall grass of the graveyard.

It was a graveyard of the old-fashioned western kind. It
was on a hill, about a mile and a half from the village. It
had a crazy board fence around it, which leaned inward in
places, and outward the rest of the time, but stood upright
nowhere. Grass and weeds grew rank over the whole
cemetery. All the old graves were sunken in. There was not
a tombstone on the place; round-topped, worm-eaten boards
staggered over the graves, leaning for support and finding none. 'Sacred to the memory of' so-and-so had been
painted on them once, but it could no longer have been
read, on the most of them, now, even if there had been
light.

A faint wind moaned through the trees, and Tom feared
it might be the spirits of the dead complaining at being disturbed. The boys talked little, and only under their breath,
for the time and the place and the pervading solemnity and
silence oppressed their spirits. They found the sharp new
heap they were seeking, and ensconced themselves within
the protection of three great elms that grew in a bunch
within a few feet of the grave.

Then they waited in silence for what seemed a long time.
The hooting of a distant owl was all the sound that troubled
the dead stillness. Tom's reflection grew oppressive. He
must force some talk. So he said in a whisper:

'Hucky, do you believe the dead people like it for us to be here?'

Huckleberry whispered:

'I wisht I knowed. It's awful solemn like, ain't it?'

'I bet it is.'

There was a considerable pause, while the boys canvassed this matter inwardly. Then Tom whispered:

'Say, Hucky – do you reckon Hoss Williams hears us talking?'

'O' course he does. Least his spirit does.'

Tom, after a pause:

'I wish I'd said *Mister* Williams. But I never meant any harm. Everybody calls him Hoss.'

'A body can't be too particular how they talk 'bout these yer dead people, Tom.'

This was a damper, and conversation died again. Presently Tom seized his comrade's arm and said:

'*Sh!*'

'What is it, Tom?' And the two clung together with beating hearts.

'*Sh!* There 'tis again! Didn't you hear it?'

'I –'

'There! Now you hear it!'

'Lord, Tom, they're coming! They're coming, sure. What'll we do?'

'I dono. Think they'll see us?'

'Oh, Tom, they can see in the dark same as cats. I wish I hadn't come.'

'Oh, don't be afeard. I don't believe they'll bother us. We ain't doing any harm. If we keep perfectly still, maybe they won't notice us at all.'

'I'll try to, Tom, but Lord, I'm all of a shiver.'

'Listen!'

The boys bent their heads together and scarcely breathed. A muffled sound of voices floated up from the far end of the graveyard.

'Look! see there!' whispered Tom. 'What is it?'

'It's devil-fire. Oh, Tom, this is awful.'

Some vague figures approached through the gloom, swinging an old-fashioned tin lantern that freckled the ground with innumerable little spangles of light. Presently Huckleberry whispered with a shudder:

'It's the devils, sure enough. Three of 'em! Lordy, Tom, we're goners! Can you pray?'

'I'll try, but don't you be afeard. They ain't going to hurt us. "Now I lay me down to sleep, I – " '

'*Sh!*'

'What is it, Huck?'

'They're *humans!* One of 'em is, anyway. One of 'em's old Muff Potter's voice.'

'No – 'tain't so, is it?'

'I bet I know it. Don't you stir nor budge. He ain't sharp enough to notice us. Drunk, same as usual, likely – blamed old rip!'

'All right, I'll keep still. Now they're stuck. Can't find it. Here they come again. Now they're hot. Cold again. Hot again. Red-hot! They're pinted right, this time. Say, Huck, I know another o' them voices; it's Injun Joe.'

'That's so – that murderin' half-breed! I'd druther they was devils a dern sight. What kin they be up to?'

The whispers died wholly out now, for the three men had reached the grave, and stood within a few feet of the boys' hiding-place.

'Here it is,' said the third voice; and the owner of it held the lantern up and revealed the face of young Dr Robinson.

Potter and Injun Joe were carrying a hand-barrow with a rope and a couple of shovels on it. They cast down their load and began to open the grave. The doctor put the lantern at the head of the grave, and came and sat down with his back against one of the elm-trees. He was so close the boys could have touched him.

68

'Hurry, men!' he said in a low voice. 'The moon might come out at any moment.'

They growled a response and went on digging. For some time there was no noise but the grating sound of the spades discharging their freight of mould and gravel. It was very monotonous. Finally a spade struck upon the coffin with a dull, woody accent, and within another minute or two the men had hoisted it out on the ground. They prised off the lid with their shovels, got out the body and dumped it rudely on the ground. The moon drifted from behind the clouds and exposed the pallid face. The barrow was got ready and the corpse placed on it, covered with a blanket, and bound to its place with the rope. Potter took out a large spring-knife and cut off the dangling end of the rope, and then said:

'Now the cussed thing's ready, Sawbones, and you'll just out with another five, or here she stays.'

'That's the talk!' said Injun Joe.

'Look here; what does this mean?' said the doctor. 'You required your pay in advance and I've paid you.'

'Yes, and you done more than that,' said Injun Joe, approaching the doctor, who was now standing. 'Five years ago you drove me away from your father's kitchen one night when I come to ask for something to eat, and you said I warn't there for any good; and when I swore I'd get even with you if it took a hundred years, your father had me jailed for a vagrant. Did you think I'd forget? The Injun blood ain't in me for nothing. And now I've got you, and you got to *settle*, you know!'

He was threatening the doctor with his fist in his face by this time. The doctor struck out suddenly, and stretched the ruffian on the ground. Potter dropped his knife, and exclaimed:

'Here, now, don't you strike my pard!' and the next moment he had grappled with the doctor, and the two were struggling with might and main, trampling the grass, and tearing the ground with their heels. Injun Joe sprang to his feet, his eyes flaming with passion, snatched up Potter's knife, and went creeping, catlike, and stooping round and round about the combatants, seeking an opportunity. All at once the doctor flung himself free, seized the heavy headboard of Williams's grave and felled Potter to the earth with it; and in the same instant the half-breed saw his chance, and drove the knife to the hilt in the young man's breast. He reeled and fell partly upon Potter, flooding him with his blood, and in the same moment the clouds blotted out the dreadful spectacle, and the two frightened boys went speeding away in the dark.

Presently, when the moon emerged again Injun Joe was standing over the two forms, contemplating them. The doctor murmured inarticulately, gave a long gasp or two, and was still. The half-breed muttered:

'That score is settled, damn you.'

Then he robbed the body. After which he put the fatal knife in Potter's open right hand, and sat down on the dismantled coffin. Three – four – five minutes passed, and then Potter began to stir and moan. His hand closed upon the knife, he raised it, glanced at it, and let it fall with a shudder. Then he sat up, pushing the body from him, and gazed at it and then around him confusedly. His eyes met Joe's.

'Lord, how is this, Joe?' he said.

'It's a dirty business,' said Joe, without moving. 'What did you do it for?'

'I! I never done it!'

'Look here! that kind of talk won't wash.'

Potter trembled and grew white.

'I thought I'd got sober. I'd no business to drink tonight. But it's in my head yet – worsen' when we started here. I'm all in a muddle; can't recollect anything of it hardly. Tell me, Joe – *honest*, now, old feller – did I do it, Joe? I never meant to; 'pon my soul and honour I never meant to, Joe.

Tell me how it was, Joe. Oh, it's awful – and him so young and promising.'

'Why, you two was scuffling, and he fetched you one with the headboard, and you fell flat; and then up you come, all reeling and staggering like, and snatched the knife and jammed it into him just as he fetched you another awful clip, and here you've laid dead as a wedge till now.'

'Oh, I didn't know what I was a doing. I wish I may die this minute if I did. It was all on accounts of the whisky and the excitement, I reckon. I never used a weapon in my life before, Joe. I've fought, but never with weapons. They'll all say that, Joe, don't tell! Say you won't tell, Joe; that's a good feller. I always liked you, Joe, and stood up for you too. Don't you remember? You won't tell, will you, Joe?' And the poor creature dropped on his knees before the stolid murderer, and clasped his appealing hands.

'No, you've always been fair and square with me, Muff Potter, and I won't go back on you. There, now, that's as fair as a man can say.'

'Oh, Joe, you're an angel! I'll bless you for this the longest day I live.' And Potter began to cry.

'Come, now, that's enough of that. This ain't any time for blubbering. You be off yonder way, and I'll go this. Move, now, and don't leave any tracks behind you.'

Potter started on a trot that quickly increased to a run. The half-breed stood looking after him. He muttered:

'If he's as much stunned with the lick and fuddled with the rum as he had the look of being, he won't think of the knife till he's gone so far he'll be afraid to come back after it to such a place by himself – chicken-heart!'

Two or three minutes later the murdered man, the blanketed corpse, the lidless coffin, and the open grave, were under no inspection but the moon's. The stillness was complete again, too.

CHAPTER X

THE two boys flew on and on towards the village, speechless with horror. They glanced backward over their shoulders from time to time apprehensively, as if they feared they might be followed. Every stump that started up in their path seemed a man and an enemy, and made them catch their breath; and as they sped by some outlying cottages that lay near the village, the barking of the aroused watch-dogs seemed to give wings to their feet.

'If we can only get to the old tannery before we break down!' whispered Tom, in short catches between breaths. 'I can't stand it much longer.'

Huckleberry's hard pantings were his only reply, and the boys fixed their eyes on the goal of their hopes, and bent to their work to win it. They gained steadily on it, and at last, breast to breast, they burst through the open door, and fell, grateful and exhausted, in the sheltering shadows beyond. By and by their pulses slowed down, and Tom whispered:

'Huckleberry, what do you reckon'll come of this?'

'If Dr Robinson dies, I reckon hanging'll come of it.'

'Do you, though?'

'Why, I know it, Tom.'

Tom thought awhile; then he said:

'Who'll tell? We?'

'What are you talking about? S'pose something happened and Injun Joe didn't hang, why he'd kill us some time or other, just as dead sure as we're a lying here.'

'That's just what I was thinking to myself, Huck.'

'If anybody tells, let Muff Potter do it, if he's fool enough. He's generally drunk enough.'

Tom said nothing – went on thinking. Presently he whispered:

'Huck, Muff Potter don't know it. How can he tell?'

'What's the reason he don't know it?'

'Because he'd just got that whack when Jnjun Joe done it. D'you reckon he could see anything? D'you reckon he knowed anything?'

'By hokey, that's so, Tom!'

'And besides, look-a-here – maybe that whack done for him!'

'No, 'tain't likely, Tom. He had liquor in him; I could see that; and besides, he always has. Well, when Pap's full, you might take and belt him over the head with a church and you couldn't phase him. He says so his own self. So it's the same with Muff Potter, of course. But if a man was dead sober, I reckon, maybe that whack might fetch him; I dono.'

After another reflective silence, Tom said:

'Hucky, you sure you can keep mum?'

'Tom, we got to keep mum. You know that. That Injun devil wouldn't make any more of drownding us than a couple of cats, if we was to squeak 'bout this and they didn't hang him. Now look-a-here, Tom, less take and swear to one another – that's what we got to do – swear to keep mum.'

'I'm agreed, Huck. It's the best thing. Would you just hold hands and swear that we – '

'Oh, no, that wouldn't do for this. That's good enough for little rubbishy common things – specially with gals, cuz they go back on you any way, and blab if they get into a huff – but there orter be writing 'bout a big thing like this. And blood.'

Tom's whole being applauded this idea. It was deep, and dark, and awful; the hour, the circumstances, the surroundings, were in keeping with it. He picked up a clean pine shingle that lay in the moonlight, took a little fragment of 'red keel' out of his pocket, got the moon on his work, and painfully scrawled these lines, emphasizing each slow downstroke by clamping his tongue between his teeth, and letting up the pressure on the up-strokes:

"Huck Finn and Tom Sawyer swears they will keep mum about This and They Wish They may Drop down dead in their Tracks if They ever Tell and Rot."

Huckleberry was filled with admiration of Tom's facility in writing and the sublimity of his language. He at once took a pin from his lapel and was going to prick his flesh, but Tom said:

'Hold on! Don't do that. A pin's brass. It might have verdigrease on it.'

'What's verdigrease?'

'It's poison. That's what it is. You just swaller some of it once – you'll see.'

So Tom unwound the thread from one of his needles, and each boy pricked the ball of his thumb and squeezed out a drop of blood.

In time, after many squeezes, Tom managed to sign his initials, using the ball of his little finger for a pen. Then he showed Huckleberry how to make an H and an F, and the oath was complete. They buried the shingle close to the wall, with some dismal ceremonies and incantations, and the fetters that bound their tongues were considered to be locked and the key thrown away.

A figure crept stealthily through a break in the other end of the ruined building now, but they did not notice it.

'Tom,' whispered Huckleberry, 'does this keep us from ever telling – always?'

'Of course it does. It don't make any difference what happens, we got to keep mum. We'd drop down dead – don't you know that?'

'Yes, I reckon that's so.'

They continued to whisper for some little time. Presently a dog set up a long, lugubrious howl just outside – within ten feet of them. The boys clasped each other suddenly, in an agony of fright.

'Which of us does he mean?' gasped Huckleberry.

'I dono – peep through the crack. Quick!'

'No, you, Tom!'

'I can't – I can't do it, Huck!'

'Please, Tom. There 'tis again!'

'Oh, Lordy, I'm thankful!' whispered Tom. 'I know his voice. It's Bull Harbison.'*

'Oh, that's good – I tell you, Tom, I was most scared to death; I'd a bet anything it was a stray dog.'

The dog howled again. The boys' hearts sank once more.

'Oh, my! that ain't no Bull Harbison!' whispered Huckleberry. 'Do, Tom!'

Tom, quaking with fear, yielded, and put his eye to the crack. His whisper was hardly audible when he said:

*If Mr Harbison had owned a slave named Bull, Tom would have spoken of him as 'Harbison's Bull'; but a son or a dog of that name was 'Bull Harbison'.

'Oh, Huck, it's A STRAY DOG!'

'Quick, Tom, quick! Who does he mean?'

'Huck, he must mean us both – we're right together.'

'Oh, Tom, I reckon we're goners. I reckon there ain't no mistake 'bout where *I'll* go to. I been so wicked.'

'Dad fetch it! This comes of playing hookey and doing everything a feller's told *not* to do. I might a been good, like Sid, if I'd tried – but no, I wouldn't, of course. But if ever I get off this time, I lay I'll just *waller* in Sunday-schools!'

And Tom began to snuffle a little.

'*You* bad!' And Huckleberry began to snuffle, too. 'Confound it, Tom Sawyer, you're just old pie 'longside o' what *I am.* Oh, *Lordy*, Lordy, Lordy, I wisht I only had half your chance.'

Tom choked off and whispered:

'Look, Hucky, look! He's got his *back* to us!'

Hucky looked with joy in his heart.

'Well he has, by jingoes! Did he before?'

'Yes, he did. But I, like a fool, never thought. Oh, this is bully, you know. *Now*, who can he mean?'

The howling stopped. Tom pricked up his ears.

'*Sh!* What's that?' he whispered.

'Sounds like – like hogs grunting. No – it's somebody snoring, Tom.'

'That *is* it? Where'bouts is it, Huck?'

'I b'leeve it's down at t'other end. Sounds so, anyway. Pap used to sleep there sometimes, 'long with the hogs, but, laws bless you, he just lifts things when he snores. Besides, I reckon he ain't ever coming back to this town any more.'

The spirit of adventure rose in the boys' souls once more.

'Hucky, do you das't to go if I lead?'

'I don't like to, much, Tom. S'pose it's Injun Joe!'

Tom quailed. But presently the temptation rose up strong again and the boys agreed to try, with the understanding that they would take to their heels if the snoring stopped. So they went tip-toeing stealthily down, the one behind the other. When they had got to within five steps of the snorer, Tom stepped on a stick, and it broke with a sharp snap. The man moaned, writhed a little, and his face came into the moonlight. It was Muff Potter. The boys' hearts had stood still, and their bodies too, when the man moved, but their fears passed away now. They tip-toed out, through the broken weather-boarding, and stopped at a little distance to exchange a parting word. That long, lugubrious howl rose on the night air again! They turned and saw the strange dog standing within a few feet of where Potter was lying, and facing Potter with his nose pointing heavenward.

'Oh, geeminy, it's *him!*' exclaimed both boys in a breath.

'Say, Tom, they say a stray dog came howling around Johnny Miller's house, 'bout midnight, as much as two weeks ago; and a whippowill come in and lit on the banisters and sung, the very same evening; and there ain't anybody dead there yet.'

'Well, I know that. And suppose there ain't. Didn't Gracie Miller fall in the kitchen fire and burn herself terrible the very next Saturday?'

'Yes, but she ain't *dead*. And what's more, she's getting better too.'

'All right; you wait and see. She's a goner, just as dead sure as Muff Potter's a goner. That's what the niggers say, and they know all about these kind of things, Huck.'

Then they separated, cogitating.

When Tom crept in at his bedroom window, the night was almost spent. He undressed with excessive caution, and fell asleep congratulating himself that nobody knew of his escapade. He was not aware that the gently snoring Sid was awake, and had been so for an hour.

When Tom awoke, Sid was dressed and gone. There was a late look in the light, a late atmosphere. He was startled. Why had he not been called – persecuted till he was up as usual? The thought filled him with bodings. Within five minutes he was dressed and downstairs, feeling sore and drowsy. The family were still at table, but they had finished breakfast. There was no voice of rebuke; but there were averted eyes; there was a silence and an air of solemnity that struck a chill to the culprit's heart. He sat down and tried to seem gay, but it was up-hill work; it roused no smile, no response, and he lapsed into silence and let his heart sink down to the depths.

After breakfast his aunt took him aside, and Tom almost brightened in the hope that he was going to be flogged; but it was not so. His aunt wept over him and asked him how he could go and break her old heart so; and finally told him to go on, and ruin himself, and bring her grey hairs with sorrow to the grave, for it was no use for her to try any more. This was worse than a thousand whippings, and Tom's heart was sorer now than his body. He cried, he pleaded for forgiveness, promised reform over and over again, and then received his dismissal, feeling that he had won but an imperfect forgiveness and established but a feeble confidence.

He left the presence too miserable to even feel vengeful towards Sid; and so the latter's prompt retreat through the back gate was unnecessary. He moped to school gloomy and sad, and took his flogging along with Joe Harper for playing hookey the day before, with the air of one whose heart was busy with heavier woes and wholly dead to trifles. Then he betook himself to his seat, rested his elbows on his desk and his jaws in his hands, and stared at the wall with the stony stare of suffering that has reached the limit and can no further go. His elbow was pressing against some hard substance. After a long time he slowly and sadly changed his position, and took up this object with a sigh. It was in a paper. He unrolled it. A long, lingering, colossal sigh followed, and his heart broke. It was his brass andiron knob! This final feather broke the camel's back.

CHAPTER XI

CLOSE upon the hour of noon the whole village was suddenly electrified with the ghastly news. No need of the as yet undreamed-of telegraph; the tale flew from man to man, from group to group, from house to house with little less than telegraphic speed. Of course the schoolmaster gave holiday for that afternoon; the town would have thought strangely of him if he had not. A gory knife had been found close to the murdered man, and it had been recognized by somebody as belonging to Muff Potter – so the story ran. And it was said that a belated citizen had come upon Potter washing himself in the 'branch' about one or two o'clock in the morning, and that Potter had at once sneaked off – suspicious circumstances, especially the washing, which was not a habit with Potter. It was also said that the town had been ransacked for this 'murderer' (the public are not slow in the matter of sifting evidence and arriving at a verdict), but that he could not be found. Horsemen had departed down all the roads in every direction, and the Sheriff was confident that he would be captured before night.

All the town was drifting towards the graveyard. Tom's heartbreak vanished, and he joined the procession, not because he would not a thousand times rather go anywhere else, but because an awful, unaccountable fascination drew him on. Arrived at the dreadful place, he wormed his small body through the crowd and saw the dismal spectacle. It seemed to him an age since he was there before. Somebody pinched his arm. He turned, and his eyes met Huckleberry's. Then both looked elsewhere at once, and wondered if anybody had noticed anything in their mutual glance. But everybody was talking, and intent upon the grisly spectacle before them.

'Poor fellow!' 'Poor young fellow!' 'This ought to be a

lesson to grave-robbers!' 'Muff Potter'll hang for this if they catch him!' This was the drift of remark, and the minister said, 'It was a judgement; His hand is here.'

Now Tom shivered from head to heel; for his eye fell upon the stolid face of Injun Joe. At this moment the crowd began to sway and struggle, and voices shouted, 'It's him! it's him! he's coming himself!'

'Who? who?' from twenty voices.

'Muff Potter!'

'Hallo, he's stopped! Look out, he's turning! Don't let him get away!'

People in the branches of the trees over Tom's head said he wasn't trying to get away – he only looked doubtful and perplexed.

'Infernal impudence!' said a bystander; 'wanted to come and take a quiet look at his work – didn't expect any company.'

The crowd fell apart now, and the Sheriff came through ostentatiously, leading Potter by the arm. The poor fellow's face was haggard, and his eyes showed the fear that was upon him. When he stood before the murdered man, he shook as with a palsy, and he put his face in his hands and burst into tears.

'I didn't do it, friends,' he sobbed; ''pon my word and honour I never done it.'

'Who's accused you?' shouted a voice.

This shot seemed to carry home. Potter lifted his face and looked around him with a pathetic hopelessness in his eyes. He saw Injun Joe, and exclaimed:

'Oh, Injun Joe, you promised me you'd never – '

'Is that your knife?' and it was thrust before him by the Sheriff.

Potter would have fallen if they had not caught him and eased him to the ground. Then he said:

'Something told me 't if I didn't come back and get – '
He shuddered; then waved his nerveless hand with a van-

quished gesture and said, 'Tell 'em, Joe, tell 'em – it ain't no use any more.'

Then Huckleberry and Tom stood dumb and staring, and heard the stony-hearted liar reel off his serene statement, they expecting every moment that the clear sky would deliver God's lightnings upon his head, and wondering to see how long the stroke was delayed. And when he had finished and still stood alive and whole, their wavering impulse to break their oath and save the poor betrayed prisoner's life faded and vanished away, for plainly this miscreant had sold himself to Satan, and it would be fatal to meddle with the property of such a power as that.

'Why didn't you leave? What did you want to come here for?' somebody said.

'I couldn't help it – I couldn't help it,' Potter moaned. 'I wanted to run away, but I couldn't seem to come anywhere but here.' And he fell to sobbing again.

Injun Joe repeated his statement, just as calmly, a few minutes afterwards on the inquest, under oath; and the boys, seeing that the lightnings were still withheld, were confirmed in their belief that Joe had sold himself to the devil. He was now become, to them, the most balefully interesting object they had ever looked upon, and they could not take their fascinated eyes from his face. They inwardly resolved to watch him, nights, when opportunity should offer, in the hope of getting a glimpse of his dread master.

Injun Joe helped to raise the body of the murdered man, and put it in a wagon for removal; and it was whispered through the shuddering crowd that the wound bled a little! The boys thought that this happy circumstance would turn suspicion in the right direction; but they were disappointed, for more than one villager remarked:

'It was within three feet of Muff Potter when it done it.'

Tom's fearful secret and gnawing conscience disturbed

his sleep for as much as a week after this; and at breakfast one morning Sid said:

'Tom, you pitch around and talk in your sleep so much that you keep me awake about half the time.'

Tom blanched and dropped his eyes.

'It's a bad sign,' said Aunt Polly, gravely. 'What you got on your mind, Tom?'

'Nothing. Nothing 't I know of.' But the boy's hand shook so that he spilled his coffee.

'And you do talk such stuff,' Sid said. 'Last night you said, "It's blood, it's blood, that's what it is!" You said that over and over. And you said, "Don't torment me so – I'll tell." Tell what? What is it you'll tell?'

Everything was swimming before Tom. There is no telling what might have happened now, but luckily the concern passed out of Aunt Polly's face, and she came to Tom's relief without knowing it. She said:

'Sho! It's that dreadful murder. I dream about it most every night myself. Sometimes I dream it's me that done it.'

Mary said she had been affected much the same way. Sid seemed satisfied. Tom got out of the presence as quickly as he plausibly could, and after that he complained of toothache for a week, and tied up his jaws every night. He never knew that Sid lay nightly watching, and frequently slipped the bandage free, and then leaned on his elbow listening a good while at a time, and afterwards slipped the bandage back to its place again. Tom's distress of mind wore off gradually, and the toothache grew irksome and was discarded. If Sid really managed to make anything out of Tom's disjointed mutterings, he kept it to himself. It seemed to Tom that his schoolmates never would get done holding inquests on dead cats, and thus keeping his trouble present to his mind. Sid noticed that Tom never was coroner at one of these inquiries, though it had been his habit to take the lead in all new enterprises; he noticed, too, that Tom never acted as a witness – and that was strange; and Sid did not overlook the fact that Tom even showed a marked aversion to these inquests, and always avoided them when he could. Sid marvelled, but said nothing. However, even inquests went out of vogue at last, and ceased to torture Tom's conscience.

Every day or two during this time of sorrow, Tom watched his opportunity and went to the little grated jail window and smuggled such small comforts through to the 'murderer' as he could get hold of. The jail was a trifling little brick den that stood in a marsh at the edge of the village, and no guards were afforded for it; indeed, it was seldom occupied. These offerings greatly helped to ease Tom's conscience. The villagers had a strong desire to tar-and-feather Injun Joe and ride him on a rail for body-snatching, but so formidable was his character that nobody could be found who was willing to take the lead in the matter, so it was dropped. He had been careful to begin both of his inquest-statements with the fight, without confessing the grave-robbery that preceded it; therefore it was deemed wisest not to try the case in the courts at present.

CHAPTER XII

ONE of the reasons why Tom's mind had drifted away from its secret troubles was that it had found a new and weighty matter to interest itself about. Becky Thatcher had stopped coming to school. Tom had struggled with his pride a few days, and tried to 'whistle her down the wind', but failed. He began to find himself hanging around her father's house, nights, and feeling very miserable. She was sick. What if she should die! There was distraction in the thought. He no longer took an interest in war, nor even in piracy. The charm of life was gone, there was nothing but dreariness left. He put his hoop away, and his bat; there was no joy in them any more. His aunt was concerned; she began to try all manner of medicines on him. She was one of those people who are infatuated with patent medicines and all new-fangled methods of producing health or mending it. She was an inveterate experimenter in these things. When something fresh in this line came out she was in a fever right away to try it; not on herself, for she was never ailing; but on any-body else that came handy. She was a subscriber for all the 'Health' periodicals and phrenological frauds; and the solemn ignorance they were inflated with was breath to her nostrils. All the rot they contained about ventilation, and how to go to bed, and how to get up, and what to eat, and what to drink, and how much exercise to take, and what frame of mind to keep oneself in, and what sort of clothing to wear, was all gospel to her, and she never observed that her health journals of the current month customarily upset everything they had recommended the month before. She was as simple-hearted and honest as the day was long, and so she was an easy victim. She gathered together her quack periodicals and her quack medicines, and, thus armed with death, went about on her pale horse, metaphorically speak-ing, with 'hell following after'. But she never suspected that she was not an angel of healing and the balm of Gilead in disguise to the suffering neighbours.

The water treatment was new, now, and Tom's low con-dition was a windfall to her. She had him out at daylight every morning, stood him up in the wood-shed and drowned him with a deluge of cold water; then she scrubbed him down with a towel like a file, and so brought him to; then she rolled him up in a wet sheet and put him away under blankets till she sweated his soul clean and 'the yellow stains of it came through his pores', as Tom said.

Yet notwithstanding all this the boy grew more and more melancholy and pale and dejected. She added hot baths, sitz baths, and plunges. The boy remained as dismal as a hearse. She began to assist the water with a slim oatmeal diet and blister plasters. She calculated his capacity as she would a jug's, and filled him up every day with quack cure-alls.

Tom had become indifferent to persecution by this time. This phase filled the old lady's heart with consternation. This indifference must be broken up at any cost. Now she heard of Pain-killer for the first time. She ordered a lot at once. She tasted it and was filled with gratitude. It was simply fire in a liquid form. She dropped the water treatment and everything else, and pinned her faith to Pain-killer. She gave Tom a teaspoonful and watched with the deepest anxiety for the result. Her troubles were instantly at rest, her soul at peace again; for the 'indifference' was broken up. The boy could not have shown a wilder, heartier interest if she had built a fire under him.

Tom felt that it was time to wake up; this sort of life might be romantic enough in his blighted condition, but it was getting to have too little sentiment and too much distracting variety about it. So he thought over various plans for relief, and finally hit upon that of professing to be fond of Pain-killer. He asked for it so often that he became a nuisance, and his aunt ended by telling him to help himself and quit bothering her. If it had been Sid she would have had no misgivings to alloy her delight; but since it was Tom she watched the bottle clandestinely. She found that the medicine did really diminish, but it did not occur to her that the boy was mending the health of a crack in the sitting-room floor with it.

One day Tom was in the act of dosing the crack when his aunt's yellow cat came along, purring, eyeing the tea-spoon avariciously, and begging for a taste. Tom said:

'Don't ask for it unless you want it, Peter.'

But Peter signified that he did want it.

'You better make sure.'

Peter was sure.

'Now you've asked for it, and I'll give it to you, because

85

there ain't anything mean about *me;* but if you find you don't like it you mustn't blame anybody but your own self.'

Peter was agreeable, so Tom pried his mouth open and poured down the Pain-killer. Peter sprang a couple of yards into the air, and then delivered a war-whoop and set off round and round the room, banging against furniture, upsetting flower-pots, and making general havoc. Next he rose on his hind feet and pranced around, in a frenzy of enjoyment, with his head over his shoulder and his voice proclaiming his unappeasable happiness. Then he went tearing around the house again, spreading chaos and destruction in his path. Aunt Polly entered in time to see him throw a few double summersets, deliver a final mighty hurrah, and sail through the open window, carrying the rest of the flower-pots with him. The old lady stood petrified with astonishment, peering over her glasses; Tom lay on the floor, expiring with laughter.

'Tom, what on earth ails that cat?'

'*I* don't know, Aunt,' gasped the boy.

'Why, I never seen anything like it. What *did* make him act so?'

''Deed I don't know, Aunt Polly; cats always act so when they're having a good time.'

'They do, do they?' There was something in the tone that made Tom apprehensive.

'Yes'm. That is, I believe they do.'

'You *do?*'

'Yes'm.'

The old lady was bending down, Tom watching with interest emphasized by anxiety. Too late he divined her 'drift'. The handle of the tell-tale teaspoon was visible under the bed-valance. Aunt Polly took it, held it up. Tom winced, and dropped his eyes. Aunt Polly raised him by the usual handle – his ear – and cracked his head soundly with her thimble.

'Now, sir, what did you want to treat that poor dumb beast so for?'

'I done it out of pity for him – because he hadn't any aunt.'

'Hadn't any aunt! – you numskull. What has that got to do with it?'

'Heaps. Because if he'd a had one she'd a burnt him out herself! She'd a roasted his bowels out of him 'thout any more feeling than if he was a human!'

Aunt Polly felt a sudden pang of remorse. This was putting the thing in a new light; what was cruelty to a cat *might* be cruelty to a boy too. She began to soften: she felt sorry. Her eyes watered a little, and she put her hand on Tom's head and said gently:

'I was meaning for the best, Tom. And, Tom, it *did* do you good.'

Tom looked up in her face with just a perceptible twinkle peeping through his gravity:

'I know you was meaning for the best, Aunty, and so was I with Peter. It done *him* good, too. I never see him get around so nice – '

'Oh, go 'long with you, Tom, before you aggravate me again. And you try and see if you can't be a good boy for once, and you needn't take any more medicine.'

Tom reached school ahead of time. It was noticed that this strange thing had been occurring every day latterly. And now, as usual of late, he hung about the gate of the school-yard instead of playing with his comrades. He was sick, he said; and he looked it. He tried to seem to be looking everywhere but whither he was really looking – down the road. Presently Jeff Thatcher hove in sight, and Tom's face lighted; he gazed a moment, and then turned sorrowfully away. When Jeff Thatcher arrived, Tom accosted him, and 'led up' warily to opportunities for remark about Becky, but the giddy lad never could see the bait. Tom watched and watched, hoping whenever a frisking frock came in sight, and hating the owner of it as soon as he saw she was not the right one. At last frocks ceased to appear, and he dropped hopelessly into the dumps; he entered the empty school-house and sat down to suffer. Then one more frock passed in at the gate, and Tom's heart gave a great bound. The next instant he was out, and 'going on' like an Indian; yelling, laughing, chasing boys, jumping over the fence at risk of life and limb, throwing handsprings, standing on his head – doing all the heroic things he could conceive of, and keeping a furtive eye out, all the while, to see if Becky Thatcher was noticing. But she seemed to be unconscious of it all; she never looked. Could it be possible that she was not aware that he was there? He carried his exploits to her immediate vicinity; came war-whooping around, snatched a boy's cap, hurled it to the roof of the school-house, broke through a group of boys, tumbling them in every direction, and fell sprawling himself under Becky's nose, almost upsetting her – and she turned, with her nose in the air, and he heard her say, 'Mf! some people think they're mighty smart – always showing off!'

Tom's cheeks burned. He gathered himself up and sneaked off, crushed and crestfallen.

CHAPTER XIII

Tom's mind was made up now. He was gloomy and desperate. He was a forsaken, friendless boy, he said; nobody loved him; when they found out what they had driven him to, perhaps they would be sorry; he had tried to do right and get along, but they would not let him; since nothing would do them but to be rid of him, let it be so; and let them blame him for the consequences – why shouldn't they? what right had the friendless to complain? Yes, they had forced him to it at last: he would lead a life of crime. There was no choice.

By this time he was far down Meadow Land, and the bell for school to 'take up' tinkled faintly upon his ear. He sobbed, now, to think he should never, never hear that old familiar sound any more – it was very hard, but it was forced on him; since he was driven out into the cold world, he must submit – but he forgave them. Then the sobs came thick and fast.

Just at this point he met his soul's sworn comrade, Joe Harper – hard-eyed, and with evidently a great and dismal purpose in his heart. Plainly here were 'two souls with but a single thought'. Tom, wiping his eyes with his sleeve, began to blubber out something about a resolution to escape from hard usage and lack of sympathy at home by roaming abroad into the great world, never to return; and ended by hoping that Joe would not forget him.

But it transpired that this was a request which Joe had just been going to make of Tom, and had come to hunt him up for that purpose. His mother had whipped him for drinking some cream which he had never tasted and knew nothing about; it was plain that she was tired of him and wished him to go; if she felt that way, there was nothing for him to do but to succumb; he hoped she would be happy, and never regret having driven her poor boy out into the unfeeling world to suffer and die.

As the two boys walked sorrowing along, they made a new compact to stand by each other and be brothers, and never separate till death relieved them of their troubles. Then they began to lay their plans. Joe was for being a hermit, and living on crusts in a remote cave, and dying, sometime, of cold, and want, and grief; but, after listening to Tom, he conceded that there were some conspicuous advantages about a life of crime, and so he consented to be a pirate.

Three miles below St Petersburg, at a point where the Mississippi river was a trifle over a mile wide, there was a long, narrow, wooded island, with a shallow bar at the head of it, and this offered well as a rendezvous. It was not inhabited; it lay far over towards the farther shore, abreast a dense and almost wholly unpeopled forest. So Jackson's Island was chosen. Who were to be the subjects of their piracies was a matter that did not occur to them. Then they hunted up Huckleberry Finn, and he joined them promptly, for all careers were one to him; he was indifferent. They presently separated, to meet at a lonely spot on the river bank two miles above the village, at the favourite hour, which was midnight. There was a small log raft there which they meant to capture. Each would bring hooks and lines, and such provisions as he could steal in the most dark and mysterious way – as became outlaws; and before the afternoon was done, they had all managed to enjoy the sweet glory of spreading the fact that pretty soon the town would 'hear something'. All who got this vague hint were cautioned to 'be mum and wait'.

About midnight Tom arrived with a boiled ham and a few trifles, and stopped in a dense undergrowth on a small bluff overlooking the meeting-place. It was starlight, and very still. The mighty river lay like an ocean at rest. Tom listened a moment, but no sound disturbed the quiet. Then he gave a low, distinct whistle. It was answered from under the bluff. Tom whistled twice more; these signals were answered in the same way. Then a guarded voice said:

'Who goes there?'

'Tom Sawyer, the Black Avenger of the Spanish Main. Name your names.'

'Huck Finn the Red-handed, and Joe Harper the Terror of the Seas.' Tom had furnished these titles from his favourite literature.

''Tis well. Give the countersign.'

Two hoarse whispers delivered the same awful word simultaneously to the brooding night:

'BLOOD!'

Then Tom tumbled his ham over the bluff and let himself down after it, tearing both skin and clothes to some extent

90

in the effort. There was an easy, comfortable path along the shore under the bluff, but it lacked the advantages of difficulty and danger so valued by a pirate.

The Terror of the Seas had brought a side of bacon, and had about worn himself out with getting it there. Finn the Red-handed had stolen a skillet, and a quantity of half-cured leaf-tobacco, and had also brought a few corn-cobs to make pipes with. But none of the pirates smoked or 'chewed' but himself. The Black Avenger of the Spanish Main said it would never do to start without some fire. That was a wise thought; matches were hardly known there in that day. They saw a fire smouldering upon a great raft a hundred yards above, and they went stealthily thither and helped themselves to a chunk. They made an imposing adventure of it, saying 'hist' every now and then and suddenly halting with finger on lip; moving with hands on imaginary dagger-hilts; and giving orders in dismal whispers that if 'the foe' stirred to 'let him have it to the hilt', because 'dead men tell no tales'. They knew well enough that the raftmen were all down at the village laying in stores or having a spree, but still that was no excuse for their conducting this thing in an unpiratical way.

They shoved off presently, Tom in command, Huck at the left oar and Joe at the forward. Tom stood amidships, gloomy-browed and with folded arms, and gave his orders in a low, stern whisper.

'Luff, and bring her to the wind!'

'Aye, aye, sir!'

'Steady, stead-y-y-y!'

'Steady it is, sir!'

'Let her go off a point!'

'Point it is, sir!'

As the boys steadily and monotonously drove the raft towards mid-stream, it was no doubt understood that these orders were given only for 'style', and were not intended to mean anything in particular.

'What sail's she carrying?'

'Courses, tops'ls, and flying-jib, sir!'

'Send the r'yals up! Lay out aloft there, half a dozen of ye, foretomast-stuns'l! Lively, now!'

'Aye, aye, sir!'

'Shake out that mainto-galans'l! Sheets and braces! *Now*, my hearties!'

'Aye, aye, sir!'

'Hellum-a-lee – hard a-port! Stand by to meet her when she comes! Port, port! *Now*, men! With a will! Stead-y-y!'

'Steady it is, sir!'

The raft drew beyond the middle of the river; the boys pointed her head right and then lay on their oars. The river was not high, so there was not more than a two or three mile current. Hardly a word was said during the next three-quarters of an hour. Now the raft was passing before the distant town. Two or three glimmering lights showed where it lay, peacefully sleeping, beyond the vague vast sweep of star-gemmed water, unconscious of the tremendous event that was happening. The Black Avenger stood still with folded arms, 'looking his last' upon the scene of his former joys and his later sufferings, and wishing 'she' could see him, now abroad on the wild sea, facing peril and death with dauntless heart, going to his doom with a grim smile on his lips. It was but a small strain on his imagination to remove Jackson's Island beyond eye-shot of the village, and so he 'looked his last' with a broken and satisfied heart. The other pirates were looking their last, too; and they all looked so long that they came near letting the current drift them out of the range of the island. But they discovered the danger in time, and made shift to avert it. About two o'clock in the morning the raft grounded on the bar two hundred yards above the head of the island, and they waded back and forth until they had landed their freight. Part of the little raft's belongings consisted of an old sail, and this they spread over a nook in the bushes for a tent to shelter their provisions; but they themselves would sleep in the open air in good weather, as became outlaws.

They built a fire against the side of a great log twenty or thirty steps within the sombre depths of the forest, and then cooked some bacon in the frying-pan for supper, and used up half of the corn 'pone' stock they had brought. It seemed glorious sport to be feasting in that wild free way in the virgin forest of an unexplored and uninhabited island, far from the haunts of men, and they said they would never return to civilization. The climbing fire lit up their faces and threw its ruddy glare upon the pillared tree-trunks of their forest temple, and upon the varnished foliage and festooning vines. When the last crisp slice of bacon was gone, and the last allowance of corn pone devoured, the boys stretched themselves out on the grass, filled with contentment. They could have found a cooler place, but they would not deny themselves such a romantic feature as the roasting camp-fire.

'*Ain't* it jolly?' said Joe.

'It's *nuts*,' said Tom.

'What would the boys say if they could see us?'

'Say? Well, they'd just die to be here – hey, Hucky?'

'I reckon so,' said Huckleberry; 'anyways *I'm* suited. I don't want nothing better'n this. I don't ever get enough to eat gen'ally – and here they can't come and kick at a feller and bullyrag him so.'

'It's just the life for me,' said Tom. 'You don't have to get up, mornings, and you don't have to go to school, and wash, and all that blame foolishness.'

'You see a pirate don't have to do *anything*, Joe, when he's ashore, but a hermit *he* has to be praying considerable, and then he don't have any fun, any way, all by himself that way.'

'Oh yes, that's so,' said Joe, 'but I hadn't thought much about it, you know. I'd a good deal ruther be a pirate now that I've tried it.'

'You see,' said Tom, 'people don't go much on hermits, now-a-days, like they used to in old times, but a pirate's always respected. And a hermit's got to sleep on the hardest place he can find, and put sackcloth and ashes on his head, and stand out in the rain, and – '

'What does he put sackcloth and ashes on his head for?' inquired Huck.

'*I* dunno. But they've *got* to do it. Hermits always do. You'd have to do that if you was a hermit.'

'Dern'd if I would,' said Huck.

'Well, what would you do?'

'I dunno. But I wouldn't do that.'

'Why, Huck, you'd *have* to. How'd you get around it?'

'Why, I just wouldn't stand it. I'd run away.'

'Run away! Well, you *would* be a nice old slouch of a hermit. You'd be a disgrace.'

The Red-handed made no response, being better employed. He had finished gouging out a cob, and now he fitted a weed stem to it, loaded it with tobacco, and was pressing a coal to the charge and blowing a cloud of fragrant smoke; he was in the full bloom of luxurious contentment. The other pirates envied him this majestic vice, and secretly resolved to acquire it shortly. Presently Huck said:

'What do pirates have to do?'

Tom said:

'Oh, they have just a bully time – take ships, and burn them, and get the money and bury it in awful places in their island where there's ghosts and things to watch it, and kill everybody in the ships – make 'em walk a plank.'

'And they carry the women to the island,' said Joe; 'they don't kill the women.'

'No,' assented Tom, 'they don't kill the women – they're too noble. And the women's always beautiful, too.'

'And don't they wear the bulliest clothes! Oh, no! All gold and silver and di'monds,' said Joe with enthusiasm.

'Who?' said Huck.

'Why, the pirates.'

Huck scanned his own clothing forlornly.

'I reckon I ain't dressed fitten for a pirate,' said he, with a regretful pathos in his voice; 'but I ain't got none but these.'

But the other boys told him the fine clothes would come fast enough after they should have begun their adventures. They made him understand that his poor rags would do to begin with, though it was customary for wealthy pirates to start with a proper wardrobe.

Gradually their talk died out and drowsiness began to steal upon the eyelids of the little waifs. The pipe dropped from the fingers of the Red-handed, and he slept the sleep of the conscience-free and the weary. The Terror of the Seas and the Black Avenger of the Spanish Main had more difficulty in getting to sleep. They said their prayers inwardly, and lying down, since there was nobody there with authority to make them kneel and recite aloud; in truth they had a mind not to say them at all, but they were afraid to proceed to such lengths as that, lest they might call down a sudden and special thunder-bolt from heaven. Then at once they reached and hovered upon the imminent verge of sleep – but an intruder came now that would not 'down'. It was conscience. They began to feel a vague fear that they had been doing wrong to run away; and next they thought of the stolen meat, and then the real torture came. They tried to argue it away by reminding conscience that they had purloined sweetmeats and apples scores of times; but conscience was not to be appeased by such thin plausibilities. It seemed to them, in the end, that there was no getting around the stubborn fact that taking sweetmeats was only 'hooking' while taking bacon and ham and such valuables was plain, simple stealing – and there was a command against that in the Bible. So they inwardly resolved that so long as they remained in the business, their piracies should not again be sullied with the crime of stealing. Then conscience granted a truce, and these curiously inconsistent pirates fell peacefully to sleep.

CHAPTER XIV

WHEN Tom awoke in the morning, he wondered where he was. He sat up and rubbed his eyes and looked around; then he comprehended. It was the cool grey dawn, and there was a delicious sense of repose and peace in the deep pervading calm and silence of the woods. Not a leaf stirred; not a sound obtruded upon great Nature's meditation. Beaded dewdrops stood upon the leaves and grasses. A white layer of ashes covered the fire, and a thin blue wreath of smoke rose straight into the air. Joe and Huck still slept. Now, far away in the woods, a bird called; another answered; presently the hammering of a woodpecker was heard. Gradually the cool dim grey of the morning whitened, and as gradually sounds multiplied and life manifested itself. The marvel of Nature shaking off sleep and going to work unfolded itself to the musing boy. A little green worm came crawling over a dewy leaf, lifting two-thirds of his body into the air from time to time, 'sniffling around', then proceeding again, for he was measuring, Tom said; and when the worm approached him of his own accord, he sat as still as a stone, with his hopes rising and falling by turns as the creature still came towards him or seemed inclined to go elsewhere; and when at last it considered a painful moment with its curved body in the air and then came decisively down upon Tom's leg and began a journey over him, his whole heart was glad – for that meant that he was going to have a new suit of clothes – without the shadow of a doubt, a gaudy piratical uniform. Now a procession of ants appeared, from nowhere in particular, and went about their labours; one struggled manfully by with a dead spider five times as big as itself in its arms, and lugged it straight up a tree-trunk. A brown spotted lady-bug climbed the dizzy heights of a grass-blade, and Tom bent down close to it and said:

> Lady-bug, lady-bug, fly away home,
> Your house is on fire, your children's alone;

and she took wing and went off to see about it – which did not surprise the boy, for he knew of old that this insect was credulous about conflagrations, and he had practised upon its simplicity more than once. A tumble-bug came next, heaving sturdily at its ball, and Tom touched the creature, to see it shut its legs against its body and pretend to be dead. The birds were fairly rioting by this time. A cat-bird, the northern mocker, lit in a tree over Tom's head, and trilled out her imitations of her neighbours in a rapture of enjoyment; then a shrill jay swept down, a flash of blue flame, and stopped on a twig almost within the boy's reach, cocked his head to one side, and eyed the strangers with a consuming curiosity; a grey squirrel and a big fellow of the 'fox' kind came scurrying along, sitting up at intervals to inspect and chatter at the boys, for the wild things had probably never seen a human being before, and scarcely knew whether to be afraid or not. All Nature was wide awake and stirring now, long lances of sunlight pierced down through the dense foliage far and near, and a few butterflies came fluttering upon the scene.

Tom stirred up the other pirates and they all clattered away with a shout, and in a minute or two were stripped and chasing after and tumbling over each other in the shallow limpid water of the white sand-bar. They felt no longing for the little village sleeping in the distance beyond the majestic waste of water. A vagrant current or a slight rise in the river had carried off their raft, but this only gratified them, since its going was something like burning the bridge between them and civilization.

They came back to camp wonderfully refreshed, glad-hearted, and ravenous; and they soon had the camp-fire blazing up again. Huck found a spring of clear cold water close by, and the boys made cups of broad oak or hickory leaves, and felt that water, sweetened with such a wild-wood charm as that, would be a good enough substitute for coffee. While Joe was slicing bacon for breakfast, Tom and Huck asked him to hold on a minute; they stepped to a promising nook in the river bank and threw in their lines; almost immediately they had reward. Joe had not had time to get impatient before they were back again with some handsome bass, a couple of sun-perch, and a small catfish – provision enough for quite a family. They fried the fish with the bacon and were astonished; for no fish had ever seemed so delicious before. They did not know that the quicker a freshwater fish is on the fire after he is caught the better he is; and they reflected little upon what a sauce open-air sleeping, open-air exercise, bathing, and a large ingredient of hunger make, too.

They lay around in the shade after breakfast, while Huck had a smoke, and then went off through the woods on an exploring expedition. They tramped gaily along, over decaying logs, through tangled underbrush, among solemn monarchs of the forest, hung from their crowns to the ground with a drooping regalia of grape-vines. Now and then they came upon snug nooks carpeted with grass and jewelled with flowers.

They found plenty of things to be delighted with, but nothing to be astonished at. They discovered that the island was about three miles long and a quarter of a mile wide, and that the shore it lay closest to was only separated from it by a narrow channel hardly two hundred yards wide. They took a swim about every hour, so it was close upon the middle of the afternoon when they got back to camp. They were too hungry to stop to fish, but they fared sumptuously upon cold ham, and then threw themselves down in the shade to talk. But the talk soon began to drag, and then died. The stillness, the solemnity, that brooded in the woods, and the sense of loneliness, began to tell upon the spirits of the boys. They fell to thinking. A sort of undefined longing crept upon them. This took dim shape presently – it was budding homesickness. Even Finn the Red-handed was dreaming of his door-steps and empty hogsheads. But they were all ashamed of their weakness, and none was brave enough to speak his thought.

For some time, now, the boys had been dully conscious of a peculiar sound in the distance, just as one sometimes is of the ticking of a clock which he takes no distinct note of. But now this mysterious sound became more pronounced, and forced a recognition. The boys started, glanced at each other, and then each assumed a listening attitude. There was a long silence, profound and unbroken; then a deep, sullen boom came floating down out of the distance.

'What is it?' exclaimed Joe, under his breath.

'I wonder,' said Tom in a whisper.

'Tain't thunder,' said Huckleberry, in an awed tone, 'becuz thunder – '

'Hark!' said Tom; 'listen – don't talk.'

They waited a time that seemed an age, and then the same muffled boom troubled the solemn hush.

'Let's go and see.'

They sprang to their feet and hurried to the shore towards the town. They parted the bushes on the bank and peered out over the water. The little steam ferry-boat was about a mile below the village, drifting with the current. Her broad deck seemed crowded with people. There were a great many skiffs rowing about or floating with the stream in the neighbourhood of the ferry-boat, but the boys could not determine what the men in them were doing. Presently a great jet of white smoke burst from the ferry-boat's side, and as it expanded and rose in a lazy cloud, that same dull throb of sound was borne to the listeners again.

'I know now!' exclaimed Tom; 'somebody's drownded!'

'That's it,' said Huck; 'they done that last summer when Bill Turner got drownded; they shoot a cannon over the water, and that makes him come up to the top. Yes, and they take loaves of bread and put quicksilver in 'em and set 'em afloat, and wherever there's anybody that's drownded, they'll float right there and stop.'

'Yes, I've heard about that,' said Joe. 'I wonder what makes the bread do that.'

'Oh, it ain't the bread so much,' said Tom; 'I reckon it's mostly what they *say* over it before they start it out.'

'But they don't say anything over it,' said Huck. 'I've seen 'em, and they don't.'

'Well, that's funny,' said Tom. 'But maybe they say it to themselves. Of *course* they do. Anybody might know that.'

The others agreed that there was reason in what Tom said, because an ignorant lump of bread, uninstructed by an incantation, could not be expected to act very intelligently when sent upon an errand of such gravity.

'By jings, I wish I was over there now,' said Joe.

'I do too,' said Huck. 'I'd give heaps to know who it is.'

The boys still listened and watched. Presently a revealing thought flashed through Tom's mind, and he exclaimed:

'Boys, I know who's drownded; it's us!'

They felt like heroes in an instant. Here was a gorgeous triumph; they were missed; they were mourned; hearts were breaking on their account; tears were being shed; accusing memories of unkindnesses to these poor lost lads were rising up, and unavailing regrets and remorse were being indulged; and, best of all, the departed were the talk of the whole town, and the envy of all the boys, as far as this dazzling notoriety was concerned. This was fine. It was worth while to be a pirate, after all.

As twilight drew on, the ferry-boat went back to her accustomed business and the skiffs disappeared. The pirates returned to camp. They were jubilant with vanity over their new grandeur and the illustrious trouble they were making. They caught fish, cooked supper, and ate it, and then fell to guessing at what the village was thinking and saying about them; and the pictures they drew of the public distress on their account were gratifying to look upon from their point of view. But when the shadows of night closed them in, they gradually ceased to talk, and sat gazing into the fire, with their minds evidently wandering elsewhere. The excitement was gone, now, and Tom and Joe could not keep back thoughts of certain persons at home who were not enjoying this fine frolic as much as they were. Misgivings came; they grew troubled and unhappy; a sigh or two escaped unawares. By-and-by Joe timidly ventured upon a roundabout 'feeler' as to how the others might look upon a return to civilization – not right now, but –

Tom withered him with derision. Huck, being uncommitted as yet, joined in with Tom, and the waverer quickly 'explained', and was glad to get out of the scrape with as little taint of chickenhearted homesickness clinging to his garments as he could. Mutiny was effectually laid to rest for the moment.

As the night deepened, Huck began to nod, and presently to snore; Joe followed next. Tom lay upon his elbow motionless for some time, watching the two intently. At last he got up cautiously on his knees, and went searching among the grass and the flickering reflections flung by the campfire. He picked up and inspected several large semi-cylinders of the thin white bark of a sycamore, and finally chose two which seemed to suit him. Then he knelt by the fire and painfully wrote something upon each of these with his 'red keel'; one he rolled up and put in his jacket-pocket, and the other he put in Joe's hat and removed it to a little distance from the owner. And he also put into the hat certain schoolboy treasures of almost inestimable value, among them a lump of chalk, an indiarubber ball, three fish-hooks, and one of that kind of marbles known as a 'sure 'nough crystal'. Then he tip-toed his way cautiously among the trees till he felt that he was out of hearing, and straightway broke into a keen run in the direction of the sand-bar.

CHAPTER XV

A FEW minutes later Tom was in the shoal water of the bar, wading towards the Illinois shore. Before the depth reached his middle he was half-way over: the current would permit no more wading now, so he struck out confidently to swim the remaining hundred yards. He swam quartering up stream, but still was swept downward rather faster than he had expected. However, he reached the shore finally, and drifted along till he found a low place and drew himself out. He put his hand on his jacket pocket, found his piece of bark safe, and then struck through the woods, following the shore with streaming garments. Shortly before ten o'clock he came out into an open place opposite the village, and saw the ferry-boat lying in the shadow of the trees and the high bank. Everything was quiet under the blinking stars. He crept down the bank, watching with all his eyes, slipped into the water, swam three or four strokes, and climbed into the skiff that did 'yawl' duty at the boat's stern. He laid himself down under the thwarts and waited, panting. Presently the cracked bell tapped, and a voice gave the order to 'cast off'. A minute or two later the skiff's head was standing high up against the boat's swell, and the voyage was begun. Tom felt happy in his success, for he knew it was the boat's last trip for the night. At the end of a long twelve or fifteen minutes the wheels stopped, and Tom slipped overboard and swam ashore in the dusk, landing fifty yards down stream, out of danger of possible stragglers. He flew along unfrequented alleys, and shortly found himself at his aunt's back fence. He climbed over, approached the 'ell' and looked in at the sitting-room window, for a light was burning there. There sat Aunt Polly, Sid, Mary, and Joe Harper's mother, grouped together, talking. They were by the bed, and the bed was between them and the door. Tom went to the door and began to softly lift the latch; then he pressed gently and the door yielded a crack; he continued pushing cautiously, and quaking every time it creaked, till he judged he might squeeze through on his knees; and so he put his head through and began, warily.

'What makes the candle blow so?' said Aunt Polly. Tom hurried up. 'Why, that door's open, I believe. Why, of course it is. No end of strange things now. Go along and shut it, Sid.'

Tom disappeared under the bed just in time. He lay and 'breathed' himself for a time, and then crept to where he could almost touch his aunt's foot.

'But as I was saying,' said Aunt Polly, 'he warn't *bad*, so to say – only misch*ee*vous. Only just giddy, and harum-scarum, you know. He warn't any more responsible than a colt. *He* never meant any harm, and he was the best-hearted boy that ever was' – and she began to cry.

'It was just so with my Joe – always full of his devilment, and up to every kind of mischief, but he was just as unselfish and kind as he could be – and, laws bless me, to think I went and whipped him for taking that cream, never once recollecting that I throwed it out myself because it was sour, and I never to see him again in this world, never, never, never, poor abused boy!' And Mrs Harper sobbed as if her heart would break.

'I hope Tom's better off where he is,' said Sid; 'but if he'd been better in some ways – '

'*Sid!*' Tom felt the glare of the old lady's eye, though he could not see it. 'Not a word against my Tom, now that he's gone! God'll take care of *him* – never you trouble *your*self, sir. Oh, Mrs Harper, I don't know how to give him up, I don't know how to give him up! He was such a comfort to me, although he tormented my old heart out of me, 'most.'

'The Lord giveth, and the Lord taketh away. Blessed be the name of the Lord! But it's *so* hard – oh, it's so hard! Only last Saturday my Joe bursted a shooting-cracker right under my nose, and I knocked him sprawling. Little did I know then, how soon – oh, if it was to do over again I'd hug him and bless him for it.'

'Yes, yes, yes, I know just how you feel, Mrs Harper, I know just exactly how you feel. No longer ago than yesterday noon, my Tom took and filled the cat full of Pain-killer, and I did think the cretur would tear the house down. And, God forgive me, I cracked Tom's head with my thimble, poor boy, poor dead boy. But he's out of all his troubles now. And the last words I ever heard him say was to reproach – '

But this memory was too much for the old lady, and she broke entirely down. Tom was snuffling now himself – and more in pity of himself than anybody else. He could hear Mary crying, and putting in a kindly word for him from time to time. He began to have a nobler opinion of himself than ever before. Still he was sufficiently touched by his aunt's grief to long to rush out from under the bed and overwhelm her with joy – and the theatrical gorgeousness of the thing appealed strongly to his nature, too, but he resisted and lay still. He went on listening, and gathered by odds and ends that it was conjectured at first that the boys had got drowned while taking a swim; then the small raft had been missed; next, certain boys said the missing lads had promised that the village should 'hear something' soon; and wise heads had 'put this and that together', and decided that the lads had gone off on that raft, and would turn up at the next town below presently; but towards noon the raft had been found, lodged against the Missouri shore some five or six miles below the village, and then hope perished; they must be drowned, else hunger would have driven them home by nightfall if not sooner. It was believed that the search for the bodies had been a fruitless effort merely because the drowning must have occurred in mid-channel, since the boys, being good swimmers, would otherwise have escaped to shore. This was Wednesday night. If the bodies continued missing until Sunday, all hope would be given over, and the funerals would be preached on that morning. Tom shuddered.

Mrs Harper gave a sobbing good night and turned to go. Then with a mutual impulse the two bereaved women flung themselves into each other's arms and had a good consoling cry, and then parted. Aunt Polly was tender far beyond her wont in her good night to Sid and Mary. Sid snuffled a bit, and Mary went off crying with all her heart.

Aunt Polly knelt down and prayed for Tom so touchingly, so appealingly, and with such measureless love in her words and her old trembling voice, that he was weltering in tears again long before she was through.

He had to keep still long after she went to bed, for she kept making broken-hearted ejaculations from time to time, tossing unrestfully, and turning over. But at last she was still, only moaning a little in her sleep. Now the boy stole out, rose gradually by the bedside, shaded the candle-light with his hand, and stood regarding her. His heart was full of pity for her. He took out his sycamore scroll and placed it by the candle. But something occurred to him, and he lingered considering. His face lighted with a happy solution of his thought; he put the bark hastily in his pocket, then he bent over and kissed the faded lips, and straightway made his stealthy exit, latching the door behind him.

He threaded his way back to the ferry landing, found nobody at large there, and walked boldly on board the boat, for he knew she was tenantless except that there was a watchman, who always turned in and slept like a graven image. He untied the skiff at the stern, slipped into it, and was soon rowing cautiously up stream. When he had pulled a mile above the village, he started quartering across, and bent himself stoutly to his work. He hit the landing on the other side neatly, for this was a familiar bit of work to him. He was moved to capture the skiff, arguing that it might be considered a ship and therefore legitimate prey for a pirate; but he knew a thorough search would be made for it, and that might end in revelations. So he stepped ashore and entered the wood. He sat down and took a long rest, torturing himself meantime to keep awake, and then started wearily down the home stretch. The night was far spent. It was broad daylight before he found himself fairly abreast the island bar. He rested again until the sun was well up and gilding the great river with its splendour, and then he plunged into the stream. A little later he paused, dripping, upon the threshold of the camp, and heard Joe say:

'No, Tom's true-blue, Huck, and he'll come back. He won't desert. He knows that would be a disgrace to a pirate, and Tom's too proud for that sort of thing. He's up to something or other. Now, I wonder what?'

'Well, the things is ours anyway, ain't they?'

'Pretty near, but not yet, Huck. The writing says they are if he ain't back to breakfast.'

'Which he is!' exclaimed Tom, with fine dramatic effect, stepping grandly into camp.

A sumptuous breakfast of bacon and fish was shortly provided, and as the boys set to work upon it Tom recounted (and adorned) his adventures. They were a vain and boastful company of heroes when the tale was done. Then Tom hid himself away in a shady nook to sleep till noon, and the other pirates got ready to fish and explore.

CHAPTER XVI

AFTER dinner all the gang turned out to hunt for turtle eggs on the bar. They went about poking sticks into the sand, and when they found a soft place they went down on their knees and dug with their hands. Sometimes they would take fifty or sixty eggs out of one hole. They were perfectly round, white things, a trifle smaller than an English walnut. They had a famous fried-egg feast that night, and another on Friday morning. After breakfast they went whooping and prancing out on the bar, and chased each other round and round, shedding clothes as they went, until they were naked, and then continued the frolic far away up the shoal water of the bar, against the stiff current, which latter tripped their legs from under them from time to time, and greatly increased the fun. And now and then they stood in a group and splashed water in each other's faces with their palms, gradually approaching each other with averted faces, to avoid the straggling sprays, and finally gripping and struggling till the best man ducked his neighbour, and then they all went under in a tangle of white legs and arms, and came up blowing, spluttering, laughing, and gasping for breath at one and the same time.

When they were well exhausted, they would run out and sprawl on the dry, hot sand, and lie there and cover them- selves up with it, and by-and-by break for the water again and go through the original performance once more. Finally it occurred to them that their naked skin represented flesh-coloured 'tights' very fairly; so they drew a ring in the sand and had a circus – with three clowns in it, for none would yield this proudest post to his neighbour.

Next they got their marbles, and played 'knucks' and 'ring-taw' and 'keeps', till that amusement grew stale. Then Joe and Huck had another swim, but Tom would not venture, because he found that in kicking off his trousers he had kicked his string of rattlesnake rattles off his ankle, and he wondered how he had escaped cramp so long without the protection of this mysterious charm. He did not venture again until he had found it, and by that time the other boys were tired and ready to rest. They gradually wandered apart, dropped into the 'dumps', and fell to gazing longingly across the wide river to where the village lay drowsing in the sun. Tom found himself writing '*Becky*' in the sand with his big toe; he scratched it out and was angry with himself for his weakness. But he wrote it again, nevertheless; he could not help it. He erased it once more, and then took himself out of temptation by driving the other boys together, and then joining them.

But Joe's spirits had gone down almost beyond resurrection. He was so homesick that he could hardly endure the misery of it. The tears lay very near the surface. Huck was melancholy too. Tom was downhearted, but tried hard not to show it. He had a secret which he was not ready to tell yet, but if this mutinous depression was not broken up soon, he would have to bring it out. He said with a great show of cheerfulness:

'I bet there's been pirates on this island before, boys. We'll explore it again. They've hid treasures here somewhere. How'd you feel to light on a rotten chest full of gold and silver – hey?'

But it roused only a faint enthusiasm, which faded out with no reply. Tom-tried one or two other seductions; but they failed too. It was discouraging work. Joe sat poking up the sand with a stick, and looking very gloomy. Finally he said:

'Oh boys, let's give it up. I want to go home. It's so lonesome.'

'Oh, no, Joe, you'll feel better by-and-by,' said Tom. 'Just think of the fishing that's here.'

'I don't care for the fishing. I want to go home.'

'But, Joe, there ain't such another swimming-place anywhere.'

'Swimming's no good; I don't seem to care for it, somehow, when there ain't anybody to say I shan't go in. I mean to go home.'

'Oh, shucks! baby! You want to see your mother, I reckon.'

108

'Yes, I *do* want to see my mother, and you would too, if you had one. I ain't any more baby than you are.' And Joe snuffled a little.

'Well, we'll let the cry-baby go home to his mother, won't we, Huck? Poor thing – does it want to see its mother? And so it shall. *You* like it here, don't you, Huck? We'll stay, won't we?'

Huck said 'Y-e-s – ' without any heart in it.

'I'll never speak to you again as long as I live,' said Joe, rising. 'There now!' And he moved moodily away and began to dress himself.

'Who cares?' said Tom. 'Nobody wants you to. Go 'long home and get laughed at. Oh, you're a nice pirate. Huck and me ain't cry-babies. We'll stay, won't we, Huck? Let him go if he wants to. I reckon we can get along without him, per'aps.'

But Tom was uneasy nevertheless, and was alarmed to see Joe go sullenly on with his dressing. And then it was discomforting to see Huck eyeing Joe's preparations so wistfully, and keeping up such an ominous silence. Presently, without a parting word, Joe began to wade off towards the Illinois shore. Tom's heart began to sink. He glanced at Huck. Huck could not bear the look, and dropped his eyes. Then he said:

'I want to go too, Tom; it was getting so lonesome anyway, and now it'll be worse. Let's go too, Tom.'

'I won't; you can all go if you want to. I mean to stay.'

'Tom, I better go.'

'Well, go 'long – who's hindering you?'

Huck began to pick up his scattered clothes. He said:

'Tom, I wisht you'd come too. Now, you think it over. We'll wait for you when we get to shore.'

'Well, you'll wait a blame long time, that's all.'

Huck started sorrowfully away, and Tom stood looking after him, with a strong desire tugging at his heart to yield his pride and go along too. He hoped the boys would stop, but they still waded slowly on. It suddenly dawned on Tom that it was become very lonely and still. He made one final struggle with his pride, and then he darted after his comrades, yelling:

'Wait! wait! I want to tell you something!'

They presently stopped and turned round. When he got to where they were, he began unfolding his secret, and they listened moodily till at last they saw the 'point' he was driving at, and then they set up a war-whoop of applause and said it was 'splendid!' and said if he had told them that at first, they wouldn't have started away. He made a plausible excuse; but his real reason had been the fear that not even the secret would keep them with him any very great length of time, and so he had meant to hold it in reserve as a last seduction.

The lads came gaily back and went at their sports again with a will, chatting all the time about Tom's stupendous plan and admiring the genius of it. After a dainty egg and fish dinner, Tom said he wanted to learn to smoke now. Joe caught at the idea, and said he would like to try too. So Huck made pipes and filled them. These novices had never smoked anything before but cigars made of grape-vine, and they 'bit' the tongue, and were not considered man y, anyway.

Now they stretched themselves out on their elbows and began to puff charily, and with slender confidence. The smoke had an unpleasant taste, and they gagged a little, but Tom said:

'Why, it's just as easy! If I'd a knowed *this* was all, I'd a learnt long ago.'

'So would I,' said Joe. 'It's just nothing.'

'Why, many a time I've looked at people smoking and thought, Well, I wish I could do that; but I never thought I could,' said Tom. 'That's just the way with me, ain't it, Huck? You've heard me talk just that way, haven't you, Huck? I'll leave it to Huck if I haven't.'

'Yes, heaps of times,' said Huck.

'Well, I have too,' said Tom; 'oh, hundreds of times. Once down there by the slaughter-house. Don't you remember, Huck? Bob Tanner was there, and Johnny Miller, and Jeff Thatcher, when I said it. Don't you remember, Huck, 'bout me saying that?'

'Yes, that's so,' said Huck. 'That was the day after I lost a white alley – no, 'twas the day before!'

'There, I told you so,' said Tom. 'Huck recollects it.'

'I believe I could smoke this pipe all day,' said Joe. '*I* don't feel sick.'

'Neither do I,' said Tom. '*I* could smoke it all day, but I bet you Jeff Thatcher couldn't.'

'Jeff Thatcher! Why, he'd keel over just with two draws. Just let him try it once; *he'd* see!'

'I bet he would, and Johnny Miller – I wish I could see Johnny Miller tackle it once.'

'Oh, don't *I?*' said Joe. 'Why, I bet you Johnny Miller couldn't any more do this than nothing. Just one little snifter would fetch *him*.'

''Deed it would, Joe. Say – I wish the boys could see us now.'

'So do I!'

'Say, boys, don't say anything about it, and some time when they're around I'll come up to you and say, "Joe, got a pipe? I want a smoke!" And you'll say, kind of careless like, as if it warn't anything, you'll say, "Yes. I got my *old* pipe, and another one, but my tobacker ain't very good." And I'll say, "Oh, that's all right, if it's *strong* enough." And then you'll out with the pipes, and we'll light up just as ca'm, and then just see 'em look!'

'By jings, that'll be gay, Tom; I wish it was *now!*'

'So do I! And when we tell 'em we learned when we was off pirating, won't they wish they'd been along!'

'Oh, I reckon not! I'll just *bet* they will!'

So the talk ran on; but presently it began to flag a trifle, and grow disjointed. The silences widened; the expectoration marvellously increased. Every pore inside the boys' cheeks became a spouting fountain; they could scarcely bale out the cellars under their tongues fast enough to prevent an inundation; little overflowings down their throats occurred in spite of all they could do, and sudden retchings followed every time. Both boys were looking very pale and miserable now. Joe's pipe dropped from his nerveless fingers. Tom's followed. Both fountains were going furiously, and both pumps baling with might and main. Joe said feebly:

'I've lost my knife. I reckon I better go and find it.'

Tom said, with quivering lips and halting utterance:

'I'll help you. You go over that way, and I'll hunt around by the spring. No, you needn't come, Huck – we can find it.'

So Huck sat down again, and waited an hour. Then he found it lonesome, and went to find his comrades. They were wide apart in the woods, both very pale, both fast asleep. But something informed him that if they had had any trouble they had got rid of it.

They were not talkative at supper that night; they had a humble look; and when Huck prepared his pipe after the meal, and was going to prepare theirs, they said no, they were not feeling very well – something they ate at dinner had disagreed with them.

CHAPTER XVII

ABOUT midnight Joe awoke, and called the boys. There was a brooding oppressiveness in the air that seemed to bode something. The boys huddled themselves together, and sought the friendly companionship of the fire, though the dull dead heat of the breathless atmosphere was stifling. They sat still, intent and waiting. Beyond the light of the fire, everything was swallowed up in the blackness of darkness. Presently there came a quivering glow that vaguely revealed the foliage for a moment and then vanished. By-and-by another came, a little stronger. Then another. Then a faint moan came sighing through the branches of the forest, and the boys felt a fleeting breath upon their cheeks, and shuddered with the fancy that the Spirit of the Night had gone by. There was a pause. Now a weird flash turned night into day, and showed every little grass-blade separate and distinct, that grew about their feet. And it showed three white startled faces, too. A deep peal of thunder went rolling and tumbling down the heavens, and lost itself in sullen rumblings in the distance. A sweep of chilly air passed by, rustling all the leaves and snowing the flaky ashes broadcast about the fire. Another fierce glare lit up the forest, and an instant crash followed that seemed to rend the tree-tops right over the boys' heads. They clung together in terror, in the quick gloom that followed. A few big rain-drops fell pattering upon the leaves.

'Quick, boys, go for the tent!' exclaimed Tom.

They sprang away, stumbling over roots and among vines in the dark, no two plunging in the same direction. A furious blast roared through the trees, making everything sing as it went. One blinding flash after another came, and peal on peal of deafening thunder. And now a drenching rain poured down, and the rising hurricane drove it in sheets along the ground. The boys cried out to each other, but the roaring wind and the booming thunder-blasts drowned their voices utterly. However, one by one they straggled in at last, and took shelter under the tent, cold, scared, and streaming with water; but to have company in misery seemed something to be grateful for. They could not talk, the old sail flapped so furiously, even if the other noises would have allowed them. The tempest rose higher and higher, and presently the sail tore loose from its fastenings, and went winging away on the blast. The boys seized each others' hands, and fled, with many tumblings and bruises, to the shelter of a great oak that stood upon the river bank. Now the battle was at its highest. Under the ceaseless conflagrations of lightnings that flamed in the skies, everything below stood out in clean-cut and shadowless distinctness; the bending trees, the billowy river white with foam, the driving spray of spume-flakes, the dim outlines of the high bluffs on the other side, glimpsed through the drifting cloud-rack and the slanting veil of rain. Every little while some giant tree yielded the fight and fell crashing through the younger growth; and the unflagging thunder-peals came now in ear-splitting explosive bursts, keen and sharp, and unspeakably appalling. The storm culminated in one matchless effort that seemed likely to tear the island to pieces, burn it up, drown it to the tree-tops, blow it away and deafen every creature in it, all at one and the same moment. It was a wild night for homeless young heads to be out in.

But at last the battle was done, and the forces retired, with weaker and weaker threatenings and grumblings, and peace resumed her sway. The boys went back to camp a good deal awed; but they found there was still something to be thankful for, because the great sycamore, the shelter of their beds, was a ruin, now, blasted by the lightnings, and they were not under it when the catastrophe happened.

Everything in camp was drenched, the camp-fire as well; for they were but heedless lads, like their generation, and had made no provision against rain. Here was matter for dismay, for they were soaked through and chilled. They were eloquent in their distress: but they presently discovered that the fire had eaten so far up under the great log it had been built against (where it curved upward and separated itself from the ground), that a hand-breath or so of it had escaped wetting; so they patiently wrought until, with shreds and bark gathered from under sides of sheltered logs, they coaxed the fire to burn again. Then they piled on great dead boughs till they had a roaring furnace and were glad-hearted once more. They dried their boiled ham and had a feast, and after that they sat by the fire and expanded and glorified their midnight adventure until morning, for there was not a dry spot to sleep on anywhere around.

As the sun began to steal in upon the boys, drowsiness came over them and they went out on the sand-bar and lay down to sleep. They got scorched out by-and-by, and drearily set about getting breakfast. After the meal they felt rusty, and stiff-jointed, and a little homesick once more. Tom saw the signs, and fell to cheering up the pirates as well as he could. But they cared nothing for marbles, or circus, or swimming, or anything. He reminded them of the imposing secret, and raised a ray of cheer. While it lasted he got them interested in a new device. This was to knock off being pirates for a while, and be Indians for a change. They were attracted by this idea; so it was not long before they were stripped, and striped from head to heel with black mud, like so many zebras, all of them chiefs, of course, and then they went tearing through the woods to attack an English settlement.

By-and-by they separated into three hostile tribes, and darted upon each other from ambush with dreadful war-whoops, and killed and scalped each other by thousands. It was a gory day. Consequently it was a satisfactory one.

They assembled in camp towards supper-time, hungry and happy. But now a difficulty arose – hostile Indians could not break the bread of hospitality together without first making peace, and this was a simple impossibility without smoking a pipe of peace. There was no other process that ever they had heard of. Two of the savages almost wished they had remained pirates. However, there was no other way, so with such show of cheerfulness as they could muster they called for the pipe and took their whiff, as it passed, in due form.

And behold they were glad they had gone into savagery, for they had gained something; they found that they could now smoke a little without having to go and hunt for a lost knife; they did not get sick enough to be seriously uncomfortable. They were not likely to fool away this high promise for lack of effort. No, they practised cautiously after supper with right fair success, and so they spent a jubilant evening. They were prouder and happier in their new acquirement than they would have been in the scalping and skinning of the Six Nations. We will leave them to smoke and chatter and brag, since we have no further use for them at present.

CHAPTER XVIII

But there was no hilarity in the little town that tranquil Saturday afternoon. The Harpers and Aunt Polly's family were being put into mourning with great grief and many tears. An unusual quiet possessed the village, although it was ordinarily quiet enough in all conscience. The villagers conducted their concerns with an abstracted air, and talked little; but they sighed often. The Saturday holiday seemed a burden to the children. They had no heart in their sports, and gradually gave them up.

In the afternoon Becky Thatcher found herself moping about the deserted school-house yard, and feeling very melancholy. But she found nothing there to comfort her. She soliloquized:

'Oh, if I only had his brass andiron knob again! But I haven't got anything now to remember him by,' and she choked back a little sob.

Presently she stopped, and said to herself:

'It was right here. Oh, if it was to do over again, I wouldn't say that – I wouldn't say it for the whole world. But he's gone now; I'll never, never, never see him any more.'

This thought broke her down, and she wandered away with the tears rolling down her cheeks. Then quite a group of boys and girls – playmates of Tom's and Joe's—came by, and stood looking over the paling fence and talking in reverent tones of how Tom did so-and-so the last time they saw him, and how Joe said this and that small trifle (pregnant with awful prophecy, as they could easily see now!) – and each speaker pointed out the exact spot where the lost lads stood at the time, and then added something like, 'and I was a standing just so – just as I am now, and as if you was him – I was as close as that – and he smiled, just this way – and then something seemed to go all over me, like – awful, you know – and I never thought what it meant, of course, but I can see now!'

Then there was a dispute about who saw the dead boys last in life, and many claimed that dismal distinction, and offered evidences more or less tampered with by the witness; and when it was ultimately decided who did see the departed last, and exchanged the last words with them, the lucky parties took upon themselves a sort of sacred importance, and were gaped at and envied by all the rest. One poor chap who had no other grandeur to offer, said, with tolerably manifest pride in the remembrance:

'Well, Tom Sawyer he licked me once.'

But that bid for glory was a failure. Most of the boys could say that, and so that cheapened the distinction too much. The group loitered away, still recalling memories of the lost heroes in awed voices.

When the Sunday-school hour was finished the next morning, the bell began to toll, instead of ringing in the usual way. It was a very still Sabbath, and the mournful sound seemed in keeping with the musing hush that lay upon nature. The villagers began to gather, loitering a moment in the vestibule to converse in whispers about the sad event. But there was no whispering in the house; only the funereal rustling of dresses, as the women gathered to their seats, disturbed the silence there. None could remember when the little church had been so full before. There was finally a waiting pause, an expectant dumbness, and then Aunt Polly entered, followed by Sid and Mary, and then by the Harper family, all in deep black, and the whole congregation, the old minister as well, rose reverently and stood, until the mourners were seated in the front pew. There was another communing silence, broken at intervals by muffled sobs, and then the minister spread his hands abroad and prayed. A moving hymn was sung, and the text followed: 'I am the resurrection and the life.'

As the service proceeded, the clergyman drew such pictures of the graces, the winning ways, and the rare promise of the lost lads, that every soul there, thinking he recognized these pictures, felt a pang in remembering that he had persistently blinded himself to them always before, and had as persistently seen only faults and flaws in the poor boys. The minister related many a touching incident in the lives of the departed, too, which illustrated their sweet, generous natures, and the people could easily see, now, how noble and beautiful those episodes were, and remembered with grief that at the time they occurred they had seemed rank rascalities, well deserving the cowhide. The congregation became more and more moved as the pathetic tale went on, till at last the whole company broke down and joined the weeping mourners in a chorus of anguished sobs, the preacher himself giving way to his feelings, and crying in the pulpit.

There was a rustle in the gallery which nobody noticed; a moment later the church door creaked; the minister raised his streaming eyes above his handkerchief, and stood transfixed! First one and then another pair of eyes followed the minister's, and then, almost with one impulse, the congregation rose and stared while the three dead boys came marching up the aisle, Tom in the lead, Joe next, and Huck, a ruin of drooping rags, sneaking sheepishly in the rear. They had been hid in the unused gallery, listening to their own funeral sermon!

Aunt Polly, Mary, and the Harpers threw themselves upon their restored ones, smothered them with kisses and poured out thanksgivings, while poor Huck stood abashed and uncomfortable, not knowing exactly what to do or where to hide from so many unwelcoming eyes. He wavered, and started to slink away, but Tom seized him and said:

'Aunt Polly, it ain't fair. Somebody's got to be glad to see Huck.'

'And so they shall! I'm glad to see him, poor motherless thing!' And the loving attentions Aunt Polly lavished upon him were the one thing capable of making him more uncomfortable than he was before.

Suddenly the minister shouted at the top of his voice:

' "Praise God from whom all blessings flow" – SING! – and put your hearts in it!'

And they did. Old Hundred swelled up with a triumphant burst, and while it shook the rafters Tom Sawyer the Pirate looked around upon the envying juveniles about him, and confessed in his heart that this was the proudest moment in his life.

As the 'sold' congregation trooped out, they said they would almost be willing to be made ridiculous again to hear Old Hundred sung like that once more.

Tom got more cuffs and kisses that day – according to Aunt Polly's varying moods – than he had earned before in a year; and he hardly knew which expressed the most gratefulness to God and affection for himself.

CHAPTER XIX

THAT was Tom's great secret – the scheme to return home with his brother pirates and attend their own funerals. They had paddled over to the Missouri shore on a log, at dusk on Saturday, landing five or six miles below the village; they had slept in the woods at the edge of the town till nearly day-light, and had then crept through back lanes and alleys and finished their sleep in the gallery of the church among a chaos of invalid benches.

At breakfast, Monday morning, Aunt Polly and Mary were very loving to Tom, and very attentive to his wants. There was an unusual amount of talk. In the course of it Aunt Polly said:

'Well, I don't say it wasn't a fine joke, Tom, to keep everybody suffering 'most a week so you boys had a good time, but it is a pity you could be so hard-hearted as to let me suffer so. If you could come over on a log to go to your funeral, you could have come over and give me a hint some way that you warn't dead, but only run off.'

'Yes, you could have done that, Tom,' said Mary; 'and I believe you would if you had thought of it.'

'Would you, Tom?' said Aunt Polly, her face lighting wistfully. 'Say, now, would you, if you'd thought of it?'

'I – well, I don't know. 'Twould a spoiled everything.'

'Tom, I hoped you loved me that much,' said Aunt Polly, with a grieved tone that discomforted the boy. 'It would been something if you'd cared enough to think of it, even if you didn't do it.'

'Now, Auntie, that ain't any harm,' pleaded Mary; 'it's only Tom's giddy way – he is always in such a rush that he never thinks of anything.'

'More's the pity. Sid would have thought. And Sid would have come and done it, too. Tom, you'll look back, some day, when it's too late, and wish you'd cared a little more for me when it would have cost you so little.'

'Now, Auntie, you know I do care for you,' said Tom.

'I'd know it better if you acted more like it.'

'I wish now I'd thought,' said Tom, with a repentant tone; 'but I dreamed about you, anyway. That's something, ain't it?'

'It ain't much – a cat does that much – but it's better than nothing. What did you dream?'

'Why, Wednesday night I dreamt that you was sitting over there by the bed, and Sid was sitting by the wood-box, and Mary next to him.'

'Well, so we did. So we always do. I'm glad your dreams could take even that much trouble about us.'

'And I dreamt that Joe Harper's mother was here.'

'Why, she was here! Did you dream any more?'

'Oh, lots. But it's so dim now.'

'Well, try to recollect – can't you?'

'Somehow it seems to me that the wind – the wind blowed the – the – '

'Try harder, Tom! The wind did blow something, come!'

Tom pressed his fingers on his forehead an anxious minute, and then said:

'I've got it now! I've got it now! It blowed the candle!'

'Mercy on us! Go on, Tom, go on!'

'And it seems to me that you said, "Why, I believe that that door – " '

'Go on, Tom!'

'Just let me study a moment – just a moment. Oh, yes – you said you believed the door was open.'

'As I'm sitting here, I did! Didn't I, Mary? Go on!'

'And then – and then – well, I won't be certain, but it seems like as if you made Sid go and – and – '

'Well? Well? What did I make him do, Tom? What did I make him do?'

'You made him – you – Oh, you made him shut it!'

'Well, for the land's sake! I never heard the beat of that in all my days! Don't tell me there ain't anything in dreams any more. Sereny Harper shall know of this before I'm an hour older. I'd like to see her get around this with her rubbage about superstitition. Go on, Tom!'

'Oh, it's all getting just as bright as day, now. Next you said I warn't bad, only mischeevous and harum-scarum, and

121

not any more responsible than – than – I think it was a colt, or something.'

'And so it was! Well! Goodness gracious! Go on, Tom!'

'And then you began to cry.'

'So I did. So I did. Not the first time, neither. And then –'

'Then Mrs Harper she began to cry, and said Joe was just the same, and she wished she hadn't whipped him for taking cream when she'd throwed it out her ownself –'

'Tom! The sperrit was upon you! You was a prophesying – that's what you was doing! Land alive! – go on, Tom!'

'Then Sid he said – he said –'

'I don't think I said anything,' said Sid.

'Yes, you did, Sid,' said Mary.

'Shut your heads and let Tom go on! What did he say, Tom?'

'He said – I think he said he hoped I was better off where I was gone to, but if I'd been better sometimes –'

'There, d'you hear that? It was his very words!'

'And you shut him up sharp.'

'I lay I did! There must a been an angel there. There was an angel there, somewheres!'

'And Mrs Harper told about Joe scaring her with a fire-cracker, and you told about Peter and the Pain-killer –'

'Just as true as I live!'

'And then there was a whole lot of talk 'bout dragging the river for us, and 'bout having the funeral Sunday, and then you and old Mrs Harper hugged and cried, and she went.'

'It happened just so! It happened just so, as sure as I'm a sitting in these very tracks. Tom, you couldn't told it more like if you'd a seen it! And then what? Go on, Tom.'

'Then I thought you prayed for me – and I could see you and hear every word you said. And you went to bed, and I was so sorry that I took and wrote on a piece of sycamore bark, "We ain't dead – we are only off being pirates", and put it on the table by the candle; and then you looked so good, laying there asleep, that I thought I went and leaned over and kissed you on the lips.'

'Did you, Tom, did you? I just forgive you everything for that!' And she seized the boy in a crushing embrace that made him feel like the guiltiest of villains.

'It was very kind, even though it was only a – dream,' Sid soliloquized just audibly.

'Shut up, Sid! A body does just the same in a dream as he'd do if he was awake. Here's a big Milum apple I've been saving for you, Tom, if you was ever found again – now go 'long to school. I'm thankful to the good God and Father of us all I've got you back, that's long-suffering and merciful to them that believe on Him and keep His word, though goodness knows I'm unworthy of it, but if only the worthy ones got His blessings and had His hand to help them over the rough places, there's few enough would smile here or ever enter into His rest when the long night comes. Go 'long, Sid, Mary, Tom – take yourselves off – you've hendered me long enough.'

The children left for school, and the old lady to call on Mrs Harper, and vanquish her realism with Tom's marvellous dream. Sid had better judgement than to utter the thought that was in his mind as he left the house. It was this:

'Pretty thin – as long a dream as that, without any mistakes in it!'

What a hero Tom was become now! He did not go skipping and prancing, but moved with a dignified swagger, as became a pirate who felt that the public eye was on him. And indeed it was; he tried not to seem to see the looks or hear the remarks as he passed along, but they were food and drink to him. Smaller boys than himself flocked at his heels, as proud to be seen with him and tolerated by him as if he had been the drummer at the head of a procession, or the elephant leading a menagerie into town. Boys of his own size pretended not to know he had been away at all, but they were consuming with envy, nevertheless. They would have given anything to have that swarthy, sun-tanned skin of his, and his glittering notoriety; and Tom would not have parted with either for a circus.

At school the children made so much of him and Joe, and delivered such eloquent admiration from their eyes, that the two heroes were not long in becoming insufferably 'stuck-up'. They began to tell their adventures to hungry listeners – but they only began; it was not a thing likely to have an end, with imaginations like theirs to furnish material. And finally, when they got out their pipes and went serenely puffing around, the very summit of glory was reached.

Tom decided that he could be independent of Becky Thatcher now. Glory was sufficient. He would live for glory. Now that he was distinguished, maybe she would be wanting to 'make up'. Well, let her – she should see that he could be as indifferent as some other people. Presently she arrived. Tom pretended not to see her. He moved away and joined a group of boys and girls, and began to talk. Soon he observed that she was tripping gaily back and forth with flushed face and dancing eyes, pretending to be busy chasing schoolmates, and screaming with laughter when she made a capture, but he noticed that she always made her captures in his vicinity, and that she seemed to cast a conscious eye in his direction at such times, too. It gratified all the vicious vanity that was in him; and so, instead of winning him, it only 'set him up' the more and made him the more diligent to avoid betraying that he knew she was about. Presently, she gave over skylarking, and moved irresolutely about, sighing once or twice and glancing furtively and wistfully towards Tom. Then she observed that now Tom was talking more particularly to Amy Lawrence than to anyone else. She felt a sharp pang and grew disturbed and uneasy at once. She tried to go away, but her feet were treacherous, and carried her to the group instead. She said to a girl almost at Tom's elbow – with sham vivacity:

'Why, Mary Austin! you bad girl, why didn't you come to Sunday-school?'

'I did come – didn't you see me?'

'Why, no! Did you? Where did you sit?'

'I was in Miss Peter's class, where I always go. I saw you.'

'Did you? Why, it's funny I didn't see you. I wanted to tell you about the picnic.'

'Oh, that's jolly. Who's going to give it?'

'My ma's going to let me have one.'

'Oh, goody; I hope she'll let me come.'

'Well, she will. The picnic's for me. She'll let anybody come that I want, and I want you.'

'That's ever so nice. When is it going to be?'

'By-and-by. Maybe about vacation.'

'Oh, won't it be fun! You going to have all the girls and boys?'

'Yes, everyone that's friends to me – or wants to be,' and she glanced ever so furtively at Tom, but he talked right along to Amy Lawrence about the terrible storm on the island, and how the lightning tore the great sycamore tree 'all to flinders' while he was 'standing within three feet of it'.

'Oh, may I come?' said Gracie Miller.

'Yes.'

'And me?' said Sally Rogers.

'Yes.'

'And me too?' said Susy Harper. 'And Joe?'

'Yes.'

And so on, with clapping of joyful hands, till all the group had begged for invitations but Tom and Amy. Then Tom turned coolly away, still talking, and took Amy with him. Becky's lips trembled and the tears came to her eyes; she hid these signs with a forced gaiety and went on chattering, but the life had gone out of the picnic, now, and out of everything else; she got away as soon as she could and hid herself, and had what her sex call 'a good cry'. Then she sat moody, with wounded pride, till the bell rang. She roused up, now, with a vindictive cast in her eye, and gave her plaited tails a shake, and said she knew what she'd do.

At recess Tom continued his flirtation with Amy with jubilant self-satisfaction. And he kept drifting about to find Becky and lacerate her with the performance. At last he spied her, but there was a sudden falling of his mercury. She was sitting cosily on a little bench behind the schoolhouse, looking at a picture-book with Alfred Temple; and so absorbed were they, and their heads so close together over the book, that they did not seem to be conscious of anything in the world beside. Jealousy ran red-hot through Tom's veins. He began to hate himself for throwing away the chance Becky had offered for a reconciliation. He called himself a fool, and all the hard names he could think of. He wanted to cry with vexation. Amy chatted happily along, as they walked, for her heart was singing, but Tom's tongue had lost its function. He did not hear what Amy was saying, and whenever she paused expectantly, he could only stammer an awkward assent, which was as often misplaced as otherwise. He kept drifting to the rear of the school-house again and again, to sear his eyeballs with the hateful spectacle there. He could not help it. And it maddened him to see, as he thought he saw, that Becky Thatcher never once suspected that he was even in the land of the living. But she did see, nevertheless; and she knew she was winning her fight, too, and was glad to see him suffer as she had suffered. Amy's happy prattle became intolerable. Tom hinted at things he had to attend to; things that must be done; and time was fleeting. But in vain – the girl chirped on. Tom thought, 'Oh, hang her, ain't I ever going to get rid of her?' At last he must be attending to those things; she said artlessly that she would be 'around' when school let out. And he hastened away, hating her for it.

'Any other boy!' Tom thought, grating his teeth. 'Any boy in the whole town but that Saint Louis smarty, that thinks he dresses so fine and is aristocracy! Oh, all right. I licked you the first time you ever saw this town, mister, and I'll lick you again! You just wait till I catch you out! I'll just take and – '

And he went through the motions of thrashing an imaginary boy – pummelling the air, and kicking and gouging.

'Oh, you do, do you? you holler 'nough, do you? Now, then, let that learn you!'

And so the imaginary flogging was finished to his satisfaction.

Tom fled home at noon. His conscience could not endure any more of Amy's grateful happiness, and his jealousy could bear no more of the other distress. Becky resumed her picture-inspections with Alfred, but as the minutes dragged along and no Tom came to suffer, her triumph began to cloud and she lost interest; gravity and absent-mindedness followed, and then melancholy; two or three times she pricked up her ear at a footstep, but it was a false hope; no Tom came. At last she grew entirely miserable, and wished she hadn't carried it so far. When poor Alfred, seeing that he was losing her he did not know how, kept exclaiming: 'Oh, here's a jolly one! look at this!' she lost patience at last and said, 'Oh, don't bother me! I don't care for them!' and burst into tears, and got up and walked away.

Alfred dropped alongside and was going to try and comfort her, but she said:

'Go away and leave me alone, can't you. I hate you!'

So the boy halted, wondering what he could have done – for she had said she would look at pictures all through the nooning – and she walked on, crying. Then Alfred went musing into the deserted school-house. He was humiliated and angry. He easily guessed his way to the truth – the girl had simply made a convenience of him to vent her spite on Tom Sawyer. He was far from hating Tom the less when this thought occurred to him. He wished there was some way to get that boy into trouble without much risk to himself. Tom's spelling-book fell under his eye. Here was his opportunity. He gratefully opened to the lesson for the afternoon, and poured ink upon the page. Becky, glancing in at a window behind him at the moment, saw the act and moved on without discovering herself. She started homeward, now, intending to find Tom and tell him: Tom would be thankful, and their troubles would be healed. Before she was halfway home, however, she had changed her mind. The thought of Tom's treatment of her when she was talking about her picnic came scorching back, and filled her with shame. She resolved to let him get whipped on the damaged spelling-book's account, and to hate him for ever into the bargain.

CHAPTER XX

Tom arrived at home in a dreary mood, and the first thing his aunt said to him showed him that he had brought his sorrows to an unpromising market:

'Tom, I've a notion to skin you alive.'

'Auntie, what have I done?'

'Well, you've done enough. Here I go over to Sereny Harper like an old softy, expecting I'm going to make her believe all that rubbage about that dream, when, lo and behold you, she'd found out from Joe that you was over here and heard all the talk we had that night. Tom, I don't know what is to become of a boy that will act like that. It makes me feel so bad to think you could let me go to Sereny Harper, and make such a fool of myself, and never say a word.'

This was a new aspect of the thing. His smartness of the morning had seemed to Tom a good joke before, and very ingenious. It merely looked mean and shabby now. He hung his head and could not think of anything to say for a moment; then he said:

'Auntie, I wish I hadn't done it – but I didn't think.'

'Oh, child, you never think. You never think of anything but your own selfishness. You could think to come all the way over here from Jackson's Island in the night to laugh at our troubles, and you could think to fool me with a lie about a dream: but you couldn't ever think to pity us and save us from sorrow.'

'Auntie, I know now it was mean, but I didn't mean to be mean; I didn't honest. And besides, I didn't come over here to laugh at you that night.'

'What did you come for, then?'

'It was to tell you not to be uneasy about us, because we hadn't got drownded.'

'Tom, Tom, I would be the thankfullest soul in this world if I could believe you ever had as good a thought as that, but you know you never did – and *I* know it, Tom.'

'Indeed and 'deed I did, Auntie – I wish I may never stir if I didn't.'

'Oh, Tom, don't lie – don't do it. It only makes things a hundred times worse.'

'It ain't a lie, Auntie; it's the truth. I wanted to keep you from grieving – that was all that made me come.'

'I'd give the whole world to believe that – it would cover up a power of sins, Tom. I'd 'most be glad you'd run off and acted so bad. But it ain't reasonable; because why didn't you tell me, child?'

'Why, you see, Auntie, when you got to talking about the funeral, I just got all full of the idea of our coming and hiding in the church, and I couldn't, somehow, bear to spoil it. So I just put the bark back in my pocket and kept mum.'

'What bark?'

'The bark I had wrote on to tell you we'd gone pirating. I wish now, you'd waked up when I kissed you – I do, honest.'

The hard lines in his aunt's face relaxed, and sudden tenderness dawned in her eyes.

'*Did* you kiss me, Tom?'

'Why, yes, I did.'

'Are you sure you did, Tom?'

'Why, yes, I did, Auntie – certain sure.'

'What did you kiss me for, Tom?'

'Because I loved you so, and you laid there moaning, and I was so sorry.'

The words sounded like truth. The old lady could not hide a tremor in her voice when she said:

'Kiss me again, Tom! – and be off with you to school, now, and don't bother me any more.'

The moment he was gone, she ran to a closet and got out the ruin of a jacket which Tom had gone pirating in. Then she stopped with it in her hand, and said to herself:

'No, I don't dare. Poor boy, I reckon he's lied about it – but it's a blessed, blessed lie, there's such comfort in it. I hope the Lord – I *know* the Lord will forgive him because it was such good-heartedness in him to tell it. But I don't want to find out it's a lie. I won't look.'

She put the jacket away, and stood by musing a minute. Twice she put out her hand to take the garment again, and twice she refrained. Once more she ventured, and this time she fortified herself with the thought: 'It's a good lie – it's a good lie – I won't let it grieve me.' So she sought the jacket pocket. A moment later she was reading Tom's piece of bark through flowing tears, and saying:

'I could forgive the boy, now, if he'd committed a million sins!'

CHAPTER XXI

THERE was something about Aunt Polly's manner when she kissed Tom, that swept away his low spirits and made him light-hearted and happy again. He started to school, and had the luck of coming upon Becky Thatcher at the head of Meadow Lane. His mood always determined his manner. Without a moment's hesitation he ran to her and said:

'I acted mighty mean today, Becky, and I'm so sorry. I won't ever, ever do it that way again as long as ever I live – please make up, won't you?'

The girl stopped and looked him scornfully in the face:

'I'll thank you to keep yourself *to* yourself, Mr Thomas Sawyer. I'll never speak to you again.'

She tossed her head and passed on. Tom was so stunned that he had not even presence of mind enough to say 'Who cares, Miss Smarty?' until the right time to say it had gone by. So he said nothing. But he was in a fine rage, nevertheless. He moped into the school-yard wishing she were a boy, and imagining how he would trounce her if she were. He presently encountered her and delivered a stinging remark as he passed. She hurled one in return, and the angry breach was complete. It seemed to Becky, in her hot resentment, that she could hardly wait for school to 'take in', she was so impatient to see Tom flogged for the injured spelling-book. If she had had any lingering notion of exposing Alfred Temple, Tom's offensive fling had driven it entirely away.

Poor girl, she did not know how fast she was nearing trouble herself. The master, Mr Dobbins, had reached middle age with an unsatisfied ambition. The darling of his desires was to be a doctor, but poverty had decreed that he should be nothing higher than a village schoolmaster. Every day he took a mysterious book out of his desk, and absorbed himself in it at times when no classes were reciting. He kept that book under lock and key. There was not an urchin in school but was perishing to have a glimpse of it, but the chance never came. Every boy and girl had a theory about the nature of that book; but no two theories were alike, and there was no way of getting at the facts in the case. Now as Becky was passing by the desk, which stood near the door, she noticed that the key was in the lock! It was a precious moment. She glanced around; found herself alone, and the next instant she had the book in her hands. The title-page – Professor somebody's *Anatomy* – carried no information to her mind; so she began to turn the leaves. She came at once upon a handsomely engraved and coloured frontispiece – a human figure. At that moment a shadow fell on the page, and Tom Sawyer stepped in at the door and caught a glimpse of the picture. Becky snatched at the book to close it, and had the hard luck to tear the pictured page half down the middle. She thrust the volume into the desk, turned the key, and burst out crying with shame and vexation:

'Tom Sawyer, you are just as mean as you can be, to sneak up on a person and look at what they're looking at.'

'How could *I* know you was looking at anything?'

'You ought to be ashamed of yourself, Tom Sawyer; you know you're going to tell on me; and, oh, what shall I do, what shall I do? I'll be whipped, and I never was whipped in school.'

Then she stamped her little foot and said:

'*Be* so mean if you want to! *I* know something that's going to happen. You just wait, and you'll see! Hateful, hateful, hateful!' – and she flung out of the house with a new explosion of crying.

Tom stood still, rather flustered by this onslaught. Presently he said to himself:

'What a curious kind of a fool a girl is. Never been licked in school! Shucks, what's a licking! That's just like a girl – they're so thin-skinned and chicken-hearted. Well, of course *I* ain't going to tell old Dobbins on this little fool, because there's other ways of getting even on her that ain't so mean; but what of it? Old Dobbins will ask who it was tore his book. Nobody'll answer. Then he'll do just the way he always does – ask first one and then t'other, and when he comes to the right girl he'll know it, without any telling. Girls' faces always tell on them. They ain't got any backbone. She'll get licked. Well, it's a kind of a tight place for Becky Thatcher, because there ain't any way out of it.' Tom conned the thing a moment longer, and then added: 'All right, though; she'd like to see me in just such a fix – let her sweat it out!'

Tom joined the mob of skylarking scholars outside. In a few moments the master arrived and school 'took in'. Tom did not feel a strong interest in his studies. Every time he stole a glance at the girls' side of the room, Becky's face troubled him. Considering all things, he did not want to pity her, and yet it was all he could do to help it. He could get up no exultation that was really worth the name. Presently the spelling-book discovery was made, and Tom's mind was entirely full of his own matters for a while after that. Becky roused up from her lethargy of distress, and showed good interest in the proceedings. She did not expect that Tom could get out of his trouble by denying that he spilt the ink on the book himself; and she was right. The denial only seemed to make the thing worse for Tom. Becky supposed she would be glad of that, and she tried to believe she was glad of it, but she found she was not certain. When the worst came to the worst, she had an impulse to get up and tell on Alfred Temple, but she made an effort and forced herself to keep still, because, said she to herself, 'he'll tell about me tearing the picture, sure. I wouldn't say a word, not to save his life!'

Tom took his whipping and went back to his seat not at all broken-hearted, for he thought it was possible that he had unknowingly upset the ink on the spelling-book himself, in some skylarking bout – he had denied it for form's sake and because it was custom, and had stuck to the denial from principle.

A whole hour drifted by; the master sat nodding in his throne, the air was drowsy with the hum of study. By-and-by Mr Dobbins straightened himself up, yawned, then un-locked his desk, and reached for his book, but seemed undecided whether to take it out or leave it. Most of the pupils glanced up languidly, but there were two among them that watched his movements with intent eyes. Mr Dobbins fingered his book absently for a while, then took it out, and settled himself in his chair to read.

Tom shot a glance at Becky. He had seen a hunted and helpless rabbit look as she did, with a gun levelled at its head. Instantly he forgot his quarrel with her. Quick, something must be done! done in a flash, too! But the very imminence of the emergency paralysed his invention. Good! he had an inspiration! He would run and snatch the book, spring through the door and fly! but his resolution shook for one little instant, and the chance was lost – the master opened the volume. If Tom only had the wasted opportunity back again! Too late; there was no help for Becky now, he said. The next moment the master faced the school. Every eye sank under his gaze; there was that in it which smote even the innocent with fear. There was silence while one might count ten; the master was gathering his wrath. Then he spoke:

'Who tore this book?'

There was not a sound. One could have heard a pin drop. The stillness continued; the master searched face after face for signs of guilt.

'Benjamin Rogers, did you tear this book?'

A denial. Another pause.

'Joseph Harper, did you?'

Another denial. Tom's uneasiness grew more and more intense under the slow torture of these proceedings. The master scanned the ranks of boys, considered a while, then turned to the girls:

'Amy Lawrence?'

A shake of the head.

'Gracie Miller?'

The same sign.

'Susan Harper, did you do this?'

134

Another negative. The next girl was Becky Thatcher. Tom was trembling from head to foot with excitement, and a sense of the hopelessness of the situation.

'Rebecca Thatcher' – (Tom glanced at her face; it was white with terror) – 'did you tear – no, look me in the face' – (her hands rose in appeal) – 'did you tear this book?'

A thought shot like lightning through Tom's brain. He sprang to his feet and shouted:

'*I* done it!'

The school stared in perplexity at this incredible folly. Tom stood a moment to gather his dismembered faculties; and when he stepped forward to go to his punishment, the surprise, the gratitude, the adoration that shone upon him out of poor Becky's eyes seemed pay enough for a hundred floggings. Inspired by the splendour of his own act, he took without an outcry the most merciless flogging that even Mr Dobbins had ever administered; and also received with indifference the added cruelty of a command to remain two hours after school should be dismissed – for he knew who would wait for him outside till his captivity was done, and not count the tedious time as loss either.

Tom went to bed that night planning vengeance against Alfred Temple; for with shame and repentance Becky had told him all, not forgetting her own treachery; but even the longing for vengeance had to give way soon to pleasanter musings, and he fell asleep at last with Becky's latest words lingering dreamily in his ear:

'Tom, how *could* you be so noble!'

CHAPTER XXII

VACATION was approaching. The schoolmaster, always severe, grew severer and more exacting than ever, for he wanted the school to make a good showing on 'Examination' day. His rod and his ferule were seldom idle now – at least among the smaller pupils. Only the biggest boys, and young ladies of eighteen and twenty, escaped lashing. Mr Dobbins's lashings were very vigorous ones too; for although he carried, under his wig, a perfectly bald and shiny head, he had only reached middle age and there was no sign of feebleness in his muscle. As the great day approached, all the tyranny that was in him came to the surface; he seemed to take a vindictive pleasure in punishing the least shortcomings. The consequence was that the smallest boys spent their days in terror and suffering and their nights in plotting revenge. They threw away no opportunity to do the master a mischief. But he kept ahead all the time. The retribution that followed every vengeful success was so sweeping and majestic that the boys always retired from the field badly worsted. At last they conspired together and hit upon a plan that promised a dazzling victory. They swore in the sign-painter's boy, told him the scheme, and asked his help. He had his own reasons for being delighted, for the master boarded in his father's family and had given the boy ample cause to hate him. The master's wife would go on a visit to the country in a few days, and there would be nothing to interfere with the plan; the master always prepared himself for great occasions by getting pretty well fuddled, and the sign-painter's boy said that when the dominie had reached the proper condition on 'Examination' evening he could 'manage the thing' while he napped on his chair; then he would have him awakened at the right time and hurried away to school.

In the fullness of time the interesting occasion arrived. At eight in the evening the school-house was brilliantly lighted and adorned with wreaths and festoons of foliage and flowers. The master sat throned in his great chair upon a raised platform, with his blackboard behind him. He was looking tolerably mellow. Three rows of benches on each side and six rows in front of him were occupied by the dignitaries of the town and by the parents of the pupils. To his left, back of the rows of citizens, was a spacious temporary platform upon which were seated the scholars who were to take part in the exercises of the evening; rows of small boys, washed and dressed to an intolerable state of discomfort; rows of gawky big boys; snow-banks of girls and young ladies clad in lawn and muslin, and conspicuously conscious of their bare arms, their grandmothers' ancient trinkets, their bits of pink and blue ribbon, and the flowers in their hair. All the rest of the house was filled with non-participating scholars.

The exercises began. A very little boy stood up and sheepishly recited 'You'd scarce expect one of my age, to speak in public on the stage,' etc., accompanying himself with the painfully exact and spasmodic gestures which a machine might have used – supposing the machine to be a trifle out of order. But he got through safely, though cruelly scared, and got a fine round of applause when he made his manufactured bow and retired.

A little shamefaced girl lisped 'Mary had a little lamb,' etc., performed a compassion-inspiring curtsey, got her meed of applause, and sat down flushed and happy.

Tom Sawyer stepped forward with conceited confidence, and soared into the unquenchable and indestructible 'Give me liberty or give me death' speech, with fine fury and frantic gesticulation, and broke down in the middle of it. A ghastly stage-fright seized him, his legs quaked under him and he was like to choke. True, he had the manifest sympathy of the house – but he had the house's silence too, which was even worse than its sympathy. The master frowned, and this completed the disaster. Tom struggled a while and then retired, utterly defeated. There was a weak attempt at applause, but it died early.

'The Boy Stood on the Burning Deck' followed; also 'The Assyrian Came Down', and other declamatory gems. Then there were reading exercises, and a spelling fight. The meagre Latin class recited with honour. The prime feature of the evening was in order, now – original 'compositions' by the young ladies. Each in her turn stepped forward to the edge of the platform, cleared her throat, held up her manuscript (tied with dainty ribbon), and proceeded to read, with laboured attention to 'expression' and punctuation. The themes were the same that had been illuminated upon similar occasions by their mothers before them, their grandmothers, and doubtless all their ancestors in the female line clear back to the Crusades. 'Friendship' was one; 'Memories of other Days'; 'Religion in History'; 'Dream Land'; 'The Adventures of Culture'; 'Forms of Political Government Compared and Contrasted'; 'Melancholy'; 'Filial Love'; 'Heart Longings', etc., etc.

A prevalent feature in these compositions was a nursed and petted melancholy; another was a wasteful and opulent gush of 'fine language'; another was a tendency to lug in by the ears particularly prized words and phrases until they were worn entirely out; and a peculiarity that conspicuously marked and marred them was the inveterate and intolerable sermon that wagged its crippled tail at the end of each and every one of them. No matter what the subject might be, a brainracking effort was made to squirm it into some aspect or other that the moral and religious mind could contemplate with edification. The glaring insincerity of these sermons was not sufficient to compass banishment of the fashion from the schools, and it is not sufficient today; it never will be sufficient while the world stands, perhaps. There is no school in all our land where the young ladies do not feel obliged to close their compositions with a sermon; and you will find that the sermon of the most frivolous and least religious girl in the school is always the longest and the most relentlessly pious. But enough of this. Homely truth is unpalatable. Let us return to the 'Examination'. The first composition that was read was one entitled 'Is this, then, Life?' Perhaps the reader can endure an extract from it:

'In the common walks of life, with what delightful emotions does the youthful mind look forward to some anticipated scene of festivity! Imagination is busy sketching rose-tinted pictures of joy. In fancy, the voluptuous votary of fashion sees herself amid the festive throng, "the observed of all observers". Her graceful form, arrayed in snowy robes, is whirling through the mazes of the joyous dance; her eye is brightest, her step is lightest in the gay assembly. In such delicious fancies time quickly glides by, and the welcome hour arrives for her entrance into the Elysian world, of which she has had such bright dreams. How fairylike does everything appear to her enchanted vision! Each new scene is more charming than the last. But after a while she finds that beneath this goodly exterior, all is vanity; the flattery which once charmed her soul, now grates harshly upon her ear; the ballroom has lost its charms; and with wasted health and embittered heart, she turns away with the conviction that earthly pleasures cannot satisfy the longings of the soul!'

And so forth and so on. There was a buzz of gratification from time to time during the reading, accompanied by whispered ejaculations of 'How sweet!' 'How eloquent!' 'So true!' etc., and after the thing had closed with a peculiarly afflicting sermon, the applause was enthusiastic.

Then arose a slim, melancholy girl, whose face had the 'interesting' paleness that comes of pills and indigestion, and read a 'poem'. Two stanzas of it will do.

A MISSOURI MAIDEN'S FAREWELL TO ALABAMA
Alabama, good-bye! I love thee well!
But yet for a while do I leave thee now!
Sad, yes, sad thoughts of thee my heart doth swell,
And burning recollections throng my brow!
For I have wandered through thy flowery woods;
Have roamed and read near Tallapoosa's stream;
Have listened to Talassee's warring floods,
And wooed on Coosa's side Aurora's beam.

Yet shame I not to bear an o'er-full heart,
Nor blush to turn behind my tearful eyes;
'Tis from no stranger land I now must part,
'Tis to no strangers left I yield these sighs.
Welcome and home were mine within this State
Whose vales I leave, whose spires fade fast from me;
And cold must be mine eyes, and heart, and *tête*,
When, clear Alabama! they turn cold on thee!

There were very few there who knew what '*tête*' meant but the poem was very satisfactory nevertheless.

Next appeared a dark-complexioned, black-eyed, black-haired young lady, who paused an impressive moment, assumed a tragic expression, and began to read in a measured tone:

A Vision

Dark and tempestuous was the night. Around the throne on high not a single star quivered; but the deep intonations of the heavy thunder constantly vibrated upon the ear; whilst the terrific lightning revelled in angry mood through the cloudy chambers of heaven, seeming to scorn the power exerted over its terrors by the illustrious Franklin! Even the boisterous winds unanimously came forth from their mystic homes, and blustered about as if to enhance by their aid the wildness of the scene. At such a time, so dark, so dreary, for human sympathy my very spirit sighed; but instead thereof,

My dearest friend, my counsellor, my comforter and guide,
My joy is grief, my second bliss in joy, came to my side.

She moved like one of those bright beings pictured in the sunny walks of fancy's Eden by the romantic and young, a queen of beauty unadorned save by her own transcendent loveliness. So soft was her step, it failed to make even a sound, and but for the magical thrill imparted by her genial touch, as other unobtrusive beauties she would have glided away unperceived – unsought. A strange sadness rested upon her features, like icy tears upon the robe of December, as she pointed to the contending elements without, and bade me contemplate the two beings presented.

This nightmare occupied some ten pages of manuscript, and wound up with a sermon so destructive of all hope to non-Presbyterians that it took the first prize. This composition was considered to be the very finest effort of the evening. The mayor of the village, in delivering the prize to the author of it, made a warm speech, in which he said that it was by far the most 'eloquent thing he had ever listened to, and that Daniel Webster himself might well be proud of it.'

It may be remarked in passing, that the number of compositions in which the word 'beauteous' was over-fondled, and human experience referred to as 'life's page', was up to the usual average.

Now the master, mellow almost to the verge of geniality, put his chair aside, turned his back to the audience, and began to draw a map of America on the blackboard, to exercise the geography class upon. But he made a sad business of it with his unsteady hand, and a smothered titter rippled over the house. He knew what the matter was, and set himself to right it. He sponged out lines and remade them; but he only distorted them more than ever, and the tittering was more pronounced. He threw his entire attention upon his work, now, as if determined not to be put down by the mirth. He felt that all eyes were fastened upon him; he imagined he was succeeding, and yet the tittering continued; it even manifestly increased. And well it might. There was a garret above, pierced with a scuttle over his head; down through this scuttle came a cat suspended around the haunches by a string; she had a rag tied about her head and jaws to keep her from mewing; she slowly descended, she curved upward and clawed at the string, she swung downward and clawed at the intangible air. The tittering rose higher and higher, the cat was within six inches of the absorbed teacher's head; down, down, a little lower, and she grabbed his wig with her desperate claws, clung to it, and was snatched up into the garret in an instant with her trophy still in her possession! And how the light did blaze abroad from the master's bald pate, for the sign-painter's boy had *gilded* it!

That broke up the meeting. The boys were avenged. Vacation was come.

NOTE. – The pretended 'compositions' quoted above are taken without alteration from a volume entitled *Prose and Poetry by a Western Lady*, but they are exactly and precisely after the school-girl pattern, and hence are much happier than any mere imitations could be.

CHAPTER XXIII

TOM joined the new order of Cadets of Temperance, being attracted by the showy character of their 'regalia'. He promised to abstain from smoking, chewing, and profanity as long as he remained a member. Now he found out a new thing – namely, that to promise not to do a thing is the surest way in the world to make a body want to go and do that very thing. Tom soon found himself tormented with a desire to drink, and swear; the desire grew to be so intense that nothing but the hope of a chance to display himself in his red sash kept him from withdrawing from the order. Fourth of July was coming: but he soon gave that up – gave it up before he had worn his shackles over forty-eight hours, and fixed his hopes upon old Judge Frazer, justice of the peace, who was apparently on his deathbed, and would have a big public funeral, since he was so high an official. During three days Tom was deeply concerned about the Judge's condition, and hungry for news of it. Sometimes his hopes ran high, so high that he would venture to get out his regalia and practise before the looking-glass. But the Judge had a most discouraging way of fluctuating. At last he was pronounced upon the mend, and then convalescent. Tom was disgusted; and felt a sense of injury, too. He handed in his resignation at once, and that night the Judge suffered a relapse and died. Tom resolved that he would never trust a man like that again. The funeral was a fine thing. The Cadets paraded in a style calculated to kill the late member with envy.

Tom was a free boy again, however; there was something in that. He could drink and swear now, but found to his surprise that he did not want to. The simple fact that he could took the desire away, and the charm of it.

Tom presently wondered to find that his coveted vacation was beginning to hang a little heavily on his hands.

He attempted a diary, but nothing happened during three days, and so he abandoned it.

The first of all the Negro minstrel shows came to town, and made a sensation. Tom and Joe Harper got up a band of performers, and were happy for two days.

Even the Glorious Fourth was in some sense a failure, for it rained hard; there was no procession in consequence, and the greatest man in the world (as Tom supposed), Mr Benton, an actual United States Senator, proved an overwhelming disappointment, for he was not twenty-five feet high, nor even anywhere in the neighbourhood of it.

A circus came. The boys played circus for three days afterwards in tents made of rag carpeting – admission, three pins for boys, two for girls – and then circusing was abandoned.

A phrenologist and a mesmerizer came – and went again and left the village duller and drearier than ever.

There were some boys' and girls' parties, but they were so few and so delightful that they only made the aching voids between ache the harder.

Becky Thatcher was gone to her Constantinople home to stay with her parents during vacation – so there was no bright side to life anywhere.

The dreadful secret of the murder was a chronic misery. It was a very cancer for permanency and pain.

Then came the measles.

During two long weeks Tom lay a prisoner, dead to the

world and its happenings. He was very ill, he was interested in nothing. When he got upon his feet at last and moved feebly down town, a melancholy change had come over everything and every creature. There had been a 'revival', and everybody had 'got religion'; not only the adults, but even the boys and girls. Tom went about, hoping against hope for the sight of one blessed sinful face, but disappointment crossed him everywhere. He found Joe Harper studying a Testament, and turned sadly away from the depressing spectacle. He sought Ben Rogers, and found him visiting the poor with a basket of tracts. He hunted up Jim Hollis, who called his attention to the precious blessing of his late measles as a warning. Every boy he encountered added another ton to his depression; and when, in desperation, he flew for refuge at last to the bosom of Huckleberry Finn and was received with a scriptural quotation, his heart broke, and he crept home and to bed, realizing that he alone of all the town was lost, for ever and for ever.

And that night there came on a terrific storm, with driving rain, awful claps of thunder and blinding sheets of lightning. He covered his head with the bedclothes and waited in a horror of suspense for his doom; for he had not the shadow of a doubt that all this hubbub was about him. He believed he had taxed the forbearance of the powers above to the extremity of endurance, and that this was the result. It might have seemed to him a waste of pomp and ammunition to kill a bug with a battery of artillery, but there seemed nothing incongruous about the getting up of such an expensive thunderstorm as this to knock the turf from under an insect like himself.

By-and-by the tempest spent itself and died without accomplishing its object. The boy's first impulse was to be grateful and reform. His second was to wait – for there might not be any more storms.

The next day the doctors were back; Tom had relapsed. The three weeks he spent on his back this time seemed an entire age. When he got abroad at last he was hardly grateful that he had been spared, remembering how lonely was his estate, how companionless and forlorn he was. He drifted listlessly down the street and found Jim Hollis acting as judge in a juvenile court that was trying a cat for murder, in the presence of her victim, a bird. He found Joe Harper and Huck Finn up an alley eating a stolen melon. Poor fellows, they, like Tom, had suffered a relapse.

CHAPTER XXIV

AT last the sleepy atmosphere was stirred, and vigorously. The murder trial came on in the court. It became the absorbing topic of village talk immediately. Tom could not get away from it. Every reference to the murder sent a shudder to his heart, for his troubled conscience and his fears almost persuaded him that these remarks were put forth in his hearing as 'feelers'; he did not see how he could be suspected of knowing anything about the murder, but still he could not be comfortable in the midst of this gossip. It kept him in a cold shiver all the time. He took Huck to a lonely place to have a talk with him. It would be some relief to unseal his tongue for a little while, to divide his burden of distress with another sufferer. Moreover, he wanted to assure himself that Huck had remained discreet.

'Huck, have you ever told anybody about that?'

' 'Bout what?'

'You know what.'

'*Oh*, 'course I haven't.'

'Never a word?'

'Never a solitary word, so help me. What makes you ask?'

'Well, I was afeard.'

'Why, Tom Sawyer, we wouldn't be alive two days if that got found out. *You* know that.'

Tom felt more comfortable. After a pause:

'Huck, they couldn't anybody get you to tell, could they?'

'Get me to tell? Why, if I wanted that half-breed devil to drown me they could get me to tell. They ain't no different way.'

'Well, that's all right then. I reckon we're safe as long as we keep mum. But let's swear again, anyway. It's more surer!'

'I'm agreed.'

So they swore again with dread solemnities.

'What is the talk around, Huck? I've heard a power of it.'

'Talk? Well, it's just Muff Potter, Muff Potter, Muff Potter all the time. It keeps me in a sweat, constant, so's I want to hide som'ers.'

'That's just the same way they go on round me. I reckon he's a goner. Don't you feel sorry for him sometimes?'

'Most always — most always. He ain't no account; but then he ain't ever done anything to hurt anybody. Just fishes a little to get money to get drunk on — and loafs around considerable; but, Lord, we all do that — leastways most of us — preachers and such like. But he's kind of good — he gives me half a fish, once, when there wasn't enough for two; and lots of times he's kind of stood by me when I was out of luck.'

'Well, he's mended kites for me, Huck, and knitted hooks on to my line. I wish we could get him out of there.'

'My! we couldn't get him out, Tom. And besides, 'twouldn't do any good; they'd ketch him again.'

'Yes — so they would. But I hate to hear 'em abuse him so like the dickens when he never done — that.'

'I do too, Tom. Lord, I hear 'em say he's the bloodiest-looking villain in this country, and they wonder he wasn't ever hung before.'

'Yes; they talk like that all the time. I've heard 'em say that if he was to get free they'd lynch him.'

'And they'd do it, too.'

The boys had a long talk, but it brought them little comfort. As the twilight drew on, they found themselves hanging about the neighbourhood of the little isolated jail, perhaps with an undefined hope that something would happen that might clear away their difficulties. But nothing happened; there seemed to be no angels or fairies interested in this luckless captive.

The boys did as they had often done before – went to the cell grating and gave Potter some tobacco and matches. He was on the ground floor, and there were no guards.

His gratitude for their gifts had always smote their consciences before – it cut deeper than ever, this time. They felt cowardly and treacherous to the last degree when Potter said:

'You've ben mighty good to me, boys – better'n anybody else in this town. And I don't forget it, I don't. Often I says to myself, says I, "I used to mend all the boys' kites and things, and show 'em where the good fishin' places was, and befriend 'em when I could, and now they've all forgot old Muff wen he's in trouble, but Tom don't, and Huck don't – *they* don't forget him," says I, "and I don't forget *them!*" Well, boys, I done an awful thing – drunk and crazy at the time, that's the only way I account for it, and now I got to swing for it, and it's right. Right, and *best*, too, I reckon; hope so, anyway. Well, we won't talk about that. I don't want to make *you* feel bad; you've befriended me. But what I want to say is, don't *you* ever get drunk, then you won't ever get here. Stand a little furder west; so, that's it; it's a prime comfort to see faces that's friendly when a body's in such a muck of trouble, and there don't none come here but yourn. Good friendly faces – good friendly faces. Get up on one another's backs, and let me touch 'em. That's it. Shake hands – yourn'll come through the bars, but mine's too big. Little hands, and weak – but they've helped Muff Potter a power, and they'd help him more if they could.'

Tom went home miserable, and his dreams that night were full of horrors. The next day and the day after, he hung about the court-room, drawn by an almost irresistible impulse to go in, but forcing himself to stay out. Huck was having the same experience. They studiously avoided each other. Each wandered away from time to time, but the same dismal fascination always brought them back presently. Tom kept his ears open when idlers sauntered out of the court-room, but invariably heard distressing news; the toils were closing more and more relentlessly around poor Potter. At the end of the second day the village talk was to the effect that Injun Joe's evidence stood firm and unshaken, and that there was not the slightest question as to what the jury's verdict would be.

Tom was out late that night, and came to bed through the window. He was in a tremendous state of excitement. It was hours before he got to sleep. All the village flocked to the court-house the next morning, for this was to be the great day. Both sexes were about equally represented in the packed audience. After a long wait the jury filed in and took their places; shortly afterwards, Potter, pale and haggard, timid and hopeless, was brought in with chains upon him, and seated where all the curious eyes could stare at him; no less conspicuous was Injun Joe, stolid as ever. There was another pause, and then the judge arrived, and the sheriff proclaimed the opening of the court. The usual whisperings among the lawyers and gathering together of papers followed. These details and accompanying delays worked up an atmosphere of preparation that was as impressive as it was fascinating.

Now a witness was called who testified that he found Muff Potter washing in the brook at an early hour of the morning that the murder was discovered, and that he immediately sneaked away. After some further questioning, counsel for the prosecution said

'Take the witness.'

148

The prisoner raised his eyes for a moment, but dropped them again when his own counsel said:

'I have no questions to ask him.'

The next witness proved the finding of the knife near the corpse. Counsel for the prosecution said:

'Take the witness.'

'I have no questions to ask him,' Potter's lawyer replied.

A third witness swore he had often seen the knife in Potter's possession.

'Take the witness.'

Counsel for Potter declined to question him.

The faces of the audience began to betray annoyance. Did this attorney mean to throw away his client's life without an effort?

Several witnesses deposed concerning Potter's guilty behaviour when brought to the scene of the murder. They were allowed to leave the stand without being cross-questioned.

Every detail of the damaging circumstances that occurred in the graveyard upon that morning which all present remembered so well was brought out by credible witnesses, but none of them were cross-examined by Potter's lawyer. The perplexity and dissatisfaction of the house expressed itself in murmurs and provoked a reproof from the bench. Counsel for the prosecution now said:

'By the oaths of citizens whose simple word is above suspicion, we have fastened this awful crime beyond all possibility of question upon the unhappy prisoner at the bar. We rest our case here.'

A groan escaped from poor Potter, and he put his face in his hands, and rocked his body softly to and fro, while a painful silence reigned in the court-room. Many men were moved, and many women's compassion testified itself in tears. Counsel for the defence rose and said:

'Your Honour, in our remarks at the opening of this trial, we foreshadowed our purpose to prove that our client did this fearful deed while under the influence of a blind and irresponsible delirium produced by drink. We have changed our mind; we shall not offer that plea. [Then to the clerk.] Call Thomas Sawyer.'

A puzzled amazement awoke in every face in the house, not even excepting Potter's. Every eye fastened itself with wondering interest upon Tom as he rose and took his place upon the stand. The boy looked wild enough, for he was badly scared. The oath was administered.

'Thomas Sawyer, where were you on the seventeenth of June, about the hour of midnight?'

Tom glanced at Injun Joe's face, and his tongue failed him. The audience listened breathless, but the words refused to come. After a few moments, however, the boy got a little of his strength back, and managed to put enough of it into his voice to make part of the house hear:

'In the graveyard!'

'A little bit louder, please. Don't be afraid. You were – '

'In the graveyard.'

A contemptuous smile flitted across Injun Joe's face.

'Were you anywhere near Horse Williams's grave?'

'Yes, sir.'

'Speak up just a trifle louder. How near were you?'

'Near as I am to you.'

'Were you hidden or not?'

'I was hid.'

'Where?'

'Behind the elms that's on the edge of the grave.'

Injun Joe gave a barely perceptible start.

'Anyone with you?'

'Yes, sir. I went there with – '

'Wait – wait a moment. Never mind mentioning your companion's name. We will produce him at the proper time. Did you carry anything there with you?'

Tom hesitated and looked confused.

'Speak out, my boy – don't be diffident. The truth is always respectable. What did you take there?'

'Only a – a – dead cat.'

There was a ripple of mirth, which the court checked.

'We will produce the skeleton of that cat. Now my boy, tell us everything that occurred – tell it in your own way – don't skip anything, and don't be afraid.'

Tom began – hesitatingly at first, but, as he warmed to his subject, his words flowed more and more easily; in a little while every sound ceased but his own voice; every eye fixed itself upon him; with parted lips and bated breath the audience hung upon his words, taking no note of time, rapt in the ghastly fascinations of the tale. The strain upon pent emotion reached its climax when the boy said, 'And as the doctor fetched the board around and Muff Potter fell, Injun Joe jumped with the knife and – '

Crash! Quick as lightning, the half-breed sprang for a window, tore his way through all opposers, and was gone!

CHAPTER XXV

Tom was a glittering hero once more – the pet of the old, the envy of the young. His name even went into immortal print, for the village paper magnified him. There were some that believed he would be President yet, if he escaped hanging.

As usual, the fickle unreasoning world took Muff Potter to its bosom, and fondled him as lavishly as it had abused him before. But that sort of conduct is to the world's credit; therefore it is not well to find fault with it.

Tom's days were days of splendour and exultation to him, but his nights were seasons of horror. Injun Joe infested all his dreams, and always with doom in his eye. Hardly any temptation could persuade the boy to stir abroad after nightfall. Poor Huck was in the same state of wretchedness and terror, for Tom had told the whole story to the lawyer the night before the great day of the trial, and Huck was sore afraid that his share in the business might leak out yet, notwithstanding Injun Joe's flight had saved him the suffering of testifying in court. The poor fellow had got the attorney to promise secrecy, but what of that? Since Tom's harassed conscience had managed to drive him to the lawyer's house by night and wring a dread tale from lips that had been sealed with the dismalest and most formidable of oaths, Huck's confidence in the human race was well-nigh obliterated. Daily Muff Potter's gratitude made Tom glad he had spoken; but nightly he wished he had sealed up his tongue. Half the time Tom was afraid Injun Joe would never be captured; the other half he was afraid he would be. He felt sure he never could draw a safe breath again until that man was dead and he had seen the corpse.

Rewards had been offered, the country had been scoured, but no Injun Joe was found. One of those omniscient and awe-inspiring marvels, a detective, came up from St Louis, moused around, shook his head, looked wise, and made that sort of astounding success which members of that craft usually achieve. That is to say, 'he found a clue'. But you can't hang a 'clue' for murder, and so after that detective had got through and gone home, Tom felt just as insecure as he was before.

The slow days drifted on, and each left behind it a slightly lightened weight of apprehension.

CHAPTER XXVI

THERE comes a time in every rightly constructed boy's life when he has a raging desire to go somewhere and dig for hidden treasure. This desire suddenly came upon Tom one day. He sallied out to find Joe Harper, but failed of success. Next he sought Ben Rogers; he had gone fishing. Presently he stumbled upon Huck Finn the Red-handed. Huck would answer. Tom took him to a private place, and opened the matter to him confidentially. Huck was willing. Huck was always willing to take a hand in any enterprise that offered entertainment and required no capital, for he had a troublesome superabundance of that sort of time which is *not* money.

'Where'll we dig?' said Huck.

'Oh, 'most anywhere.'

'Why, is it hid all around?'

'No, indeed it ain't. It's hid in mighty particular places, Huck – sometimes on islands, sometimes in rotten chests under the end of a limb of an old dead tree, just where the shadow falls at midnight; but mostly under the floor in ha'nted houses.'

'Who hides it?'

'Why, robbers, of course – who'd you reckon? Sunday-school sup'rintendents?'

'I don't know. If it was mine I wouldn't hide it; I'd spend it and have a good time.'

'So would I; but robbers don't do that way, they always hide it and leave it there.'

'Don't they come after it any more?'

'No, they think they will, but they generally forget the marks, or else they die. Anyway it lays there a long time and gets rusty; and by-and-by somebody finds an old yellow paper that tells how to find the marks – a paper that's got to be ciphered over about a week because its mostly signs and hy'roglyphics.'

'Hyro – which?'

'Hy'roglyphics – pictures and things, you know, that don't seem to mean anything.'

'Have you got one of them papers, Tom?'

'No.'

'Well, then, how you going to find out the marks?'

'I don't want any marks. They always bury it under a ha'nted house, or on an island, or under a dead tree that's got one limb sticking out. Well, we've tried Jackson's Island a little, and we can try it again sometime; and there's the old ha'nted house up the Still-House branch, and there's lots of dead-limb trees – dead loads of 'em.'

'Is it under all of them?'

'How you talk! No!'

'Then how you going to know which one to go for?'

'Go for all of 'em.'

'Why, Tom, it'll take all summer.'

'Well, what of that? Suppose you find a brass pot with a hundred dollars in it, all rusty and gay, or a rotten chest full of di'monds. How's that?'

Huck's eyes glowed.

'That's bully, plenty bully enough for me. Just you gimme the hundred dollars, and I don't want no di'monds.'

'All right. But I bet you *I* ain't going to throw off on di'monds. Some of 'em's worth twenty dollars apiece. There ain't any, hardly, but's worth six bits or a dollar.'

'No! Is that so?'

'Cert'nly – anybody'll tell you so. Hain't you ever seen one, Huck?'

'Not as I remember.'

'Oh, kings have slathers of them.'

'Well, I don't know no kings, Tom.'

'I reckon you don't. But if you was to go to Europe you'd see a raft of 'em hopping around.'

'Do they hop?'

'Hop? – your granny! No!'

'Well, what did you say they did for?'

'Shucks! I only meant you'd *see* 'em – not hopping, of course – what do they want to hop for? But I mean you'd just see 'em – scattered around, you know, in a kind of a general way. Like that old hump-backed Richard.'

'Richard! What's his other name?'

'He didn't have any other name. Kings don't have any but a given name.'

154

'No?'

'But they don't.'

'Well, if they like it, Tom, all right; but I don't want to be a king and have only just a given name, like a nigger. But say – where you going to dig first?'

'Well, I don't know. S'pose we tackle that old dead limb tree on the hill t'other side of Still-House branch?'

'I'm agreed.'

So they got a crippled pick and a shovel, and set out on their three-mile tramp. They arrived hot and panting, and threw themselves down in the shade of a neighbouring elm to rest and have a smoke.

'I like this,' said Tom.

'So do I.'

'Say, Huck, if we find a treasure here, what you going to do with your share?'

'Well, I'll have a pie and a glass of soda every day, and I'll go to every circus that comes along. I'll bet I'll have a gay time.'

'Well, ain't you going to save any of it?'

'Save it? What for?'

'Why, so as to have something to live on by-and-by.'

'Oh, that ain't any use. Pap would come back to thish yer town some day and get his claws on it if I didn't hurry up, and I tell you he'd clean it out pretty quick. What you going to do with yourn, Tom?'

'I'm going to buy a new drum, and a sure-'nough sword, and a red necktie, and a bull-pup, and get married.'

'Married!'

'That's it.'

'Tom, you – why, you ain't in your right mind.'

'Wait – you'll see.'

'Well, that's the foolishest thing you could do, Tom. Look at Pap and my mother. Fight! why they used to fight all the time. I remember, mighty well.'

'That ain't anything. The girl I'm going to marry won't fight.'

'Tom, I reckon they're all alike. They'll all comb a body. Now you better think about this a while. I tell you you better. What's the name of the gal?'

'It ain't a gal at all – it's a girl.'

'It's all the same, I reckon; some says gal, some says girl – both's right, like enough. Anyway, what's her name, Tom?'

'I'll tell you some time – not now.'

'All right – that'll do. Only if you get married I'll be more lonesomer than ever.'

'No, you won't, you'll come and live with me. Now stir out of this, and we'll go to digging.'

They worked and sweated for half an hour. No result. They toiled another half hour. Still no result. Huck said:

'Do they always bury it as deep as this?'

'Sometimes – not always. Not generally. I reckon we haven't got the right place.'

So they chose a new spot and began again. The labour dragged a little, but still they made progress. They pegged away in silence for some time. Finally Huck leaned on his shovel, swabbed the beaded drops from his brow with his sleeve, and said:

'Where you going to dig next, after we get this one?'

'I reckon maybe we'll tackle the old tree that's over yonder on Cardiff Hill, back on the widow's.'

'I reckon that'll be a good one. But won't the widow take it away from us, Tom? It's on her land.'

'She take it away! Maybe she'd like to try it once. Whoever finds one of these hid treasures, it belongs to him. It don't make any difference whose land it's on.'

That was satisfactory. The work went on. By-and-by Huck said:

'Blame it, we must be in the wrong place again. What do you think?'

'It is mighty curious, Huck. I don't understand it. Sometimes witches interfere. I reckon maybe that's what's the trouble now.'

156

'Shucks! witches ain't got no power in the daytime.'

'Well, that's so. I didn't think of that. Oh, I know what the matter is! What a blamed lot of fools we are! You got to find out where the shadow of the limb falls at midnight, and that's where you dig!'

'Then confound it, we've fooled away all this work for nothing. Now hang it all, we got to come back in the night. It's an awful long way. Can you get out?'

'I bet I will. We've got to do it tonight, too, because if somebody sees these holes they'll know in a minute what's here and they'll go for it.'

'Well, I'll come around and meow tonight.'

'All right. Let's hide the tools in the bushes.'

The boys were there that night about the appointed time. They sat in the shadow waiting. It was a lonely place, and an hour made solemn by old traditions. Spirits whispered in the rustling leaves, ghosts lurked in the murky nooks, the deep baying of a hound floated up out of the distance, an owl answered with his sepulchral note. The boys were subdued by these solemnities, and talked little. By-and-by they judged that twelve had come; they marked where the shadow fell and began to dig. Their hopes commenced to rise. Their interest grew stronger, and their industry kept pace with it. The hole deepened and still deepened, but every time their hearts jumped to hear the pick strike upon something, they only suffered a new disappointment. It was only a stone or a chunk. At last Tom said:

'It ain't any use, Huck, we're wrong again.'

'Well, but we can't be wrong. We spotted the shadder to a dot.'

'I know it, but then there's another thing.'

'What's that?'

'Why, we only guessed at the time. Like enough it was too late or too early.'

Huck dropped his shovel.

'That's it,' said he. 'That's the very trouble. We got to

give this one up. We can't ever tell the right time, and besides, this kind of thing's too awful, here this time of night with witches and ghosts a fluttering around so. I feel as if something's behind me all the time; and I'm afeard to turn around, becuz maybe there's others in front a waiting for a chance. I been creeping all over ever since I got here.'

'Well, I've been pretty much so too, Huck. They 'most always put in a dead man when they bury a treasure under a tree, to look out for it.'

'Lordy!'

'Yes, they do. I've always heard that.'

'Tom, I don't like to fool around much where there's dead people. A boy's bound to get into trouble with 'em, sure.'

'I don't like to stir 'em up, either, Huck. S'pose this one here was to stick his skull out and say something!'

'Don't, Tom! It's awful.'

'Well, it just is, Huck. I don't feel comfortable a bit.'

'Say, Tom, let's give this place up, and try somewheres else.'

'All right, I reckon we better.'

'What'll it be?'

Tom considered awhile, and then said:

'The ha'nted house. That's it.'

'Blame it. I don't like ha'nted houses, Tom. Why, they're a dern sight worse'n dead people. Dead people might talk maybe, but they don't come sliding around in a shroud when you ain't noticing, and peep over your shoulder all of a sudden and grit their teeth the way a ghost does. I couldn't stand such a thing as that, Tom – nobody could.'

'Yes; but, Huck, ghosts don't travel around only at night – they won't hinder us from digging there in the daytime.'

'Well, that's so. But you know mighty well people don't go about that ha'nted house in the day nor the night.'

'Well, that's mostly because they don't like to go where a man's been murdered, anyway. But nothing's ever been seen around that house in the night – just some blue light slipping by the window – no regular ghosts.'

'Well, where you see one of them blue lights flickering around, Tom, you can bet there's a ghost mighty close behind it. It stands to reason. Becuz you know that they don't anybody but ghosts use 'em.'

'Yes, that's so. But anyway they don't come around in the daytime, so what's the use of our being afeard?'

'Well, all right. We'll tackle the ha'nted house if you say so; but I reckon it's taking chances.'

They had started down the hill by this time. There in the middle of the moonlit valley below them stood the 'haunted' house, utterly isolated, its fences gone long ago, rank weeds smothering the very door-step, the chimney crumbled to ruin, the window-sashes vacant, a corner of the roof caved in. The boys gazed awhile, half expecting to see a blue light flit past a window; then talking in a low tone, as befitted the time and the circumstances, they struck far off to the right, to give the haunted house a wide berth, and took their way homeward through the woods that adorned the rearward side of Cardiff Hill.

CHAPTER XXVII

ABOUT noon the next day the boys arrived at the dead tree; they had come for their tools. Tom was impatient to go to the haunted house; Huck was measurably so, also, but suddenly said:

'Looky here, Tom, do you know what day it is?'

Tom mentally ran over the days of the week and then quickly lifted his eyes with a startled look in them:

'My! I never once thought of it, Huck!'

'Well, I didn't, neither, but all at once it popped on to me that it was Friday.'

'Blame it; a body can't be too careful, Huck. We might a got into an awful scrape, tackling such a thing on a Friday.'

'Might! Better say we would! There's some lucky days, maybe, but Friday ain't.'

'Any fool knows that. I don't reckon you was the first that found it out, Huck.'

'Well, I never said I was, did I? And Friday ain't all, neither. I had a rotten bad dream last night – dreamt about rats.'

'No! Sure sign of trouble. Did they fight?'

'No.'

'Well, that's good, Huck. When they don't fight, it's only a sign that there's trouble around, you know. All we got to do is to look mighty sharp and keep out of it. We'll drop this thing for today, and play. Do you know Robin Hood, Huck?'

'No. Who's Robin Hood?'

'Why, he was one of the greatest men that was ever in England – and the best. He was a robber.'

'Cracky, I wisht I was. Who did he rob?'

'Only sheriffs and bishops and rich people and kings, and such like. But he never bothered the poor. He loved 'em. He always divided up with 'em perfectly square.'

'Well, he must a ben a brick.'

'I bet you he was, Huck. Oh, he was the noblest man that ever was. They ain't any such men now, I can tell you. He could lick any man in England with one hand tied behind him; and he could take his yew bow and plug a ten cent piece every time, a mile and a half.'

'What's a *yew* bow?'

'I don't know. It's some kind of a bow, of course. And if he hit that dime only on the edge he could set down and cry – and curse. But we'll play Robin Hood – it's noble fun. I'll learn you.'

'I'm agreed.'

160

So they played Robin Hood all the afternoon, now and then casting a yearning eye down upon the haunted house and passing a remark about the morrow's prospects and possibilities there. As the sun began to sink into the west, they took their way homeward athwart the long shadows of the trees and soon were buried from sight in the forests of Cardiff Hill.

On Saturday, shortly after noon, the boys were at the dead tree again. They had a smoke and a chat in the shade, and then dug a little in their last hole, not with great hope, but merely because Tom said there were so many cases where people had given up a treasure after getting down within six inches of it, and then somebody else had come along and turned it up with a single thrust of a shovel. The thing failed this time, however, so the boys shouldered their tools and went away, feeling that they had not trifled with fortune, but had fulfilled all the requirements that belong to the business of treasure-hunting.

When they reached the haunted house, there was something so weird and grisly about the dead silence that reigned there under the baking sun, and something so depressing about the loneliness and desolation of the place, that they were afraid, for a moment, to venture in. Then they crept to the door and took a trembling peep. They saw a weed-grown, floorless room, unplastered, an ancient fire-place, vacant windows, a ruinous staircase; and here, there, and everywhere, hung ragged and abandoned cobwebs. They presently entered softly, with quickened pulses, talking in whispers, ears alert to catch the slightest sound, and muscles tense and ready for instant retreat.

In a little while familiarity modified their fears, and they gave the place a critical and interested examination, rather admiring their own boldness, and wondering at it, too. Next they wanted to look upstairs. This was something like cutting off retreat, but they got to daring each other, and of course there could be but one result – they threw their

161

tools into a corner and made the ascent. Up there were the same signs of decay. In one corner they found a closet that promised mystery, but the promise was a fraud – there was nothing in it. Their courage was up now, and well in hand. They were about to go down and begin work when –

'*Sht!*' said Tom.

'What is it?' whispered Huck, blanching with fright.

'*Sh!* There! Hear it?'

'Yes! Oh, my! Let's run!'

'Keep still! Don't you budge! They're coming right towards the door.'

The boys stretched themselves upon the floor with their eyes to knot-holes in the planking, and lay waiting in a misery of fear.

'They've stopped – No – coming – Here they are. Don't whisper another word, Huck. My goodness, I wish I was out of this!'

Two men entered. Each boy said to himself:

'There's the old deaf and dumb Spaniard that's been about town once or twice lately – never saw t'other man before.'

'T'other' was a ragged, unkempt creature, with nothing very pleasant in his face. The Spaniard was wrapped in a *serape;* he had bushy white whiskers, long white hair flowed from under his sombrero, and he wore green goggles. When they came in, 't'other' was talking in a low voice; they sat down on the ground, facing the door, with their backs to the wall, and the speaker continued his remarks. His manner became less guarded and his words more distinct as he proceeded.

'No,' said he, 'I've thought it all over, and I don't like it. It's dangerous.'

'Dangerous!' grunted the 'deaf and dumb' Spaniard, to the vast surprise of the boys. 'Milksop!'

This voice made the boys gasp and quake. It was Injun Joe's! There was silence for some time. Then Joe said:

'What's any more dangerous than the job up yonder – but nothing's come of it.'

'That's different. Away up the river so, and not another house about. 'Twon't ever be known that we tried, anyway, long as we didn't succeed.'

'Well, what's more dangerous than coming here in the daytime? – anybody would suspicion us that saw us.'

'I know that. But there wasn't any other place as handy after that fool of a job. I want to quit this shanty. I wanted to yesterday, only it wasn't any use trying to stir out of here with those infernal boys playing over there on the hill right in full view.'

'Those infernal boys' quaked again under the inspiration of this remark, and thought how lucky it was that they had remembered it was Friday and concluded to wait a day. They wished in their hearts they had waited a year. The two men got out some food and made a luncheon. After a long and thoughtful silence Injun Joe said:

'Look here, lad, you go back up the river where you belong. Wait there till you hear from me. I'll take the chances on dropping into this town just once more, for a look. We'll do that "dangerous" job after I've spied around a little and think things look well for it. Then for Texas! We'll leg it together!'

This was satisfactory. Both men presently fell to yawning, and Injun Joe said:

'I'm dead for sleep! It's your turn to watch.'

He curled down in the weeds and soon began to snore. His comrade stirred him once or twice, and he became quiet. Presently the watcher began to nod; his head drooped lower and lower; both men began to snore now.

The boys drew a long grateful breath. Tom whispered:

'Now's our chance – come!'

Huck said: 'I can't – I'd die if they was to wake.'

Tom urged – Huck held back. At last Tom rose slowly and softly, and started alone. But the first step he made

163

wrung such a hideous creak from the crazy floor that he sank down almost dead with fright. He never made a second attempt. The boys lay there counting the dragging moments till it seemed to them that time must be done and eternity growing grey; and then they were grateful to note that at last the sun was setting.

Now one snore ceased. Injun Joe sat up, stared around – smiled grimly upon his comrade, whose head was drooping upon his knees – stirred him up with his foot and said:

'Here! You're a watchman, ain't you!'

'All right, though – nothing's happened.'

'My! Have I been asleep?'

'Oh, partly, partly. Nearly time for us to be moving, pard. What'll we do with what little swag we've got left?'

'I don't know – leave it here as we've always done, I reckon. No use to take it away till we start south. Six hundred and fifty in silver's something to carry.'

'Well – all right – it won't matter to come here again.'

'No – but I'd say come in the night as we used to do – it's better.'

'Yes, but look here; it may be a good while before I get the right chance at that job; accidents might happen, 'tain't in such a very good place; we'll just regularly bury it – and bury it deep.'

'Good idea,' said the comrade, who walked across the room, knelt down, raised one of the rearward hearth-stones and took out a bag that jingled pleasantly. He subtracted from it twenty or thirty dollars for himself and as much for Injun Joe, and passed the bag to the latter, who was on his knees in the corner, now, digging with his bowie-knife.

The boys forgot all their fears, all their miseries in an instant. With gloating eyes they watched every movement. Luck! – the splendour of it was beyond all imagination! Six hundred dollars was money enough to make half a dozen boys rich! Here was treasure-hunting under the happiest auspices – there would not be any bothersome uncertainty

164

as to where to dig. They nudged each other every moment – eloquent nudges and easily understood, for they simply meant, 'Oh, but ain't you glad now we're here!'

Joe's knife struck upon something.

'Hello!' said he.

'What is it?' said his comrade.

'Half-rotten plank – no, it's a box, I believe. Here bear a hand, and we'll see what it's here for. Never mind, I've broke a hole.'

He reached his hand in and drew it out.

'Man, it's money!'

The two men examined the handful of coins. They were gold. The boys above were as excited as themselves, and as delighted.

Joe's comrade said:

'We'll make quick work of this. There's an old rusty pick over amongst the weeds in the corner, the other side of the fire-place – I saw it a minute ago.'

He ran and brought the boys' pick and shovel. Injun Joe took the pick, looked it over critically, shook his head, muttered something to himself, and then began to use it.

The box was soon unearthed. It was not very large; it was iron-bound and had been very strong before the slow years had injured it. The men contemplated the treasure awhile in blissful silence.

'Pard, there's thousands of dollars here,' said Injun Joe.

''Twas always said that Murrel's gang used around here one summer,' the stranger observed.

'I know it,' said Injun Joe; 'and this looks like it, I should say.'

'Now you won't need to do that job.'

The half-breed frowned. Said he:

'You don't know me. Least you don't know all about that thing. 'Tain't robbery altogether – it's revenge!' and a wicked light flamed in his eyes. 'I'll need your help in it.

When it's finished – then Texas. Go home to your Nance and your kids, and stand by till you hear from me.'

'Well, if you say so. What'll we do with this – bury it again?'

'Yes. [Ravishing delight overhead.] No! by the great Sacham, no! [Profound distress overhead.] I'd nearly forgot. That pick had fresh earth on it! [The boys were sick with terror in a moment.] What business has a pick and a shovel here? What business with fresh earth on them? Who brought them here – and where are they gone? Have you heard anybody? – seen anybody? What! bury it again and leave them to come and see the ground disturbed? Not exactly – not exactly. We'll take it to my den.'

'Why, of course! Might have thought of that before. You mean number one?'

'No – number two – under the cross. The other place is bad – too common.'

'All right. It's nearly dark enough to start.'

Injun Joe got up and went about from window to window, cautiously peeping out. Presently he said:

'Who could have brought those tools here? Do you reckon they can be upstairs?'

The boys' breath forsook them. Injun Joe put his hand on his knife, halted a moment, undecided, and then turned towards the stairway. The boys thought of the closet, but their strength was gone. The steps came creaking up the stairs – the intolerable distress of the situation woke the stricken resolution of the lads – they were about to spring for the closet, when there was a crash of rotten timbers, and Injun Joe landed on the ground amid the *débris* of the ruined stairway. He gathered himself up cursing, and his comrade said:

'Now what's the use of all that? If it's anybody, and they're up there, let them stay there – who cares? If they want to jump down, now, and get into trouble, who objects? It will be dark in fifteen minutes – and then let them follow us if they want to; I'm willing. In my opinion, whoever hove those things in here caught a sight of us, and took us for ghosts or devils or something. I'll bet they're running yet.'

Joe grumbled awhile; then he agreed with his friend that what daylight was left ought to be economized in getting things ready for leaving. Shortly afterwards they slipped out of the house in the deepening twilight, and moved towards the river with their precious box.

Tom and Huck rose up, weak but vastly relieved, and stared after them through the chinks between the logs of the house. Follow? Not they – they were content to reach the ground again without broken necks, and take the townward track over the hill. They did not talk much, they were too much absorbed in hating themselves – hating the ill-luck that made them take the spade and the pick there. But for that, Injun Joe never would have suspected. He would have hidden the silver with the gold to wait there till his 'revenge' was satisfied, and then he would have had the misfortune to find that money turn up missing. Bitter, bitter luck that the tools were ever brought there! They resolved to keep a look-out for that Spaniard when he should come to town spying out for chances to do his revengeful job, and follow him to 'number two', wherever that might be. Then a ghastly thought occurred to Tom:

'Revenge? What if he means *us*, Huck!'

'Oh, don't,' said Huck, nearly fainting.

They talked it all over, and as they entered town they agreed to believe that he might possibly mean somebody else – at least that he might at least mean nobody but Tom, since only Tom had testified.

Very, very small comfort it was to Tom to be alone in danger! Company would be a palpable improvement, he thought.

CHAPTER XXVIII

THE adventure of the day mightily tormented Tom's dreams that night. Four times he had his hands on that rich treasure, and four times it wasted to nothingness in his fingers as sleep forsook him, and wakefulness brought back the hard reality of his misfortune. As he lay in the early morning recalling the incidents of his great adventure he noticed that they seemed curiously subdued and far away, somewhat as if they had happened in another world, or in a time long gone by. Then it occurred to him that the great adventure itself must be a dream! There was one very strong argument in favour of this idea, namely, that the quantity of coin he had seen was too vast to be real. He had never seen as much as fifty dollars in one mass before, and he was like all boys of his age and station in life, in that he imagined that all references to 'hundreds' and 'thousands' were mere fanciful forms of speech, and that no such sums existed in the world. He never had supposed for a moment that so large a sum as a hundred dollars was to be found in actual money in anybody's possession. If his notions of hidden treasure had been analysed, they would have been found to consist of a handful of real dimes, and a bushel of vague, splendid, ungraspable ones.

But the incidents of his adventure grew sensibly sharper and clearer under the attrition of thinking them over, and so he presently found himself leaning to the impression that the thing might not have been a dream after all. This uncertainty must be swept away. He would snatch a hurried breakfast, and go and find Huck.

Huck was sitting on the gunwale of a flat boat, listlessly dangling his feet in the water, and looking very melancholy. Tom concluded to let Huck lead up to the subject. If he did not do it, then the adventure would be proved to have been only a dream.

'Hello, Huck!'

'Hello, yourself.'

Silence for a minute.

'Tom, if we'd a left the blame tools at the dead tree we'd a got the money. Oh, ain't it awful!'

''Tain't a dream, then, 'tain't a dream! Somehow I 'most wish it was. Dog'd if I don't.'

'What ain't a dream?'

'Oh, that thing yesterday. I ben half thinking it was.'

'Dream! If them stairs hadn't broke down you'd a seen how much dream it was! I've had dreams enough all night, with that patch-eyed Spanish devil going for me all through 'em, rot him!'

'No, not rot him. Find him! Track the money!'

'Tom, we'll never find him. A feller don't only have one chance for such a pile, and that one's lost. I'd feel mighty shaky if I was to see him, anyway.'

'Well, so'd I; but I'd like to see him anyway, and track him out – to his number two.'

'Number two; yes, that's it. I ben thinking 'bout that. But I can't make nothing out of it. What do you reckon it is?'

'I dono. It's too deep. Say, Huck – maybe it's the number of a house!'

'Goody! – No, Tom, that ain't it. If it is, it ain't in this one-horse town. They ain't no numbers here.'

'Well, that's so. Lemme think a minute. Here – it's the number of a room – in a tavern, you know!'

'Oh, that's the trick! They ain't only two taverns. We can find out quick.'

'You stay here, Huck, till I come.'

Tom was off at once. He did not care to have Huck's company in public places. He was gone half an hour. He found that in the best tavern number two had long been occupied by a young lawyer, and was still so occupied. In the less ostentatious house number two was a mystery. The tavern-keeper's young son said it was kept locked all the time, and he never saw anybody go into it or come out of it except at night; he did not know any particular reason for this state of things; had had some little curiosity, but it was rather feeble; had made the most of the mystery by entertaining himself with the idea that that room was 'ha'nted'; had noticed that there was a light in there the night before.

'That's what I've found out, Huck. I reckon that's the very number two we're after.

'I reckon it is, Tom. Now what you going to do?'

'Lemme think.'

Tom thought a long time. Then he said:

'I'll tell you. The back door of that number two is the door that comes out into that little close alley between the tavern and the old rattle-trap of a brick-store. Now you get hold of all the door keys you can find and I'll nip all of Auntie's, and the first dark night we'll go there and try 'em. And mind you keep a look out for Injun Joe, because he said he was going to drop into town and spy around once more for a chance to get his revenge. If you see him, you just follow him; and if he don't go to that number two, that ain't the place.'

'Lordy, I don't want to foller him by myself!'

'Why, it'll be night, sure. He mightn't ever see you – and if he did, maybe he'd never think anything.'

'Well, if it's pretty dark I reckon I'll track him. I dono – I dono. I'll try.'

'You bet I'll follow him if it's dark, Huck! Why, he might a found out he couldn't get his revenge, and be going right after that money.'

'It's so, Tom, it's so. I'll foller him; I will, by jingoes.'

'Now you're talking! Don't you ever weaken. Huck, and I won't.'

CHAPTER XXIX

THAT night Tom and Huck were ready for their adventure. They hung about the neighbourhood of the tavern until after nine, one watching the alley at a distance and the other the tavern door. Nobody entered the alley or left it; nobody resembling the Spaniard entered or left the tavern door. The night promised to be a fair one; so Tom went home with the understanding that if a considerable degree of darkness came on, Huck was to come and 'meow', whereupon he would slip out and try the keys. But the night remained clear, and Huck closed his watch and retired to bed in an empty sugar hogshead about twelve.

Tuesday the boys had the same ill-luck. Also Wednesday. But Thursday night promised better. Tom slipped out in good season with his aunt's old tin lantern, and a large towel to blindfold it with . He hid the lantern in Huck's sugar hogshead and the watch began. An hour before midnight the tavern closed up, and its lights (the only one thereabouts) were put out. No Spaniard had been seen. Nobody had entered or left the alley. Everything was auspicious. The blackness of darkness reigned, the perfect stillness was interrupted only by occasional mutterings of distant thunder.

Tom got his lantern, lit it in the hogshead, wrapped it closely in the towel, and the two adventurers crept in the gloom towards the tavern. Huck stood sentry and Tom felt his way into the alley. Then there was a season of waiting anxiety that weighed upon Huck's spirits like a mountain. He began to wish he could see a flash from the lantern – it would frighten him, but it would at least tell him that Tom was alive yet.

It seemed hours since Tom had disappeared. Surely he must have fainted; maybe he was dead; maybe his heart had burst under terror and excitement. In his uneasiness Huck found himself drawing closer and closer to the alley, fearing all sorts of dreadful things, and momentarily expecting some catastrophe to happen that would take away his breath. There was not much to take away, for he seemed only able to inhale it by thimblefuls, and his heart would soon wear itself out, the way it was beating. Suddenly there was a flash of light, and Tom came tearing by him:

'Run!' said he; 'run for your life!'

He needn't have repeated it; once was enough; Huck was making thirty or forty miles an hour before the repetition was uttered. The boys never stopped till they reached the shed of a deserted slaughter-house at the lower end of the village. Just as they got within its shelter the storm burst and the rain poured down. As soon as Tom got his breath he said:

'Huck, it was awful! I tried two of the keys just as soft as I could; but they seemed to make such a power of racket that I couldn't hardly get my breath, I was so scared. They wouldn't turn in the lock either. Well, without noticing what I was doing, I took hold of the knob, and open comes the door! It wasn't locked! I hopped in and shook off the towel, and, *great Caesar's ghost!*'

'What! – what'd you see, Tom?'

'Huck, I most stepped on to Injun Joe's hand!'

'No!'

'Yes. He was laying there, sound asleep on the floor, with his old patch on his eye and his arms spread out.'

'Lordy, what did you do? Did he wake up?'

'No, never budged. Drunk, I reckon. I just grabbed that towel and started!'

'I'd never a thought of the towel, I bet!'

'Well, I would. My aunt would make me mighty sick if I lost it.'

'Say, Tom, did you see that box?'

'Huck, I didn't wait to look around. I didn't see the box, I didn't see the cross. I didn't see anything but a bottle and a tin cup on the floor by Injun Joe! Yes, and I saw two barrels and lots more bottles in the room. Don't you see, now, what's the matter with that ha'nted room?'

'How?'

'Why, it's ha'nted with whisky! Maybe all the Temperance Taverns have got a ha'nted room, hey, Huck?'

'Well, I reckon maybe that's so. Who'd a thought such a thing? But say, Tom, now's a mighty good time to get that box, if Injun Joe's drunk.'

'It is that! You try it!'

Huck shuddered.

'Well, no – I reckon not.'

'And I reckon not, Huck. Only one bottle alongside of Injun Joe ain't enough. If there'd been three he'd be drunk enough and I'd do it.'

There was a long pause for reflection, and then Tom said:

'Looky here, Huck, less not try that thing any more till we know Injun Joe's not in there. It's too scary. Now if we watch every night, we'll be dead sure to see him go out some time or other, then we'll snatch that box quicker'n lightning.'

'Well, I'm agreed. I'll watch the whole night long, and I'll do it every night, too, if you'll do the other part of the job.'

'All right, I will. All you got to do is to trot up Hooper Street a block and meow – and if I'm asleep, you throw some gravel at the window and that'll fetch me.'

'Agreed, and good as wheat!'

'Now, Huck, the storm's over, and I'll go home. It'll begin to be daylight in a couple of hours. You go back and watch that long, will you?'

'I said I would, Tom, and I will. I'll ha'nt that tavern every night for a year. I'll sleep all day and I'll stand watch all night.'

'That's all right. Now where are you going to sleep?'

'In Ben Roger's hay-loft. He lets me, and so does his pap's nigger man, Uncle Jake. I tote water for Uncle Jake whenever he wants me to, and any time I ask him he gives me a little something to eat if he can spare it. That's a mighty good nigger, Tom. He likes me, becuz I don't ever act as if I was above him. Sometimes I've set right down and eat with him. But you needn't tell that. A body's got to do things when he's awful hungry he wouldn't want to do as a steady thing.'

'Well, if I don't want you in the daytime, Huck, I'll let you sleep. I won't come bothering around. Any time you see something's up in the night, just skip right around and meow.'

CHAPTER XXX

THE first thing Tom heard on Friday morning was a glad piece of news – Judge Thatcher's family had come back to town the night before. Both Injun Joe and the treasure sank into secondary importance for a moment, and Becky took the chief place in the boy's interest. He saw her, and they had an exhausting good time playing 'hi-spy' and 'gully-keeper' with a crowd of their schoolmates. The day was completed and crowned in a peculiarly satisfactory way: Becky teased her mother to appoint the next day for the long-promised and long-delayed picnic, and she consented. The child's delight was boundless, and Tom's not more moderate. The invitations were sent out before sunset, and straightway the young folks of the village were thrown into a fever of preparation and pleasurable anticipation. Tom's excitement enabled him to keep awake until a pretty late hour, and he had good hopes of hearing Huck's 'meow' and of having his treasure to astonish Becky and the picnickers with, next day; but he was disappointed. No signal came that night.

Morning came eventually, and by ten or eleven o'clock

a giddy and rollicking company were gathered at Judge Thatcher's, and everything was ready for a start. It was not the custom for elderly people to mar picnics with their presence. The children were considered safe enough under the wings of a few young ladies of eighteen and a few young gentlemen of twenty-three or thereabouts. The old steam ferry-boat was chartered for the occasion: presently the gay throng filed up the main street laden with provision baskets. Sid was sick and had to miss the fun; Mary remained at home to entertain him. The last thing Mrs Thatcher said to Becky was:

'You'll not get back till late. Perhaps you'd better stay all night with some of the girls that live near the ferry landing, child!'

'Then I'll stay with Susy Harper, mamma.'

'Very well. And mind and behave yourself, and don't be any trouble.'

Presently, as they tripped along, Tom said to Becky:

'Say – I'll tell you what we'll do. 'Stead of going to Joe Harper's, we'll climb right up the hill and stop at Widow Douglas's. She'll have ice-cream! She has it 'most every day – dead loads of it. And she'll be awful glad to have us.'

'Oh, that will be fun!'

Then Becky reflected a moment, and said:

'But what will mamma say?'

'How'll she ever know?'

The girl turned the idea over in her mind, and said reluctantly:

'I reckon it's wrong – but – '

'But – shucks! Your mother won't know, and so what's the harm? All she wants is that you'll be safe; and I bet you she'd a said go there if she'd a thought of it. I know she would!'

The Widow Douglas's splendid hospitality was a tempting bait. It and Tom's persuasions presently carried the day. So it was decided to say nothing to anybody about the night's programme.

Presently it occurred to Tom that maybe Huck might come this very night and give the signal. The thought took a deal of the spirit out of his anticipations. Still he could not bear to give up the fun at Widow Douglas's. And why should he give it up, he reasoned – the signal did not come the night before, so why should it be any more likely to come tonight? The sure fun of the evening outweighed the uncertain treasure; and, boy-like, he determined to yield to the stronger inclination and not allow himself to think of the box of money another time that day.

Three miles below town the ferry-boat stopped at the mouth of a woody hollow and tied up. The crowd swarmed ashore, and soon the forest distances and craggy heights echoed far and near with shoutings and laughter. All the different ways of getting hot and tired were gone through with, and by-and-by the rovers straggled back to camp fortified with responsible appetites, and then the destruction of the good things began. After the feast there was a refreshing season of rest and chat in the shade of spreading oaks. By-and-by somebody shouted:

'Who's ready for the cave?'

Everybody was. Bundles of candles were produced, and straightway there was a general scamper up the hill. The mouth of the cave was high up the hill-side, an opening shaped like the letter A. Its massive oaken door stood unbarred. Within was a small chamber, chilly as an ice-house, and walled by Nature with solid lime-stone that was dewy with a cold sweat. It was romantic and mysterious to stand here in the deep gloom and look out upon the green valley shining in the sun. But the impressiveness of the situation quickly wore off, and the romping began again. The moment a candle was lighted, there was a general rush upon the owner of it; a struggle and a gallant defence followed, but the candle was soon knocked down or blown out, and then there was a glad clamour of laughter and a new chase. But all things have an end. By-and-by the procession went filing down the steep descent of the main avenue, the flickering rank of lights dimly revealing the lofty walls of rock almost to their point of junction sixty feet overhead. This main avenue was not more than eight or ten feet wide. Every few steps other lofty and still narrower crevices branched from it on either hand, for McDougal's cave was but a vast labyrinth of crooked aisles that ran into each other and out again and led nowhere. It was said that one might wander days and nights together through its intricate tangle of rifts and chasms, and never find the end of the cave; and that he might go down and down, and still down into the earth, and it was just the same – labyrinth underneath labyrinth, and no end to any of them. No man 'knew' the cave. That was an impossible thing. Most of the young men knew a portion of it, and it was not customary to venture much beyond this known portion. Tom Sawyer knew as much of the cave as anyone.

The procession moved along the main avenue some three-quarters of a mile, and then groups and couples began to slip aside into branch avenues, fly along the dismal corridors, and take each other by surprise at points where the corridors joined again. Parties were able to elude each other for the space of half an hour without going beyond the 'known' ground.

By-and-by, one group after another came straggling back to the mouth of the cave, panting, hilarious, smeared from head to foot with tallow drippings, daubed with clay, and entirely delighted with the success of the day. Then they were astonished to find that they had been taking no note of time, and that night was about at hand. The clanging bell had been calling for half an hour. However, this sort of close to the day's adventures was romantic and therefore satisfactory. When the ferry-boat with her wild freight pushed into the stream, nobody cared sixpence for the wasted time but the captain of the craft.

Huck was already upon his watch when the ferry-boat's

lights went glinting past the wharf. He heard no noise on board, for the young people were as subdued and still as people usually are who are nearly tired to death. He wondered what boat it was, and why she did not stop at the wharf – and then he dropped her out of his mind and put his attention upon his business. The night was growing cloudy and dark. Ten o'clock came, and the noise of vehicles ceased, scattered lights began to wink out, all straggling foot-passengers disappeared, the village betook itself to its slumbers and left the small watcher alone with the silence and the ghosts. Eleven o'clock came, and the tavern lights were put out; darkness everywhere, now. Huck waited what seemed a weary long time, but nothing happened. His faith was weakening. Was there any use? Was there really any use? Why not give it up and turn in?

A noise fell upon his ear. He was all attention in an instant. The alley door closed softly. He sprang to the corner of the brick-store. The next moment two men brushed by him, and one seemed to have something under his arm. It must be that box! So they were going to remove the treasure. Why call Tom now? It would be absurd – the men would get away with the box and never be found again. No, he would stick to their wake and follow them; he would trust to the darkness for security from discovery. So communing with himself, Huck stepped out and glided along behind the men, cat-like, with bare feet, allowing them to keep just far enough ahead not to be invisible.

They moved up the river street three blocks, then turned to the left up a cross street. They went straight ahead, then, until they came to the path that led up Cardiff Hill; this they took. They passed by the old Welshman's house, half way up the hill, without hesitating, and still climbed upward. Good, thought Huck, they will bury it in the old quarry. But they never stopped at the quarry. They passed on, up the summit. They plunged into the narrow path between the tall sumach bushes, and were at once hidden in the gloom. Huck closed up and shortened his distance, now, for they would never be able to see him. He trotted along a while; then slackened his pace, fearing he was gaining too fast; moved on a piece, then stopped altogether; listened; no sound; none, save that he seemed to hear the beating of his own heart. The hooting of an owl came from over the hill – ominous sound! But no footsteps. Heaven was everything lost? He was about to spring with winged feet, when a man cleared his throat not four feet from him! Huck's heart shot into his throat, but he swallowed it again; and then he stood there shaking as if a dozen agues had taken charge of him at once, and so weak that he thought he must surely fall to the ground. He knew where he was. He knew he was within five steps of the stile leading into Widow Douglas's grounds. 'Very well,' he thought, 'let them bury it there; it won't be hard to find.'

Now there was a low voice – a very low voice – Injun Joe's:

'Damn her, maybe she's got company – there's lights, late as it is.'

'I can't see any.'

This was that stranger's voice – the stranger of the haunted house. A deadly chill went to Huck's heart – this, then, was the 'revenge' job! His thought was to fly. Then he remembered that the Widow Douglas had been kind to him more than once, and maybe these men were going to murder her. He wished he dared venture to warn her; but he knew he didn't dare – they might come and catch him. He thought all this and more in the moment that elapsed between the stranger's remark and Injun Joe's next – which was:

'Because the bush is in your way. Now – this way – now you see, don't you?'

'Yes. Well, there is company there, I reckon. Better give it up.'

'Give it up, and I just leaving this country for ever! Give

it up, and maybe never have another chance. I tell you again, as I've told you before, I don't care for her swag – you may have it. But her husband was rough on me – many times he was rough on me – and mainly he was the justice of the peace that jugged me for a vagrant. And that ain't all! It ain't the millionth part of it! He had me horsewhipped! – horsewhipped in front of the jail, like a nigger! – with all the town looking on! Horsewhipped! – do you understand? He took advantage of me and died. But I'll take it out of her!'

'Oh, don't kill her! Don't do that!'

'Kill? Who said anything about killing? I would kill him if he was here; but not her. When you want to get revenge on a woman you don't kill her – bosh! you go for her looks. You slit her nostrils – you notch her ears like a sow's!'

'By God, that's – '

'Keep your opinion to yourself! It will be safest for you. I'll tie her to the bed. If she bleeds to death, is that my fault? I'll not cry if she does. My friend, you'll help me in this thing – for my sake – that's why you're here – I mightn't be able alone. If you flinch, I'll kill you! Do you understand that? And if I have to kill you, I'll kill her – and then I reckon nobody'll ever know much about who done this business.'

'Well, if it's got to be done, let's get at it. The quicker the better – I'm all in a shiver.'

'Do it now? – and company there? Look here – I'll get suspicious of you, first thing, you know. No – we'll wait till the lights are out – there's no hurry.'

Huck felt that a silence was going to ensue – a thing still more awful than any amount of murderous talk; so he held his breath and stepped gingerly back; planted his foot carefully and firmly, after balancing, one-legged, in a precarious way and almost toppling over, first on one side and then on the other. He took another step back with the same elaboration and the same risks; then another and another, and a twig snapped under his foot! His breath stopped and he listened. There was no sound – the stillness was perfect. His gratitude was measureless. Now he turned in his tracks between the walls of sumach bushes – turned himself as carefully as if he were a ship – and then stepped quickly but cautiously along. When he emerged at the quarry he felt secure, so he picked up his nimble heels and flew. Down, down he sped till he reached the Welshman's. He banged at the door, and presently the heads of the old man and his two stalwart sons were thrust from windows.

'What's the row there? Who's banging? What do you want?'

'Let me in – quick! I'll tell everything.'

'Why, who are you?'

'Huckleberry Finn – quick, let me in!'

'Huckleberry Finn, indeed! It ain't a name to open many doors, I judge! But let him in, lads, and let's see what's the trouble?'

'Please don't ever tell I told you,' were Huck's first words when he got in. 'Please don't – I'd be killed sure – but the widow's been good friend to me sometimes, and I want to tell – I will tell if you'll promise you won't ever say it was me.'

'By George, he has got something to tell, or he wouldn't act so!' exclaimed the old man. 'Out with it, and nobody here'll ever tell, lad.'

Three minutes later the old man and his sons, well armed, were up the hill, and just entering the sumach path on tiptoe, their weapons in their hands. Huck accompanied them no farther. He hid behind a great boulder and fell to listening. There was a lagging, anxious silence, and then all of a sudden there was an explosion of firearms and a cry. Huck waited for no particulars. He sprang away and sped down the hill as fast as his legs could carry him.

CHAPTER XXXI

As the earliest suspicion of dawn appeared on Sunday morning, Huck came groping up the hill and rapped gently at the old Welshman's door. The inmates were asleep, but it was a sleep that was set on a hair-trigger, on account of the exciting episode of the night. A call came from a window:

'Who's there?'

Huck's scared voice answered in a low tone:

'Do please let me in! It's only Huck Finn!'

'It's a name that can open this door night or day, lad! – and welcome!'

These were strange words to the vagabond boy's ears, and the pleasantest he had ever heard. He could not recollect that the closing word had ever been applied in his case before.

The door was quickly unlocked and he entered. Huck was given a seat, and the old man and his brace of tall sons speedily dressed themselves.

'Now, my boy, I hope you're good and hungry, because breakfast will be ready as soon as the sun's up, and we'll have a piping hot one, too – make yourself easy about that. I and the boys hoped you'd turn up and stop here last night.'

'I was awful scared,' said Huck, 'and I run. I took out when the pistols went off, and I didn't stop for three mile. I've come now becuz I wanted to know about it, you know; and I come before daylight becuz I didn't want to run across them devils, even if they was dead.'

'Well, poor chap, you do look as if you'd had a hard night of it – but there's a bed here for you when you've had your breakfast. No, they ain't dead, lad – we are sorry enough for that. You see, we knew right where to put our hands on them, by your description; so we crept along on tip-toe till we got within fifteen feet of them – dark as a cellar that sumach path was – and just then I found I was going to sneeze. It was the meanest kind of luck! I tried to keep it back, but no use – 'twas bound to come, and it did come! I was in the lead, with my pistol raised, and when the sneeze, started those scoundrels a rustling to get out of the path, I sang out "Fire, boys!" and blazed away at the place where the rustling was. So did the boys. But they were off in a jiffy, those villains, and we after them, down through the woods. I judge we never touched them. They fired a shot apiece as they started, but their bullets whizzed by and didn't do us any harm. As soon as we lost the sound of their feet we quit chasing, and went down and stirred up the constables. They got a posse together, and went off to guard the river bank and as soon as it is light the sheriff and a gang are going to beat up the woods. My boys will be with them presently. I wish we had some sort of a description of those rascals – 'twould help a good deal. But you couldn't see what they were like in the dark, lad, I suppose?'

'Oh, yes, I saw them down town, and follered them.'

'Splendid! Describe them – describe them, my boy!'

'One's the old deaf and dumb Spaniard that's been around here once or twice, and t'other's a mean-looking, ragged –'

'That's enough, lad, we know the men! Happened on them in the woods back of the widow's one day, and they slunk away. Off with you, boys, and tell the sheriff – get your breakfast tomorrow morning!'

The Welshman's sons departed at once. As they were leaving the room Huck sprang up and exclaimed:

'Oh, please don't tell anybody it was me that blowed on them! Oh, please!'

'All right if you say it, Huck, but you ought to have the credit of what you did.'

'Oh, no, no! Please don't tell!'

When the young men were gone, the old Welshman said:

'They won't tell – and I won't. But why don't you want it known?'

Huck would not explain further than to say that he already knew too much about one of those men, and would not have the man know that he knew anything against him for the whole world – he would be killed for knowing it, sure.

The old man promised secrecy once more, and said:

'How did you come to follow these fellows, lad? Were they looking suspicious?'

Huck was silent, while he framed a duly cautious reply. Then he said:

'Well, you see, I'm a kind of a hard lot – least everybody says so, and I don't see nothing agin it – and sometimes I can't sleep much, on accounts of thinking about it, and sort of trying to strike out a new way of doing. That was the way of it last night. I couldn't sleep, and so I came along up street 'bout midnight a turning it all over, and when I got to that old shackly brick-store by the Temperance Tavern, I backed up agin the wall to have another think. Well, just then along comes these two chaps slipping along close by me, with something under their arm, and I reckoned they'd stole it. One was a smoking, and t'other one wanted a light; so they stopped right before me, and the cigars lit up their faces, and I see that the big one was the deaf and dumb Spaniard, by his white whiskers and the patch on his eye, and t'other one was a rusty, ragged-looking devil.'

'Could you see the rags by the light of the cigars?'

This staggered Huck for a moment. Then he said:

'Well, I don't know, but somehow it seems as if I did.'

'Then they went on, and you –'

'Followed 'em – yes. That was it. I wanted to see what was up – they sneaked along so. I dogged 'em to the widder's stile, and stood in the dark, and heard the ragged one beg for the widder, and the Spaniard swear he'd spile her looks, just as I told you and your two –'

'What! the deaf and dumb man said all that?'

Huck had made another terrible mistake! He was trying his best to keep the old man from getting the faintest hint of who the Spaniard might be, and yet his tongue seemed determined to get him into trouble in spite of all he could do. He made several efforts to creep out of his scrape, but the old man's eye was upon him, and he made blunder after blunder. Presently the Welshman said:

'My boy, don't be afraid of me, I wouldn't hurt a hair of your head for all the world. No – I'd protect you – I'd protect you. This Spaniard is not deaf and dumb; you've let that slip without intending it; you can't cover that up now. You know something about that Spaniard that you want to keep dark. Now trust me – tell me what it is, and trust me – I won't betray you.'

Huck looked into the old man's honest eyes a moment, then bent over and whispered in his ear:

''Tain't a Spaniard – it's Injun Joe!'

The Welshman almost jumped out of his chair. In a moment he said:

'It's all plain enough now. When you talked about notching ears and slitting noses, I judged that that was your own embellishment, because white men don't take that sort of revenge. But an Injun! That's a different matter, altogether.'

During breakfast the talk went on, and in the course of it the old man said that the last thing which he and his sons had done, before going to bed, was to get a lantern and examine the stile and its vicinity for marks of blood. They found none, but captured a bulky bundle of –

'Of WHAT?'

If the words had been lightning, they could not have leaped with a more stunning suddenness from Huck's blanched lips. His eyes were staring wide, now, and his breath suspended – waiting for the answer. The Welshman started – started in return – three seconds – five seconds – ten – then replied:

'Of burglar's tools.'

'Why, what's the matter with you?'

Huck sank back, panting gently, but deeply, unutterably grateful. The Welshman eyed him gravely, curiously – and presently said:

'Yes, burglar's tools. That appears to relieve you a good deal. But what did give you that turn? What were you expecting we'd found?'

Huck was in a close place; the inquiring eye was upon him – he would have given anything for material for a plausible answer. Nothing suggested itself; the inquiring eye was boring deeper and deeper – a senseless reply offered – there was no time to weigh it, so at a venture he uttered it, feebly:

'Sunday-school books, maybe.'

Poor Huck was too distressed to smile, but the old man laughed loud and joyously, shook up the details of his anatomy from head to foot, and ended by saying that such a laugh was money in a man's pocket, because it cut down the doctor's bills like everything. Then he added:

'Poor old chap, you're white and jaded; you ain't well a bit. No wonder you're a little flighty and off your balance. But you'll come out of it. Rest and sleep will fetch you all right, I hope.'

Huck was irritated to think he had been such a goose and betrayed such a suspicious excitement, for he had dropped the idea that the parcel brought from the tavern was the treasure as soon as he had heard the talk at the widow's stile. He had only thought it was not the treasure, however; he had not known that it wasn't; and so the suggestion of a captured bundle was too much for his self-possession. But on the whole he felt glad the little episode had happened, for now he knew beyond all question that the bundle was not *the* bundle, and so his mind was at rest and exceedingly comfortable. In fact everything seemed to be drifting just in the right direction, now; the treasure must be still in number two, the men would be captured and jailed that day, and he and Tom could seize the gold that night without any trouble or any fear of interruption.

Just as breakfast was completed there was a knock at the door. Huck jumped for a hiding-place, for he had no mind to be connected even remotely with the late event. The Welshman admitted several ladies and gentlemen, among them the Widow Douglas, and noticed that groups of citizens were climbing the hill to stare at the stile. So the news had spread.

The Welshman had to tell the story of the night to the visitors. The widow's gratitude for her preservation was outspoken.

'Don't say a word about it, madam. There's another that you're more beholden to than you are to me and my boys maybe, but he don't allow me to tell his name. We wouldn't ever have been there but for him.'

Of course this excited a curiosity so vast that it almost belittled the main matter; but the Welshman allowed it to eat into the vitals of his visitors, and through them he transmitted it to the whole town, for he refused to part with his secret. When all else had been learned the widow said:

'I went to sleep reading in bed, and slept straight through all that noise. Why didn't you come and wake me?'

'We judged it wasn't worth while. Those fellows weren't likely to come again; they hadn't any tools left to work with, and what was the use of waking you up and scaring you to death? My three Negro men stood guard at your house all the rest of the night. They've just come back.'

More visitors came, and the story had to be told and retold for a couple of hours more.

There was no Sabbath-school during day-school vacation, but everybody was early at church. The stirring event was well canvassed. News came that not a sign of the villains had been yet discovered. When the sermon was finished Judge Thatcher's wife dropped alongside of Mrs Harper as she moved down the aisle with the crowd, and said:

'Is my Becky going to sleep all day? I just expected she would be tired to death.'

'Your Becky?'

'Yes,' with a startled look. 'Didn't she stay with you last night?'

'Why, no.'

Mrs Thatcher turned pale, and sank into a pew just as Aunt Polly, talking briskly with a friend, passed by. Aunt Polly said:

'Good morning, Mrs Thatcher. Good morning, Mrs Harper. I've got a boy that's turned up missing. I reckon my Tom stayed at your house last night – one of you. And now he's afraid to come to church. I've got to settle with him.'

Mrs Thatcher shook her head feebly and turned paler than ever.

'He didn't stay with us,' said Mrs Harper, beginning to look uneasy. A marked anxiety came into Aunt Polly's face.

'Joe Harper, have you seen my Tom this morning?'

'No'm.'

'When did you see him last?'

Joe tried to remember, but was not sure he could say. The people had stopped moving out of church. Whispers passed along, and a brooding uneasiness took possession of every countenance. Children were anxiously questioned, and young teachers. They all said they had not noticed whether Tom and Becky were on board the ferry-boat on the homeward trip; it was dark; no one thought of inquiring if anyone was missing. One young man finally blurted out his fear that they were still in the cave! Mrs Thatcher swooned away; Aunt Polly fell to crying and wringing her hands.

The alarm swept from lip to lip, from group to group, from street to street; and within five minutes the bells were wildly clanging, and the whole town was up! The Cardiff

Hill episode sank into instant insignificance, the burglars were forgotten, horses were saddled, skiffs were manned, the ferry-boat ordered out, and before the horror was half an hour old two hundred men were pouring down high-road and river towards the cave.

All the long afternoon the village seemed empty and dead. Many women visited Aunt Polly and Mrs Thatcher, and tried to comfort them. They cried with them, too, and that was still better than words.

All the tedious night the town waited for news; but when the morning dawned at last, all the word that came was 'Send more candles, and send food.' Mrs Thatcher was almost crazed, and Aunt Polly also. Judge Thatcher sent messages of hope and encouragement from the cave, but they conveyed no real cheer.

The old Welshman came home towards daylight, spattered with candle-grease, smeared with clay, and almost worn out. He found Huck still in the bed that had been provided for him, and delirious with fever. The physicians were all at the cave, so the Widow Douglas came and took charge of the patient. She said she would do her best by him, because, whether he was good, bad, or indifferent, he was the Lord's and nothing that was the Lord's was a thing to be neglected. The Welshman said Huck had good spots in him, and the widow said:

'You can depend on it. That's the Lord's mark. He don't leave it off. He never does. Puts it somewhere on every creature that comes from His hands.'

Early in the forenoon parties of jaded men began to straggle into the village, but the strongest of the citizens continued searching. All the news that could be gained was that remotenesses of the cavern were being ransacked that had never been visited before; that every corner and crevice was going to be thoroughly searched; that wherever one wandered through the maze of passages, lights were to be seen flitting hither and thither in the distance, and shoutings and pistol-shots sent their hollow reverberations to the ear down the sombre aisles. In one place, far from the section usually traversed by tourists, the names 'BECKY' and 'TOM' had been found traced upon the rocky wall with candle smoke, and near at hand a grease-soiled bit of ribbon. Mrs Thatcher recognized the ribbon and cried over it. She said it was the last relic she should ever have of her child; and that no other memorial of her could ever be so precious, because this one parted latest from the living body before the awful death came. Some said that now and then in the cave a far-away speck of light would glimmer, and then a glorious shout would burst forth and a score of men go trooping down the echoing aisle – and then a sickening disappointment always followed; the children were not there; it was only a searcher's light.

Three dreadful days and nights dragged their tedious hours along, and the village sank into a hopeless stupor. No one had heart for anything. The accidental discovery, just made, that the proprietor of the Temperance Tavern kept liquor on his premises, scarcely fluttered the public pulse, tremendous as the fact was. In a lucid interval, Huck feebly led up to the subject of taverns and finally asked, dimly dreading the worst, if anything had been discovered at the Temperance Tavern since he had been ill.

'Yes,' said the widow.

Huck started up in bed, wild-eyed:

'What! What was it?'

'Liquor! – and the place has been shut up. Lie down, child – what a turn you did give me!'

'Only tell me one thing – only just one – please! Was it Tom Sawyer that found it?'

The widow burst into tears.

'Hush, hush, child, hush! I've told you before, you must *not* talk. You are very, very sick!'

Then nothing but liquor had been found; there would have been a great pow-pow if it had been the gold. So the treasure was gone for ever – gone for ever. But what could she be crying about? Curious that she should cry.

These thoughts worked their dim way through Huck's mind, and under the weariness they gave him he fell asleep. The widow said to herself:

'There – he's asleep, poor wreck. Tom Sawyer find it! Pity but somebody could find Tom Sawyer! Ah, there ain't many left, now, that's got hope enough, or strength enough either, to go on searching.'

CHAPTER XXXII

Now to return to Tom and Becky's share in the picnic. They tripped along the murky aisles with the rest of the company, visiting the familiar wonders of the cave – wonders dubbed with rather over-descriptive names, such as 'The Drawing-room', 'The Cathedral', 'Aladdin's Palace', and so on. Presently the hide-and-seek frolicking began, and Tom and Becky engaged in it with zeal until the exertion began to grow a trifle wearisome; then they wandered down a sinuous avenue, holding their candles aloft and reading the tangled web-work of names, dates, post-office addresses, and mottoes with which the rocky walls had been frescoed (in candle smoke). Still drifting along and talking, they scarcely noticed that they were now in a part of the cave whose walls were not frescoed. They smoked their own names under an overhanging shelf and moved on. Presently they came to a place where a little stream of water, trickling over a ledge and carrying a limestone sediment with it, had, in the slow-dragging ages, formed a laced and ruffled Niagara in gleaming and imperishable stone. Tom squeezed his small body behind it in order to illuminate it for Becky's gratification. He found that it curtained a sort of steep natural stair-way which was enclosed between narrow walls, and at once the ambition to be a discoverer seized him. Becky responded to his call, and they made a smoke mark for future guidance and started upon their quest. They wound this way and that, far down into the secret depths of the cave, made another mark, and branched off in search of novelties to tell the upper world about. In one place they found a spacious cavern, from whose ceiling depended a multitude of shining stalactites of the length and circumference of a man's leg; they walked all about it, wondering and admiring, and presently left it by one of the numerous passages that opened into it. This shortly brought them to a bewitching spring, whose basin was encrusted with a frostwork of glittering crystals; it was in the midst of a cavern whose walls were supported by many fantastic pillars which had been formed by the joining of great stalactites and stalagmites together, the result of the ceaseless water-drip of centuries. Under the roof vast knots of bats had packed themselves together, thousands in a bunch; the lights disturbed the creatures, and they came flocking down by hundreds, squeaking and darting furiously at the candles. Tom knew their ways, and the danger of this sort of conduct. He seized Becky's hand and hurried her into the first corridor that offered; and none too soon, for a bat struck Becky's light out with its wing while she was passing out of the cavern. The bats chased the children a good distance; but the fugitives plunged into every new passage that offered, and at last got rid of the perilous things. Tom found a subterranean lake, shortly, which stretched its dim length away until its shape was lost in the shadows. He wanted to explore its borders, but concluded that it would be best to sit down and rest a while first. Now for the first time the deep stillness of the place laid a clammy hand upon the spirits of the children. Becky said:

'Why, I didn't notice, but it seems ever so long since I heard any of the others.'

'Come to think, Becky, we are away down below them,

and I don't know how far away north, or south, or east, or whichever it is. We couldn't hear them here.'

Becky grew apprehensive.

'I wonder how long we've been down here, Tom. We better start back.'

'Yes, I reckon we better. P'raps we better.'

'Can you find the way, Tom? It's all a mixed-up crookedness to me.'

'I reckon I could find it, but then the bats. If they put both our candles out it will be an awful fix. Let's try some other way, so as not to go through there.'

'Well, but I hope we won't get lost. It would be so awful!' and the child shuddered at the thought of the dreadful possibilities.

They started through a corridor, and traversed it in silence a long way, glancing at each new opening, to see if there was anything familiar about the look of it; but they were all strange. Every time Tom made an examination, Becky would watch his face for an encouraging sign, and he would say cheerily:

'Oh, it's all right. This ain't the one, but we'll come to it right away!' But he felt less and less hopeful with each failure, and presently began to turn off into diverging avenues at sheer random, in the desperate hope of finding the one that was wanted. He still said it was 'All right', but there was such a leaden dread at his heart, that the words had lost their ring, and sounded as if he had said, 'All is lost!' Becky clung to his side in an anguish of fear, and tried hard to keep back the tears, but they would come. At last she said:

'Oh, Tom, never mind the bats; let's go back that way! We seem to get worse and worse off all the time.'

Tom stopped.

'Listen!' said he.

Profound silence; silence so deep that even their breathings were conspicuous in the hush. Tom shouted. The call went echoing down the empty aisles, and died out in the distance in a faint sound that resembled a ripple of mocking laughter.

'Oh, don't do it again, Tom, it is too horrid,' said Becky.

'It is horrid, but I better, Becky; they *might* hear us, you know,' and he shouted again.

The 'might' was even a chillier horror than the ghostly laughter, it so confessed a perishing hope. The children stood still and listened; but there was no result. Tom turned upon the back track at once, and hurried his steps. It was but a little while before a certain indecision in his manner revealed another fearful fact to Becky; he could not find his way back!

'Oh, Tom, you didn't make any marks!'

'Becky, I was such a fool! such a fool! I never thought we might want to come back! No, I can't find the way. It's all mixed up.'

'Tom, Tom, we're lost! we're lost! We never, never can get out of this awful place! Oh, why did we ever leave the others?'

She sank to the ground, and burst into such a frenzy of crying that Tom was appalled with the idea that she might die, or lose her reason. He sat down by her and put his arms around her; she buried her face in his bosom, she clung to him, she poured out her terrors, her unavailing regrets, and the far echoes turned them all to jeering laughter. Tom begged her to pluck up hope again, and she said she could not. He fell to blaming and abusing himself for getting her into this miserable situation; this had a better effect. She said she would try to hope again, she would get up and follow wherever he might lead, if only he would not talk like that any more. For he was no more to blame than she, she said.

So they moved on again – aimlessly – simply at random – all they could do was to move, keep moving. For a little while hope made a show of reviving – not with any reason to back it, but only because it is its nature to revive when the spring has not been taken out of it by age and familiarity with failure.

By-and-by Tom took Becky's candle and blew it out. This economy meant so much. Words were not needed. Becky understood, and her hope died again. She knew that Tom had a whole candle and three or four pieces in his pocket – yet he must economize.

By-and-by fatigue began to assert its claims; the children tried to pay no attention, for it was dreadful to think of sitting down when time was grown to be so precious; moving, in some direction, in any direction, was at least progress and might bear fruit; but to sit down was to invite death and shorten its pursuit.

At last Becky's frail limbs refused to carry her farther. She sat down. Tom rested with her, and they talked of home, and the friends there, and the comfortable beds, and above all, the light! Becky cried, and Tom tried to think of some way of comforting her, but all his encouragements were grown threadbare with use, and sounded like sarcasms. Fatigue bore so heavily upon Becky that she drowsed off to sleep. Tom was grateful. He sat looking into her drawn face and saw it grow smooth and natural under the influence of pleasant dreams; and by-and-by a smile dawned and rested there. The peaceful face reflected somewhat of peace and healing into his own spirit, and his thoughts wandered away to bygone times and dreamy memories. While he was deep in his musings, Becky woke up with a breezy little laugh: but it was stricken dead upon her lips, and a groan followed it.

'Oh, how *could* I sleep! I wish I never, never had waked! No, no, I don't, Tom! Don't look so! I won't say it again.'

'I'm glad you slept, Becky; you'll feel rested, now, and we'll find the way out.'

'We can try, Tom; but I've seen such a beautiful country in my dream. I reckon we are going there.'

'Maybe not, maybe not. Cheer up, Becky, and let's go on trying.'

They rose up and wandered along hand, in hand and hopeless. They tried to estimate how long they had been in the cave, but all they knew was that it seemed days and weeks, and yet it was plain that this could not be, for their candles were not gone yet.

A long time after this – they could not tell how long – Tom said they must go softly and listen for dripping water – they must find a spring. They found one presently, and Tom said it was time to rest again. Both were cruelly tired, yet Becky said she thought she could go a little farther. She was surprised to hear Tom dissent. She could not understand it. They sat down, and Tom fastened his candle to the wall in front of them with some clay. Thought was soon busy; nothing was said for some time. Then Becky broke the silence:

'Tom, I am so hungry!'

Tom took something out of his pocket.

'Do you remember this?' said he.

Becky almost smiled.

'It's our wedding-cake, Tom.'

'Yes – I wish it was as big as a barrel, for it's all we've got.'

'I saved it from the picnic for us to dream on, Tom, the way grown-up people do with wedding-cake – but it'll be our – '

She dropped the sentence where it was. Tom divided the cake, and Becky ate with good appetite, while Tom nibbled at his moiety. There was abundance of cold water to finish the feast with. By-and-by Becky suggested that they move on again. Tom was silent a moment. Then he said:

'Becky, can you bear it if I tell you something?'

Becky's face paled, but she said she thought she could.

'Well, then, Becky, we must stay here, where there's water to drink. That little piece is our last candle!'

Becky gave loose to tears and wailings. Tom did what he

could to comfort her, but with little effect. At length Becky said:

'Tom!'

'Well, Becky?'

'They'll miss us and hunt for us!'

'Yes, they will! Certainly they will!'

'Maybe they're hunting for us now, Tom?'

'Why, I reckon maybe they are! I hope they are.'

'When would they miss us, Tom?'

'When they get back to the boat, I reckon.'

'Tom, it might be dark, then – would they notice we hadn't come?'

'I don't know. But anyway, your mother would miss you as soon as they got home.'

A frightened look in Becky's face brought Tom to his senses, and he saw that he had made a blunder. Becky was not to have gone home that night! The children became silent and thoughtful. In a moment a new burst of grief from Becky showed Tom that the thing in his mind had struck hers also – that the Sabbath morning might be half spent before Mrs Thatcher discovered that Becky was not at Mrs Harper's. The children fastened their eyes upon their bit of candle and watched it melt slowly and pitilessly away; saw the half inch of wick stand alone at last: saw the feeble flame rise and fall, rise and fall, climb the thin column of smoke, linger at its top a moment, and then – the horror of utter darkness reigned.

How long afterwards it was that Becky came to a slow consciousness that she was crying in Tom's arms, neither could tell. All that they knew was that after what seemed a mighty stretch of time, both awoke out of a dead stupor of sleep, and resumed their miseries once more. Tom said it might be Sunday now – maybe Monday. He tried to get Becky to talk, but her sorrows were too oppressive, all her hopes were gone. Tom said that they must have been missed long ago, and no doubt the search was going on. He would shout, and maybe someone would come. He tried it; but in the darkness the distant echoes sounded so hideously that he tried it no more.

The hours wasted away, and hunger came to torment the captives again. A portion of Tom's half of the cake was left; they divided and ate it. But they seemed hungrier than before. The poor morsel of food only whetted desire.

By-and-by Tom said:

'*Sh!* Did you hear that?'

Both held their breath and listened. There was a sound like the faintest far-off shout. Instantly Tom answered it, and leading Becky by the hand, started groping down the corridor in its direction. Presently he listened again; again the sound was heard, and apparently a little nearer.

'It's them!' said Tom; 'they're coming! Come along, Becky – we're all right now!'

The joy of the prisoners was almost overwhelming. Their speed was slow, however, because pitfalls were somewhat common, and had to be guarded against. They shortly came to one, and had to stop. It might be three feet deep, it might be a hundred – there was no passing it, at any rate. Tom got down on his breast, and reached as far down as he could. No bottom. They must stay there and wait until the searchers came. They listened; evidently the distant shoutings were growing more distant! A moment or two more, and they had gone altogether. The heart-sinking misery of it! Tom whooped until he was hoarse, but it was of no use. He talked hopefully to Becky; but an age of anxious waiting passed and no sound came again.

The children groped their way back to the spring. The weary time dragged on; they slept again, and awoke famished and woe-stricken. Tom believed it must be Tuesday by this time.

Now an idea struck him. There were some side-passages near at hand. It would be better to explore some of these than bear the weight of the heavy time in idleness. He took

198

a kite-line from his pocket, tied it to a projection, and he and Becky started, Tom in the lead, unwinding the line as he groped along. At the end of twenty steps the corridor ended in a 'jumping-off place'. Tom got down on his knees and felt below, and then as far around the corner as he could reach with his hands conveniently; he made an effort to stretch yet a little further to the right, and at the moment, not twenty yards away, a human hand, holding a candle, appeared from behind a rock! Tom lifted up a glorious shout, and instantly that hand was followed by the body it belonged to – Injun Joe's! Tom was paralysed; he could not move. He was vastly gratified the next moment to see the 'Spaniard' take to his heels and get himself out of sight. Tom wondered that Joe had not recognized his voice and come over and killed him for testifying in court. But the echoes must have disguised the voice. Without doubt that was it, he reasoned. Tom's fright weakened every muscle in his body. He said to himself that if he had strength enough to get back to the spring he would stay there, and nothing should tempt him to run the risk of meeting Injun Joe again. He was careful to keep from Becky what it was he had seen. He told her he had only shouted 'for luck'.

But hunger and wretchedness rise superior to fears in the long run. Another tedious wait at the spring, and another long sleep brought changes. The children awoke, tortured with a raging hunger. Tom believed it must be Wednesday or Thursday, or even Friday or Saturday, now, and that the search had been given over. He proposed to explore another passage. He felt willing to risk Injun Joe and all other terrors. But Becky was very weak. She had sunk into a dreary apathy, and would not be roused. She said she would wait, now, where she was, and die – it would not be long. She told Tom to go with the kite-line and explore if he chose; but she implored him to come back every little while and speak to her; and she made him promise that when the awful time came, he would stay by her and hold her hand until all was over. Tom kissed her, with a choking sensation in his throat, and made a show of being confident of finding the searchers or an escape from the cave; then he took the kite-line in his hand and went groping down one of the passages on his hands and knees, distressed with hunger and sick with bodings of coming doom.

CHAPTER XXXIII

TUESDAY afternoon came, and waned to the twilight. The village of St Petersburg still mourned. The lost children had not been found. Public prayers had been offered up for them, and many and many a private prayer that had the petitioner's whole heart in it; but still no good news came from the cave. The majority of the searchers had given up the quest and gone back to their daily avocations, saying that it was plain the children could never be found. Mrs Thatcher was very ill, and a great part of the time delirious. People said it was heart-breaking to hear her call her child, and raise her head and listen a whole minute at a time, then lay it wearily down again with a moan. Aunt Polly had drooped into a settled melancholy, and her grey hair had grown almost white. The village went to its rest on Tuesday night, sad and forlorn.

Away in the middle of the night a wild peal burst from the village bells, and in a moment the streets were swarming with frantic half-clad people, who shouted, 'Turn out! turn out! they're found! they're found!' Tin pans and horns were added to the din, the population massed itself and moved towards the river, met the children coming in an open carriage drawn by shouting citizens, thronged around it, joined its homeward march, and swept magnificently up the main street roaring huzza after huzza!

The village was illuminated; nobody went to bed again;

it was the greatest night the little town had ever seen. During the first half-hour a procession of villagers filed through Judge Thatcher's house, seized the saved ones and kissed them, squeezed Mrs Thatcher's hand, tried to speak but couldn't, and drifted out raining tears all over the place.

Aunt Polly's happiness was complete, and Mrs Thatcher's nearly so. It would be complete, however, as soon as the messenger despatched with the great news to the cave should get the word to her husband.

Tom lay upon a sofa with an eager auditory about him, and told the history of the wonderful adventure, putting in many striking additions to adorn it withal; and closed with a description of how he left Becky and went on an exploring expedition; how he followed two avenues as far as his kite-line would reach; how he followed a third to the fullest stretch of the kite-line, and was about to turn back when he glimpsed a far-off speck that looked like daylight; dropped the line and groped towards it, pushed his head and shoulders through a small hole and saw the broad Mississippi rolling by! And if it had only happened to be night he would not have seen that speck of daylight, and would not have explored that passage any more! He told how he went back for Becky and broke the good news, and she told him not to fret her with such stuff, for she was tired, and knew she was going to die, and wanted to. He described how he laboured with her and convinced her, and how she almost died for joy when she had groped to where she actually saw the blue speck of daylight; how he pushed his way out of the hole and then helped her out; how they sat there and cried for gladness; how some men came along in a skiff, and Tom hailed them and told them their situation and their famished condition; how the men didn't believe the wild tale at first, 'because', said they, 'you are five miles down the river below the valley the cave is in'; then took them aboard, rowed to a house, gave them supper, made them rest till two or three hours after dark, and then brought them home.

Before day-dawn Judge Thatcher and the handful of searchers with him were tracked out in the cave by the twine clues they had strung behind them, and informed of the great news.

Three days and nights of toil and hunger in the cave were not to be shaken off at once, as Tom and Becky soon discovered. They were bedridden all of Wednesday and Thursday, and seemed to grow more and more tired and worn all the time. Tom got about a little on Thursday, was down town Friday, and nearly as whole as ever Saturday; but Becky did not leave her room until Sunday, and then she looked as if she had passed through a wasting illness.

Tom learned of Huck's sickness, and went to see him on Friday, but could not be admitted to the bedroom; neither could he on Saturday or Sunday. He was admitted daily after that, but was warned to keep still about his adventure and introduce no exciting topic. The Widow Douglas stayed by to see that he obeyed. At home Tom learned of the Cardiff Hill event; also that the ragged man's body had eventually been found in the river near the ferry landing; he had been drowned while trying to escape perhaps.

About a fortnight after Tom's rescue from the cave he started off to visit Huck, who had grown plenty strong enough, now, to hear exciting talk, and Tom had some that would interest him, he thought. Judge Thatcher's house was on Tom's way, and he stopped to see Becky. The judge and some friends set Tom to talking, and someone asked him ironically if he wouldn't like to go to the cave again. Tom said yes, he thought he wouldn't mind it.

The Judge said:

'Well, there are others just like you, Tom, I've not the least doubt. But we have taken care of that. Nobody will get lost in that cave any more.'

'Why?'

'Because I had its big door sheathed with boiler iron two weeks ago, and triple locked; and I've got the keys.'

Tom turned as white as a sheet.

'What's the matter, boy? Here, run, somebody! Fetch a glass of water!'

The water was brought and thrown into Tom's face.

'Ah, now you're all right. What was the matter with you, Tom?'

'Oh, Judge, Injun Joe's in the cave!'

CHAPTER XXXIV

WITHIN a few minutes the news had spread, and a dozen skiff-loads of men were on their way to McDougal's cave, and the ferry-boat, well filled with passengers, soon followed. Tom Sawyer was in the skiff that bore Judge Thatcher. When the cave door was unlocked, a sorrowful sight presented itself in the dim twilight of the place. Injun Joe lay stretched upon the ground, dead, with his face close to the crack of the door, as if his longing eyes had been fixed to the latest moment upon the light and the cheer of the free world outside. Tom was touched, for he knew by his own experience how this wretch had suffered. His pity was moved, but nevertheless he felt an abounding sense of relief and security, now, which revealed to him in a degree which he had not fully appreciated before, how vast a weight of dread had been lying upon him since the day he lifted his voice against this bloody-minded outcast.

Injun Joe's bowie-knife lay close by, its blade broken in two. The great foundation-beam of the door had been chipped and hacked through with tedious labour; useless labour, too, it was, for the native rock formed a sill outside it, and upon that stubborn material the knife had wrought no effect; the only damage done was to the knife itself. But if there had been no stony obstruction there, labour would have been useless still, for if the beam had been wholly cut away Injun Joe could not have squeezed his body under the door, and he knew it. So he had only hacked that place in order to be doing something – in order to pass the weary time – in order to employ his tortured faculties. Ordinarily one could find half a dozen bits of candle stuck around in the crevices of this vestibule, left by tourists; but there were none, now. The prisoner had searched them out and eaten them. He had also contrived to catch a few bats, and these, also, he had eaten, leaving only their claws. The poor unfortunate had starved to death. In one place near at hand, a stalagmite had been slowly growing up from the ground for ages, builded by the water-drip from a stalactite overhead. The captive had broken off the stalagmite, and upon the stump had placed a stone wherein he had scooped a shallow hollow to catch the precious drop that fell once in every twenty minutes with the dreary regularity of a clock-tick – a dessert-spoonful once in four-and-twenty hours. That drop was falling when the Pyramids were new; when Troy fell when the foundations of Rome were laid; when Christ was crucified; when the Conqueror created the British Empire; when Columbus sailed; when the massacre at Lexington was 'news'. It is falling now; it will still be falling when all these things shall have sunk down the afternoon of history and the twilight of tradition, and been swallowed up in the thick night of oblivion. Has everything a purpose and a mission? Did this drop fall patiently during five thousand years to be ready for this flitting human insect's need, and has it another important object to accomplish ten thousand years to come? No matter. It is many and many a year since the hapless half-breed scooped out the stone to catch the priceless drops, but to this day the tourist stares longest at that pathetic stone and that slow-dropping water when he comes to see the wonders of McDougal's cave. Injun Joe's cup stands first in the list of the cavern's marvels; even 'Aladdin's Palace' cannot rival it.

Injun Joe was buried near the mouth of the cave; and

people flocked there in boats and wagons from the town and from all the farms and hamlets for seven miles around; they brought their children, and all sorts of provisions, and confessed that they had had almost as satisfactory a time at the funeral as they could have had at the hanging.

This funeral stopped the further growth of one thing – the petition to the Governor for Injun Joe's pardon. The petition had been largely signed; many tearful and eloquent meetings had been held, and a committee of sappy women appointed to go in deep mourning and wail around the Governor, and implore him to be a merciful ass, and trample his duty underfoot. Injun Joe was believed to have killed five citizens of the village, but what of that? If he had been Satan himself, there would have been plenty of weaklings ready to scribble their names to a pardon-petition, and drip a tear on it from their permanently impaired and leaky waterworks.

The morning after the funeral Tom took Huck to a private place to have an important talk. Huck had learned all about Tom's adventure from the Welshman and the Widow Douglas by this time, but Tom said he reckoned there was one thing they had not told him; that thing was what he wanted to talk about now. Huck's face saddened. He said:

'I know what it is. You got into number two, and never found anything but whisky. Nobody told me it was you, but I just knowed it must a ben you, soon as I heard 'bout that whisky business; and I knowed you hadn't got the money becuz you'd a got at me some way or other, and told me, even if you was mum to everybody else. Tom, something's always told me we'd never get hold of that swag.'

'Why, Huck, I never told on that tavern-keeper. You know his tavern was all right the Saturday I went to the picnic. Don't you remember you was to watch there that night?'

'Oh, yes! Why, it seems 'bout a year ago. It was that very night that I follered Injun Joe to the widder's.'

'You followed him?'

'Yes – but you keep mum. I reckon Injun Joe's left friends behind him. I don't want 'em souring on me, and doing me mean tricks. If it hadn't been for me he'd be down in Texas now, all right.'

Then Huck told his entire adventure in confidence to Tom, who had only heard of the Welshman's part of it before.

'Well,' said Huck, presently, coming back to the main question, 'whoever nipped the whisky in number two nipped the money too, I reckon – anyways it's a goner for us, Tom.'

'Huck, that money wasn't ever in number two!'

'What!' Huck searched his comrade's face keenly. 'Tom, have you got on the track of that money again?'

'Huck, it's in the cave!'

Huck's eyes blazed.

'Say it again, Tom!'

'The money's in the cave!'

'Tom – honest injun, now – is it fun or earnest?'

'Earnest, Huck – just as earnest as ever I was in my life. Will you go in there with me and help get it out?'

'I bet I will! I will if it's where we can blaze our way to it and not get lost.'

'Huck, we can do that without the least little bit of trouble in the world.'

'Good as wheat! What makes you think the money's – '

'Huck, you just wait till we get in there. If we don't find it, I'll agree to give you my drum and everything I've got in the world. I will, by jings.'

'All right – it's a whiz. When do you say?'

'Right now, if you say it. Are you strong enough?'

'Is it far in the cave? I ben on my pins a little three or four days, now, but I can't walk more'n a mile, Tom – least I don't think I could.'

'It's about five miles into there the way anybody but me would go, Huck, but there's a mighty short cut that they don't anybody but me know about. Huck, I'll take you right to it in a skiff. I'll float the skiff down there, and I'll pull it back again, all by myself. You needn't ever turn your hand over.'

'Less start right off, Tom.'

'All right. We want some bread and meat, and our pipes, and a little bag or two, and two or three kite-strings, and some of those new-fangled things they call lucifer-matches. I tell you many's the time I wished I had some when I was in there before.'

A trifle after noon the boys borrowed a small skiff from a citizen who was absent, and got under way at once. When they were several miles below 'Cave Hollow', Tom said:

'Now you see this bluff here looks all alike all the way down from the cave hollow – no houses, no woodyards, bushes all alike. But do you see that white place up yonder where there's been a land-slide? Well, that's one of my marks. We'll get ashore now.'

They landed.

'Now, Huck, where we're a standing you could touch that hole I got out of with a fishing-pole. See if you can find it.'

Huck searched all the place about, and found nothing. Tom proudly marched into a thick clump of sumach bushes and said:

'Here you are! Look at it, Huck; it's the snuggest hole in this country. You just keep mum about it. All along I've been wanting to be a robber, but I knew I'd got to have a thing like this, and where to run across it was the bother. We've got it now, and we'll keep it quiet, only we'll let Joe Harper and Ben Rogers in – because of course there's got to be a gang, or else there wouldn't be any style about it. Tom Sawyer's Gang – it sounds splendid, don't it, Huck?'

'Well, it just does, Tom. And who'll we rob?'

'Oh, 'most anybody. Waylay people – that's mostly the way.'

'And kill them.'

'No – not always. Hive them in the cave till they raise a ransom!'

'What's a ransom?'

'Money. You make them raise all they can off'n their friends, and after you've kept them a year, if it ain't raised then you kill them. That's the general way. Only you don't kill the women. You shut up the women, but you don't kill them. They're always beautiful and rich, and awfully scared. You take their watches and things, but you always take your hat off and talk polite. They ain't anybody as polite as robbers – you'll see that in any book. Well, the women get to loving you, and after they've been in the cave a week or two weeks they stop crying, and after that you couldn't get them to leave. If you drove them out, they'd turn right around and come back. It's so in all the books.'

'Why, it's real bully, Tom. I b'lieve it's better to be a pirate.'

'Yes, it's better in some ways, because it's close to home, and circuses, and all that.'

By this time everything was ready and the boys entered the hole, Tom in the lead. They toiled their way to the farther end of the tunnel, then made their spliced kite-strings fast and moved on. A few steps brought them to the spring, and Tom felt a shudder quiver all through him. He showed Huck the fragment of candle-wick perched on a lump of clay against the wall, and described how he and Becky had watched the flame struggle and expire.

The boys began to quiet down to whispers, now, for the stillness and gloom of the place oppressed their spirits. They went on, and presently entered and followed Tom's other corridor until they reached the 'jumping-off place'. The candles revealed the fact that it was not really a precipice, but only a steep clay hill, twenty or thirty feet high. Tom whispered:

'Now I'll show you something, Huck.'

He held his candle aloft and said:

208

'Look as far around the corner as you can. Do you see that? There – on the big rock over yonder – done with candle smoke.'

'Tom, it's a *cross!*'

'Now where's your number two? "*Under the cross*", hey? Right yonder's where I saw Injun Joe poke up his candle, Huck!'

Huck stared at the mystic sign a while, and then said with a shaky voice:

'Tom, less git out of here!'

'What! and leave the treasure?'

'Yes – leave it. Injun Joe's ghost is round about there, certain.'

'No it ain't, Huck, no it ain't. It would ha'nt the place where he died – away out at the mouth of the cave – five mile from here.'

'No, Tom, it wouldn't. It would hang round the money. I know the ways of ghosts, and so do you.'

Tom began to fear that Huck was right. Misgivings gathered in his mind. But presently an idea occurred to him.

'Looky here, Huck, what fools we're making of ourselves! Injun Joe's ghost ain't a going to come around where there's a cross!'

The point was well taken. It had its effect.

'Tom, I didn't think of that. But that's so. It's luck for us, that cross is. I reckon we'll climb down there and have a hunt for that box.'

Tom went first, cutting rude steps in the clay hill as he descended. Huck followed. Four avenues opened out of the small cavern which the great rock stood in. The boys examined three of them with no result. They found a small recess in the one nearest the base of the rock, with a pallet of blankets spread down in it; also an old suspender, some bacon rind, and the well-gnawed bones of two or three fowls. But there was no money-box. The lads searched and re-searched this place, but in vain. Tom said:

'He said *under* the cross. Well, this comes nearest to being under the cross. It can't be under the rock itself, because that sets solid on the ground.'

They searched everywhere once more, and then sat down discouraged. Huck could suggest nothing. By-and-by Tom said:

'Looky here, Huck; there's foot-prints and some candle-grease on the clay about one side of this rock, but not on the other sides. Now what's that for? I bet you the money *is* under the rock. I'm going to dig in the clay.'

'That ain't no bad notion, Tom!' said Huck, with animation.

Tom's 'real Barlow' was out at once, and he had not dug four inches before he struck wood.

'Hey, Huck! you hear that?'

Huck began to dig and scratch now. Some boards were soon uncovered and removed. They had concealed a natural chasm which led under the rock. Tom got into this and held his candle as far under the rock as he could, but said he could not see to the end of the rift. He proposed to explore. He stooped and passed under; the narrow way descended gradually. He followed its winding course, first to the right, then to the left, Huck at his heels. Tom turned a short curve by-and-by, and exclaimed:

'My goodness, Huck, looky here!'

It was the treasure-box, sure enough, occupying a snug little cavern, along with an empty powder-keg, a couple of guns in leather cases, two or three pairs of old moccasins, a leather belt, and some other rubbish well soaked with the water drip.

'Got it at last!' said Huck, ploughing among the tarnished coins with his hands. 'My, but we're rich, Tom!'

'Huck, I always reckoned we'd get it. It's just too good to believe, but we *have* got it, sure! Say, let's not fool around here, let's snake it out. Lemme see if I can lift the box.'

It weighed about fifty pounds. Tom could lift it after an awkward fashion, but could not carry it conveniently.

'I thought so,' he said; 'they carried it like it was heavy that day at the ha'nted house – I noticed that. I reckon I was right to think of fetching the little bags along.'

The money was soon in the bags, and the boys took it up to the cross rock.

'Now let's fetch the guns and things,' said Huck.

'No, Huck, leave them there. They're just the tricks to have when we go to robbing. We'll keep them there all the time, and we'll hold our orgies there, too. It's an awful snug place for orgies.'

'What's orgies?'

'I dunno. But robbers always have orgies, and of course we've got to have them too. Come along, Huck, we've been in here a long time. It's getting late, I reckon. I'm hungry, too. We'll eat and smoke when we get to the skiff.'

They presently emerged into the clump of sumach bushes, looked warily out, found the coast clear, and were soon lunching and smoking in the skiff. As the sun dipped towards the horizon they pushed out and got under way. Tom skimmed up the shore through the long twilight, chatting cheerily with Huck, and landed shortly after dark.

'Now, Huck,' said Tom, 'we'll hide the money in the loft of the widow's wood-shed, and I'll come up in the morning and we'll count and divide, and then we'll hunt up a place out in the woods for it where it will be safe. Just you lay quiet here and watch the stuff till I run and hook Benny Taylor's little wagon. I won't be gone a minute.'

He disappeared, and presently returned with the wagon, put the two small sacks into it, threw some old rags on top of them, and started off, dragging his cargo behind him. When the boys reached the Welshman's house they stopped to rest. Just as they were about to move on the Welshman stepped out and said:

'Hallo, who's that?'

'Huck and Tom Sawyer.'

'Good! Come along with me, boys, you are keeping everybody waiting. Here, hurry up, trot ahead; I'll haul the wagon for you. Why, it's not as light as it might be. Got bricks in it, or old metal?'

'Old metal,' said Tom.

'I judged so; the boys in this town will take more trouble and fool way more time hunting up six bits' worth of old iron to sell to the foundry, than they would to make twice the money at regular work. But that's human nature. Hurry along, hurry along!'

The boys wanted to know what the hurry was about.

'Never mind; you'll see when we get to the Widow Douglas's.'

Huck said with some apprehension, for he was long used to being falsely accused:

'Mr Jones, we haven't been doing nothing.'

The Welshman laughed.

'Well, I don't know, Huck, my boy. I don't know about that. Ain't you and the widow good friends?'

'Yes. Well, she's ben a good friend to me, anyways.'

'All right, then. What do you want to be afraid for?'

This question was not entirely answered in Huck's slow mind before he found himself pushed, along with Tom, into Mrs Douglas's drawing-room. Mr Jones left the wagon near the door and followed.

The place was grandly lighted, and everybody that was of any consequence in the village was there. The Thatchers were there, the Harpers, the Rogerses, Aunt Polly, Sid, Mary, the minister, the editor, and a great many more, and all dressed in their best. The widow received the boys as heartily as anyone could well receive two such looking beings. They were covered with clay and candle-grease. Aunt Polly blushed crimson with humiliation, and frowned and shook her head at Tom. Nobody suffered half as much as the two boys did, however. Mr Jones said:

'Tom wasn't at home, yet, so I gave him up; but I stumbled on him and Huck right at my door, and so I just brought them along in a hurry.'

'And you did just right,' said the widow. 'Come with me, boys.'

She took them to a bedchamber and said:

'Now wash and dress yourselves. Here are two new suits of clothes – shirts, socks, everything complete. They're Huck's – no, no thanks, Huck – Mr Jones bought one and I the other. But they'll fit both of you. Get into them. We'll wait – come down when you are slicked up enough.'

Then she left.

CHAPTER XXXV

Huck said:

'Tom, we can slope if we can find a rope. The window ain't high from the ground.'

'Shucks! what do you want to slope for?'

'Well, I ain't used to that kind of a crowd. I can't stand it. I ain't going down there, Tom.'

'Oh, bother! It ain't anything. I don't mind it a bit. I'll take care of you.'

Sid appeared.

'Tom,' said he, 'Auntie has been waiting for you all the afternoon. Mary got your Sunday clothes ready, and everybody's been fretting about you. Say, ain't this grease and clay on your clothes?'

'Now, Mr Siddy, you just 'tend to your own business. What's all this blow-out about, anyway?'

'It's one of the widow's parties that she's always having. This time it's for the Welshman and his sons, on account of that scrape they helped her out of the other night. And say– I can tell you something, if you want to know.'

'Well, what?'

'Why, old Mr Jones is going to try to spring something on the people here tonight, but I overheard him tell Auntie today about it, as a secret, but I reckon it's not much of a secret now. Everybody knows – the widow, too, for all she tries to let on she don't. Oh, Mr Jones was bound Huck should be here – couldn't get along with his grand secret without Huck, you know!'

'Secret about what, Sid?'

'About Huck tracking the robbers to the widow's. I reckon Mr Jones was going to make a grand time over his surprise, but I bet you it will drop pretty flat.'

Sid chuckled in a very contented and satisfied way.

'Sid, was it you that told?'

'Oh, never mind who it was. Somebody told, that's enough.'

'Sid, there's only one person in this town mean enough to do that, and that's you. If you had been in Huck's place you'd a sneaked down the hill and never told anybody on the robbers. You can't do any but mean things, and you can't bear to see anybody praised for doing good ones. There – no thanks, as the widow says.' And Tom cuffed Sid's ears and helped him to the door with several kicks. 'Now go and tell Auntie if you dare, and tomorrow you'll catch it!'

Some minutes later the widow's guests were at the supper table, and a dozen children were propped up at little side tables in the same room, after the fashion of that country and day. At the proper time Mr Jones made his little speech, in which he thanked the widow for the honour she was doing himself and his sons, but said that there was another person whose modesty –

And so forth and so on. He sprang his secret about Huck's share in the adventure in the finest dramatic manner he was master of, but the surprise it occasioned was largely counterfeit, and not as clamorous and effusive as it might have been under happier circumstances. However, the widow made a pretty fair show of astonishment, and heaped so many compliments and so much gratitude upon Huck, that he almost forgot the nearly intolerable discomfort of his new clothes in the entirely intolerable discomfort of being set up as a target for everybody's gaze and everybody's laudations.

The widow said she meant to give Huck a home under her roof and have him educated; and that when she could spare the money she would start him in business in a modest way. Tom's chance was come. He said:

'Huck don't need it. Huck's rich!'

Nothing but a heavy strain upon the good manners of the company kept back the due and proper complimentary laugh at this pleasant joke. But the silence was a little awkward. Tom broke it.

'Huck's got money. Maybe you don't believe it, but he's got lots of it. Oh, you needn't smile; I reckon I can show you. You just wait a minute.'

Tom ran out of doors. The company looked at each other with a perplexed interest, and inquiringly at Huck, who was tongue-tied.

'Sid, what ails Tom?' said Aunt Polly. 'He – well, there ain't ever any making of that boy out. I never – '

Tom entered, struggling with the weight of his sacks, and Aunt Polly did not finish her sentence. Tom poured the mass of yellow coin upon the table and said:

'There – what did I tell you? Half of it's Huck's, and half of it's mine!'

The spectacle took the general breath away. All gazed, nobody spoke for a moment. Then there was a unanimous call for an explanation. Tom said he could furnish it, and he did. The tale was long, but brimful of interest. There was scarcely an interruption from anyone to break the charm of its flow. When he had finished, Mr Jones said:

'I thought I had fixed up a little surprise for this occasion, but it don't amount to anything now. This one makes it sing mighty small, I'm willing to allow.'

The money was counted. The sum amounted to a little over twelve thousand dollars. It was more than anyone present had ever seen at one time before, though several persons were there who were worth considerably more than that in property.

CHAPTER XXXVI

THE reader may rest satisfied that Tom's and Huck's windfall made a mighty stir in the poor little village of St Petersburg. So vast a sum, all in actual cash, seemed next to incredible. It was talked about, gloated over, glorified, until the reason of many of the citizens tottered under the strain of the unhealthy excitement. Every 'haunted' house in St Petersburg and the neighbouring villages was dissected, plank by plank, and its foundations dug up and ransacked for hidden treasures – and not by boys, but men – pretty grave, unromantic men, too, some of them. Wherever Tom and Huck appeared they were courted, admired, stared at. The boys were not able to remember that their remarks had possessed weight before; but now their sayings were treasured and repeated; everything they did seemed somehow to be regarded as remarkable; they had evidently lost the power of doing and saying commonplace things; moreover, their past history was raked up and discovered to bear marks of conspicuous originality. The village paper published biographical sketches of the boys.

The Widow Douglas put Huck's money out at six per cent and Judge Thatcher did the same with Tom's at Aunt Polly's request. Each lad had an income now that was simply prodigious – a dollar for every weekday in the year and half of the Sundays. It was just what the minister got – no, it was what he was promised – he generally couldn't collect it. A dollar and a quarter a week would board, lodge, and school a boy in those old simple days – and clothe him and wash him, too, for that matter.

Judge Thatcher had conceived a great opinion of Tom. He said that no commonplace boy would ever have got his daughter out of the cave. When Becky told her father, in strict confidence, how Tom had taken her whipping at school, the Judge was visibly moved; and when she pleaded grace for the mighty lie which Tom had told in order to shift that whipping from her shoulders to his own, the Judge said with a fine outburst that it was a noble, a generous, a magnanimous lie – a lie that was worthy to hold up its head and march down through history breast to breast with George Washington's lauded Truth about the hatchet! Becky thought her father had never looked so tall and so superb as when he walked the floor and stamped his foot and said that. She went straight off and told Tom about it.

Judge Thatcher hoped to see Tom a great lawyer or a great soldier some day. He said he meant to look to it that Tom should be admitted to the National Military Academy, and afterwards trained in the best law-school in the country, in order that he might be ready for either career, or both.

Huck Finn's wealth, and the fact that he was under the Widow Douglas's protection, introduced him into society – no, dragged him into it, hurled him into it – and his sufferings were almost more than he could bear. The widow's servants kept him clean and neat, combed and brushed, and they bedded him nightly in unsympathetic sheets that had not one little spot or stain which he could press to his heart and know for a friend. He had to eat with knife and fork; he had to use napkin, cup, and plate; he had to learn his book; he had to go to church; he had to talk so properly that speech was become insipid in his mouth; whithersoever he turned, the bars and shackles of civilization shut him in and bound him hand and foot.

He bravely bore his miseries three weeks, and then one day turned up missing. For forty-eight hours the widow hunted for him everywhere in great distress. The public were profoundly concerned; they searched high and low, they dragged the river for his body. Early the third morning Tom Sawyer wisely went poking among some old empty hogsheads down behind the abandoned slaughterhouse, and in one of them he found the refugee. Huck had slept there; he had just breakfasted upon some stolen odds and ends of food, and was lying off, now, in comfort with his pipe. He was unkempt, uncombed, and clad in the same old ruin of rags that had made him picturesque in the days when he was free and happy. Tom routed him out, told him the trouble he had been causing, and urged him to go home. Huck's face lost its tranquil content and took a melancholy cast. He said:

'Don't talk about it, Tom. I've tried it, and it don't work; it don't work, Tom. It ain't for me; I ain't used to it. The widder's good to me, and friendly; but I can't stand them ways. She makes me git up just at the same time every morning; she makes me wash, they comb me all to thunder; she won't let me sleep in the woodshed; I got to wear them blamed clothes that just smothers me, Tom; they don't seem to any air git through 'em, somehow; and they're so rotten nice that I can't set down, or lay down, nor roll around anywheres; I ain't slid on a cellar door for – well, it 'pears to be years; I got to go to church, and sweat and sweat – I hate them ornery sermons! I can't ketch a fly in there, I can't chaw, I got to wear shoes all Sunday. The widder eats by a bell; she goes to bed by a bell; she gits up by a bell – everything's so awful reg'lar a body can't stand it.'

'Well, everybody does that way, Huck.'

'Tom, it don't make no difference. I ain't everybody and I can't stand it. It's awful to be tied up so. And grub comes too easy – I don't take no interest in vittles that way. I got to ask to go a fishing; I got to ask to go in a swimming – dern'd if I hain't got to ask to do everything. Well, I'd got to talk so nice it wasn't no comfort; I'd got to go up in the

218

attic and rip out a while every day to git a taste in my mouth, or I'd a died, Tom. The widder wouldn't let me smoke, she wouldn't let me yell, she wouldn't let me gape, nor stretch, nor scratch before folks.' Then with a spasm of special irritation and injury: 'And dad fetch it, she prayed all the time! I never see such a woman! I had to shove, Tom, I just had to. And besides, that school's going to open, and I'd a had to go to it; well, I wouldn't stand that, Tom. Looky here, Tom, being rich ain't what it's cracked up to be. It's just worry and worry, and sweat and sweat, and a wishing you was dead all the time. Now these clothes suits me and this bar'l suits me, and I ain't ever going to shake 'em any more. Tom, I wouldn't ever got into all this trouble if it hadn't a ben for that money; now you just take my sheer of it along with yourn, and gimme a ten-center sometimes – not many times, becuz I don't give a dern for a thing 'thout it's tollable hard to git – and you go and beg off for me with the widder.'

'Oh, Huck, you know I can't do that. 'Tain't fair; and besides, if you'll try this thing just a while longer you'll come to like it.'

'Like it! Yes – the way I'd like a hot stove if I was to set on it long enough. No Tom, I won't be rich, and I won't live in them cussed smothery houses. I like the woods, and the river, and hogsheads, and I'll stick to 'em too. Blame it all! just as we'd got guns, and a cave, and all just fixed to rob, here this dern foolishness has got to come up and spile it all!'

Tom saw his opportunity:

'Looky here, Huck, being rich ain't going to keep me back from turning robber.'

'No! Oh, good licks, are you in real dead-wood earnest, Tom?'

'Just as dead earnest as I'm a sitting here. But, Huck, we can't let you into the gang if you ain't respectable, you know.'

Huck's joy was quenched.

'Can't let me in, Tom? Didn't you let me go for a pirate?'

'Yes, but that's different. A robber is more high-toned than what a pirate is – as a general thing. In most countries they're awful high up in the nobility – dukes and such.'

'Now, Tom, hain't you always ben friendly to me? You wouldn't shet me out, would you, Tom? You wouldn't do that, now, would you, Tom?'

'Huck, I wouldn't want to and I don't want to, but what would people say? Why, they'd say, "Mph! Tom Sawyer's Gang! pretty low characters in it!" They'd mean you, Huck. You wouldn't like that, and I wouldn't.'

Huck was silent for some time, engaged in a mental struggle. Finally he said:

'Well, I'll go back to the widder for a month and tackle it and see if I come to stand it, if you'll let me b'long to the gang, Tom.'

'All right, Huck, it's a whiz! Come along, old chap, and I'll ask the widow to let up on you a little, Huck.'

'Will you, Tom, now will you? That's good. If she'll let up on some of the roughest things, I'll smoke private and cuss private, and crowd through or bust. When you going to start the gang and turn robbers?'

'Oh, right off. We'll get the boys together and have the initiation tonight, maybe.'

'Have the which?'

'Have the initiation.'

'What's that?'

'It's to swear to stand by one another, and never tell the gang's secrets, even if you're chopped all to flinders, and kill anybody and all his family that hurts one of the gang.'

'That's gay – that's mighty gay, Tom, I tell you.'

'Well, I bet it is. And all that swearing's got to be done at midnight, in the lonesomest, awfulest place you can find – a ha'nted house is the best, but they're all ripped up, now.'

'Well, midnight's good, anyway, Tom.'

'Yes, so it is. And you've got to swear on a coffin, and sign it with blood.'

'Now that's something like! Why, it's a million times bullier than pirating. I'll stick to the widder till I rot, Tom; and if I git to be a reg'lar ripper of a robber, and everybody talking 'bout it, I reckon she'll be proud she snaked me in out of the wet.'

CONCLUSION

So endeth this chronicle. It being strictly a history of a boy, it must stop here; the story could not go much further without becoming the history of a man. When one writes a novel about grown people, he knows exactly where to stop – that is, with a marriage; but when he writes of juveniles, he must stop where he best can.

Most of the characters that perform in this book still live, and are prosperous and happy. Some day it may seem worth while to take up the story of the younger ones again, and see what sort of men and women they turned out to be; therefore it will be wisest not to reveal any of that part of their lives at present.

PENGUIN POPULAR CLASSICS

Titles published or forthcoming

PENGUIN POPULAR CLASSICS

Titles published or forthcoming

Elizabeth Gaskell	Cranford
	North and South
Thomas Hardy	Far from the Madding Crowd
	Jude the Obscure
	The Mayor of Casterbridge
	A Pair of Blue Eyes
	The Return of the Native
	Tess of the D'Urbervilles
	Under the Greenwood Tree
	The Woodlanders
Nathaniel Hawthorne	The Scarlet Letter
Henry James	The Aspern Papers
	The Turn of the Screw
Rudyard Kipling	Kim
	Plain Tales from the Hills
Herman Melville	Moby Dick
Walter Scott	Ivanhoe
William Shakespeare	Hamlet
	King Lear
	Macbeth
	The Merchant of Venice
	A Midsummer Night's Dream
	Romeo and Juliet
Mary Shelley	Frankenstein
Robert Louis Stevenson	Dr Jekyll and Mr Hyde
	Treasure Island
Bram Stoker	Dracula
Jonathan Swift	Gulliver's Travels
W. M. Thackeray	Vanity Fair
Anthony Trollope	Barchester Towers
	The Warden
Mark Twain	Huckleberry Finn
	Tom Sawyer
Jules Verne	Around the World in Eighty Days
Oscar Wilde	Lord Arthur Saville's Crime
	The Picture of Dorian Gray